EMPOWERMENT OF WOMEN THROUGH ENTREPRENEURSHIP

EMPOWERMENT OF WOMEN THROUGH ENTREPRENEURSHIP

Edited by
Dr. L. Rathakrishnan
(Editor)

GYAN

GYAN PUBLISHING HOUSE

NEW DELHI-110002

Empowerment of Women Through Entrepreneurship

Rs. 900

ISBN: 81-212-0965-X

Published in 2008 in India by
Gyan Publishing House,
5, Ansari Road, Darya Ganj,
New Delhi-110002
Phones : 23282060, 23261060
Fax : 011-23285914
E-mail: books@gyanbooks.com
Website: www.gyanbooks.com

Lasser Type Setting by: Quick Media, Delhi
Printed at : Singhal Print Media, Delhi

Dedicated to
My
Mother

CONTENTS

IV. Women Entrepreneurs: Problems and Prospects

PREFACE

Compared to men, women in India are disempowered. In India, men outnumber women: the ratio is 1000 men to 927 women. The women were denied the opportunities for education and economic independence. Again women have little control over assets, health, fertility and disproportionately suffer from malnourishment and anemia. Women are often under-paid or un-paid for their work. Their contributions to society and the economy are often ignored. Thus, women's contribution to the family and society development cannot be measured economically. In developing countries like India, women participation in the formal sector is only about 15 per cent not withstanding the fact that in the developed countries it is as high as 72–80 per cent.

In India, the trickle down effects of macroeconomic policies have failed to resolve the problem of gender inequality. Women have been the vulnerable section of society and constitute a sizeable segment of the poverty-struck population. Women face gender specific barriers in access to education, health and employment. Although the development activities in entrepreneurial efforts are vital factors in developing the livelihood and thereby eradicating poverty, the role of women is to be considered in a different angle as equitable women involvement is necessary in enterprise development.

An entrepreneur is a catalyst of development, with him/her, we prosper, without him/her we are poor. In the absence of entrepreneurial traits, development of the country is inconceivable. The entrepreneur is critical person who strives to reorient the national strategies and bring out the desired changes in the development pattern. The entrepreneur is mainly a catalyst who can mobilise different resources and put them to effective use. In fact, entrepreneurship is reckoned as a factor of production along with land, labour, capital and organisation.

Most of the micro enterprises base on home level depends on individual and neighboring market, which is low cost and affordable with a good cash flow and as a result more women want to be within this range. Results and experiences from thousands of micro entrepreneurial activities clearly established the fact that the projects led by women have a better potential for growth. If the women have the ability and proper guidance, they can be extremely successful. Micro entrepreneurship thereby makes significant contribution to the family, community and the local economy.

Schumpeter defined entrepreneur as a "person who possesses enterprising capacity to allocate, organize and manage factors of production more efficiently so as to maximise the profit and minimise cost". Government of India defined "women entrepreneur as an enterprise owned and controlled by a women having a maximum financial interest of 51 per cent of the capital and giving at least 51 per cent of the employment generated in the enterprise to women".

Now-a-days women play a vital role as income earners. In advanced countries there is a phenomenal increase in the number of self-employed women. In US women own 25 per cent of all business, in Canada 1/3rd of small business are owned by women. In France, it is 1/5. In India the self-employed women account for only 5.2 per cent. However, in recent times, rural women are very dynamic and innovative in development activities and also the self confidence among women enhanced status of the society. Participation of the rural women in the village work is a land mark to achieve the aspiration reflected in the governmental programmes.

Women can involve in the following entrepreneurial activities, namely (i) livestock-based - dairy, poultry, fisheries, piggery; (ii) Agro-based— mushroom cultivation, cultivation of medicinal plants, seed production, bee keeping, nursery raising, ornamental fish culture, processing of milk dairy, processing of fruits and vegetables, production and marketing of green gram, soyabean and sunflower; (iii) Non-farm based - beauty parlours, tailoring, bakery, carpenters, rope making, stone carving, leaf cup making, puffed rice preparation, oil crushing, binding and printing, 'restaurants, mini-food stall, tailoring and embroidery, tie & die, toy making, packaging for grain, spice and food, small retail shop, agarbathi/ chalk/candle, etc.

Women attain success through hard work, dedication and commitment. However, they face lot of problems, namely high cost of production, shortage of raw materials, problems of middlemen, difficulties in finding a space for establishment, difficulties in tracing resources, financial problems, problems of marketing and competition, problem related to awareness and information on recent trends, managerial problems, socio-cultural problems and family conflict.

In order to promote the welfare of the women and their empowerment a number of supporting agencies were involved, namely KVIC, National Dairy Development Board, Tribal Cooperative Development

Organisation, Commercial Banks – Lead Bank, DIC. Block adoption programmes by Industrial Development Bank of India (IDBI), and Entrepreneurship Development Institute of India.

In this respect, NABARD had introduced short-term (repayment in 18 months), medium-term (repayment in 3 to 7 years) and long-term (repayment in 3 to 15 years) credit facilities to women entrepreneurs. NABARD have also introduced exclusive schemes for women, namely promotion of women self-help groups, women clubs under Vikas Volunteer Vahini (VVV) programmes; Assistance to Rural Women in Non-farm Development (ARWIND); assistance for marketing of non-farm products of rural women (MAHIMA), and setting up of women development cells.

Research studies have proved that women are successful in many entrepreneurial activities. Some to quote are SEWA in Ahmedabad; milk cooperatives under operation Flood - Anand in Gujarat and Orissa Industrial and Technical Consultancy Organisation (ORITCO) –Orissa. They promote a better market for traditional arti-crafts produced by tribes. Nevertheless, women entrepreneurs need to go a long journey to show her strength, power and identity in the male dominated society. Hence this book has been brought out for wide reading and understanding the hidden strength of women.

(L. Rathakrishnan)

ACKNOWLEDGEMENT'S

I wish to express my deep sense of gratitude to all those contributors of this edited volume. Few of them are known to me and many are unknown. When I started to send e-mail and letter correspondence about the topic and its outcome, I have received prompt response and also prompt contribution. Many have not contributed but extended their hearty wishes for successful completion of the edited volume. The list of such persons is long. The chapter contributors have done their job perfectly, without aspiring for any return. I am thankful to all of them. I consider myself lucky having met many such dignitaries personally as well as corresponded through letter and e-mail. I would like to express my gratitude to the numerous well wishers who have shared their experience in getting the book published. I am under obligation to acknowledge gratefully the kind co-operation of all of them.

My thanks are also due to the reviewers whose comments have led to improvements in the content and presentation of the book. A special acknowledgement to my teachers, namely Dr. M. Ramadoss, Dr. B.S. Nagarajan, Dr. S. Ramachandran, Dr. N. Meenakshi Sundaram, Dr. B. Ramasamy, Dr. S. Ramamoorthy, Dr. P.N. Ramani for their care and unflinching support at all times. I am deeply indebted to them all. They all inspired me to take up the venture of writing this book. I also thank all teaching and non-teaching members of the Department of Rural Industries and Management, Gandhigram Rural University, Gandhigram for their kjjad support and encouragement.

I gratefully acknowledge the assistance and guidance of a number of friends and colleagues who guided me to go for this venture. I greatly appreciate the silent contributions from my family members. Many have helped me in proof reading. I would like to mention the help I received from Ms.P.Uma, H.O.D of Management Studies, Fathima College, Madurai and her colleagues in English Department in proof reading and correction. A special thanks to Gyan publication House New Delhi for his patients and timely publications.

There are many others who also helped me indirectly without whose 'cooperation and support this work could not have been completed in time. I thank them all.

(L. Rathakrishnan)

LIST OF CONTRIBUTORS

1. Dr. Mrs. V. Gomathi, Head, Department of Commerce, Cauvery College for Women, Tiruchirapalli–620 018.
2. Dr. K. Selvarani, Reader in commerce, V.V. Vannia Perumal College for Women, Virudhunagar.
3. Dr. G. Varadharajan, Director, G.V. Siddha & Herbal Research Foundation, Kainangarai, Mathur (Post), Kulathur, Pudukkottai (District)–622 515.
4. Dr. D. Pulla Rao, Reader, Department of Cooperation and Applied Economics, Andhra University, Visakhapatnam.
5. Dr. G. Vijayalakshmi, Reader in Home Science, Gandhigram Rural Univesity, Gandhigram–624 302.
6. Ms. B. Prajeetha, Lecturer in Home Science, Fatima College, Madurai–18.
7. Dr. Kiran Mishra, Department of English, Ranchi Women's College, Ranchi, Jharkhand.
8. Dr. B. Padma Narayan, Faculty Association, GITAM Institute of Foreign Trade, GITAM Campus, Rushikonda, Visakhapatna–45.
9. Dr. B.V. Suryanarayana, Reader, Departm,ent of Statistics, Andhra University, Visakhapatnam–3.
10. Dr. B. Ratnakumari, Reader, Dr. Durgabhai Deshmuki Centre for Women's studies, Andha University, Visakhapatnam–3.
11. Ms. Zilani Begum, Research Scholar, Department of Applied Economics, Andhra University, Viskhapatnam–3.
12. Ms. M. anitha, Research Scholar, Department of Applied Economics, Andhra University, visakhapatnam–3.
13. Dr. L. Rathakrishnan, Reader in Rural Indistries and Management, Gandhigram Rural University, Gandhigram–624 302.
14. Dr. U. Arabi, Reader, Department of Studies and Research in Economics, Mangalore University, Mangalgangothri, Karnataka–574 199.

15. Dr. Nilabja Ghosh, Institute of Economic Growth, University of Delhi Enclave, Delhi–110 007. Tel: 91-11-2766-7424.

    email:nila@iegindia.org, nilabia@yahoo.com.

16. Dr. R. Ganesan, Research Coordinator, Centre for Research & consultancy,Sree Saraswathi Thyagaraja College, Pollachi Taluk, Coimbatore District–642 107.

    email: drganesan.nfed@redifmail.com

17. Dr. I. Narendra Kumar, Academic Consultant, Department of Economics, S.V. University, Tirupati–2, Andhra Pradesh.

18. Dr. G. Chandrasekar Rao, Principal, S.V.V. College of Arts, S.V. University, Tirupati–2, Andhra Pradesh.

19. Dr. V.K. Reddy, Professor, Department of Economics, S.V. University, Tirupati–2, Andhra Pradesh.

20. Dr. V.B. Naidu, Reader, Department of Economics, S.V. University, Tirupati–2, Andhra Pradesh.

21. Mr. Arpita Sharma, Senior Scientist, Central Institute of Fisheries Education (Deemed University), Indian Council of Agricultural Research, Seven Bungalows, Versova, Mumbai–400 061.

    Email: arpita sharma@yahoo.com, a.Sharma@cife.in

22. Dr. T. Sobhasir, Reader, Department of Social Work, Andhra University, Visakhapatnam–530 003.

23. Dr. G. Sanjeevayya. Teching Associate, Department of Social Work, Andhra University, Visakhapatnam–530003, Andhra Pradesh, emai: sanjeev962001@yahoo.com.

24. Dr. (Mrs.). P. Tarakumari, Reader, Department of Economics, Andhra University, Visakhapatnam–530 003, Andhra Pradesh.

25. Mrs. Shanthi Nachiappan, Asst. Professors Velammal College of Management and Computer Studies, Chennai.

26. Dr. B. Dharmalingam, Director i/c, Centre for Rural Development, Alagappa University, Karaikudi.

27. Dr. R. Seerangarajan, Professor in Rural Industries and Management, Gandhigram Rural University, Gandhigram–624 302.

28. Er. A.T. Narasimhan, Asst. Exe. Engineer, P.W.D. Madurai (Part Time Research Scholar, Department or Rural Industries and

Management, Gandhigram Rural University Gandhigram)–624 302.

29. A Ingarsal, Research Assistant, IDARA, Gandhigram Rural University, Gandhigram–624 302.

30. A.V. Yadappanayar, Centre for Women Development, N.I>R.D., Rajendranagar, Hyderabad–500 030.

31. Dr. K. Thiripura Sundari, Reader in Commerce, Sri Parasakthi College for Women, Courtallam–627 802.

32. Mr. Raj. Santan, Research Scholar, M.S. University, Tirunelveli–627 012.

33. Mr. G. Saravanan, Research Scholar, Department of Rural Industries and Mangement,Gandhigram Rural University, Gandhigram–624 302.

34. Dr. D.P. Angadi, Lecturer, Department of Geography, University College, Hampanakatta, Mangalore.

35. Dr. Jayaseela, Reader, Department of Economics, Mangalore University, Mangalagangothri–574 199.

36. Dr. Yathish Kumar, Senior Scale Lecturer, Department of Commerce, University Collgece, Mangalore–575 011.

37. Dr. A. Ranga Reddi, professor in Economics, J.V. University, Tirupati–517 502.

38. Mr. P. Balamuruan, Research Scholar, Department of Economcis, Bharathidasan University, Tiruchirappalli–620 024.

39. Mr. V. Basil Hans, Teacher Fellows, Department of Studies and Research in Economcis, Magalore University, Mangalagangothri–574 199.

40. Mr. V.P. Sriraman, Assistant Professor, Bharathidasan Institute of Management, Tiruchirapalli.

41. Dr. R. Balasubramaniyan, Reader in Economics, D.G. Vaishnav College, Chennai–600 106.

42. Ms. Prabha Mathur, No. 3, Mahindra Society, Nagar Road, Pune–411 006.

43. Dr. A. Balakrishnan, Reader, Department of Applied Research, Gandhigram Rural University, Gandhigram.

44. Dr. M. Soundara Pandan, Professor in R.I.M. Gandhigram Rural University, Gandhigram–624 302.

Chapter 1

WOMEN EMPOWERMENT—STILL A PIPE DREAM

***Dr. A. Ranga Reddy**

ABSTRACT

The chapter highlights the components of women empowerment and their future. The national policy for "Empowerment of Women" (2001) states that "Empower the Women in Order to bring Socio-economic Change and Development". How for this has been practiced in reality is discussed in this chapter.

Introduction

During the period of Vedas and Upanishads, Women's progress kept pace with that of men. Man precepted that women donot deserve independence. Historically women at no point in time, showed signs of incompetence in matters relating to any socio-economic, political and cultural activities provided male dominance society liberalizes their mind and action.

Educate your women first and leave them of themselves, then they will tell you what reforms are necessary for them, Vivekanda said. It is still a great disadvantage to be born female. Presently, women produce 50 per cent of the world's food supply, account for 60 per cent of working force and contribute upto 30 per cent of the official labour force, but receive only 10 per cent of the world economy and more surprisingly own less than 1 per cent of world's real estate.

India is one of the few countries where women population is lower than the men in 2001 Census. There is a continuous decline in the sex ratio due to high mortality rate among females in all age groups, the maternal mortality, mortality of female child due to sex identification

Professor, Department of Economics Sri Venkateswara University, Tirupati-517502 before birth, poverty and malnutrition, etc. This inverse sex ratio confirms the poor status of women and women's health. Girls get less vaccination, less education and less nutrition than their brothers and when they grow up, they are less healthy than their male counterparts and succumb more easily to sickness and disease.

Gender Discrimination at World Level

Women, men literacy ratio was 70:85 for world. Developed countries like East Europe, Ex-USSR, East Asia, the difference of literacy ratio among male and female is very low. Whereas in China the literacy ratio is 75:90 and in India 40:68. In developed countries 80 per cent of women are in economic activies. In South Asia and in Latin America women are participating 41 to 60 per cent in economic activities. In Arab countries, women labourers are 40 per cent. Extreme Islam and Christian countries, were not allowed women to enter into economic activities. Women is a dominant and leading earner in Tanzania among all world countries. Sweden, Kenya and USA were stood as second, third and fourth countries, respectively[1].

Economic Empowerment

Employment of women in the organized sector (both public and private) at end March 2003 was 4.97 million constituted 18.4 per cent of the total organized sector employment compared to 18.1 per cent in 2002. as regards sectoral distribution, community, social and personal services sectors employed 56.6 per cent of women workers followed by manufacturing (20.3 per cent), agriculture and allied occupations (9.4 per cent) and finance, insurance, real estate and business (5.5 per cent). States with high female literacy rates have high proportion of women in organized sector employment[2].

The Government has been implementing various schemes for the socio-economic advancement and development of women in the country. The "National Policy for Empowerment of Women" was adopted in 2001 with an objective of ensuring women, their rightful place in society by empowering them as agents of socio-economic change and development. To eliminate all types of discrimination against women and girl child and their empowerment, major strategies including social empowerment, economic empowerment and gender justice. Two important schemes in the areas of education viz., 'Sarva Shiksha Abhiyan' and Mahila Samakhya' are being implemented by Department of Elementary Education and literacy as special efforts to stretch the reach of education especially to the girl child. To achieve economic empowerment and welfare of women, a number of schemes are being implemented. These include Swayamsidha, Swashaki, Rastriya Mahila Kosh, Swalamban and support to Training-cum-Employment Programme (STEP), Swadhar and Hostel for working women[3].

Empowerment of Socially Disadvantages

Empowerment deals the welfare of persons belonging to the scheduled castes, religious and linguistic minorities, socially and educationally backward classes, welfare of persons with disabilities and programmes of social defence relating to victims of alcoholism, drug addiction, juvenile social maladjustment, welfare of prisoners, children in need of care and protection, welfare of aged and matters relating to the administration.

Women job Sectors

The number of women job seekers, especially Scheduled Castes and Scheduled Tribes has increased. The number of women increased from 95.3 lakhs in 1998 to 107.5 lakhs in 2003 and of the SCs and STs from 58.0 lakhs and 16.9 lakhs to 66.3 lakhs and 23.1 lakhs. The number of physically handicapped persons seeking employment also rose from 4.2 lakhs to 6.6 lakhs. The age-wise analysis shows that approximately 71 per cent of the job-seekers are below 29. Among women, 73.5 per cent were inexperienced, followed by 12.1 per cent in category of professional, technical and related workers[4].

Excluding the percentage of contract labourers, the national percentage of women, who are directly employed by a unit works out to 14.47 per cent. This includes employment for all types of jobs in the private, public and government sector. Southern states have much higher ratio of employed women than the national average. It is almost 62 per cent in Kerala, 37 per cent Karnataka, but only 2.44 per cent in Uttar Pradesh[5].

Hindu Succession (Amendment) Act

On August 29, 2005 Indian Parliament passed Hindu succession Amendment bill that gives women of the community equal rights in inheritance of property. The act would also remove gender bias by giving equal rights to daughters as sons had. Even in agricultural land also can get share, provided states have to make law. In 1986, Government of Andhra Pradesh also brought an amendment similar to it[6].

Need of Empowerment even Before Birth

It is better to stop 'unacceptable' crime being encouraged by the widespread misuse of modern technology—'Pre-Natal Diagnostic Technique Regulation and Prevention Misuse Act, 1994 and its mindless commercial exploitation. This dastardly social phenomenon must be socially boycotted and legally punished. This hazardous effect of this practice is already there for us to see in some of our most developed states and it has created a gender imbalance, which was harmful to society. Unfortunately, present political system has forgotten the sacrifices made by women during the British rule. Manmohan Singh's Government is confident that equitable representation of women in the highest decision making bodies is urgently required. Time had come to give due place to women in political institutions and economic processes. No nation could stand proud of its discrimination against any of its citizens and no society could claim to bepart of the modern civilized world unless it treated its women on par with men[7]. domestic violence, as per the act, constitutes physical or mental harm, including sexual, verbal, emotional or economical abuse by a male member of the family or any one living under the same roof. Harassment of the victim with a view to coercing her or any other person related to her to meet any unlawful demand for dowry or property is also covered under the new law[8].

August 24th 2005 marks an important event in the history of the women's movement in India. In an unanimous vote, the Lok Sabha passed the protection of women from Domestic Violence Bill, 2005. recognizes the right of a women to live in a violence-free home. Close examination of domestic violence statistics show that women barely use the law and if and why they do, it is only when they have been subjected to extreme violence. The ultimate objective of the law is to pin accountability for illegal conduct. This law is unique in legislative history[9].

The status of women in Indian society will not materially change till mindsets are altered. Over the last five years dowry deaths virtually no change in their number. In few states registered cases declined, but bride burning increased, despite existence of a most draconian anti-dowry law. The anti-dowry yet is more abused than used. Very few convictions take place in genuine cases of victimization or cold blooded murder. To bring change in social structure, Non-Governmental Organisations (NGOs) do play a positive role in many cases. It is a theoretical triumph. Pseudo-progressive, which includes pseudo-secularism, has done more damage to the country than any other-ideology[10].

Women's Reservation Bill

The fact is that Parliamentarians are simply not interested in passing Bill, which will leave a third of them jobless. By all means, two National parties has accepted to pass the bill but spanner was thrown by two regional parties of Yadavas, who have been advocating a quota for OBCs within the women quota.

The experience of a decade of women's reservation in the Panchayats shows that of its 10 lakh women, many are mere rubber-stamps for husbands who cannot contest elections from reserved constituencies. The process of empowerment has been set in motion at the grassroots through the efforts of NGOs which train women in their political roles, women are yet to graduate from the first school of political empowerment are deep-rooted patriarchal bias and caste and class issues. The Bill will not remedy these (however unfortunate) aspects of the Indian electorate. Reservation is also an ineffective tool for meeting social ends unless accompanied with effective of socio-economic empowerment, training and inculcating self-confidence among vulnerable sections[11].

Conclusion

Women are not inferior in any field of activity, provided they are given liberal and equality by male dominant society. Historically, women fought with British people equally to achieve freedom and joined in many socio-economic, political movements. In organized sector, Central and States had given less opportunities to grow fast in many spheres. Women are exploited by men of all classes and castes. Many Government schemes in education, employment had not achieved anticipated results. Infact, SCs, STs and minority religious women are worst sufferers. Parliamentary Acts on women empowerment may not bring quick results, unless continuous training by NGOs at Panchayats to Parliament level.

REFERENCES

1. *Andhra Jyothi* (2005): Still Women in discrimination, *Telugu daily*, September 1.
2. Govt. of India, (2004): *Economic Survey*, 2004-2005, p. 231.
3. Govt. of India, (2004): *Economic Survey*, 2004-2005, p. 241.
4. Special Correspondent (2005): Women, SC/ST Job Seekers on the rise, *The Hindu,* September 4.
5. Special Correspondent (2005): Poor deal for fairer sex in Government jobs, *The Economic Times*, August 30, p. 1.
6. Special Correspondent (2005): Hindu Women get equal property Rights, *The Hindu*, August 30, 2005.
7. Special Correspondent (2005): Manmohan Confident of Passage of Bill, *The Hindu* August 24.
8. Special Correspondent (2005): President gives assent to domestic violence Act, *The Hindu*, September 17, p. 13.
9. Astima Basu (2005): Magic Bill, *Sunday Vijaya Times,* September 4, Mangalore, p. 6.
10. Chandan Mitra (2005): Women on Top, *Sunday Vijaya Times*, September 4, Mangalore, p. 6.
11. Yoga Rangatia (2005): Political Foot Ball, *Sunday Vijaya Times*, September 4, Mangalore, p. 6.

Chapter 2
STATUS OF WOMEN IN INDIA : SOME DIMENSIONS

*Dr. D. Pulla Rao

ABSTRACT

The status of women in India is discussed in this chapter. Women are still treated as second rated citizen or subordinate to men. Whatever may be the efforts of the government, they remain in backward position. Government is providing special efforts to utilize women's talent. Women do take advantages of such support, they are also proving their worthiness in education, health, household enterprises and I.T. Now they made it clear that without active involvement of women sustainable development is not possible.

Introduction

Women though equal to men in population, is subjected to a lot of deprivations even in this modern sophisticated world. Women are still treated as the second rated citizen or subordinate to men in all major fields of life i.e., social, economical and political. Though various efforts are being made to improve the status of women, women folk could not make maximum use of them and hence remained backward. In almost all countries, the Governments are providing special provisions for women's development and efforts are being made to extract maximum use of women's talent. It has been clear for decades that women in many parts of the world make key contributions in areas of development such as agriculture, health, education, water resources management etc.

In India, the shift from "welfare" to "development" of women took place in the Sixth Five Year Plan (1980-85). The Eighth Five-Year Plan

* Associate Professor, Dept. of Cooperation & Applied Economics, Andhra University, Visakhapatnam.

(1992-97) promised to ensure that the benefits of development from different sectors do not bypass women. The Rashtriiya Mahila Kosh was set up in 1993 to meet the credit needs of the poor and the assetless women. The Ninth Five-Year Plan (1997-2002) made two significant changes in the strategy of planning for women. Firstly, "empowerment of women" became a primary first objective and second, the plan attempted "convergence of existing services" available in both women-specific and women related sectors. The Tenth Five-Year Plan (2002-2007) has made a major commitment towards "empowering women as the agent of socio-economic change and development". Based on the recommendation of National Policy for Empowerment of Women, the Tenth Five-Year Plan suggests a three- fold strategy for empowering women, through social empowerment, economic empowerment and gender justice.

Demographic Dimensions

(*i*) Sex Ratio : Sex ratio is defined as number of females per 1000 males. Sex ratio is a useful indicator to understand women's health and position in any society. India has distinction along with China and few other South Asian countries having a deficit of females for a long period. This is largely interpreted as the symptom of low status of women and discrimination of females existing in the country. Unusually high mortality Indian women faced relative to males until recently confirmed this fact. The female mortality registered significantly high rates than males at the younger ages, though it reverted recently.

Ashish Bose (2001) and Agnihotri (2001) stated that census has given a shocking aspect, namely a sharp decline in the female – male ratio in several states. They further stated that migration cannot explain this phenomenon, which must be the consequence of female foeticide on a massive scale, if not female infanticide and higher female child mortality rates. Sex ratio is a useful indicator to understand women's health and position in any society. India has distinction along with China and few other South Asian countries having a deficit of females for a long period. This is largely interpreted as the symptom of low status of women and discrimination of females existing in the county. Unusually high mortality Indian women faced relative to males until recently confirmed this fact. The female mortality registered significantly high rates than males at the younger ages, though it reverted recently. This is revealed through a study of the sex ratios existing in our country from 1901 onwards. Strangely enough, in spite of the advances in medical sciences, the drop in death rate from 42.6 per cent in 1901 – 1911 to 8.4 per cent in 2001, the tremendous advances made in eradication of malaria and control of infectious diseases like tuberculosis, as well as, an increase in life expectancy for women from 23.3 years in 1901 – 1910 to 64.2 in 1996 – 2001. The sex ratios of our population continue to be adverse for women. In 1901, the sex ratio was 972 females per 1000 men. This ratio has been continuously declining from 1901 onwards except in 1951, 1981 and 2001. It is 933 in 2001 (Table –1).

Table – 1 : Population And Sex Ratios In India: 1901-2001

Census year	*Total population (in millions)*	*Sex ratios (females per 1,000 males)*
1901	238.10	972
1911	252.09	964
1921	252.32	955
1931	278.98	950
1941	318.66	945
1951	361.09	946
1961	439.24	941
1971	548.16	930
1981	685.18	933
1991	844.33	927
2001	1027.02	933

Source: Census of India, 2001.

***(ii)* Juvenile (0 – 6 age group) Sex Ratio :** The age distribution of population in the Indian census follows five yearly groupings like 0 - 4, 5-9, 10-14 and so on. In 1991, it was decided to calculate literacy rates for the population seven years and over. Therefore, a new category of 0-6 age group was introduced in the primary census abstract, and literacy data for the age group seven and above were sorted out. Besides 0-6 age

Table – 2 : Sex Ratio In 0-6 Age Group: 1961-2001

Year	*Sex ratio in 0-6 age group*	*Variation*
1961	976	—
1971	964	-12
1981	962	-2
1991	945	-17
2001	927	-18

Source: Census of India, 2001.

group was convenient to study the import of the Integrated Child Development Services etc. In keeping with this practice, the 2001 census tables give data on literacy after excluding 0-6 age groups. In this process separate figures are available for the sex composition of the 0-6 age group.

Table – 2 shows a sharp decline in the sex ratio of the under 0-6-age population in the last 40 years, i.e., 976 in 1961, 964 in 1971, 962 in 1981, 945 in 1991 and 927 in 2001, a decline of 18 points in this last decade.

Literacy Dimensions

(*i*) Female Literacy Rate : The most important characteristic of population is literacy, which is a pre – requisite for the overall development of the country both socially and economically. Female literacy is considered to be a more sensitive index of social development compared to overall literacy rates. Female literacy is negatively related with fertility rates, population growth rates, infant and child mortality rates, and shows a positive association with female age at marriage, life expectancy and participation in modern sectors of the economy. In spite of all the special constitutional provisions and governmental efforts in the field of education, the disparities between males and females are still large. The gap between the literacy rates of males and females has been presented since 1901 when the female literacy rate was only 0.60 per cent as against 9.83 per cent among males. The disparity index (ratio of male literacy rate to female literacy rate) in 1901 was 16.4. On the eve of the initiation of planned economic development in 1951 the literacy rate of women was 7.93 per cent. And women education received a phenomenal jerk from 1961. One can notice a double-digit growth rate in that year and it continued to grow at an increasing rate thereafter and even surpassed the cut off level of 50:50 by the year 2001 (Table –3).

Table – 3 : Sex Differences In Literacy Rates In India: (1901 to 2001)

Year	*Male literacy rates*	*Female literacy rates*	*Disparity index*
1901	9.83	0.60	16.4
1911	10.56	1.05	10.1
1921	12.21	1.81	7.6
1931	15.59	2.93	5.3
1941	24.90	7.30	3.4
1951	24.95	7.93	3.1
1961	34.44	12.95	2.6
1971	39.45	18.69	2.1
1981	56.50	29.85	1.9
1991	64.13	39.29	1.6
2001	75.85	54.16	1.4

Source: Census Report, 2001.

***(ii)* Female Enrollment At Various Levels Of Education :** After Independence, the government of India has designed several strategies for promotion of girls / women education. Separate institutions for girls / women education were opened. Special incentives to attract the girls / women into the academic institutions were introduced. As a result, the female literacy rate has gone up from 7.93 per cent in 1951 to 54.16 per cent by 2001. In the field of higher education also the share of females enrollment into various faculties has increased very substantially. The increase in women enrollment in the educational institutions has its impact on the women employment in educational institutions.

Let us now examine the progress of females' enrollment in primary, upper primary, secondary / high secondary and higher education stages. As shown in Table - 4 in 1950-51, the enrollment of girls was 28.1 per cent at primary school stage, 16.1 per cent at the upper primary stage, 13.3 per cent at secondary / higher secondary level and 10.0 per cent in higher education level compared with the corresponding percentage of 71.9, 83.9, 86.7 and 90.0 per cent among boys / men.

Table – 4 : Percentage Of Females' Enrollment Of The Total Enrollment By Stages

Year	*Primary I-V*	*Upper Primary VI-VIII*	*Secondary Hr. Secondary 10+2/ Intermediate*	*Higher Education (Degree and above)*
1	*2*	*3*	*4*	*5*
1950-51	28.1	16.1	13.3	10.0
1955-56	30.5	20.8	15.4	14.6
1960-61	32.6	23.9	20.5	16.0
1965-66	36.2	26.7	22.0	20.4
1970-71	37.4	29.3	25.0	20.0
1975-76	38.1	31.3	26.9	23.2
1980-81	38.6	32.9	29.6	26.7
1985-86	40.3	35.6	30.3	33.0
1990-91	41.5	36.7	32.9	33.3
1995-96	43.1	39.5	36.1	37.2
2000-01	43.7	40.9	38.6	36.9

Source: Selected Educational Statistics 2000-2001.

By 2000-01, the situation has considerably improved at all levels, in favour of females to 43.7 per cent at primary level, 40.9 per cent at upper primary level, 38.6 per cent at secondary / higher secondary level and 36.9 per cent in higher education as against 56.3 per cent in primary stage, 59.1 per cent in upper primary stage, 61.4 per cent in secondary / higher secondary level and 63.1 per cent in higher education stage among boys / men.

Career counseling is being actively promoted to ensure that the skills acquired by girls and they appropriately utilize women. These positive initiatives have helped in improving the participation of girls/women at all levels of education especially in higher education since the post-independent period. It is evident that the enrollment of girls/ women has increased at a faster rate than that of boys at primary, upper primary, secondary / higher secondary and higher education stage. The foregoing analysis shows that during the whole period of five decades after implementation of our constitution, the growth rate of enrollment of girls/ women in all stages of education has been higher than that of boys / men.

Mortality Rates

***(i)* Infant Mortality :** Infant mortality rate reflects a country's level of socio-economic development and quality of life and is used for monitoring and evaluating population and health programmes and policies.

The main reasons for decreasing sex ratio of the child population in India are:

1. Neglect of the girl child resulting in their higher mortality at younger ages.
2. Sex selective female abortion.
3. Female infanticide, and
4. Change in sex ratio at birth.

There is no doubt that increasing use of pre-natal sex determination tests and female foeticide must have contributed significantly to the significant decline in the sex ratio in the last two decades.

The infant mortality rate (IMR) for the world in 1990 was 73 per thousand live births, only 16 in the more developed nations, and as high as 81 in the developing nations. The IMR in Asia in 1990 was 74 per thousand. As per the report from publication reference bureau, Washington, USA, 2001, the estimated infant mortality rate for the world for the year 2001 was 56 per thousand live births, only 8 in the more developed nations, and as high as 61 per thousand in the developing nations. The estimated IMR in Asia for the year 2001 was 55 per thousand live births.

Table – 5 : Infant Mortality Rates By Sex And Residence In India

Year	*Rural*			*Urban*			*Total*		
	Males	*Females*	*Persons*	*Males*	*Females*	*Persons*	*Males*	*Females*	*Persons*
1972	141	161	150	85	85	85	132	148	139
1973	141	144	143	88	90	89	132	135	134
1976	133	146	139	78	82	80	124	134	129
1977	136	146	140	80	82	81	126	135	130
1978	132	143	137	74	75	74	123	131	127
1979	129	131	130	73	71	72	119	121	120
1980	123	125	124	65	65	65	113	115	114
1981	119	119	119	63	62	62	110	111	110
1982	114	114	114	70	60	65	106	104	105
1983	113	114	114	69	63	66	105	105	105
1984	113	114	113	68	64	66	104	104	104
1985	106	107	107	56	62	59	96	98	97
1986	104	106	96	64	60	62	96	97	96
1987	103	106	104	63	57	61	95	96	95

Year	Rural			Urban			Total		
	Males	*Females*	*Persons*	*Males*	*Females*	*Persons*	*Males*	*Females*	*Persons*
1988	103	102	102	65	59	62	96	94	94
1989	100	98	91	100	98	58	92	90	91
1990	54	88	86	50	49	50	78	81	80
1991	87	87	87	53	52	53	81	80	80
1992	84	86	85	54	52	53	79	80	79
1993	81	84	82	47	44	45	73	75	74
1994	NA	NA	80	NA	NA	52	75	73	74
1995	NA	NA	80	NA	NA	NA	49	NA	74
1998	NA	NA	77	NA	NA	45	69.8	73.5	72
2001	70	74	72	41	44	42	64	68	66

Source: Sample Registration System, Registrar general and Commissioner, Census Operations, Government of India, New Delhi for various years.

Once the child is born, the infant mortality rate in the first year of life is often adverse as far as female children are concerned. We have data available through the Sample Registration System (SRS) conducted by the Registrar General of Census from the year 1972 onwards. The total infant mortality rate in 1972 was 139; it was 132 (for males) and 148 (for females) per thousand live births (Table-5). The adversarial relationship of female IMR with male IMR continued right up to 1987. Since then, after the introduction of the Universal Immunization Programme at the end of 1985, the gap between male and female mortality rates narrowed down and from 1988 onwards, except for 1990, the female IMR has been lower than the male IMR. It may also be noted that females in urban areas have generally had lower IMR than their counterparts in rural areas. Ultimately, the total infant mortality rate in 2001 was 66, for males it was 64 and for females it was 68 per thousand births. The female IMR is higher than the male IMR in total, rural and urban areas also in 2001. Although the significant drop in IMR is largely due to the grand success of the Expanded Programme of Immunization started in 1978 and the universal immunization launched in 1985, which has succeeded in getting more than 85 per cent children, immunized.

(*ii*) Maternal Mortality : World Health Organization (WHO) defines maternal death as the death of a woman while pregnant or within 42 days of the termination of pregnancy, from any cause related to or aggravated by the pregnancy or its management but not from accidental or incidental causes.

Every minute of every day, at least one woman dies from causes related to pregnancy, childbirth and abortion. There are about 6,00,000 of these deaths each year and 99 per cent of them occur in developing countries.

The maternal mortality ratio is the number of women's deaths from causes related to pregnancy and child birth per 1,00,000 live births. The level of maternal mortality varies more than any other health indicator that researchers use to compare levels of development. Even the best estimates of maternal mortality do not capture all deaths related to pregnancy. There is strong evidence that official statistics seriously underestimate maternal mortality even in developed countries.

The maternal mortality ranges from less than five in some European countries to over 1000 in some of the world's poorest countries. The maternal mortality ratio in developing countries may be as much as 50 times higher than that found in developed countries.

(*iii*) Maternal Mortality Rates In India : The decadal census data does not give any indication of maternal mortality rates (MMR) but

Sample Registration Survey (SRS) rates are available and also some data from the Registrar General of India Census Office indicates maternal mortality rates state-wise (Table - 6). The national data seems to reveal a maternal mortality rate of 408 per 1,00,000 births. The state-wise data is available for 1992 and 1997.

There are wide inter-state variations in mortality rates as seen from Table 3. States with low female status in health and education and large percentage of tribal population like Assam, Bihar, Madhya Pradesh, Orissa and Uttar Pradesh have the highest maternal mortality rates. Some states have shown dramatic decreases in these rates, like Bihar, Assam, Madhya Pradesh in the four-year period 1992-97.

Table – 6 : Maternal Mortality Rates: 1992 and 1997

State	*Per 100,000 live births*	
	MMR 1992	*MMR 1997**
India	500	408
Andhra Pradesh	100	154
Assam	1,210	401
Bihar	1,490	451
Gujarat	810	29
Haryana	320	105
Himachal Pradesh	580	—
Karnataka	400	195
Kerala	130	195
Madhya Pradesh	1,370	498
Maharashtra	180	135
Orissa	1,110	361
Punjab	200	196
Rajasthan	640	677
Tamil Nadu	230	76
Uttar Pradesh	1,120	707
West Bengal	780	264

Note: *Annual Report, Ministry of Health and Family Welfare, Government of India, New Delhi, 1999-2000.

Sources: Col.1. Occasional paper No.1, 1994, Census of India, Registrar General and Commissioner, Census Operations, Government of India, New Delhi.

Col.2 based on Sample Registration System estimates Registrar General and Commissioner, Census Operations, Government of India, New Delhi.

Economic Dimensions

(*i*) Work Force Participation Rate (WFPR) In India : The Work Force Participation Rate (WFPR), also called Labour Force Participation Rate (LFPR) is the percentage of working population to total population of a country. It is an important factor which affects production, saving and capital formation. It helps in analysing the occupational structure of a country and thus its level of employment. WFPR depends up on the age and sex structure of the population, age of marriage, average size of family, education, health, attitude to work, availability of work, etc. The work force participation rates in India for the Census years 1901 to 2001 are shown in Table-7. WFPR in the pre-independence period from 1901-31 was higher than in the post-independence period from 1951-91, except for the Census year 1961. The reason being the use of different definition of the 'work force' in the censuses. In the pre-independence census, main workers were linked with unpaid family workers. But in the 1951 Census, unpaid family workers were excluded from the main workers. That is why the WFPR in 1951 was 39.1 per cent as compared to more than 43 per cent in the pre-independence years (1901-1931). Again in 1961, WFPR increased to 43 per cent because persons whose main activity was not economic were included in the main workers. WFPR declined to 34.2 per cent in 1971 because persons engaged in part time activities were excluded from the category of the main workers. But since the Census of 1981, WFPR had risen to 36.7 per cent in1981 to 37.7 per cent in 1991 and to 39.3 per cent in 2001. This has been due to the adoption of a rigorous of "worker" in terms of main workers and marginal workers.

Table -7: Gender-Wise Work Force Participation Rate in India: 1901-2001

(In Percentage)

Year	*Females*	*Males*	*Persons*
1901	31.1	61.1	46.6
1911	33.7	61.9	48.1
1921	32.7	60.5	46.9
1931	27.6	58.3	43.3
1951	23.3	54.0	39.1
1961	28.0	57.1	43.0
1971	14.2	52.7	34.2
1981	19.7	52.6	36.7
1991	22.7	51.6	37.7
2001	25.7	51.9	39.3

Source: Census Reports for various years.

In the case of WFPR by sex, it had been much higher for males as compared to females. This is because of the social status of women. They are generally not allowed to undertake productive work outside home. But since 1971, their work participation rate has been on the increase. It rose from 14.2 per cent in 1971 to 25.7 per cent in 2001. This is due to increasing literacy and declining birth rate. Now more and more women are entering the industrial and service sectors. With urbanisation and expansion of dairy and poultry farming, fisheries, horticulture, etc., more women are participating in such activities. On the other hand, the work participation rate for men declined from 52.7 per cent in 1971 to 51.9 per cent in 2001. This again shows that more women are taking the place of men in productive activities.

Political Dimensions

Participation of women in political arena and in decision-making role is an important tool for empowerment. The extent of this participation is monitoring standards of political performance at all levels. In India the particiapation of women in politics have been actually nominal since the days of freedom movement while in many other countries women are moving forward. Although their electoral participation has increased over the years, yet voting is only one aspect of political participation. In fact there is no correlation between their population and voting percentage with their numbers in the legislatures or Government or other political offices. Inspite of a congenial political environment in the country, we find psychological obstacles, economic hurdles and socio-cultural barriers restricting women's effective participation.

As politics became more centralized as well as criminalized, thus undermining all other institutions of civil society, women were pushed out of leadership positions to function on the margins, at best relegated to the domain of social work at the local level. Even that tradition eroded from 1970s onwards. The setback to women's participation is even more severe at the state level than in Lok Sabha.

(*i*) Women's Representation In Lok Sabha : The representation of women in Lok Sabha has basically remained stagnant. It reached a 'high' of 8.1 per cent in 1984, then it increased to 9.0 per cent in 1999 and declined to 8.2 per cent in 2004 (Table-8). This despite the fact that all major national parties in recent years have declared through their manifestos that they would implement 33 per cent reservation for women in all legislatures. The ugly scenes and stalemate over tabling the Women's Reservation Bill in Parliament seems to be entangled in the web of male-dominated politics. Political parties have no unanimous stand on the bill.

Table – 8 : Women's Representation In Lok Sabha

Year	*Seats*	*No. of Women*	*% of Women*
1952	499	22	4.4
1957	500	27	5.4
1962	503	34	6.8
1967	523	31	'5.9
1971	521	22	4.2
1977	544	19	3.5
1980	544	28	5.1
1984	544	44	8.1
1989	517	27	5.2
1991	544	39	7.2
1996	543	39	7.2
1998	543	43	7.9
1999	543	49	9.0
2004	539	44	8.2

Source: CSDS, Data Unit.

(*ii*) Women's Representation In Rajya Sabha : The presence of women in Rajya Sabha has been only slightly higher, probably due to

Table – 9 : Women's Representation In Rajya Sabha

Year	*Seats*	*No. of Women*	*% of Women*
1952	219	16	7.3
1957	237	18	7.6
1962	238	18	7.6
1967	240	20	8.3
1971	243	17	7.0
1977	244	25	10.2
1980	244	24	9.8
1984	244	23	11.5
1989	245	24	9.8
1991	245	38	15.5
1996	223	24	9.0
1998	245	15	6.1
1999	245	19	7.8
2004	245	28	11.4

Source: CSDS, Data Unit.

indirect elections and nomination of some women members. The representation of women in Rajya Sabha has reached a "high" of 11.5 per cent in 1984. It increased to 15.5 per cent in 1991, then it decreased to 6.1 per cent in 1998 and ultimately it reached to 11.4 per cent on 2004 (Table-9). Nonetheless, this representation does not come close to the 33 per cent mark. The number of women contesting elections have always been low. It is interesting to note that the percentage of winners among women has been consistently more than that of men.

Conclusions

Women community though equal to men in population, it is a subject of concern to note that, in this modern sophisticated world also she is treated as the second rated citizen or subordinate to men in all major fields of life. Though various efforts are being made to improve the status of women, women folk could not take their maximum use and remained still backward. In almost all countries, the Governments are providing special provisions for women's development and efforts are being made to utilize women's talent to the maximum extent. It is well known fact that, in many parts of the world women have started making key contributions in areas of development such as agriculture, health, education, household enterprises, water resource management etc. And by now it is made clear, that without the active involvement of women sustainable development is not possible.

Gender discrimination or inequality from womb to tomb is a patent fact in the traditional cultures of the developing countries. In India too, discrimination on the basis of sex often starts at the earliest stages of life. The development processes of independent India, at a pace never achieved before, have also not succeeded in stopping the decline of sex ratios. A large number of migrant males who come to work in some cities may be responsible for the adverse female sex ratio. The other reasons for decline in sex ratio are differential mortality between males and females, differential undercount of females than males and drop in the female births leading to adverse sex ratio at birth.

There is a sharp decline in the sex ratio of the under 0-6 age population in the last 40 years in India. In most of the States and Union Territories the child sex ratio (0-6 age group) has gone down in 2001 while in 7+ age group there has been an increase in the sex ratio in almost all the states. Maharastra, the first state which has been passed the PNDT act also registered a decline in the under – 6 sex – ratio, from 946 in 1991 to 917 in 2001 (29 points). There is no doubt that increasing use of pre-natal sex determination tests and female foeticide must have contributed significantly to the significant decline in the sex ratio in the last two decades.

In spite of all the special constitutional provisions and governmental efforts, in the field of education, the disparities between males and females are still large. The total literacy rate in 2001 was 65.38 per cent, for males it was 75.85 per cent and for females it was 54.16 per cent. In literacy rate Kerala retained its position by being on top with 90.9 per cent literacy rate in 2001 in the country, this rate among males was 94.2 per cent and among females it was 87.9 per cent. Bihar stood at the bottom with a literacy rate of 47.5 per cent (60.30 per cent for males and 33.6 per cent for females).

However, as time passed by, females made rapid progress in all stages of education, the constitutional provisions and special efforts made by the 'state' coming in handy. A process has set in motion where by the gap between males and females in literacy rate is getting reduced, the growth rate of enrollment of females at all stages of education is exceeding that of boys, and more importantly, more and more females are taking to teaching in schools. These are favorable trends and need to be nurtured. Attempts to promote female education should be given greater priority than ever and there can be no better way to raise to self-respect of females than to employ them in schools and make them shape the careers of future citizens of India.

Maternal mortality and infant mortality are directly related to health care facilities available in the nearest place. But this is only the necessary condition. The sufficient condition is that the woman/man must be capable enough by way of education to know the importance of such a health care provision. This is more so with regard to maternal mortality.

In the case of WFPR by sex, it had been much higher for males as compared to females. This is because of the social status of women. They are generally not allowed to undertake productive work outside home. But since 1971, their work participation rate has been on the increase. It rose from 14.2 per cent in 1971 to 25.7 per cent in 2001. This is due to increasing literacy and declining birth rate. Now more and more women are entering the industrial and service sectors. With urbanisation and expansion of dairy and poultry farming, fisheries, horticulture, etc., more women are participating in such activities. On the other hand, the work participation rate for men declined from 52.7 per cent in 1971 to 51.9 per cent in 2001. This again shows that more women are taking the place of men in productive activities.

Still women's representation in Lok Sabha and Rajya Sabha is very low. Special measures are needed to accelerate the process of political participation of women. Various women's organizations should impart political education to the women, to make them aware of their political rights and civic duties, through an organized movement. It is also imperative that national political parties should adopt specific programmes for women, and mobilize them for electoral purposes and also provide them opportunities in public life. Certain endeavours should be made in this direction to create proper environment to empower women and to enhance their capacity.

REFERENCES

1. Agnihotri, S.B. (2001): "Rising sons and setting daughters provisional results of the 2001 census", in Vina Mazumdar and M. Krishnaji (eds.) Enduring conundrum: India's Sex Ratio, Centre for women's Development Studies, Rainbow Publishers, Delhi.
2. Ashish Bose. (2001): Population of India, 2001 Census results and Methodology, B.R. Publishing Corporation, Delhi.
3. Ashish Bose.(2001): "Fighting Female Foeticide: Grouping greed and shrinking child sex ratio", Economic and Political Weekly, Sept. 8, pp. 3427-29.
4. Chandra Sekhar, S. (1959): Infant Mortality in India 1901-1955, Allen and Unwin, London.
5. Coale, A. (1991): "Excess Female Mortality and the Balance of the sexes: An estimate of the number of Missing Females," publication and Development Review, 17, pp. 517-23.
6. Government of India. (2001): SRS Bulletin, Vol.35, No.1 Registrar General, New Delhi.
7. Harriss, B. (1989): "Differential Child Mortality and Health care in South Asia" Journal of Social Studies, 44, pp. 21-23.
8. Karl Marilee. (1995): Women and Empowerment, Participation and Decision Making, Zed Books Ltd., London.
9. Mahendra K.Premi. (2001): "The Missing Girl Child" Economic and Political Weekly, May 26, pp. 1875-80.
10. Neeta Tapan. (2000): Need for women Empowerment, Rawat Publications, Jaipur.
11. Pulla Rao, D. (1998): Economics of Primary Education, Rawat Publications, Jaipur.
12. The Annual Reports of the Department of Women and Child Development, Ministry of Human Resource Development, Government of India, New Delhi, 1985-86, 1997-98.
13. The Annual Reports of the Ministry of Health and Family Welfare, Government of India, New Delhi, 1985-86, 1997-98.
14. Visalia, Pravin. (1961): The Sex Ratio of the Population of India, Census of India, 1961, Monograph No.10, New Delhi: Registrar General of India.
15. Vitz, M.D. (1987): Women Entrepreneurs in India, Mittal Publications, New Delhi.

Chapter 3

WOMEN ENTREPRENEURSHIP IN INDIA : AN ANALYSIS

*Dr. D. Pulla Rao

ABSTRACT

Women represent half the resources and half the potential in all the societies. Efforts to promote greater equality between women and men can also contribute to the overall development of human society. The empowerment and autonomy of women and the improvement of women's social, economic and political status is essential for the achievement of sustainable development in all areas of life. Throughout the world, women's participation in economic activities is fast increasing. The role of women in entrepreneurship is also increasing. In India too, women are participating in large number in almost all the spheres of economic activity. In the case of Work Force Participation Rate (WFPR) by sex, it had been much lower for females as compared to males. But due to increasing literacy rate of females, their work participation rate has been on the increase. It increased from 14.2 per cent in 1971 to 25.7 per cent in 2001. In the case of work participation rate women have a lower participation rate than men. Compared to the urban areas, there had been a steady increase in the participation rate among women during 1971- 2001 in rural areas. As per 2001 Census, the share of females in total work force was 31.6 per cent and that of males was 68.4 per cent. Among the rural workers, the share of females was 35.9 per cent and that

* Associate Professor, Dept. of Cooperation & Applied Economics, Andhra University, Visakhapatnam.

of males was 64.1 per cent. The share of urban females work force was 17 per cent and that of males was 83 per cent. Working women are major part of labour market of India. Their problems cannot be ignored. They are engaged in gainful employment and contributing to home and national economy. But they are still over burdened and there is a need to correlate education and employment among women. To conclude, the working women have become a major part of labour market of India and hence their problem cannot be ignored. When they are engaged in gainful employment and contributing to the household and national economy, they should be given the due respect and status they deserve in the family and the society. In the changing socio-cultural environment of India, women are entering in a new era. But they are still over burdened with the household cores. So some measures should be introduced to reduce their household burden. This requires a drastical change in the mind set of the men folk towards women in general and working women in particular.

Introduction

Women community though equal to men in population, it is a subject of concern to note that, in this modern sophisticated world, she is treated as the second rated citizen or subordinate to men. Though various efforts are being made to improve the status of women, women folk could not take their maximum use and remained still backward. In almost all countries, the Governments are providing special provisions for women's development and efforts are being made to extract maximum use of women's talent.

In India, though during Veda, Upanishad periods, women were given much respect and they enjoyed equal right with men in all fields. Slowly women's position deteriorated and now we can see that she is being exploited and harassed in all respects.

Though during British era steps were taken to improve the status of women in India it was only after the independence, she enjoyed privileged rights. As per constitution, she is given equal status with man and several special provisions are made for her upliftment. Yet it is sad to note that women could not utilize the legal advantages properly. Only a small percentage of women have taken maximum advantage of the legislations and facilities available to them and have shined in various fields. Now, we can see the ladies working not only in the Primary and Secondary sectors, but also successful in the Military and Defence field as well. There are women Doctors, Lawyers, Scientists and Teachers and have shown that they are not less efficient to men, but are equally efficient, intelligent and hard working. In the field of business and commerce, women are lagging behind as compared to other fields. However, there are certain exceptions that a few ladies have shined in the industrial and commerce sectors also, and earned name and fame outside the country too. Due to increased cost of living, it becomes necessary for women also to undertake economic activity and support their families. Now the attitude of the society has also changed and working women is not seen with suspicious eyes as in the past. She is more liberated now and the modern woman leads a very happy and peaceful family life with her husband and family.

Again the modern woman has realized her values. She wants to make use of her intelligence, knowledge and education. She wants to make her children more efficient than earlier through her prestigious role. Even the time has changed so much so that, the lady having a job or profession will get easily married. She can enjoy all the comforts and luxuries of life being economically independent. Throughout the world, women's participation in economic activities is increasing. The role of women entrepreneurship is also increasing. In India too, women are participating in large number in almost all the spheres of economic activity. From village to city, we can see large number of women workers and entrepreneurs contributing towards the national income of the country.

During the early decades of planning, women's role in economic activity was not given much importance and only the Draft of Sixth Five-Year plan (1980-85) had stressed for special emphasis on the issues of women entrepreneurship and the steps were undertaken in that direction. The Eighth Five-Year Plan (1992-97) promised to ensure that benefits of development from different sectors do not bypass women. The Rashtriiya Mahila Kosh was set up in 1993 to meet the credit needs of poor and asset less women. The Ninth Five-Year Plan (1997-2002) made two significant changes in the strategy of planning for women. First, "empowerment of women" became a primary objective and secondly the plan attempted "convergence of existing services" available in both women-specific and women related sectors. The Tenth Five-Year Plan (2002-2007) has made a major commitment towards "empowering women as the agent of socio-economic change and development". Based on the recommendation of National Policy for Empowerment of Women, the

Tenth Five-Year Plan suggests a three- fold strategy for empowering women, through social empowerment, economic empowerment and gender justice.

The Concept of Entrepreneurship

Websters' Dictionary defines the term 'entrepreneur' as 'one who undertakes an enterprise' and becomes employer. An 'enterprise' has been defined as a bold or dangerous undertaking or an adventure. Various experts on entrepreneurship have defined the terms 'entrepreneur' and 'entrepreneurship' in different words. But most acceptable definition of the term 'entrepreneur' may be a "person or group of persons who assume(s) risk and undertake(s) an economic activity and provides goods, services and employment to society". Similarly, the term 'entrepreneurship' may be defined as risk-bearing and innovativeness capacity, capability and activity of a person or group of persons leading to starting and managing self-employment oriented economic activity.

Characteristics of Entrepreneur

To be a successful entrepreneur, a person has to acquire and develop certain qualities, which can be included by training and motivation. The essential entrepreneurial traits/qualities are:

1. High achievement motivation
2. Insatiable drive and persistent enthusiasm
3. Readiness for challenge
4. Persistent problem solving
5. Goal setting
6. Dealing with failure
7. Technical background
8. Experience in the line
9. Willingness to introduce something new (Sprit of innovation)
10. Taking initiative and seeking personal responsibility
11. Competing against self imposed standards
12. Tolerance to ambiguity and uncertainty
13. Hard working
14. Regularity and dedication to work
15. Self control
16. Self confidence

17. Confidence in self capability
18. Use of feed back
19. Willingness to take advice
20. Time management
21. Money as a measure
22. Drive and energy
23. Long term involvement
24. Total commitment and immersion

Women Entrepreneurship: Indian Scenario

Traditionally it was believed that women are physically and mentally weak and, hence, they are not fit for hard, and hazardous and risky tasks. But with the increasing empowerment of women in the world, now no job, profession or enterprise is such which women cannot undertake. Contrary to it, it can be observed that in oriental societies the women are born-risk seekers. They grow up with the feeling of management of risk and adjustment/adaptation with the changing environment.

Women entrepreneurship is the process where women take lead and organise a business or industry and provide employment opportunities to others. Though women entrepreneurship is a recent phenomenon in India, which came into prominence in late 1970's, now we see that more and more women are venturing as entrepreneurs in all kinds of business and economic activities and service sectors. Though at the initial stage women entrepreneurship developed only at urban areas, lately it has extended its wings to rural and semi-urban areas too.

Women industries mainly fall into informal sector where less than 10 persons with or without power and less than 20 persons without power are engaged and they will be of labour intensive and rely on indigeneous resources, family ownership and only small scale skills are sufficient. Though earlier women concentrated much on traditional activities, due to the spread of education, favourable government policies towards development of women entrepreneurship, women have changed their attitudes and diverted towards non-traditional activities too. They show favourable response to changing situations and get adjusted to them and have improved their position.

The Government and Non-Government organizations are giving more prominence to promote self-employment among women and build women entrepreneurship. Special financial assistance is provided and training programmes are organized for women to start their ventures.

Women Entrepreneurs

There has been a rapid growth of women entrepreneurs all over the world. In the fields of fashion, beauty and career counseling, many fashion designers are women with their own labels. To name a few: Ritu Kumar, known as the queen of Indian textiles, Ritu Beri, who has had a stint in the French fashion industry and Rina Dhaka among others. The Indian fashion industry is now conscious of the opportunities available in this industry abroad and the need to be globally competitive. The world of beauty culture has opened up many opportunities for women entrepreneurs. Women are setting up successfully small establishments as beauticians and hair stylists. Apart from clothes, women are successful in producing design accessories as well. Indian women have established brands in the world. Vinita Jain of Biotique and Shahnaz Husain of Shahnaz Herbals are global brands today. It is time to collate data on small and big business run by women. In the field of education, counsellors are mostly women, primarily because men did not see it as a lucrative sector. As disposable incomes increase with the opening up of the economy; women are taking to opening up restaurants as well.

Gender Wise Total Workers and Work Participation Rate According to 2001 Census

According to 2001 Census, out of total population of 1,025 million, 402.5 million persons were workers, of these 275.5 million are males and 127.0 million are females (See Table-1). In relative terms, the share of

Table – 1: Total Workers And Work Participation Rates In India: 2001

		Females	*Males*	*Persons*
Total	Population	494.8	530.4	1025.2
	Workers	127.0 (31.6)	275.5 (68.4)	402.5 (100)
	% of workers	25.7	51.9	39.2
Rural	Population	359.8	380.4	740.2
	Workers	111.5 (35.9)	199.2 (64.1)	310.6 (100)
	% of workers	31.0	52.4	42.0
Urban	Population	135.0	150.0	285.0
	Workers	15.6 (17)	76.3 (83)	91.9 (100)
	% of workers	11.6	50.9	32.2

Note: Figures in brackets indicate percentage of female and male work force.

Source: Registrar General of India.

males in total work force was 68.4 per cent and that of females was 31.6 per cent. Out of total rural population of 740.2 million, workers accounted for 310.6 million with 199.2 million being males and 111.5 million being females. Among the rural workers, the share of males was of the order of 64.1 per cent and that of females was of the order of 35.9 per cent. In the urban population, out of a total of 285.0 million, 91.9 million persons constituted the urban work force. Among them, 76.3 million were males and 15.6 million were females. This implies that the share of males in urban work force was 83 per cent and that of females was 17 per cent. From the data is concerned, the conclusion emerges that rural women are more burdened; not only they participate in large numbers in economic activity, they have to return home from that activity to undertake domestic work like cooking, cleaning, tending of cattle, not to mention child bearing and child rearing. As against them, vast majority of the urban women have withdrawn from economic activity outside the home and look after only domestic work.

Discrimination Against Women

We naturally require a change in mindset to allow economic participation of women on an equal footing with men in society. Women need to move away to a certain extent from the traditional roles of homemakers and child-rearing to more progressive roles where their economic contribution to society is regarded in a positive light. The UN Convention on the Elimination of All Forms of Discrimination Against Women (CEDAW), that India has ratified, mentions that, "State parties shall take all appropriate measures to eliminate discrimination against women in the field of employment in order to ensure, on a basis of equality of men and women, the same rights, in particular (a) The right to work as an inalienable right of all human beings; (b) The right to the same employment opportunities, including the application of the same criteria for selection in matters of employment; (c) The right to free choice of profession and employment, the right to promotion, job security and all benefits and conditions of service and the right to receive vocational training and retraining, including apprenticeships, advanced vocational training and recurrent training; (d) The right to equal remuneration, including benefits and to equal treatment in respect of work of equal values, as well as equality of treatment in the evaluation of the equality of work..." Given this and given the fact that India has ratified the Convention, it is important to put these rights into practice. Of course, the Indian Constitution guarantees equality to all its citizens, but this remains largely on paper due to feudal mindset in most parts of the country.

Suggestions for Improving the Status of Women Workers

The problems of women workers in India are multifarious and multidimensional. These problems can be solved through changes in the attitude of family, society and nation towards the women. Some suggestions are given below:

- There shall be compulsory education for women. When she is educated, she can manage her dual responsibility of home and work.
- Women should be given vocational training in their work so that their efficiency increases. They should be trained to develop their capabilities of decision-making and individual thinking.
- Women should be made aware of their constitutional and legal rights both in their work and in the social sphere.
- The attitude of the husband and family members should be changed towards the working women. Husband should come forward to share her burden.
- She should be given adequate facilities.
- She should be given financial freedom.
- Baby care centre should be opened at the work place where she can leave her child.
- Maternity benefit schemes should be enhanced in private sectors.
- Wage gapes between men and women should be reduced. Better medical facilities and congenial atmosphere should be provided to them.
- Another suggestion is to increase part time jobs for women in various organizations, which will give a sense of dignity and identity to the women.
- Women should change their attitude about themselves. They should be self confident in their approach.
- More seminars, conferences and workshops on women should be organized. They should be encouraged to participate in them and express their views.

Conclusions

Now working women have become a major part of labour market of India and hence their problem cannot be ignored. When they are engaged in gainful employment and contributing to the household and national economy, they should be given the due respect and status they deserve in the family and the society. In the changing socio-cultural environment of India, women are entering in a new era. But they are still over burdened with the household cores. So some measures should be introduced to reduce their household burden. This requires a drastical change in the mind set of the men folk towards women in general and working women in particular.

REFERENCES

1. Birley, S. (1989): "Female Entrepreneurs: Are they really any different", Journal of small business management, 27 (1), pp. 32-37.
2. Garg, R.B.L. (2004): "Women Entrepreneurs: Problems and Prospects", Social Welfare, 50 (12), March, pp. 16-18.
3. Khurana, I.R. (1988): "Strategy for Rural Development", Khadi Gram Udyog, 34 (8), pp. 335-344.
4. Mohiuddin, A. (1987): "Entrepreneurship in Rural Women", Kurukshetra, 35 (12), pp. 22-25.
5. Nelson, R.E.(1985): Entrepreneurship and Self Employment Training, Asian Development Bank, Manila.
6. Rao, S.K. (1976): Entrepreneur Development in India - Is achievement training the answer, Laghu Udyog, 4. pp. 9-12.
7. Sinha, Poonam. (2003): "Women Entrepreneurship in the North East India: Motivation, Social Support and Constraints", Indian Journal of Industrial Relations, 28 (4), April, pp. 425-41.
8. Sundaram, I. Satya. (2004): "Encouraging Women's Entrepreneurship", Social Welfare, 50 (12), March, pp. 15-19.
9. Vidyu Lata. (1990): Developing Rural Women, Discovery Publishing House, New Delhi.
10. Vitz, M.D. (1987): Women Entrepreneurs in India, Mittal Publications, New Delhi.

Chapter 4

WOMAN ENTREPRENEURSHIP IN INDIA—A GENDER PERSPECTIVE

***P. Balamurugan**

"My greatest hope is women.

They want a helping hand to lift them out of the well".

Mahatma Gandhi

ABSTRACT

Owing to various socio-cultural and economic reasons, India has failed to attain gender equality even after the 50 years of its Independence. It is a fact that gender discrimination is high in India when compared with Western countries. There has been a gradual improvement in the participation of women in the various activities of the country in the last two decades though there has not been significant and satisfactory level of improvement. In India, the majority of woman entrepreneurs are involved only in the small and tiny scale units. In general, woman entrepreneurs are constrained with problems like lack of finance, lack of technical knowledge and lack of moral support from the family members etc. The paper finds that Government initiatives taken for the promotion of woman entrepreneurs are yet to reach the beneficiaries. Hence, the paper suggests that necessary steps should be taken to promote the woman entrepreneurs in the present globalized era for the rapid economic development of the country.

* Research Scholar, Department of Economics, Bharathidasan University, Tiruchirappalli-620 024.

Introduction

In India, gender discrimination is high and more visible when compared with Western countries. Owing to various socio and cultural reasons women are prohibited to enter into the entrepreneurial world. In many fields, women participation is very low in India. Entrepreneurship is one such a field where women's participation is very low, though some improvements in women literacy rate are observed. In 1971, the women constituted only two per cent of the total entrepreneurs. Now it has increased nearly 10 per cent. In the present modern world, women entrepreneurs are recognized as powerful instruments for the economic development of any nation as well as the catalyst in bringing out the changes in the society. It is noteworthy that increased women participation in the economic platforms of USA was greatly helpful to the country to come out from the Great Depression. In this context, the present paper attempts to study the present status and the problems faced by the women as entrepreneurs.

Definition of Woman Entrepreneur

The meaning and definition of an entrepreneur is common to all irrespective of the sex, caste, religion and race. The wisdom of entrepreneurship is not gender specific. In general, those who are playing the entrepreneurial role can be called as entrepreneurs, irrespective of their sex. Hence, there is no need to define the woman entrepreneurs separately. However, in the practical sense, the woman entrepreneur is regarded as a woman who accepts or taking a challenging role in any business venture to become economically strong by making suitable adjustments in both family and social life.

Global Situation in Brief

Women owned business are becoming increasingly important in the national economy of many countries in the world. It is estimated that in US economy, women contribute more than $ 250 billion annually and create new business at two to three times the rate of their male counterparts. Since 1970, the share of women owned business has grown from only 5 per cent to more than 30 per cent, representing nearly 6 million of the nation's 16.5 million non-formal sole proprietorship. Women-owned business can today be found in every sector of the economy and in every region of the US. In Britain, the role played by the woman entrepreneurs are satisfactory, they occupy one third in the total self-employed in the country. It is estimated that the share of woman entrepreneurs in small businesses in UK is about 40 per cent and it is expected to grow further due to some external factors like improvement in technology, new communication means and improvement in child care, etc. In India, the share of woman entrepreneurs is not satisfactory and significant. However, there has been a remarkable improvement in their share due to their increased literacy rate, urbanization and changing life styles, etc.

Need for Woman Entrepreneurship in India

In India, a very substantial portion of women are unemployed though they have the ability to undertake varied activities including industrial activity. It is estimated that unemployment rate is higher among women when compared with men; and, the improvement in women's education is not proportionate to their employment levels in India. It is estimated that women constitute 60 per cent of the rural unemployment and 56 per cent of the total unemployed in the country. To reduce the unemployment rate among women, it is essential to develop women entrepreneurship in order to expose the women to various employment and profit-generating avenues. To speed up the economic development of a country, it is essential that the available work force should be optimally utilized. Hence, in India, it is necessary to bring the women into the hold of entrepreneurship with a motive to attain rapid economic development in the present globalized era.

Avenues for Woman Entrepreneurs in India

Classifying the job, business and industrial activity etc on the basis of gender is absolutely a backward thinking. In the modern world, women can venture into any area of business and industrial activities. However, this depends on their interest and their educational background, family, social status, income level, technical knowledge, entrepreneurial background and so on. The major portions of housewives are treated as unemployed. The following activities are considered and identified as the convenient business ventures for housewives: They are hand made papers, bee-keeping, black smithy, carpentry, bio-gas, making of palmgur, non-edible oils and soaps, gur and pulses processing, fruit-processing and preservation, bamboo and cane work, gums, weaving of door-mats, manufacturing of candles etc. It does not, however, mean that housewives could be engaged only in small scale business units; for there are lots of successful married women involved in large-scale manufacturing businesses in India. But this is only meager.

Historical Development of Woman Entrepreneurship in India

Before the Independence, Indian women were not encouraged to enter into entrepreneurial world. However, the situations changed in India after the Independence. In the Fifties, generally, woman entrepreneurs were come from the families where there was no income generating male. In the Sixties, many women educated in schools and colleges and began to start one-woman enterprises at home and from home. In the Seventies, mass of women completed their education and entered the work force as professionals. The women in this decade opened up new frontiers. Women in this decade wanted homes, marriage and children as well as an occupation. In the Eighties, women were educated in highly sophisticated technological and professional education. Many had medical, engineering and similar degrees and diplomas. Women in this decade opened their own clinics and nursing homes and many more opened up small boutiques, small enterprises of manufacturing and entered garment exports. This was the decade of the breakthrough for women in many fields and many frontiers. In the Nineties, there was a qualitative improvement in the women entrepreneurs in the country. In this decade, many women entered into the big enterprises and proved their talent with their competencies and capabilities. Women in India are potentially competing with men in almost all the sectors of the economy. However, it has to be improved to a remarkable extent.

Status of Women Entrepreneurs in India

In India, for a long time, women were prohibited to enter into any serious business ventures due to various socio and cultural reasons. The concept of women entrepreneurship is a recent phenomenon in India which came into prominence in the late 1970's. In India, in the initial stage of women entrepreneurship, it was concentrated only in the urban areas; however, lately it has extended its wings to rural and semi-urban areas too. Now, there has been a remarkable improvement in the share of women entrepreneurs in the country. However, still, it has not reached the satisfactory level. In India, the female population is 495 million as per the Census in 2001 contributing to nearly half of the country's population. But, the businesses owned and operated by women constitute only less than 10 per cent. The women's participation in corporate and large-scale business ventures in India is very meager; even in the small-scale sector they contribute only less than 8 per cent. It is estimated that in India, majority of the women entrepreneurs are involved only in the micro enterprises. It is obvious that in the last 20 years, there has been a qualitative shift in women entrepreneurs from low cost, low technology to high cost, high technology and more socially respectable entrepreneurial areas.

In India, the wisdom of women entrepreneurship has been mainly occupied by the upper community educated urban women. The share of dalit and rural women entrepreneurs is meager. Though there has been improvement in their participation, yet, it has to be increased to a remarkable extent.

Among the Indian States, Kerela ranks first in motivating women entrepreneurs. In this state women are well equipped with education and are highly encouraged to do their business independently and are prepared to face any challenge. It is said that this is the outcome of high women literacy in the state. The Kerela should be taken as an example to create favorable atmosphere to women entrepreneurs. In 1975-76, the number of industrial units run by women entrepreneurs in Kerela was 73. It had increased to 4,190 industrial units in 1993-94. The women entrepreneurs in Kerela now constitute a significant position in all the industrial activities ranging from readymade garments to high-tech computers.

Barriers to Women Entrepreneurs in India

In India, women entrepreneurs face several challenges like the problems of finance, marketing, production and personal and social problems.

In the social front, the major problem faced by the Indian women entrepreneurs is that they have to work amidst social taboos and restrictions, etc. It is said that the sense of inferiority in women fostered by custom is a great barrier to their entrepreneurial skill. In India, women are forced to be lacking in knowledge. Women's social interaction is less when compared with men. As a result, they do not have enough practical knowledge about the society and other entrepreneurial related issues. This would be the same even in the case of an educated women. Majority of the women lack in confidence and always feel that they may not be successful and hence hesitate to take risks. Thereby, their risk bearing capacity is significantly less. It is obvious that the general attitude of the society is not healthy towards women in India. Many of the Indian women entrepreneurs are constrained with lack of support from their family members. Moreover, the employed and self-employed women are seen with suspicious eyes by the society and even by their family members. As women entrepreneurs have to play a dual role, they have to strive hard to balance their family life and hence many women feel better to be housewives.

In the economic front, getting the required financial support is a big problem to the women entrepreneurs. The officials in the financial institutions think that the majority of women entrepreneurs are dummy and they are there to extract all the benefits from the financial institutions to support their male companion. Moreover, women entrepreneurs lack in property on their own. The International Labour Organization (ILO) states that though women constitute 50 per cent of the world's population, they own only less than 1 per cent of the world property. Hence, the officials in the financial institutions are hesitating to sanction loans to women entrepreneurs. It is obvious that availing the required financial assistance is the major problem faced by the women entrepreneurs in India. The marketing is another important problem faced by the women entrepreneurs in India, as majority of Indian women own only small scale business units and hence they have strived hard to sell their products in the present modern competitive world. It is said that their marketing knowledge and skill are also less. Another important problem faced by the women entrepreneurs is the management of labourers working in their unit. In general, the male workers feel inferior and inconvenient to work under the women entrepreneurs.

It is said that the government support for women entrepreneurs are inadequate. It is alleged that government has not introduced any important exclusive schemes to promote women entrepreneurs in the country. In the absence of adequate support from the government, the women entrepreneurs have to face severe problems to emerge and maintain as an entrepreneur in a traditional society like India.

Initiatives Taken for the Promotion of Women Entrepreneurs in India

In India, the Government initiatives so far taken for the over all empowerment of women are satisfactory. However, the government efforts for the promotion of women entrepreneurs are meager. The followings are the few important efforts thereof.

In India, during the early decades of planning, women's role in economic activity were not given much importance and only the Draft of Sixth Five-year Plan (1980-85) stressed for special emphasis on the issues of women entrepreneurship and the steps were undertaken.

In 1985, the Government of India established a National Level Standing Committee on Women Entrepreneurs with a motive to promote women entrepreneurs in the country.

In the Industrial Policy 1991, the need for special training programmes to support women entrepreneurs had been greatly emphasized. Product and process-oriented courses enabling women to start small scale industry are also recommended in the policy statement.

In India, banks play a key role in promoting women entrepreneurship through various Government programmes. As per the recommendations of National perspective plan for women, Women Development Corporations have been set up to provide various supports to the women entrepreneurs in the country. The Government of India has introduced schemes like Support to Training and Employment Programmes (STEP), Mahila Samirddhi Yojana (MSY) and Rashtriya Mahila Kosh (RMK) to promote women entrepreneurs in the country.

To promote women entrepreneurs in the country, so far, several organizations have been established. In 1966, the Federation of Indian Women Entrepreneurs was established with a motive to attain economic empowerment of women by helping them to become successful entrepreneurs. The federation continuously interacts with the policy makers in order to make them to support women entrepreneurs. The federation gives entrepreneurial training to the women entrepreneurs and helps them to get financial assistance from the banks. Since its dawn, it has been playing its rightful role to promote women entrepreneurs in India. The organizations like Indian Council of Women Entrepreneurs and FICCI Ladies Organization, are playing their rightful role for the development of women entrepreneurs in the country.

Suggestions

The following are the few important suggestions to promote the women entrepreneurs in the country.

It is obvious that education plays an important role in the entrepreneurial performance of an entrepreneur. Among the women entrepreneurs, the major portion is occupied by the educated women. By realizing the importance of education, due attention should be given to the women's education to promote women entrepreneurs in the country.

By keeping in view the socio-cultural set-up of India, more motivational training should be organized at the regional levels across the country. It is necessary to increase the number of professional schools for women.

Government should introduce a package of schemes exclusively for the promotion of women entrepreneurs in the country. In order to promote the women entrepreneurship, the government should come forward to give more subsidies to women entrepreneurs. By realizing the worsening status of women in the down trodden communities, a special package of schemes should be introduced to increase their share in the entrepreneurs in the country.

As women entrepreneurs have to face severe marketing problems, they should be taken into consideration by the Government and steps should be taken to solve them. Markets should be developed in rural and semi-urban areas so that women entrepreneurs can sell them easily in the nearest markets. More and more fares and exhibitions should be arranged for women products.

Conclusion

The socio-economic development of a country cannot be fully realized as long as its women are confined to subordinate position and their talents are unexplored. Women form a large component of the human resources of any country. They are the potential contributors towards development and productivity. Their contribution could be realized only when they get opportunities and also the freedom to use them. Hence, for the well-being of the society, the gender equalization should be maintained and the women should be used as productive agents. For a country's economic development, those who are having the ability to sustain and compete in the market should be encouraged to enter into any business venture irrespective of their sex, because market is not gender biased. It should be remarked that in many fields, women have proved and established their talents as successful entrepreneurs. In the present wage employment shrinking situation, there is need to orient women towards opting for entrepreneurship.

REFERENCES

- Anna. V (1990), "Socio-Economic Basis of Women Entrepreneurship", ***SEDME,*** Vol. 17, No. 1.
- Anil Kumar (2005), "Women Entrepreneurship in Metropolitan Cities" edited by Verma S. B in "Entrepreneurship & Employment: Strategies for Human Resource Development", ***Deep and Deep Publication Pvt. Ltd***, New Delhi.
- Bharti Kollan and Indira J Parikh (2005), "A Reflection of the Indian Women in Entrepreneurial World", ***Working Paper No. 2005-08-07, Indian Institute of Management,*** Ahmedabad.
- Dhameja S.K (2004), "Women Entrepreneurs: Opportunities – Performance – Problems", ***Deep and Deep Publication Pvt. Ltd***, New Delhi.
- Gopalakrishnan. V (2004), "Financial and Social Constraints of Rural Women Entrepreneurs" edited by Maria John. S (e. t) in "Rural Women Entrepreneurship" ***Discovery Publishing House***, New Delhi.
- Sumangala Naik (2005), "The Need for Developing Women Entrepreneurs" edited by Verma S. B in "Entrepreneurship & Employment: Strategies for Human Resource Development", ***Deep and Deep Publication Pvt. Ltd***, New Delhi.
- Padmini. M (2005), "Opportunities for Women Entrepreneurs in Rural India" edited by Maria John. S (e. t) in "Rural Women Entrepreneurship" ***Discovery Publishing House***, New Delhi.

Chapter 5

MARGINALIZATION IN THE MIDST OF MODERNIZATION—WOMEN'S HEALTH EMPOWERMENT

*V. Basil Hans

"Indian society has always recognized the need for special consideration for women in its traditional health sciences"

– Mira Seth

ABSTRACT

This chapter tries to focus on women health status in India today and its linkages to empowerment. It analyses the present scenario of women health, the emerging trends in women health status, health care structure and policy-making, and also recommends certain policy predictions to the existing problems and challenges. The main focus of this research paper stems out of the prevailing inadequate access and utilization of health care services in India. The findings are the outcome of the author's research in health economics in general and health infrastructure in particular, with reference to the Indian economy.

Introduction

Indian society is a marginalized society consisting of diverse groups of dalits, backward classes and women who have different socio-economic characteristics and problems. The term 'marginalisation' implies that a group or class in society is in someway obstructed by another class or group in the context of development from one rung to another or from one phase to another. The marginalized group is at the 'margin' of the benefits of progress and is deprived of its rightful share in the gains that

* Teacher Fellow, Dept. of Studies & Research in Economics, Mangalore University, Mangalagangothri-574199, D.K. district, Karnataka State.

accrue from any improvements that take place in economic, social and cultural life of the society at large. The simplest way to define marginalization is to describe the bias to which the concerned class or group is subjected to. The bias manifests itself in inequalities (of opportunities, responsibilities and returns), discrimination(from social cultural, political, economic and even biological perspectives), and deprivation (of rights, status, dignity, and even justice).

In India the roots of discrimination against women lie in the religious and cultural practices. Although some studies point to the equal status and rights that women enjoyed in the Vedic period (2500 B.C. to 1500 B.C.), patriarchy seems to have been the norm throughout history. The status of women in the contemporary context is reflected in the state of their health, education, employment and life in society (Madhok: 2006). Some feel that the pace of marginalization of rural people, women, tribals, dalits, etc has accelerated with the adoption of structural adjustment programmes in many countries. If we are to assess its impact in the coming times, we need to be aware of the deterioration in their health and welfare status, already becoming visible. Women are especially affected by these policies given that their health status has shown little improvement in recent decades (Karkal et.al:1995:25).

One important marginalized group in India that is known for its historical sufferings is that of 'women'. Apparently this is a gender problem. Hence the cliché calls of "gender equity" and "empowerment of women". Underlying the problem of empowerment is the plea of shared responsibilities, resources and returns (gains) between the male and the female. One of the chief areas of gender disability/denial/deprivation is health. In fact one of the important reasons for the call for women empowerment in general or rural women empowerment in particular is the poor health condition and/or poor access to health infrastructure of India. This assumes significance in the context of the development of physical infrastructure and human capital.

While human capital is a clear determinant of economic growth, only recently was health's role in this process become a focus of serious academic inquiry[1]. by marrying the separate fields of health economics and Women's development. This paper explores the explicit mechanisms by which a population's individual and collective health status affects a nation's economic development and performance.

In India women in reproductive age (15-44 years) and children (below 5 years of age) comprise 62 per cent of the total population. This proportion is equal to the total population of USA, Russia, Japan, and

Canada put together (Siddhagangamma: 2005:102). And they are the most vulnerable group in the society (Neeraja: 2003:1). Low health status of women in India is in fact a sad part of the story of India's social and economic development, particularly in the post-independence period. What is even more unfortunate that this state of affairs is still continuing in the present era of modern economic development labeled as liberalization, privatization, and globalization. There is ample empirical evidence to show how females – both children and elders – are discriminated vis-à-vis their male counterparts in the matter of health care. This proves that there is marginalization in the midst of modernization.

The health care scenario in India has changed significantly after independence. Despite developmental efforts and overall gains, majority of women in India – working as well as non-working – are still baffling with basic threats to their health and human dignity. Health inequities between rich and poor, men and women still exist. It is unfair that the fair sex always has been at the receiving end of the health management. New and re-emerging diseases and dilemmas have undermined gains and pose new challenges. Health has been accepted as a fundamental right of all people by the Constitution of the World Health Organisation (WHO). Health is key factor in national prosperity and so it should be a national priority too. While the health needs of the country are enormous, its financial resources are mismatching the needs (Iefai: 2004:13)[2]. Even the social framework for health care needs a cure. The WHO has defined 'health' as a state of complete well-being. But the health scenario in many a society shows that all is not well with regards to women health. They have a poor quality of life, both when they are men-dependent and self determined[3].

In Asia 41 per cent of women do not get prenatal care; of the 5 lakh pregnant women dying annually across the world, one lakh are in India alone, says the World Health Report 2005 whose theme is 'Make Every Mother and Child Count'. With this background, the twin *objective* of this paper is to identify the conundrums of women's health in the context of their access to resources of health care and to devise mechanisms to augment their status. Herein I try to look at the gender perspective of human development as regards women-health status in India. This is very important because unless the Indian society in general and women themselves in particular, do not address the emerging issues related to health crisis of women it would not be possible to bring the marginalized to the national mainstream. Such an analysis is important for another reason as well, that is the on-going structural change in health care in India.

Gender Divide in Health care – a bitter truth

When we look at the scenario of healthcare facilities for women, we have to evaluate this through their mortality, morbidity and demographic pattern. In fact they indicate their health status. The data on life expectancy for men and women indicate that women had lesser life expectancy than men upto 1981 (see Table 1) (Mira: op cit: 158- 59).

Thus, Life expectancy in India is low. In 1998 in India life expectancy rate for males was 62.5 and for females 63.3 while in Japan it was 76.9 for males and 80.2 for females, and in Sri Lanka it was 71.1 for males and 75.6 for females. There are also wide inter-regional and inter-state variations in life expectation rates. Life expectancy rate in rural India is around 58 years compared to around 66 years in urban India. Some more facts and figures related to India will aid us in understanding health status of women clearly.

- Out of 1 lakh delivery cases 453 women die in India
- Lakhs of women die due to poverty, dowry, and rape.

Table 1: Expectations of Life at Birth-All India, 1901-2016

Year	*Male (years)*	*Female (years)*	*Combined (years)*
1901-10	22.6	23.3	22.9
1911-20	19.4	20.9	20.0
1921-30	26.9	26.6	26.8
1931-40	32.1	31.4	31.8
1941-50	32.4	31.7	32.1
1951-60	41.9	40.6	41.3
1961-70	46.4	44.7	45.6
1970-75	50.5	49.0	49.7
1976-80	52.5	52.1	52.3
1981-85	55.4	55.7	55.4
1986-90	57.7	58.1	57.7
1991-96 (P)	60.6	61.1	61.2
1996-2001(P)	62.8	64.2	63.5
2001(P)	64.1	65.6	64.9
2001-06(P)	64.11	66.91	NA
2006-11(P)	65.63	67.22	NA
2011-16(P)	66.93	68.80	NA

Source: Census Estimates, Government of India, New Delhi and Report of the Expert Committee on population Projections (various years).
Note: P=Projection; NA= Not Available

- As many as 58 per cent of women reduce their food intake during pregnancy instead of increasing it.
- 50 per cent of women are malnourished.
- 70 per cent of women do not get adequate health care.
- 41 per cent of females suffer chronic energy deficiency.
- Two-thirds of deliveries still take place at home, with only 43 per cent supervised by health professionals.
- Only 52 per cent of couples in the reproductive age groups use contraception.
- India loses 12.6 per cent of women due to abortion, 23.7 per cent due to loss of blood and 13.1 per cent due to anaemia.
- 80 per cent of women are anaemic.
- Close to 125,000 women die from pregnancy and pregnancy related causes each year.
- Out of the deaths occurring during pregnancy and childbirth 20 per cent is due to anaemia alone.
- Maternal mortality rate (MMR) in India is around 450 while it is very low in Canada (6), Switzerland (7) and other countries. In Pakistan MMR is 340. India's MMR is the second-highest in the world.
- In India about 2 lakh female foeticides take place every year.
- Indians seem to very much believe that marriages are made in heaven. Every year about 4.5 lakh marriages take place, of which 50 per cent of the brides are between 15-10 years of age.
- In rural India almost 60 per cent of girls are married before they are 18. Nearly 60 per cent of married girls bear children before they are 19. Almost one third of all babies are born with low birth weight.
- An alarming number of HIV positive cases among women have been recorded in India.
- Although diarrhea is the second largest killer of babies, only 43 per cent of mothers know about ORS and only 26 per cent report ever having used it.
- Social restrictions of women's mobility also contribute to lesser heath care for women and children. For example, 90 per cent of married women in Uttar Pradesh and Jammu and Kashmir and about 80 per cent in Bihar, Madhya Pradesh, Rajasthan, Haryana,

West Bengal, Andhra Pradesh and Assam need permission to visit even friends and relatives.

- The privatization of the health sector has increased the burden of the poor. Studies suggest that illness is the second highest cause for rural indebtedness.
- Only 50 per cent of villages have any government health facility.

The UNDP's Human Development Report, 1995 made a comprehensive analysis at the disparities between men and women around the world. It came out with two new concepts in human development, i.e., the gender – related development index (GDI) and the gender empowerment measure (GEM). The former takes into account the achievement in life expectancy, educational attainment and per capita real GDP (same as the Human Development Index), while the latter is more a measure of empowerment and reflects women's participation in decision-making too. On the GDI India ranked 99 out of 130 countries. On the GEM, India fared worse, coming in 101 out of 16, well below Bangladesh (at 80). Thus, today we take note of inequality in the attainment of health status between men and women. Gender inequity is a moral and social hazard in India (Misra: 1997:205). This is a matter to worry because while biologically women are endowed with better strength to survive the survival rate as well as the sex ratio in India is unfavourable to the fair sex. The Population Census 2001 for instance shows only 933 women for very 100 men. In the words of Noble Laureate Amartya Sen, India with its present 1 billion has to account for some 25 million 'missing women' (Sarojini: 14)[3].

A country that has a tradition of treating women as gods, a country that has named several of its rivers after women, shows a different picture when it comes to the status of women health. In every state of India women are the neglected underclass virtually in every city and village there are thousands of women whose greatest disadvantage in access to health care are concern is gender. Gender is the most neglected component in the entire discourse on health, particularly in under-developed countries like India. It starts in the unit of family and grows in communities and classes until this disease spreads in the whole body of society. This has led to a general imbalance in the socio-economic development process in Indian society because health status is a vital component of human development. In fact, health care itself can provide gains provided it is not gender-biased and if there is close collaboration between those who receive care and those who provide it.

The poor health of women is also indicted by the high maternal mortality rate (MMR) of 400 to 500 per 1,00,000 births in India compared with 15 or 20 in the developed countries and 40-60 in some 'developing' countries such as Sri Lanka. Neglect of Women's health and high female infant mortality is clearly linked with the neglect of women from birth and the lower status accorded to women in our society. Their health is at the root of the health and population problems in the country. The problems get neglected throughout the life cycle, starting from sex preferences during infancy, discrimination in feeding practices, food and medical care, biological vulnerability during reproductive span, and the resultant high level of fertility and its ill consequences (Karkal and Divya: 1989:3)

Health is a factor of one's body, mind and soul. It helps in the formation of total personality of an individual. Discrimination[4] in health care – in any form – hampers peaceful co-existence, progress and prosperity. Man needs woman to make a family. Family building and maintenance is possible only with healthy co-existence based on mutual respect, concern and love (Ousepparampil: 2004:3). A society that alienates women from facilities of improving health status is an ailing society. This is a bitter truth not only for patients but also for doctors[5]. What is more blantant is that this sort of discrimination continues shamelessly with modernization all around. Rather modern technology has come to the aid of perpetuating the culture of discrimination in a sophisticated way, as in the case of prenatal diagnostic techniques such as amniocentesis and ultrasound scan to find out the sex of the child in order to selectively abort female fetuses.

The discrimination of females in health care is not confined to childhood. It continues through adolescence to adulthood. According to the National Family Health Survey 2, about a third of women in reproductive age (15-49 years) were malnourished and 13 per cent stuned, and what is worse, half the women in the group were anaemic. No wonder old women have hardly any better chance. There is thus, a 'compromise state health's in India. Not only those women are denied the right to make their own choices and decisions regarding their health, they are also exposed avoidable risks of morbidity and mortality. They don't get (or men forget women?) when it comes to the question of access to good food, health and hygiene.

In the matter of medical treatment also women are taken for granted. There is enough research evidence to show that shows women are discriminated against medical treatment.

With regard to health care, discrimination against females is also reflected in the type and relative frequency in utilizing the same… males receive better medical treatment than females in all age groups but this is more prominent in case of children (Mohanty: 1995: 347).

More than five decades of economic planning, and active participation in the International year of the woman (1975) and International Women's Decade (1975-1985), setting up of the Central Social Welfare Board in 1956, Department of Women and Child Development (WCD) under the Ministry of Human Resource Development in 1985, signing the Health For All by 2000 Declaration in 1977, National Commission of Women in 1992, Rashtiya Mahila Kosh (National Women's Bank) in 1992, drawing up the National Perspective Plan for Women (1998-2000), and declaring 2001 as the Year of Women's Empowerment or Swashakti, are part of India's rich experience in highlighting the cause of women and their development. The Ninth five-year Plan virtually and forcefully recognized that empowered women are agents of social change and development. Yet the process mainstreaming gender, gender sensitization and gender equity is anything but slow in India. This is not to deny the fact that in certain other fields like education, science, administration, entertainment and sports, women's position has improved quite a lot. In several cases they even occupy the centre stage. But a break even in women's welfare has still eluded India. What little has happened so far is only a shift in perspective from 'women in development approach' to a 'gender approach'. This is reflected in population and birth control strategies of the family welfare programme, viz., reproductive health approach. Thus gender discrimination has with it various complexities which cannot be ignored while focusing on the status of women's health.

Focus on Women's Health: Concerns, Challenges and Opportunities

Development that is not equitable is not sustainable. Investment in human resource development is therefore vital for "growth with human face". Gender issues cannot be separated from the process of developed even under privatization and liberalization. 'How they are' influences 'what they are'. Providing for good health is therefore called for Health is a merit food in the public finance parlance. Even under privatization, if and when market fails to deliver the goods, government intervention is justified. Women and Health, therefore is vital (and common) area of concern in sociology and economics. A developing society can leave women at the periphery only at the cost of development itself. The role of women as catalytic agents in spreading the knowledge of health and health care begins from their own household itself. What happens in the family spread to the community and then to the country. What we have to strive for is to meet the genuine demands of women without damaging the family fabric in society (Hans: 1997:219). It is in this context we need to have some concern, identify the challenges as well as opportunities for health development of women. The main areas of concern are:

- Food and Nutrition - bread-bakers or bread-winners, women still are the largest component of malnourished population; they suffer from anaemia, vitamin deficiencies etc; they have poor food security[6].
- Education, specifically health education – much of health education does not go beyond women's maternal role; there is no concept of life view of women's health[7] . Public knowledge campaigns are woefully lacking. A new information-education-communication (IEC) model has to be evolved to mobilize resources and realize the goals.
- Marriage and family systems that exploit women – polugamy, child and early marriages (low mean age at marriage) still continue to attack women's health status.
- Age and stage of development, say adolescence – specific nutritional requirements for girl during adolescence and general growth patter of her body receives inadequate attention in our society.
- Violence against women – young, married or unmarried, even widows are the victims of physical and psychological abuses and atrocities even in the modern era. They lack security, health included.
- Occupational hazards – beginning from home (kitchen smoke causing respiratory diseases) to farms(contaminated water and insect bites causing rheumatism) and firms (poor working conditions affecting mentural function, limb functions and productivity).
- Health care providers – women doctors are few, women are highlighted more in advertisements of medicines, fitness concepts etc, but their health needs are taken lightly. There is a felt-need for ethical framework for medical treatment to bring out good life (Brock: 1995:126-7) Stereotype roles of men and women need to be removed in and by the media.
- Interventions and Responses – even when some action is taken to prevent casualty and crimes against women more often than not it is too, little and too late. There are instances where genuine responses get delayed for want of sponsors!

- Strategies to be devised and implemented: the voice and choice of women – the question of responsiveness and responsibility.
- Women health policy: debate of public vs. private – there is more heat and dust than light and crust, less pragmatism, more dogmatism.
- Role of women's organizations in the context of modernization and globalization – less coverage, more glamour than armour for women against health deprivation cause concern; women have to be trained to demand access to health care.

A few of the Challenges are as Follows

- Women in India are by and large poor than men and they are economically dependent. (By official estimates 30-40 per cent of women are living below the poverty line). Therefore, they can't afford best food, medicine and other inputs for a healthier and longer life.
- Women do exhausting work at home as well outside in poor environmental conditions. There is larger threat to their health and life under these circumstances (e.g., beedi rolling industry, fireworks industry, mining etc).
- The social and ethical atmospheres in which women live and work in several cases leave much to be desired. Often the atmosphere/treatment they get is dirtiest and degrading.
- In terms of time they have little access to health care.
- Adverse sex is still demographic characteristic in India.
- Health indicators such as maternal mortality, malnutrition etc remain unacceptably high.
- Family Welfare Programme is unduly highlighting the target of control of numbers rather than improving the quality of life.
- Even where women have some access to health care, the places of treatment and persons who treat them are ill-equipped to deal with them: there are biased doctors, unhealthy surroundings, lack of privacy and faith in women. (For instance even today in some places, including the cities, the age-old belief that most women are irrational and hysterical exists and their genuine health problems are often dismissed as psychosomatic).
- There is a health crisis in India: and deplorable low status of women health in India is one of its ugly faces). Women's health for many is not a serious issue at all. They view women's health

only in terms of motherhood and not in terms of womanhood! Hence large many of our women are uncared, unheard, disabled, disaster-affected disadvantaged and deprived. What solutions, therefore have to be worked for addressing the challenges? We can consider the following:

1. Creating a sound awareness about women health problems both among women themselves and the males.
2. Revitalizing the governmental machinery at all places where women approach for the demand of health care.
3. Having women's cells in all places where women learn, work and undertake a host of other activities.
4. Raising the allocations for health care sector in India.
5. Promoting Women health care organizations for collective work and protection of rights.
6. Poverty alleviation for raising health care demand and creating healthy women, healthy homes, and healthy environment.
7. Integrating, monitoring and coordinating all schemes and projects of food, nutrition, health, occupation etc with respect to the female population.
8. Humane treatment to human resource, even when the most sophisticated techniques are used.
9. Multi-sectoral interventions by all players in the health and other related field – for having a holistic approach to the issues.
10. Saying 'no' to injustice.

Conclusion

Policies and programme are being prepared at global (e.g. Safe Mother hood Campaign), and national levels for improving the health care situation in developing countries. What remains to be done are concrete efforts at the grass root level. it is here that the women folk are directly confronted with the challenges, day in and day out. New women-friendly initiatives and a gender equity stance need to be taken not only in the interest of the fair (weaker?) sex but also in the interest of the whole society, as women health is a subject that affects the present and future generations to a large extent. This engulfs all forms of health care: preventive, curative, rehabilitative and promotive. A strong and active female population has to be built. For this, their health status has to be enhanced, quantitatively and qualitatively, combining nationalistic values with human values. Health should become women's point of strength, not of weakness.

If women have to be active receivers of health care, a life-cycle approach from cradle to the grave has to be initiated (Misra: op.cit:186). Simply it means giving some more space to women, in fact their rightful place in all circles, and considering the female force as a decisive one even while making decisions for development. From house-keeping to horse-riding, from handicrafts to spacecrafts women have traveled along way. The question that don't they have right to keep up their health? It is not just in homes, jobs and markets but also in minds that they get an honoured position. Mere income does not guarantee improved female health status[8] (Karkal: op.cit:44). A new insight and a cultural revolution can benefit women and men together. That means we must strive collectively for welfare mode, equity mode, anti-poverty mode, efficiency mode, and empowerment mode. We need to view issues related to women's health as a collective social responsibility (CSR), and not as a charity.

Ultimately a unifying concept of holistic health for all – without discrimination of sex, income, job or environment has to be evolved and actualised[9]. This is the part of new paradigm of "sustainable human development". This requires that the condition of women in India today changes from that of powerlessness to empowerment, from denial to development, from exploitation to enhancement of quality of life, and from gender conflict to gender co-operation. That is possible. We can make it happen if we are prepared to make a difference, and make it now.

Endnotes

[1] Women and children are the most vulnerable assets on earth. It is therefore vital to improve their health and well-being in order to achieve complete development of overall human resources. It is for this reason that the Millennium Development Goals call for a two third reduction in child mortality and three fourth in maternal mortality by 2015.

[2] For instance, at present about 6-7 per cent of the gross domestic product (GDP) is spent on health sector. The central budgetary allocation for health sector has been almost stagnant at 1.3 per cent, while that in the States, declined from 7.0 per cent to 5.5 per cent. So, it is not surprising that the quality of public health services has been low.

[3] The slogan for world health day 2005 is "Make every mother and child count", which reflects the reality that today, the health of women and children is not a high enough priority for many governments and the international community.

[4] Discrimination means treating one or more members of a specified group unfairly as compared with other people. It impairs the recognition, enjoyment and exercise by women of human and fundamental freedoms in political, economic and social or any other field. (Ravindran: 2004:4).

[5] A doctor once wrote: "I spent years in medical college, studying the basic medical sciences. I developed my clinical skills, first rate hospital, and acquired all the conceivable medical, technical, diagnostic, and therapeutic abilities. I graduated with absolute confidence in my ability to undertake patient care. What my education did not prepare me was how to deal with my first patient, and elderly widow with 5 children lying ill at home in a room without light, running water or sanitary facilities". (Mira op cit: 207)

[6] For women on many occasions fasting is feasting. They serve but are not served. Their special foods are often called left-overs. There are socio-cultural food fetters in Indian society, a clear case of exclusion and seclusion.

[7] Traditionally, in Indian society mother is revered as 'matrishkti' – the giver of life and the nurturer of children. Maternal feelings are considered a force to be reckoned with girls. Becoming a mother is considered essential. Indian women have regardless of passion, fashion and more importantly their health, always tried to bear children. Even now 28 million women conceive childreneery year out of which 25 million births occur. What is ironical is that women's health is neglected during pregnancy and during child birth too. Information about health is least provided to woman.

[8] There is a non-income index of economic development in the concept of physical quality of life index (PQLI) prepared by the Overseas Development Council. It comprises of three elements, viz., life expectancy, infant mortality, and literacy. For details about this index and other indices, and India's position in them see Hans, V.B., *Nature and scope of Health Economics in India: a Survey of Literature* (1997: 283 – 337).

Questions about the quality of life are questions about human lives themselves. Complications arising from sex division, cultural division etc., in an all known societies make the questions difficult. For an elaborate discussion on quality of life and norms of division see Annas Julias, 'Women and the Quality of life: Two norms or One?' in Marth C. Nussabaum and Amartya Sen (ed.), *The Quality of Life*, Oxford University Press, New York, 1995, pp.279-302.

[9] In the holistic concepts of health and development which perceive women as an integral part that needs to be developed along with men, lies the true future of Indian society. It is gratifying that the realization that women's issues cannot be compartmentalized and isolated as secondary issues is slowly dawning in and around us. This realization has a constant value. Indian women are beginning to get a better deal. Some positive changes in their health status are also taking place. But the size and speed of all these outcomes do not measure up to the need of the hour. (Tapan: 2000:11-13). Hence a discussion on women's health status is still relevant.

REFERENCES

- Brock, Dan, 'Quality of Life Measures in Health Care and Medical Ethics' in Marth C. Nussbaum and Amartya Sen (ed.), *The Quality of Life,* Oxford University Press, New york, 1995 00.95-131.
- Hans, VB, *Nature and Scope of Health Economics in India: a Survey of Literature,* unpublished M.Phil dissertation submitted to the Mangalore Univeristy, Mangalagangothri, 1997.
- Icfai, Study @ 'Healthcare', Vol. V No. 9 September 2004, pp.12-13.
- Karkal, Malini and Divya Pandey, 'Introduction' in Karkal and Pandey (ed.), *Studies on Women and Population*, Himalalya Publishing House, Bombay, 1989, pp.1-9.
- Karkal, Malini; Manisha Gupte: and Mira Sadgopal ' Women, Health and Development. Radical Journal of Health' Vol.1, No. 1, 1995 pp. 25-34. Available at http://www.hsp.harvard.edu/organizations/healthnet/SAsia/suchana/0909/rh332html. Accessed n January 19, 2006.
- Madhok, Sujata, 'Infochange Women' Available at at http://www.infochangeindia.org/womenIbp.jsp Accessed on January 19, 2006.
- Misra, Baidyanath, *Economic Profile of India,* APH Publiching Corporation, New Delhi.
- Mohanty, Bidyut, 'Panchayat Raj, 73rd Constitutional Amendment and Women', *Economic and Political Weekly,* December 30, p.3347, cited in Doshi, SL and PC Jain, *Rural Sociology,* Rawat Publications, Jaipur, 2002, Chapter 15 Panchayat Raj, An Era of Empowerment, pp. 329-344.

- Neeraja, K.P., *Rural Women – Maternal, Child Health, and Family Planning Services,* Discovery Publishing House, New Delhi, 2003, pp.1-8.
- Ravindran, TK Sundari, 'Zeroing on Gender Discrimination', *Health Action,* Vol. 13, No. 9, September 2004, p. 4.
- Sarojini, NB. 'Starting form the Womb', *Health Action,* Vol. 17. No.7, July 2004, pp. 14-15.
- Siddhagangamma, 'Health Conditions of Women and Children in Karnataka', *Development Studies* (Kannada journal), Vol.4, No. 1, 2005, vf, pp. 102-125.
- Seth, Mira 'Women's Health' in Mira Seth (ed.), *Women and Development-The Indian Experience,* Sage Publications, New Delhi, 2001, pp. 157-188.
- Tapan, Neeta, (Preface) in Neeta Tapan, *Need for Women Empowerment,* Rawat Publication, Jaipur, 2000, pp. 11-14.

Chapter 6

WHO SAYS WOMEN CAN'T PRO-CREATE ON THEIR OWN?

*Dr. L. Rathakrishnan
**V.P. Sriram

ABSTRACT

Development experience shows that gender inequalities are a major impeding progress towards Millennium Development Goals of poverty reduction. Women SHGs are increasingly being used as a tool for various developmental interventions. Credit an amentin for women empowerment was advocated later. These groups represents a new culture in rural development, breaking traditional bureaucracy and top-down management. One of the interesting observation noticed in recent time is that the group empower in managing rural micro enterprises and make decisions collectively for their common economic interest. This chapter illustrate some of the successful women entrepreneurs either as a member of SHGs or as a group.

Introduction

"In most of the developing countries today, more and more emphasis is laid on the need for development of women and their active participation in the main stream of development process. It is also widely recognized that apart from managing household, bearing children, rural women bring income with productive activities ranging from traditional work in the fields to working in factories or running small and petty businesses. They have also proven that they can be better entrepreneurs

* Reader, Department of Rural Industries and Management, Gandhigram Rural University, Gandhigram.

** Assistant Professor, Bharathidasan Institute of Management, Tiruchirapalli.

and development managers in any kind of human development activities. Therefore, it is important and utmost necessary to make rural women empowered in taking decisions to enable them to be in the central part of any human development process. The empowerment of women also considered as an active process enabling women to realize their full identity power in all spheres of life.

Development experience shows that gender inequalities are a major impeding progress towards the Millennium Development Goals of poverty reduction. This is particularly true in rural areas, where women are generally very involved in productive work but lack access to assets they need to play that role effectively. As a result of this imbalance, rural women are often more vulnerable to poverty than men, and their limited ability to secure assets independently makes them more likely to be negatively affected by ongoing changes in rural markets and institutions.

Women are Critical for Development

In his book "The Fortune at the bottom of the Pyramid", Prof. C.K. Prahlad comments, "A well-understood but poorly articulated reality of development is the role of women. Women are central to the entire development process. There are also at the vanguard of social transformation. For example, Grameen bank's success is based on lending only to women. The entrepreneurs who were able to use the microfinance made available were women. The grameen phone 'ladies' are the entrepreneurs. There are adequate evidence from various studies undertaken so far that the role of women in building a new society is inevitable. The SHGs at ICICI bank are all women, as are the shakti ammas at HLL. The women are entrepreneurs responsible for saving and accessing credit. In the case of CEMEX, the company works only with women. Amul, a milk cooperative, depends on women for their milk origination in villages. Women also collect the cash for the milk and therefore have achieved a new social status. Access to economic independence can change the long tradition of suppression of women and denial of opportunities. The success of Avon, Mary Kay and Tupperware in US and other parts of the world are also based on the role of women entrepreneurship. Although the evidence is overwhelming, very little explicit attention has been paid to actively co-opting women in the efforts to build markets and lead the development process".

When asked with Muhammad Yunus, managing director of Grameen Bank in Bangladesh, a pioneer in the practice of microcredit lending as to why loaned primarily to women, he replied, that "It has to do with the decision to have a separate bank for the poor people. From the beginning,

I had complained about the banking system on two grounds. One complaint was that the banking system was denying financial services to the poor people through certain rules it had set up. The second allegation was that the banking system also was not treating women fairly. If you look at the gender composition of all the borrowers of all the banks in Bangladesh, not even 1 per cent of the borrowers happen to be women. I said this is a very gender-biased organization. So when I began, I wanted to make sure half the borrowers in my program are women so that they are even. I did that. It was not easy because women themselves didn't think that they should borrow money. I had to do a lot of convincing. I encouraged them to believe that they should borrow money and make money. Part of that effort was to overcome fears – cultural fears – and the fact that they never had any experience with business and so on. Soon we saw that money going to women brought much more benefit to the family than money going to the men. So we changed our policy and gave a high priority to women. As a result, now 96 per cent of our four million borrowers in Grameen Bank are women".

In one of the speeches of Shabana Azmi on gender and population in South Asia, she revealed the disadvantaged position held by women in India embedded in the Indian psyche: endless cases of female infanticide, dowry deaths and abysmal access to literacy and health care. She noted that it is this differential treatment that lays the foundation for not only rapidly increasing population, but also in making millions of women endure lives of weakness and subjugation. In addition, she emphasizes education that reinforces gender equality as the most important element leading to women empowerment. However, there is not enough attention being given to the quality of education. Although she acknowledges the importance of legislation, she said that laws alone cannot bring about change. What are needed, according to Azmi, are a change of mindset, a change of attitudes, and a commitment to gender equality.

Women Self-help Groups

"Women self-help groups are increasingly being used as tool for various developmental interventions. Credit and its delivery through self-help groups have also been taken as a means for empowerment of rural women. This integrated approach, whereby, credit is only an entry point, and an instrument to operationalise other aspects of group dynamics and management, also caters to the need for social intermediation of these groups. A self-help group is conceived as a sustainable people's institution that provides the poor rural women with space and support necessary for them to take effective steps towards achieving greater control of their lives.

Through organizing informal self-help groups (SHGs), rural women in India are provided credit and extension support for various production-oriented income-generating activities. These activities usually include garment making, embroidery, food processing, bee keeping, basketry, gem cutting, weaving, and knitting. SHGs are self-governed, with decisions about production and marketing taken collectively, although the group leader is responsible for identifying potential marketing centers and consumers. These groups represent a new culture in rural development, breaking with traditional bureaucracy and top-down management. Informal groups empower rural women to manage rural industries and make decisions collectively for their common economic interests. Studies on the development of informal women's groups in India, show how it is possible to avoid the 'top-down management' and bureaucracy that often contribute to the failure of other schemes. Informal self-help groups in rural areas serve to empower women, and provide a basis for the provision of credit and other support for various production and income-generation activities.

The benefits that can be reaped by the grouping together of poor women in rural areas are many. A case in the point is a program of The Association of the Women of village of Canglon (ASOMUCA) in Panama. Investing in just a few women in the rural community has benefited the community as a whole, suggesting that similar projects can be replicated in other areas.

The project has yielded a number of benefits:

- There is greater grassroots participation in the region;
- The initiative has led to improving living conditions in the community;
- There is greater understanding on the part of the residents of Canglon and nearby communities about the importance and potential benefits of living in the vicinity of a protected area;
- The project has demonstrated that empowerment and the broader participation of women in community affairs benefits the community as a whole.

Another case in the same line in India is the effort of a group of rural women belonging to the untouchable "Paraiya" caste in South India to initiate and build an organization of their own to stand up for their rights and to challenge their oppression. The description covers the evolution from literacy to health action; the orientation workshop (which included building confidence through sharing experiences, participatory training techniques, reflecting on women's position in society, creating new attitudes of self value, identifying oppressive attitudes and structures in society, and the socio-economic and political causes of disease); and the role of animators. Rural Women's Social Education Center (RUWSEC) in Chingleput, South India, was initiated in 1981 by 10 women who belonged to the villages of Chingleput. The women had come together because of involvement in a nationwide literacy campaign in which the 10 village women as literacy teachers in their respective villages. Through their work, the women realized their own worth and potential and felt committed to working with other women in their communities to change their exploited situation. RUWSEC has focused on activities and issues related to women and health. 10 women "animators" began working in their villages carrying out health care, health education, and working towards building a women's organization in those villages. The animators' approach was to help women understand their own and/or communities' health problems and participate in their own healing. As a result of the efforts of RUWSEC, there were requests from several villages in the neighborhood for the creation of women's centers, and the animators decided to extend their work to 5 more villages. They visited the 5 villages and asked the community to nominate their own animators. The animators chosen were introduced to the work and philosophy of RUWSEC through a 6-day orientation program organized by the senior animators. The animators, RUWSEC, after 2 years of training in administration, accounting and management, and in conducting training programs, now are in charge of all their own activities. They have ventured also to further build and expand their organization.

Organizations for the Women and by the Women

There are many successful women forums and organizations that are trying to bring the rural women together for developmental works. The examples that we will take are Working Women's Forum (WWF), SEWA and Shri Mahila Griha Udyog Lijjat Papad, or Lijjat.

The Working Women's Forum (WWF), established in Madras in 1978, has brought together over 13,000 poor urban women around the issue of credit. Most women who live in the slums of Madras work as small-scale traders and vendors, their earnings often providing over half the family income. Interviews with these women revealed that their primary concern was increasing their earning capacity. The WWF was set up to enable these women to obtain low interest loans to expand their businesses. The key element in the WWF structure is the neighborhood loan group, comprised of 10-20 women from the same area who act as mutual guarantors for the loans of all group members. Over 7000 women have received loans and the repayment rate has been over 90 per cent.

About 2800 new jobs or businesses have been created, and earnings have increased an average of 50 per cent in existing enterprises. Women report that they are eating better quality and more varied foods as a result of their increased income. The WWF is expanding its activities to address the political and social problems of working women as well. The Forum operates day care centers, skills training centers, and remedial classes for school children. In 1980 the WWF launched family planning programs in which field workers (who are drawn from the WWF membership and paid $18 per month) disseminate information on helath, nutrition, and family planning to families in their communities. According to a staff member, this program was an outcome of the realization that "income generation and large families do not go together." The WWF also promotes intercaste, no dowry marriages and lobbies for public services. Women have become more confident of the possibility of gaining control over their lives, including their fertility. The WWF experience demonstrates that an organization does not need a lot of money, educated staff, or technical expertise to reach poor women. The Forum's success is attributed to its selection of one critical issue, utilization of local leadership, organization of women around existing neighborhood ties, and decentralized management.

The Self-Employed Women's Association (SEWA) is an Ahmedabad-based union of women workers established in, 1972. backed by more than 220,000 association members and has set up 16 organizations, including the SEWA. Bank has organized to fight poverty through full employment and self-reliance. SEWA has fought to gain the recognition of home-based and outside workers' legitimate rights. However, it was realized during the course of such struggle that struggle alone could not fulfill the demands, needs, and priorities of workers. There was also a need to create alternative economic organizations of workers in terms of access to capital, markets, raw materials, and knowledge and skills; social security; and enabling policies. The joint action of union and cooperatives has therefore been SEWA's organizing strategy for all these decades.

Shri Mahila Griha Udyog Lijjat Papad, or Lijjat, is an organization that has acted as a catalyst in empowering poor urban women across India during the last four decades. Starting as a small group of seven women in 1959, today Lijjat has more than 40,000 members in 62 branches across 17 Indian states. Only women can become members of Lijjat, and all of its members, addressed as "sisters", own the organization. Lijjat's main product is a thin, round, savory snack called *papad,* and papad rolling is the major activity of the "member sisters". Remuneration is the same for everyone, and profits and losses are shared equally among the member sisters, so there is no possibility of concentration of assets and wealth. Lijjat refuses to accept donations, but instead provides donations to the needy. Besides papad, Lijjat has also introduced other products, such as Sasa detergent and soap. However, papad has remained as its core identity product.

Key Factors for Success of Lijjat

- The merging of ownership with membership has encouraged uniform and sustained organizational growth.
- The consistent quality of the product has been a primary factor in establishing and maintaining Lijjat's brand image in the market for the last four decades.
- The Sarvodaya philosophy proved vital in forming Lijjat's foundation.
- Lijjat has emerged as an innovative organization in which women from any religion, caste, or class can become members. The pledge and all-religion prayer also encourage cooperative work among women, irrespective of caste of religion.
- Transparency in operations and a nonhierarchical structure has helped in establishing organizational accountability among member sisters.
- Lijjat encourages its members to give to others whatever they can, instead of expecting help from others. Lijjat does not accept donations, but gives donations, which enhances members' self-esteem and pride in their own organization.
- Calling the members "sisters" creates an informal work environment. Frequent meetings, open interaction, and consensual distribution of tasks reduce the possibility of disputes resulting from communication gaps and help work to go smoothly.
- Lijjat provides economic opportunities through a domestic activity. Once involved in this activity, the women acquire confidence and status as they make money in a respectable manner. The more enterprising, responsible, and experienced member sisters climb the administrative ladder. Lijjat exemplifies a remarkable way of making leaders out of ordinary women.

Microfinance and Women Empowerment

Links between microfinance and women's empowerment are viewed as optimistic, limited by design, cost effective in eliminating poverty, and a misplaced diversion of resources. Microfinance programs range from small scale self-help groups to large poverty-targeted banks. One model may vary in delivery, group functions and structures, and complementary services. There could be 3 contrasting approaches to microfinance and women's empowerment: the financial sustainability approach, the integrated community development approach, and the feminist empowerment approach. However, program evaluations revealed the need to question the assumptions underlying all 3 approaches. In most programs, women are benefited to a limited degree. Many women did not control the loan use. Most women were engaged in low paid, traditionally female activities, and increases in income were small. Resources and time invested in economic activity were limited by responsibility for household consumption and unpaid domestic work. Microfinance programs sometimes created domestic tension between spouses and loss of spousal income and support. Group repayment pressures sometimes created pressures between women. Many women focused on personal rather than social objectives. The author proposes a gender strategy for microfiance and sets priorities for further research.

Women Entrepreneurs

Empowering Women has become the key element in the development of any economy. It is been found that there are various forums and NGOs that are working hard towards this direction. There is lot of research studies supporting this view.

The Indian Economy has been substantially liberalized in recent years with an increasing role for small-scale private enterprise. Alongside economic liberalization has come a drive to enhance the role of women with moves to ensure that women have at least 30 per cent of seats in local councils and many other elected bodies (though not as yet in the national parliament).

As a result women are playing a more important economic role. There has always been a tradition of education for middle class women in India and increasingly there is a strong and growing group of professional women holding positions in Indian Universities and Government service. However, there are no sex discrimination laws within the labour market.

Women have also traditionally been involved in the informal economy, working in family businesses without formal position or pay. Thus their economic contribution is often undervalued or just not mentioned at all. The Indian Government and the state governments have taken some steps to encourage women to set up small businesses. For example the Karnataka State Government was offering help to widows to set up kitting businesses in 1997. However, whilst some statistical information is available (e.g. Singh, 1991) this focuses on work participation, unemployment, work seekers, wage rates, differentials and trades union membership. There is some information available on women entrepreneurs in the UK. Johnson and Storey (1994) suggest that women entrepreneurs are less likely to be married or have a professional qualification or to start self-employment under 30. Whereas Vokins (1994) study of successful women entrepreneurs suggested they had a different approach: an ability to do several things at once; ability to admit mistakes; keen to develop the workforce; less concerned with outward trappings. Women also faced different problems. Simpson (1991) found that their partners do not help with domestic chores or the business, whilst the reverse is true for men. Simpson also suggested that women have to work harder to gain credibility. Truman (1994) found that the advice services for entrepreneurs do not gear themselves for women. They also have problems with childcare and raising finance. However, the Microcredit Programme run by the India/Indian Government does help provide finance for small businesses. Rajasekhar in his study of NGOs has produced some research on the effects of the Micro Credit Programmes on Poverty, Wellbeing and Gender Equality. This study would therefore focus on the different motivation of women entrepreneurs in India and their contribution to the local economy for which there does not appear to be specific research.

Chapter 7

A STUDY OF THE STATUS OF WOMEN ENTREPRENEURS AND DETERMINANTS OF THEIR EMPOWRMENT IN INDIA

*Dr. R. Balasubramaniyan

ABSTRACT

Women have a good combination of entrepreneurial spirit, ambition, discipline and human relations. All these help them to succeed in highly volatile business and cut-throat competition. Women Entrepreneurship is an enterprise owned and controlled by women having a minimum financial interest of 51 percent of the capital and giving at least 51 percent of the employment generated in the enterprise to women. This paper attempts to examine the status of women entrepreneurs and determinants of their empowerment in India. The study used the Goalposts and formulae appeared in the HDR (2005) to calculate Life Expectancy Index, Education Index and Gender Related Development Index for females and males value. The results indicate a very insignificant Human Development Index (0.493) for females and also shows the presence of moderate to high gender inequality in India across States.

Introduction

Indian Society is a developing society. It is passing through a transitional stage. The attitude towards women is not so rigidly unfavorable as it was in the past. Women are trying hard to establish themselves as most sensible entrepreneurs. But many women faces challenging constraints which includes chorus household duties, the

* Reader, Department of Economics, D.G. Vaishnav College, Chennai - 600 106.

atmosphere or living conditions and burden of debt were actually keeping them away from the active work of entrepreneurship. Today, the changing attitude, outlook and attributes of women and the ever rising economic needs has led women to work outside the families and to financially support their families. When women moves forward, the family moves, the village moves and the nation moves. These are the golden words of Pandit Jawaharlal Nehru which are often repeated because it is an accepted fact that only when women are in the main stream of progress can make any economic and social development be meaningful.

Women have a good combination of entrepreneurial spirit, ambition, discipline and restrains. All these help them to succeed in these highly volatile markets. There has been an almost 10-15 percent increase in women investors during the last five years in beauty parlour industry. Most of these investors are married. The spurt in women investors started from 1997. Since then markets have been providing an easy opportunity to make fast money. Education levels among women are also going up. Women are endowed with a spirit of entrepreneurship, common sense, empowered trade and financial support of their family. A women entrepreneur is a person, who is an enterprising individual with an eye for opportunities and an uncanny vision, commercial acumen, with tremendous perseverance and above all a person, who is willing to take risks with the unknown because of the adventurous spirit she possess (Medha, 1997). Women entrepreneurs represent a group of women who have been broken away from the beaten track for exploring new avenues of economic participation (Gopalan, 1981).

Gender inequality is now receiving greater attention. Women and children constitute nearly 67 per cent of the India's total population. Women, better known as half of the humanity, have long been neglected in their role as beneficiaries in the process of development. Though they contribute 2/3rd of the World's work hours, earn only 1/3rd of the total income and own less than 1/10th of the World's resources (Indira and Rao, 2005), Women have to face problems under various circumstances solely and shoulder the increasing responsibilities. Emotional incompatibility with husband, in-laws and relatives, generation gap and gender discrimination create role conflicts even now and then, and on every step of their career. In general, educated women have internalized their roles and the resultant positions. They are ready to pay the price for the benefits of economic independence, equal status and position of self respect (Renuka Devi, 2005).

Section one of this paper attempts to examine the status of Women entrepreneurs and its determinants of empowerment in India. The rest of the paper is organised as follows. Section II explores the review of literature. Section III specifies the objectives and methodology of the study. Section IV underscores the results and discussion by considering the plaussible determinants of women entrepreneurial empowerment in India. Finally, section V presents the summary and conclusion.

Review of Literature

Women's economic empowerment is absolutely essential for raising their status in society. Women's prime aspiration for independence motivated them to take up entrepreneurship. The significant interactions with rural and urban Women and questioning them about their needs always elicited the same answer : 'give us finance and we can do the rest and best' (Renuka Devi, 2005). Entrepreneur is a person who possesses enterprising capacity to allocate, organise and manage factors of production more efficiently so as to maximise the profit and minimise the cost (Schumpeter).

Entrepreneurs are the innovators who introduce some thing new into the economy through new combination of resources and new methods of trade and commerce. The Government of India has defined a Women Entrepreneurship as " an enterprise owned and controlled by a women having a minimum financial interest of 51 per cent of the capital and giving at least 51 percent of the employment generated in the enterprise to women".

The first National Convention of Women Entrepreneurs held in New Delhi in november, 1981 recommended to give more priority to women entrepreneurship particularly in the allotment of lands, sanction of power supply, industrial licenses and adequate capital etc. In 1986, the National Policy on Education (NPE) highlighted the significance of education as a strategy for achieving a basic change in the life of a women (Sukumar, 2005). Further, the New Industrial Policy (NIP) 1991 underscores the need for conducting special entrepreneurship development programmes for women with a view to encourage women to enter into business. The Government of India declared the year 2001, as the year of 'empowerment of women'. The National Policy on Women Empowerment, 2002 recommended creating an environment for equal access to women in all fields by eliminating all kinds of discrimination in order to improve women's bargaining power (Sukumar, 2005).

Women's empowoerment consists of four dimensions, each are equally important but none sufficient by itself to enable women to act on their own behalf (Stromquest, 1995). These are the cognitive (Critical Understanding of one's reality), the psychological (self-esteem), the political (awareness of power) and the economic aspects (Capacity to generate income). Amartya Sen's work on human capabilities stresses empowerment as both a means and an end. It is a process of developing individuals capacity through gaining education and skills in order to empower men and women to fight for a better quality of life (Amartya Sen, 1990 and 1995). Naila Kabeer (1994) emphasises collective grass roots participatory action to boost women entrepreneurship with the power to work with others, to frame agenda and to make collective decisions. Deepa Narayan (2000) defines empowerment as a procoess which increases the assets and capability of the poor people and other excluded groups to participate, negotiate, change and hold accountable institution.

Objective of the Study

1. To examine the role of women entrepreneurs in India
2. To calculate the women's life expectancy index, education index and gender related development index (GDI)
3. To find out determinants and respective role of each variable in determining women's empowerment.
4. To suggest suitable policy measures to further empower women in India

Methodology

The study is predominantly based on secondary data. The women entrepreneurship data at the state and National level is primarily considered to gauge the women's status, educational level, life-expectancy at birth, number of children born to ever married women by age of women, distribution of rural women by employement status, number of women workers in rural India, economic well-being of women and cross-country comparisons. Largely, the data base is derived from Census Tables, Census of India, Department of Health and Family Welfare, Govt. of India, National Family Health Survey, 2001, IIPS, Mumbai, Pocket book of labour statistics 2000, Ministry of Labour, Govt. of India and Human Development Report, 2005, UNDP. The study attempts to calculate the women's life Expectancy Index, Education Index and Gender Related Development Index (GDI) by considering Human Development Report (2005) Model. Further, the study used the well established methodology for calculating HDI and GDI as recommended by UNDP / world Bank. They are as follows:

(*i*) Goalposts for calculating the HDI

Indicator	*Maximum Value*	*Minimum Value*
Life expectancy at birth (years)	85	25
Adult literacy rate (%)	100	0
Combined gross enrolment ratio (%)	100	0
GDP per Capita (US$)	40,000	100
(*ii*) Goalposts for calculating the GDI		
Female life expectancy at birth (year)	87.5	27.5
Male life expectancy at birth (years)	82.5	22.5
Adult literacy rate (%)	100	0
Combined gross enrolment ratio (%)	100	0
Estimated earned income (PPP US$)	40,000	100

Results and Discussion

In Japan, women do most of the farm work. To be able to manage their house holds and farms efficiently, farm wives have turned to mechanisation. Women in Ceylon have formed industrial cooperatives which produce baskets, mats, cane goods, textiles etc., Doll-making is a well – known Japanese craft. In India, there are a variety of industrial cooperatives in which women are active, producing food stuffs such as spices, pickles, papads, readymade garments, embroidered goods, and numerous other articles for use in the home. Table 1 covers the percentage of Male and Female workers engaged in various sectors of the Indian economy. Number of women workers engaged in primary sector in rural areas accounted to be as 81.2 per cent. The tertiary sector accounts for 10.8 percent and only 8.0 percent of women workers are engaged in secondary sector. The Table 1 clearly demonstrates that female workers outnumbering male workers in the primary sector.

Table 2 presents the state – wise distribution of rural women entrepreneurs by employment status, 2001. The rural female work forces are distributed in such a way that their contribution to GDP is not as significant as expected. However, female workers working in family farm business accounts for 15.3 percent, 17.4 percent working for some one else and only 2.7 percent are in self-employed business at the all – India level. The state-wise data on female workers generates hetrogeneity in contributions. States like Himachal Pradesh (44.5 percent), Maharashtra (31.2 percent), Rajastan (28 percent), Gujarat (27.4 percent) and Jammu and Kashmir (25 percent) chronologically stands for having largest female work force engaged in family farm business. North- eastern States like Nagaland (25.6 percent), Manipur (23.7 percent) and Arunachal Pradesh (21.5 percent) are having significant women entrepreneurs as self – employed.

Table 3 shows the percentage of women workers in rural India, 1999-2000. It clearly captures the distribution of women workers in rural India according to 2001 census provisional across major occupational categories. The number of women workers engaged in primary sector in rural areas accounts for 85.3 percent, secondary sector (9 percent) and Tertiary sector (5.7 percent) respectively. Among the lowest strata of women workers engaged are in Trade and Hotel Industry (2 percent), construction (1.1 percent), mining (0.3 percent) and Transport (0.1 percent) respectively.

Table 4 pictures the state-wise position of different age groups of women giving birth as on 2000-2001. It shows that the number of children ever-born to ever married women of different age ranging from 15-19 to 30- 34. The states like Manipur (1.43 percent), Delhi (1.33 percent) and Mizoram (1.09 percent) are having largest young ever married women in the age group of 15 – 19 giving birth of infants as against all – India figure (0.62 percent). The states like Utar Pradesh (4.70 percent), Assam (4.56 percent) and Bihar (4.41 percent) are having significant and proportion of ever married women in the age group of 30-34 giving birth to children as against all – India (3.92 percent) data. The Table 4 clearly indicates that women by and large until 35 years of age are giving birth and they are posting danger signal to Indian demography.

Table 5 presents the total population of India as per 2001 census. It shows the rural – urban break up of population and population explosion. In 2001, India's population stood at 102.7 crore of which, rural population account for 741 million and urban population account for 285 million clearly demonstrates that India is the second most populated country in the world.

Table 6 captures the literacy rate of India as per 2001 census. According to 1991 census, the literacy rate in India was 51.63 per cent and it is increased to 65.38 per cent by 2001. The change in literacy rate between 1991-2001 is 13.75 per cent. The male literacy rate (75.96 percent) and female literacy rate (54.28 percent) provide a big gap on educational status as per 2001 census. Table 7 shows the rural – urban differences in literacy status of women between 1961 – 2001. During the 30 year period (1961 – 91), the rural female literacy has registered a rise of 20.5 points and the corresponding value in urban areas is 23.5 but between 1991 – 2001 female literacy rate has shown declined marginally for obvious reasons. The urban female literacy rate has significantly increased over the years. In 1961, it was just 40.46 per cent has now increased to 79.46 per cent.

Table 8 presents the economic status of the World and India. The proportion of female headed households is on the rise globally. Female headed households account for one – fourth of households in Eastern and southern Africa, the Caribbean, North America and central Asia. Women headed house holds result from divorce, widowhood, migration for work and unmarried women.

The connections between gender and poverty have attracted more attention recently, because women's lack of social power and lack of resources can be mutually reinforcing. The economic status of the world shows (Table 8) percentage of female labour force was 57 in 1980 marginally increased to 61 in 2000. Women participation in the labour force are greater in numbers but they receive lower pay than men even when they work in the same sector.

Table 9 underscores the summary results of calculated HDI and GDI for India, 2001. The Dimension index for HDI female value is:

$$\frac{\text{actual value} - \text{minimum value}}{\text{maximum value} - \text{minimum value}}$$

The HDI is then calculated as a simple average of the dimension indices. Hence, Human Development Index (HDI) is the simple average of the three dimension indices (LEI + EI + GDP Index). The results indicate a very insignificant index value of 0.493 . Drop-out rates of girl students is one of the important reason for lower HDI value. As regards Gender related Development Index (GDI) both male and female life expectancy, literacy rate, gross enrolment ratio and income are considered for calculation. It is simply the un weighted average of the three component indices namely, equally distributed LEI, equally distributed EI and equally distributed income index. The result shows that there is a presence of moderate to high gender inequality in India across states.

Summary and Conclusion

More than 15 million girls aged 15 – 19 gave birth each year. Motherhood at a very young age entails complications during pregnancy and delivery. The children of young mothers have higher levels of morbidity and mortality. Discrimination and neglect in childhood can initiate a life long downward spiral of deprivation and exclusion from the social mainstream. Gender biased educational processes including curricula, teachers attitudes and classroom interaction reinforce existing gender inequalities. Girls are less encouraged than boys to participate in and learn about the social, economic and political functioning of society, with the result they are neglected. An estimated 450 million adult women in developing countries are affected as a result of childhood malnutrition. The UNDP has estimated that 1.3 billion people in the developing countries are poor. Siginificantly, women represent about 70 percent of this figure (Subbha Ray, 2005).

More than 5 lakh women die very year from causes relating to pregnancy, childbirth and abortion. Globally, women account for 48 per cent of adults who are infected with HIV / AIDS. Young women are vulnerable to HIV injection for both biological and social reasons. Poverty is a curse on women, as girls exchange sex for money for survival.

While discussing the status and role of women entrepreneurs in economic development, certain change indicators which are dynamic have to be considered. The impact of modernisation on changes in the status of women could be visualised through social, economic, occupational and cultural changes, changes in education, health and political awareness. The classification of status on dependency and organisation has its own limitations for women projecting a leading role. Time and again participation of women in socio-economic development has not received its due recognition. In developing countries like India, women participation in the formal sector is only about 15 per cent, notwithstanding the fact that in the developed countries it is as high as 72 – 80 per cent.

To sum up, women today can no longer be regarded as weaker sex and discriminated as second class citizens. Women are making efforts around the world to see that their rights are respected, their voices heeded, their opportunities widened. Women have more experience in business ability and they are the organiser of the family and the people. Hence, women put the foundation to build entrepreneurs. Women are the mothers and masters of entrepreneus. But it is a herculean task for the government to evolve a policy to eradicate female illeteracy, gender discrimination, female unemployment and poverty.

Table 1 : Percentage of Male/Female workers Engaged in Major Sectors

Sector	*Persons*	*Males*	*Females*
Primary	67.5	63.6	81.2
Secondary	12.0	13.1	8.0
Tertiary	20.5	23.3	10.8
Total	100.00	100.00	100.00

Source: Pocket book of labour stratistics, Ministry of labour, Govt. of India.

Table 2 : State-Wise Distribution of Rural Women By Employment Status, 2001.

S.No.	*State*	*Not Working*	*Working in family farm / for some Business*	*Working*	*Self employed one else*
1.	Andhra Pradesh	36.1	23.7	34.7	5.5
2.	Assam	81.4	0.9	15.7	2.0
3.	Bihar	73.0	7.6	16.9	2.6
4.	Goa	67.2	6.9	17.6	8.3
5.	Gujarat	45.1	27.4	25.6	2.0
6.	Haryana	67.5	24.3	6.9	1.2
7.	Himachal Pradesh	50.3	44.5	4.4	0.8
8.	Jammu & Kashmir	69.8	25.0	4.0	1.3
9.	Karnataka	44.1	22.7	31.5	1.8
10.	Kerala	75.2	1.2	19.4	4.2
11.	Madhya Pradesh	64.4	24.7	9.1	1.7
12.	Maharashtra	35.2	31.2	31.6	2.0
13.	Manipur	47.2	18.7	10.4	23.7
14.	Meghalaya	55.5	19.9	18.3	6.3
15.	Mizoram	64.8	20.8	10.4	4.0
16.	Nagaland	51.9	18.5	4.0	25.6
17.	Orissa	73.5	2.9	19.5	4.2
18.	Punjab	92.5	2.0	4.5	1.0
19.	Rajasthan	64.5	28.0	5.8	1.8
20.	Tamil Nadu	43.7	12.0	42.3	1.9

21.	Tripura	72.0	12.7	12.2	3.1
22.	Uttar Pradesh	85.9	8.7	3.1	2.4
23.	West Bengal	74.9	7.6	14.4	3.2
24.	Arunachal Pradesh	48.8	21.5	8.1	21.5
25.	Delhi	86.9	3.4	6.0	3.7
	India	64.6	15.3	17.4	2.7

Source : National Family Health Survey 2000–2001.

Table 3 : Percentage of Women Workers in Rural India, 1999-2000

(in per cent)

Sector description	*Number of women workers*
Primary Sector	85.3
Mining and Quarrying	0.3
Manufacturing	7.6
Construction	1.1
Secondary sector	9.0
Trade, Hotelling etc.	2.0
Transport and communications	0.1
Services	3.6
Tertiary sector	5.7
All Non-Agricultural	13.7

Source : National Family Health Survey 2000 – 2001.

Table 4 : State-Wise Position of Number of Children Ever Born to Ever Married Women by Age of Women, 2000-2001.

S.No.	*State*	*Age (%)*			
		15-19	*20-24*	*25-29*	*30-34*
1.	Andhra Pradesh	0.70	1.83	2.89	3.38
2.	Assam	0.95	2.08	3.38	4.56
3.	Bihar	0.49	1.63	3.08	4.41
4.	Goa	0.97	1.74	2.51	—
5.	Gujarat	0.61	1.85	3.14	4.00
6.	Haryana	0.61	1.85	3.14	4.00
7.	Himachal Pradesh	0.46	1.44	2.73	3.43
8.	Jammu & Kashmir	0.45	1.41	2.69	3.75
9.	Karnataka	0.82	2.08	2.93	3.78

10.	Kerala	0.40	1.22	1.85	2.48
11.	Madhya Pradesh	0.56	1.73	3.4	4.15
12.	Maharashtra	0.92	2.08	2.93	3.78
13.	Manipur	1.43	2.57	3.53	—
14.	Meghalaya	0.58	1.42	2.61	4.02
15.	Mizoram	1.09	2.14	3.38	—
16.	Nagaland	0.86	1.25	2.35	3.80
17.	Orissa	0.62	1.50	2.70	3.61
18.	Punjab	0.57	1.32	2.67	3.42
19.	Rajasthan	0.48	1.47	2.91	3.89
20.	Tamil Nadu	0.55	1.53	2.31	3.04
21.	Tripura	0.84	1.70	2.85	3.32
22.	Uttar Pradesh	0.54	1.63	3.27	4.70
23.	West Bengal	0.62	1.82	2.90	3.70
24.	Arunachal Pradesh	0.66	1.72	2.93	3.76
25.	Delhi	1.33	2.56	3.5	—
	India	0.62	1.70	2.93	3.92

Source : National Family Health Survey 2000 – 2001.

Table 5 : Total Population of India as per 2001 Census

Categories	*Males*	*Females*	*Persons*
Rural Population	381,141,184	360,519,109	741,660,293
Urban Population	150,135,894	135,219,060	285,354,954
Total Population	531,277,078	495,738,169	1,027,015,247
Literates 7 years & Above	339,969,048	226,745,947	566,714,995

Sources : Census of India, 2001.

Table 6 : Literacy Rate of India as per 2001 Census

(in per cent)

Country	*Persons*	*Males*	*Females*	*Literacy Rate Change in*	*(1991 Census) Literacy rate (1991-2001)*
India	65.38	75.96	54.28	51.63	13.75

Sources : Census of India, 2001.

Table 7 : Rural-Urban Differences in Literacy Status of Women in India, 1961-2001

(in per cent)

Year	*Rural*	*Urban*	*Overall*
1961	10.13	40.46	15.33
1971	15.52	48.84	21.97
1981	20.66	54.40	28.47
1991	30.62	64.05	39.29
2001	30.57	79.46	55.18

Sources: Census of India, 2001.

Table 8 : Economic Status of the World and India

(in per cent)

Categories		*Percent of Female Headed Households* Female	*Percent in Labour Force (ages 15-64) 1980* Female	*Percent in Labour Force (ages 15-64) 2000* Male	*Gross National income per Capita US$*
WORLD	—	57	61	86	6,650
More Developed	—	59	65	81	20,520
Less Developed	—	57	60	87	3,300
India	9	48	45	87	2,230

Sources : World Development Report, 2003.

Table 9 : Summary Results of Calculated HDI and GDI for India, 2001.

(in per cent)

S.No.	*HDI Indicator (Female)*	*Value*		*GDI (Female / Male) Value*
1.	Life Expectancy Index	0.699		0.676
2.	Educational Index	0.563		0.751
3.	GDP Index	0.217		0.418
	HDI Value	0.493	GDI Value	0.615

Note : The Table is constructed based on the Goalposts given in the Methodology section of this paper and Formule Prescribed in the Technical Note 1, Human Dvelopment Report, 2005, pp.340-344.

REFERENCES

- **Anand, Sudhir and Amartya Sen (1994),** "Human Development Index: Methodology and Measurement". Occasional paper 12, UNDP, New York.
- **Ashine Roy,** Development of women: An Assessment, Rajat Publications, New Delhi, 2003.
- **Bardhan et al (1999),** " UNDP's Gender- Related Indices : A critical Review, World Development 27 (6), pp. 985 – 1010.
- **Census Tables,** Census of India Govt. of India, 2001.
- **Human Development Report, 2005,** UNDP Reports, Various years.
- **Indira Kumari and Sambasiva Rao,** Empowerment of Women and Rural Development, Serials Publications, New Delhi, 2005.
- **Ponnuswamy, B. (2005),** "The Role of Non formal Education in the Empowerment of Poor Women in India," Quantonomics, pp. 17-24.
- **Renuka Devi (2005)** "Legal Rights of Women Entrepreneurship in India," Quantonomics, Chennai, pp. 5-12.
- **__________ (2005),** "The Role of Indian Working Women and Socio-Economic Transformation," Quantonomics, Chennai, pp. 13-18.
- **Sukumar, S.N. (2005),** "Women Entrepreneurs - Myth and Realities," Quantonomics, pp. 21-30.
- **Tamil Nadu**—An Economic Appraisal, 2001 – 2004.
- **Todaro, M.P.** Economic Development, Longman Ltd., London, 1997.
- **World Development Report, 2005.**

Chapter 8
STATUS OF WOMEN IN INFORMAL SECTOR

*Dr. D. Pulla Rao

The 'informal sector', which essentially covers the unorganized spectrum of economic activities in commerce, agriculture, construction, manufacturing, transportation and services, now absorbs as much as 60 per cent of the labour force in urban areas of developing countries.—ILO

ABSTRACT

The informal sector activities can be grouped under two broad categories, namely (i) coping strategies (survival activities) such as casual / temporary / unpaid jobs, subsistence agriculture and multiple job holding, and (ii) unofficial earning strategies (illegality in business) such as unofficial business activity (tax evasion) and underground activities (crime, corruption etc). This chapter discuss the characteristics of the informal sector, especially women workforce in the unorganized sector.

Introduction

The informal sector covers a wide range of labor market activities that may be categorised into two broad groups. The first category covers those individuals and families in economic environment whose earning opportunities are scarce and do not come under state regulations. The second category covers those individuals and families that desire to willfully escape state regulations.

The two types of informal sector activities can be described as follows:

1. Coping strategies (survival activities): casual jobs, temporary jobs, unpaid jobs, subsistence agriculture, multiple job holding etc.

2. Unofficial earning strategies (illegality in business): (1) Unofficial business activities: tax evasion, avoidance of labor regulation and other government or institutional regulations, no registration of the company; and (2) Underground activities: crime, corruption - activities not registered by statistical offices.

The informal sector plays an important and controversial role. It provides jobs and reduces unemployment and underemployment, but in many cases the jobs are low-paid and the job security is poor. It bolsters entrepreneurial activity, but at the detriment of state regulations compliance, particularly regarding tax and labor regulations. It helps alleviate poverty, but in many cases informal sector jobs are low-paid and the job security is either totally absent or very inadequate. The size of the informal labor market varies from the estimated 4-6 per cent in the high-income countries to over 50 per cent in the low-income countries. Its size and role in the economy increases during economic downturns and periods of economic adjustment and transition.

The concept of the informal sector was introduced into international usage in 1972 by the International Labor Organization (ILO) in its Kenya Mission Report, which defined informality as a "way of doing things characterized by (*a*) ease of entry; (*b*) reliance on indigenous resources; (*c*) family ownership; (*d*) small scale operations; (*e*) labor intensive and adaptive technology; (*e*) skills acquired outside of the formal sector; (*g*) unregulated and competitive markets". Since that time, many definitions were introduced by different authors and the ILO itself. The ILO/ICFTU international symposium on the informal sector in 1999 proposed that the informal sector workforce can be categorized into three broad groups: (*a*) owner-employers of micro enterprises, which employ a few paid workers, with or without apprentices; (*b*) own-account workers, who own and operate one-person business, who work alone or with the help of unpaid workers, generally family members and apprentices; and (*c*) dependent workers, paid or unpaid, including wage workers in micro enterprises, unpaid family workers, apprentices, contract labor, home workers and paid domestic workers.

Operationalizing the concept of informality for the purpose of measurement is not easy both because the two categories of the informal sector overlap and also the border between the informal and the formal sector is blurry. First, if unofficial earning strategies are exercised by a low-profit small enterprise with low quality working conditions, then workers of this enterprise and the enterprise itself can be classified as belonging to both informal market categories. An example of such a case is an unregistered one-person low-profit street trade enterprise - these characteristics combine unofficial and survival activities. Second, some formal market jobs or enterprises can be classified as informal if it is found that they have poor work protection or if the life style and opportunities they entail are considered undesirable. If the street trader from the previous example registers her enterprise, the enterprise and the trader herself could be categorized as belonging to the formal sector if the profit is considered above the survival level.

CHARACTERISTICS OF THE INFORMAL SECTOR

Employment

1. Absence of official protection and recognition
2. Non coverage by minimum wage legislation and social security system
3. Predominance of own-account and self-employment work
4. Absence of trade union organization
5. Low income and wages
6. Little job security
7. No fringe benefits from institutional sources.

Enterprise

1. Unregulated and competitive markets
2. Small scale operation with individual or family ownership
3. Ease of entry
4. Reliance on locally available resources
5. Family ownership of enterprises
6. Labour intensive and adapted technology
7. Absence of access to institutional credit or other supports and protections.

Habitat

1. Unauthorized use of vacant public or private land
2. Illegal subdivision and/or rental of land
3. Unauthorized construction of structures and buildings
4. Reliance on low cost and locally available scrap construction materials
5. Absence of restrictive standards and regulations
6. Reliance on family labour and artisanal techniques for construction
7. Non-availability of mortgage *or* any other subsidized finance.

Credit

1. Unregulated and non-subsidized
2. Easy accessibility
3. Availability in very small size and for short terms
4. Low administrative and procedural costs
5. Little of no collateral requirements
6. Flexible interest rates (from very high to no interest at all)
7. Highly flexible transactions and repayments tailored to individual needs.

Women and Work

The Declaration of Philadelphia (1944) annexed to the ILO Constitution proclaims that "all human beings have the right to pursue their material well-being and their spiritual development in conditions of freedom and dignity, of economic security and equal opportunity." "All human beings are born equal in dignity and before the law" is the essence of the Universal Declaration of Human Rights.

The need for total involvement of women in the process of change, progress and development may be defined as a social, political and economic process of change. To be just and to sustain the development participation of all classes, races and gender is to be ensured. Development has also been termed as a process which enlarged people's choices, reducing their vulnerabilities and increasing their capacities. Discrimination of any nature to any gender, class or group is a serious threat to the development and progress of a country.

Women and men as equal members of the society have the right to the equality of opportunities and treatment. The right to support oneself and to contribute to the economic well-being of one's family is as important for women as men. In fact, majority of women want and need to work, and their income earning capacity is essential for thir own survival and that of their families.

The Report of the National Commission on Self-Employed Women and Women in the Informal Sector observes that 90 per cent of the working women are in the informal and unorganized sector, and only 10 per cent work in the formal sector. According to World Bank Report, 1991, the percentage of women in the non-agricultural formal sector ranges between 2 and 5 per cent of the total female labour force and the non-agricultural informal sector between 7 and 15. Women in agriculture account for 81 per cent of the work force.

Non-agricultural informal sector includes hawkers and endors, construction workers, bidi workers, handloom workers, mine workers and domestic workers; while agricultural informal sector includes women in agriculture related activities like fishery, animal husbandry, dairy, agro and social forestry, sericulture, khadi, handicrafts and handloom. Agriculture itself is classified as an informal sector.

Activity wise Distribution of Women Workers

Agriculture is the most important activity of the women workforce (84%) in the rural areas, with the highest number of women workers engaged as agricultural labourers. (Table-1).

However, the percentage of women workforce in agriculture is declining. Manufacturing and services are the other two sectors where women are employed in large numbers.

Table 1 : Percentage of Workers in various Industrial Categories (1999-2000)

Activity	*% of Female Workers*	
	Rural	*Urban*
Agriculture	84.0	14.6
Mining and Quarrying	0.4	0.4
Manufacturing	7.7	23.2
Electricity, Water et.	—	0.2
Construction	1.2	5.5
Trade, Hotels and Restaurant	2.3	16.4
Transport, storage	0.1	2.0
Services	4.3	37.8
Total	100.0	100.0

Source: NSSO, 55th round, 1999-2000, Report No. 455.

In the rural areas, the pattern of changes in the distribution of workers by employment, status categories during the last fifteen years has generally been similar for men and women workers. There has been a fall in self-employment and an increase in casual labour for both categories. In the urban sector, employment status distribution for women workers has undergone substantial change, with regular employment having recorded an increase, while casual labour has decreased correspondingly (Table-2).

The trends show distinct signs of casualisation, i.e., increase in the number of casual workers, for both males and females. In rural areas,

Table-2 : Changes in the Distribution of Employment Status Categories Over Time

Year	*NSS round*	*Rural*						*Urban*					
		Male			*Female*			*Male*			*Female*		
		Self-employed	*Regular*	*Casual*	*Self-employed*	*Regular*	*Casual*	*Self-employed*	*Regular*	*Casual*	*Self-employed*	*Regular*	*Casual*
1983	38th	60.5	10.3	29.2	61.9	2.8	35.3	40.9	43.7	15.4	45.8	25.8	28.4
1987-88	43rd	58.6	10.0	31.4	60.8	3.7	35.5	41.7	43.7	14.6	47.1	27.5	25.4
1993-94	50th	57.9	8.3	33.8	58.5	2.8	38.7	41.7	42.1	16.2	45.4	28.6	26.2
1999-2000	55th	55.0	8.8	36.2	57.3	3.1	39.6	41.9	41.7	16.8	45.3	33.3	21.4

Source: NSS Reports, 1999-2000.

while women have been predominantly self-employed / family helpers, the proportion of casual employees is on the increase. The trends of casualisation, for both – females and males have been more pronounced in rural areas. It has been pointed out that a large proportion of semi-landless and marginal landholders work as casual wage labourers. The increase in landless households and precariously small holding, in turn, accentuates the pressure on the casual labour wage market. While men in landless households were able to find other kinds of work, women in such households were confined to wage work. Options of diversification to non-agricultural employment, which is more paying, are fewer for women.

The Unorganised Sector

Globally, the unorganized sector has been growing in relation to the organized sector. In this sector, there are no defined or regulated conditions of work or employment. It includes a high percentage of agricultural workers and also workers who are not attached to any particular employer. It has been estimated that this sector contributes over 60 per cent to the NDP and over 60 per cent to household savings. The unorganized sector also contributes substantially to the exports of the country, accounting for Rs.46, 000 crores, (1996-97) which approximates to 40 per cent of the total export earnings.

Women Workers in the Unorganised Sector

Women constitute a large percentage of the workforce in the unorganised sector. Data from the 55th Round of NSS (1999-2000) show that in the non-agricultural sector, Own Account Enterprises (OAEs) have a higher concentration of women workers (Table-3). OAEs provide women the freedom to organize their time in such a way that they can undertake activities along with their domestic chores. Even under OAEs, most women are not working as owners or hired workers, but are put in the residual category of 'other workers'. In rural areas, they account for 35 per cent of all 'other workers'.

Table 3 : Distribution of Workers by Gender, 1999-2000 (Percentage)

	Gender	*Rural*	*Urban*	*Combined*
Male	OAE	72.18	81.28	75.76
	Estb.	83.75	91.1	89.32
Female	OAE	27.8	18.7	24.2
	Estb.	16.2	8.9	10.7

Source: NSS 55th round, 1999-2000.

The percentage of self employed women is higher in Own Account Enterprises (OAEs) as compared to those in Establishments. It can be seen that a slightly higher percentage of women are working as owners in rural areas than in urban areas-in both establishments as well as in OAEs (Table-4). But the most significant form of employment for women in rural as well as urban areas is as 'other workers'. i.e., unpaid family hands in OAEs.

Table-4: Percentage of female workers in different activities, 1999-2000

Activities	*Working owner*		*Hired worker*		*Other worker/helper*	
	Full Time	*Part Time*	*Full Time*	*Part Time*	*Full Time*	*Part Time*
All Enterprises						
Rural	16.2	6.32	15.69	3.04	35.05	22.07
Urban	10.94	3.23	8.97	1.31	19.57	9.48
Establishments						
Rural	6.93	2.06	16.6	2.37	23.11	6.84
Urban	4.73	1.21	9.04	1.18	7.28	3.73
OAEs						
Rural	16.77	6.58	7.33	9.16	35.73	22.93
Urban	12.79	3.84	7.63	3.92	23.11	11.13

Source: NSS 55th round, 1999-2000.

Within the unorganized sector, women have an overwhelming presence in agriculture, forestry, fishing, plantation and allied activities with the highest proportion working as agricultural labourers and cultivators. They predominate in certain industries such as garments, textiles, food and electronics. The seasonality of work in the agriculture sector and the lack of other avenues of work, make them vulnerable to all types of exploitative practices including attempts to depress their wages or remunerations. Though women are economically active and contribute to the national economy, they remain invisible and poor.

Conclusions

Working women are facing so many problems in the informal sector. They face specific problems in each occupation depending upon the nature and area of work, level of their education and prevailing social setup. Women have restricted opportunities for public participation because their family responsibilities are organized around homes. These affect their chances of employment. They often have interrupted labour force participation and consequently, suffer downward mobility and increased risk of poverty and vulnerability. The overall effect is lower lifetime earnings and less employment security which further increases their dependency on a male 'provider'. Women's work participation can increase substantially if the supportive services such as day care and maternity benefits are provided to them.

Women's disadvantaged position as far as employment is concerned cannot be changed unless there is a social awakening in the society regarding the rights of women at par with men. Women should come forward and mobilize themselves in trade unions and women's organizations and establish their rights in various spheres. Women's organization can play a major role in addressing women's issues, mobilizing public opinion against any gender discrimination in the society and in lobbing for desired changes.

Change and improvement in the employment status of women in India is not possible without a major change in the traditional dominating attitude of men towards women in our society. Men should realize that women workers are no longer a secondary labour force whose income is simply a complement to the family unit, and that both men and women as equal members of the society have right to equality of opportunity and treatment. In the case of working women, men should realize and appreciate the plurality of roles women have to play as house-wives and as economic contributors. In such families men should come forward to lessen the burden of double work load of their women by assuming greater responsibility in domestic matters and extending a helping hand in day-to-day household activities.

Women have the right to work and their work is essential for their survival. They form an integral part of the process of national development.

REFERENCES

- Kundu, A. (1999): "Urban Informal Sector in India: Macro Trends and Policy Perspectives", Development Policy Department, ILO, Geneva.
- Kundu, A. and A.N. Sharma. (2001): "Informal Sector in India: Perspective and Policies", IHD and IAMR, New Delhi.
- Mitra, A. (1998): "Employment in the Informal Sector", *The Indian Journal of Labour Economics*, Vol. 41, No.3.
- Paul-Majumder, P. (2001): "Impact of Working condition and terms of Employment on the Women's labour force participation and their labour Productivity", *Empowerment,* Vol. 8.

- Reardon, T., J. Berdegue and G. Escobar. (2001): "Rural Non-form Employment and incomes in Latin America: Overview and Policy Implications", *World Development.* Vol. 29, No. 3, March.
- Start, Daniel. (2001): "The Rise and Fall of the Rural Non-farm Economy: Poverty Impacts and Policy Options", *Development Policy Review*, December.
- Venkateswarlu, A. (2003): "Changing Workforce Structure in India and Andhra Pradesh: 1961- 2001 "The Indian Journal of Labour Economics", Vol.46, No.4, October-December.

Chapter 9

WOMEN ENTREPRENEURS : CURRENT TRENDS AND FUTURE AVENUES

*Prabha Mathur

ABSTRACT

The current trends and future avenues for women in entrepreneurial activity is discussed. The women are progressing in all fields but they need support and encouragement from the community and also from the family. It's predicted that women have better prospects in the future. Ambition, systematic approach and sincerity are essential if the women want to be successful in their entrepreneurial activity.

Current Trends

Women in India though professionally qualified are still a minority as far as entrepreneurship is concerned. Baring a few most women at the top positions are in jobs, service industry and allied occupations which in itself is creditable. Not everyone has the grit and enterprise to be an entrepreneur but women at large are born leaders. They are homemakers, good mothers, wives and family makers having a basic knack of managing things. This talent if channelised properly in the right direction can lead to some outstanding entrepreneurs.

However, sadly, lack of capital, money, resources, opportunities and the required exposure doesn't give a very conducive environment for women to venture into full scaled businesses. Most of them choose safe tried and tested occupations like jewellary designing, interior decorators, homemakers, catering, fashion designing, pottery painting etc, which provide both creative and monetary benefits. But there is no long term stability.

Social workers, NGO's are the other common lines which women predominantly make a mark because of the right kind of environment it provides apart from the inherent need to do good to mankind.

* No. 3 Mahindra Society, Nagar Road, Pune-411006.

A large section of the women operate small businesses from their homes be it providing lunch to office goers & students or offices & industries. They start off in a small way with small shop snack stalls at reasonable rates and expand as the business grows. A classic admirable example of this is the lady who was behind the Bedekar pickles & masala's empire. She started with average 10 jars and went door to door selling, the stuff which slowly turned into a roaring business chain. But how many women have this kind of determination to go forward and do their own thing? The family constraints play a major role in women becoming entrepreneurs.

With a few exceptions like Kiran Majumdar Shaw who proved herself in an entirely different field not many women come forward for areas like farming, carpentry, service based repair centers etc. the comparatively lesser knowledge base of these areas, no formal education/avenues in both the technical & non technical aspects and the fight in a Man's World pose some of the few hurdles to women who want to make a mark in these fields.

What is needed is the availability of resources and equal opportunities with infrastructure support from the Government, social organizations, business houses, banking sector, industries etc. Some of the practical aspects of providing the right environment for initial capital, manpower and a basic place of work are the areas which need to be highlighted and addressed. The moral encouragement from the family and society is another very important aspect of successful women entrepreneurs. And the fact that the woman being the Boss is not always a bad thing.

Future Avenues

The choice is unlimited. But hardwork only is not the answer. The behavioral attitude biased against women hamper new avenues being explored. A simple co-operative society movement among the village women was immensely successful in Gujarat but failed almost every where else. Why? A Multitude of reasons among them being the attitude problems of society, the labor resistance, marketing inabilities all played an important role for the failure.

But all is not lost. Many women especially in the present modern day in towns, cities and metros are realizing the need for an independent identity and the various avenues available.

Teaching, Consultancy, CA's/MBA's are the common fields where women are excelling, however, it is the non allied areas which need encouragement. Biotechnology, Medicine, Engineering Units, service based industries like petrol pump service stations etc, are some of the key future avenues a women entrepreneur can look forward to.

Travel & Tourism, Hospitality sector, Vermiculture are some of the fast emerging business opportunities for women entrepreneurs. The immense market potential today with the fast growing metro population gives enough encouragement.

Setting up small scale industries / factories is another future avenue. However, most of the time the women entrepreneurs are not taken seriously and face innumerable problems for marketing their products, material supply, finance & banking. They try making a name for oneself.

The possibilities are endless. All that is needed the determination and encouragement. Not everyone has to go to space like Kalpana Chawla to prove themselves, a courtyard of flowers is enough if you can and want to. Ambition, systematic approach and sincerity will go a long way.

Women entrepreneurs have the world waiting for them today in almost any field but they need to break the traditional grounds to emerge as the educated young dynamic leader of today.

Chapter 10

SELF-HELP GROUPS A VIABLE ALTERNATIVE FOR SUSTAINABLE DEVELOPMENT

*Dr. R. Seerengarajan
**Er. A.T. Narasimhan

ABSTRACT

Self help group is a group of rural women / people, who have volunteered to organize themselves into a group for eradication of poverty of is members and to have sustainable income. A self-employed women is getting better status and it enables her to take part in decision making in the family affairs and outside the family as well. Entrepreneurial activities are suitable for economic empowerment of rural women. The suggested micro enterprises are (i) livestock based – dairy poultry, fishery and piggery, (ii) agro based – mushroom cultivation & medicinal plants, (iii) value added products based, bee keeping processing or fruits and vegetables; and (iv) non-farm based – beauty parlour, tailoring, bakery, computer, assembling work and textile related.

Introduction

Economic Empowerment has changed the lives of many people including the poorest women, by providing them economic gains on an on-going and sustained basis. Without economic empowerment, social and political empowerment has little relevance. Entrepreneurship is suitable for economic empowerment of rural women. Therefore, mobilization and organization of women into self-help groups is equally

*Reader, Department of Rural Industries and Management, GRU, Gandhigram.
**Part-time Research Scholar, Department of Rural Industries and Management, GRU, Gandhigram. (Asst. Exe. Engineer, PWD, Madurai.)

important, because these groups form the basis of solidarity, strength and action and thereby, economic empowerment is achieved.

SHGs are informal groups, where members come together toward collective action for a common cause. The common need without being dependent on outside help. The main objective of SHGs is to inculcate the habit of thrift, savings, banking culture *i.e.,* availing the loan and repaying the same over a given period of time. In this process, they gain economic prosperity through credit. SHGs are organized in the selected villages for economic and social development of rural poor and women in particular. As a result of group activities, the women are able to protect themselves from all types of exploitations.

'Self-Help Group' is a group of rural women/people, who have volunteered to organize themselves into a group for eradication of poverty of its members and to have sustainable income.

In recent years, the individual approach to poverty alleviation programmes has been increasingly replaced by group mode. This was particularly experienced in delivering micro-finance to the poor. Delivery of micro-finance to the poor is smooth, effective and less costly, if they are organized into SHGs. People come together to form SHGs groups can address a wide range of problems from alcoholism to micro-credit. The group dynamics of self-help groups micro enterprises under SGSY has been explained and entrepreneurial attributes developed in rural women after joining SHGs has been explained.

Self Help Groups : An Alternative for Sustainable Development

'Economic Empowerment' as an approach to development and gender equality has acquired greater importance in India and elsewhere over the last decade. "Economic empowerment is an economic change / material gain plus increased bargaining power and / or structural change which enables women to secure economic gains on an on-going and sustained basis". It has two aspects, one is income or livelihood and the other is whether or not women have effective control over this income or livelihood. There is a special opportunity offered by this approach to change the lives of many people including the poorest women. Without economic empowerment, the development of women is an empty promise plans, policies, legislations and laws provide only philosophical blueprint for directing the progress of society. In practical terms, these plans fructify only when women receive economic power in their hands. The status of women is instantly uplifted with economic independence.

The multidimensional process of empowerment requires awareness, access to education and training, participation in decision-making and politics and mobilization of women for economic self-reliance.

The process of empowerment helps in identifying areas to be targeted, planning strategies for action and outcomes. Empowerment is not a process, which is horizontal or vertical, but a process, which goes round in a circle. Here, the beginning ends in change and change leads to another beginning. No one magic formula can exist for empowerment. It has to be tailor made to suit the clients. The process of empowerment has provided a broad-based activity schedule to the national, regional and global agencies in which participation has been highlighted. By this method, participation of women in the decision-making process could be enhanced many fold and progress attained in a much shorter time.

Entrepreneurship is suitable for women and it is possible to do work when she has free time. A self-employed woman is getting better status and it enables her to take part in decision-making in the family affairs. Through the economic independence, women automatically get empowerment also. Development of women entrepreneurship enables men to understand and appreciate women's abilities.

Credit is the lifeline of any enterprise and lack of adequate finances to establish and operate a unit in rural areas is a major obstacle to rural industrialization. Even though the government agencies have established credit-lending institutions for such activities, but due to bureaucratic bottlenecks and lack of collateral, adequate credit is not made available to these units. As a result, these units cannot adopt innovative technologies and increase productivity through mechanization as well as market their products to areas where the demand as well as prices of their finished products to high.

Economic empowerment has changed the lives of many people including the poorest women, by providing them economic gains on an on-going and sustained basis. Without economic empowerment, social and political empowerment has little relevance. Entrepreneurship is suitable for economic empowerment of rural women. Therefore, mobilization and organization of women into self-help groups is equally important, because these groups form the basis of solidarity, strength and action and thereby, economic empowerment is achieved.

SHGs are informal groups, where members come together toward collective action for a common cause. The common need here is meeting their emergent economic needs without being dependent on outside help. The main objective of SHGs is to inculcate the habit of thrift, savings, banking culture i.e. availing the loan and repaying the same over a given period of time. In this process, they gain economic prosperity through credit. SHGs are organized in the villages for economic and social development of the rural poor and women, in particular. As a result of group activities, the women are able to protect themselves from all types of exploitations.

'Self Help Group' is a group of rural women/people, who have volunteered to organize themselves into a group for eradication of poverty of its members and to have sustainable income.

In recent years, the individual approach to poverty alleviation progrmmes has been increasingly replaced by group mode. This was particularly experienced in delivering micro-finance to the poor. Delivery of micro-finance to the poor is smooth, effective and less costly, if they are organized into SHGs. People come together to form SHGs when they are mutually aided to over come common problems. Such groups can address a wide range of problems from alcoholism to micro-credit.

Providing micro-credit to rural women through an organized set up will make them enterprising women. Regional Rural Banks, cooperative banks and commercial banks are not successful in rural micro-credit. Many rural poor (women) feel reluctant to approach the banks or financing agencies and do not have enough courage because of the low status of their livelihood as well as illiteracy. The Self-Help Group (SHG) is a viable alternative to achieve the objective of rural development and to get community participation in all rural development programmes. SHG is a viable organized set up to disburse micro-credit to rural women for the purpose of encouraging them to enter into entrepreneurial activities.

Initiating and monitoring the credit programmes for the poor can be made more effective and less costly if banks make attempts to organize the poor in self-help groups. Undoubtedly, self-help groups have the advantages of better knowledge about their members as compared to the bank staff. Proper utilisation of credit and timely repayment are ensured in self-help groups. Self-help groups enhance the equality of women as particpators, decision-makers and beneficieries in the democratic, economic, social and cultural spheres of life.

The maximum experimentation with micro-credit can be seen in Bangladesh, where it has been extensively used for reaching, the poorest sections of society. It has proved to be a most powerful weapon to fight poverty. Micro credit is not a charity, it is a loan facility in a convenient manner without procedural constrains and bureaucratic delays.

Mahila Samajans (Women's group) in Trivandrum, provided a good organization base for economic activites for the women in the community. The Samajans played a crucial role in highlighting the central position of grass root organizations in improving the employment conditions for women. The experiment showed that efforts involving poor people require the building up of firm linkages to various power structures. The case studies concluded that welfare-oriented organizations could form the basis for more economically oriented activities. It is suggested that a trained field worker should be attached to a self help group with sufficient time to listen, watch, answer questions and give whatever support is needed.

Shylendra (1998) evaluated the performance of eight women's self-help groups (SHGs) promoted by IRMA, Anand. He gave some lessons viz; the need of forming SHGs based on the assessment; ensuring clear understanding of the concept of SHGs among team members involved in promoting SHGs; and the need to enhance the relevance of SHGs to their members by enabling them to meet effectively their requirements, be it savings or credit or income generating activities.

Sustainable Micro Enterprises for Women

India is a land of villages and more than 74 per cent of population is living in the rural areas. The development of Indian depends on the development of rural masses. It was for this reason that Gandhiji laid the greatest emphasis on the development of villages in India-culturally, economically as well as politically and said, "If the villages perish, India will perish too". Gandhiji believed that India's progress would remain rather marginal or cosmetic unless it reaches and shows up in the remotest corners of the nation's vast countryside or until the villages become the main "repository of progress and power". Manifestly, therefore, rural development has been high on India's agenda ever since the advent of Independence.

Government of India, in the Five Year Plans, has launched several programmes for the alleviation of poverty and socio-economic upliftment of rural people. The percentage of people living below poverty line has declined over the last two decades, but because of population growth, the total number of poor people has remained more or less constant. According to National Sample Survey Organisation (NSSO, 2000), the national percentage of people below poverty line is 26.1 per cent. there are few states having higher than national level of people below poverty line and these are Orissa (47.15%), Bihar (42.6%), Madhya Pradesh (37.43%), Sikkim (36.55% and Tripura (34.44%). Although poverty alleviation programmes have been in existence but they have not reached the poor and the extent of poverty is still high after more than 50 years of independence.

Table 1: Percentage of People below Poverty Line

Years	*Rural*	*Urban*	*All India*
1973-74	56.4	47.0	54.9
1977-78	53.1	45.2	51.3
1983	45.7	40.8	44.5
1987-88	38.1	38.2	36.9
1993-94	37.3	32.4	36.0
1999-2000	27.1	23.6	26.1

Source: Economic Survey 2000-2001.

As most of the welfare needs arise from poverty, therefore, poverty alleviation for welfare and upgradation of standard of living has to be the main agenda for the development of country. Involvement of voluntary agencies, mass media and the corporate sector with 'mission-mode' approach is vital for the success of poverty alleviation programmes.

Poverty hits women the hardest as they balance 'means and ends' at the household level and many a time skip a meal to let rest of the household avail of the little that is available. These women are subjected to economic and social discrimination and credit is not easily available to them. Millions of Indian women live below poverty line and their social empowerment would have little relevance without first empowering them on economic front. The World Bank studies have shown that enhancement of women's earnings would have a more profound effect on the welfare of the family as a whole, since increase in women's income result more directly into better health and nutrition for children.

Women are moving to the forefronts of the global agenda for socio-economic and political development process. Though, there is a great gap between agenda to policies to practice, yet their contribution are attracting attention of policy makers, planners and implementation system on continuous basis. The indicators of development with respect to women like health, education, nutrition, and decision-making have so far attained unsatisfactory progress, consequently, making women's development more crucial.

It has been recorded that either type of development may not help women until or unless their status is raised in terms of economic, education and political participation, both in rural and urban settings. Women can determine the nature of development when they are given the space and opportunity. Economic participation of women can safely be designed; if things are worked out for benefit of women to carry out some skill based economic activities out of routine labour intensive activities.

Rural women constitute 75 per cent of the total female population of the country. On any given indicator of development, the rural women is disadvantaged compared to her urban counterparts. The profile of rural women is that of a poor, ignorant, illiterate, superstitious and suppressed being with low level of skills. She is unorganized and underrepresented. Her access to information, assets and opportunities is also low. Rural women are a major work force in informal sector. Hence, skill development, income generation and credit availability are the main planks of economic empowerment of women.

Government has emphasized the need for development of resources for women in numerous ways for the purpose of development. The high illiteracy and low socio-economic status of rural women stress the need for greater attention for the economic emancipation. The constitutional provisions have been made for equal rights and privileges for both men and women with special provisions for women to help them to improve their status in the society. Constant efforts are being made by government to include women, who are below the poverty line in different schemes.

Poverty and unemployment are the major issues, which confront our nation. Micro enterprise development in rural areas is a one step towards employment generation and economic empowerment. Rural areas are potential business hubs offering tremendous scopes for self employment creating through micro enterprises development.

Sustainable development of country depends on development of the rural sector, where majority of population lives. Poverty alleviation is best achieved through employment generation; promotion of sustainable micro-enterprises could be a solution. This requires technological skills, finance, marketing and management skills so as to become self-promoted micro-enterprises sustainable in the rural sector. Special efforts must be made to include women, who are otherwise left out of mainstream of development.

To promote micro enterprise in rural India, the development of human factor *i.e.,* entrepreneur himself must be considered. Government of India has launched a number of programmes to promote rural employment by providing the economically viable opportunities at doorsteps. Such launching of programmes requires a well planned strategy *i.e.,* organizing technical trainings, market outlook, availability of resources etc. so that the micro-enterprise is smooth, effective and profitable.

For micro enterprises to be sustainable it is highly required that the micro enterprise developed should be based on the resources, occupational skills of people and availability of markets as in Swarna Jayanthi Gram Swarojgar Yojana (SGSY). The advantages of micro enterprises are that, the women themselves could run the business within their capacity. Risks involved in micro enterprises are minimum, since these can be guided by careful management and consultation at the minimum level. Marketing of the products can be obtained easily, since span of control can be kept well within the limit.

Development of livestock enterprises in rural areas on a commercial scale can change the employment and income scenario of Indian villages Livestock is a source of employment. A survey of Rural India by National Sample Survey organization (NSSO) of the Government of India has revealed that the livestock development activities are preferred by rural folks as a source of supplementing their income besides regular farm activities.

The suggested micro enterprises can be classified into three categories as:

- Livestock based-Dairy, Poultry, Fishery, Piggery,
- Agro-based Mushroom Cultivation, Cultivation of Medicinal Plants.
- Bee keeping, Processing of Fruits and Vegetables,
- Non farm based Beauty Parlour, tailoring, Bakery etc.

REFERENCES

1. Gangal. SC. (1996). Developing and Uplifting India's Villages. Yojana 40 (I): 19.
2. Naik. Chitra (1996). Social Welfare and Poverty Alleviation. Some Reflections. Yojana. 40 (I). 6.
3. Saguna. B. (2002). Strategies for Empowerment of Rural Women. Social Welfare. 49 (5): 3-6.
4. Samuel. John and Prabhakar, Ghana (2001). Withering of the Welfare State–India. Social Watch, p. 114-115.
5. Vishwanathan, Sujatja (1997). Grouping Women for Economic Empowerment. Yojana, 41 (3) 37.

Chapter 11
SELF HELP GROUPS AND WOMEN EMPOWRMENT

*A. Ingarsal
**Dr. A. Bala Krishnan

ABSTRACT

The chapter discuss the formation of SHGs, objectives, operation modalities, strategy benefits and indicators of good SHGs etc. The SHGs are a media for the development of savings habit among women folk. It's a window for developing better technology and skill upgradation. The SHGs collective action and solidarity are called an important women empowerment mechanism.

Introduction

It is not surprising that the development of women in India has been the centre stage of its development planning since independence though the concept has been evolving from plan to plan. In most South Asian countries, the status of women is low and their socio-economic conditions are much more depressed than that of men. In India, while the constitutional and legal status of women is equal to that of men in all respects, the reality is that they suffer in all spheres of social and economic life. Poverty, in fact, is one of the aspects of their deprived condition. Low earning, lower wages, low level of skills, limited access of the factors of production, low literacy, malnutrition, poor standard of health, and greater exposure to domestic violence.

Self-help groups have emerged as a popular method of working with people in the recent years. Power to the people signifies a new social

* Research Assistant & Part—Time Research Scholar, IDARA Gandhigram Rural Institute, Gandhigram.

** Reader, Dept. of Applied Research, G.R.V, Gandhigram.

movement, which has probably has born out of the realization that society's traditional arrangements for solving their problems and inadequate. This movement stems from the people's desire to meet their needs and determine their own destinies though the principle of "by the people, for the people, and of the people". Ordinarily self-help refers to provision of aid to self, but here self is also taken to mean internal. Self-help emphasizes self-determination, self-reliance, self-production, and self-empowerment by mobilizing internal resources for the persons the group, or the community.

Meaning of Self-Help Groups

Self-Help Group (SHGs) is a small voluntary association of poor people, preferably from the same socio-economic background. They come together for the purpose of solving their common problems through self-help and mutual help. The SHGs promotes small savings among its members. The savings are kept with a bank. This common fund is in the name of the SHGs. Usually, the number of members in one SHGs does not exceed twenty.

Objectives of Self-Help Groups

The SHGs comprise very poor people who do not have access to formal financial institutions. They act as the forum for the members to provide space and support to each other. It also enables the members to learn to cooperate and work in a group environment. The SHGs provide savings mechanism, which suits the needs of the members. It also provides a cost effective delivery mechanism for small credit to its members. The SHGs significantly contribute to the empowerment of poor women.

Specific Objectives of Women SHGs

- To create awareness among the women about their social and economic problems.
- To identify the common interest of the group members
- To carry out the common interest in the most efficient and economic way.
- To enable the women to cross all social and economic barriers.
- To get equality of status in democratic, economic, social and cultural spheres of life.
- To empower women to work together with men as equal in all respect.
- To promote and ensure the human rights of women at all stages of their life cycle.

Formation of SHGs

Non Governmental Organisations (NGOs) Social Workers, health workers, village level workers, etc. Informal Associations of local people Development oriented government departments, Banks, Bank personnel and other individuals (in their personal capacities) Farmers' Clubs under the Programme of NABARD Other development institutions.

Operation of Women SHGs

The group members must meet every week for savings, repayment collection and every fortnight for discussing all other matters. The agenda is prepared and discussed in each meeting.

The matters regarding saving, rotation of group funds, bank loans and repayments, social and community action programme are discussed in every meeting. Since the group functions in a democratic way, one animator and two representatives are selected among the member, instead of President and Secretary and others. Animators will be the role models and change agents for the groups and for the villages as a whole. The animator position will be rotated amongst the representative every two years.

SHG Members Comprise Only Poor People

The SHGs-bank linkage programme is targeted to reach the poorest sections, which are by passed by the formal banking system. Therefore, it is essential that only the very poor be considered as the target group for the SHGs-bank linkage programme.

SHGs comprise only women members

SHGs can be all-women group, all-men group, or even a mixed Group. However, it has been the experience that women's groups perform better in all the important activities of SHGs. Mixed group is not preferred in many of the places, due to the presence of conflicting interests.

Success of SHGs strategy

Training can contribute significantly to the success of the SHGs. Appropriate training (formal or informal) at each state of SHGs growth is one of the essential inputs required.

Promotion of SHGs

Training is essential for all partner agencies who participate in the SHGs bank linking programme. The details regarding the different types of training needs, organizational facilities, modules, etc.

Role of SHGs in Women's Empowerment

SHGs are voluntary association of people who have come together to attain certain social and economic goals. SHGs are informal groups which have emerged on other own or are formed by voluntary agencies/ banks. It consists members of poor households who are economically and socially backward. Since the poor did not have access to formal financial institutions and the banks also found it difficult to reach many people of small means, the group approach has been evolved for promotion of thrift and savings among the poor. The savings of the members are collected in weekly/fortnightly/monthly intervals and are lent among members for their emergent credit needs. When the group successfully mobilized saving and extended credit of its own funds with a good repayment record, the group is linked to a bank for availing credit facilities.

The objectives of SHGs is to inculcate the habit of thrift, savings, banking culture, that is availing loan and repaying the same over a given peiod of time and in the process, gain economic prosperity through credit. The principles underlying the SHGs are financing the poorest of the poor, ensuring excellent recovery level, and empowering women not just by meeting their needs for consumption and productive loans but also through more holistic educative programmes on issues such as sanitation, family planning and the evil effects of liquor consumption in the family.

Benefits from Women SHGs

- A viable media for development of saving habit among the poor.
- Access to larger quantum of resources.
- A window for better technology / skill-up gradation,
- Availability of emerging consumption / production credit at the door step,
- Access to various promotional assistance,
- Assurance of freedom, equality, self-reliance and empowerment,
- In self help group collective action and solidarity is an important empowering mechanism. Collective action implies cohesion of the group to perceive commointerest and act collectively.

Indicators of good SHGs

Homogeneous membership

As far as possible, the membership of SHGs may comprise people from comparable socio-economic background. Though difficult to define in clear terms, a major indicator of homogeneity in membership is absence of conflicting interests among members.

No discrimination

There should not be any discrimination among members based on caste, religion or political affiliations.

Small membership

Ideally, the group size may be between 15 and 20, so that the members are participative in all activities of the SHGs. In a smaller group, members get opportunity to speak openly and freely. However, the membership may not be too small that its financial transactions turn out to be insignificant.

Regular Attendance

Total participation in regular group meeting lens strength to the effectiveness of SHGs. To achieve this, the SHGs should place strong emphasis on regular attendance in the group meetings. Transparency in functioning.

It is important that all financial and non-financial transactions are transparent in SHGs. This promotes trust, mutual faith and confidence among its members. Maintenance of books of accounts and also other records like the minute's book, attendance register, etc., are important.

Set of Byelaws

The SHGs may discuss and fianlise a set of byelaws, indicating rules and regulations for the SHGs functioning and also roles and responsibilities of members. It is better to have a written set of byelaws. The Self Help Promoting Institution (SHPI) and bank may guide the SHGs in this.

Thrift

The habit of thrift (small savings) is fundamental to the SHGs and helps in building up a strong common fund.

Utilizing Savings for Loaning

Once SHGs has accumulated sizeable amount in the form of savings say for a period of about 3-6 months, the members may be allowed to avail loans against their savings for emergent consumption and supplementary income generating credit needs.

Conclusion

SHGs are a media for the development of savings habit among the women folk. It mobilizes a large quantum of resources. It is a window for better technology and skill upgradation. It helps to increase an income of the family. The SHGs collective action and solidarity are important empowering mechanisms. Moreover, the Government and bankers are giving whole-hearted support for providing credit either directly or thoroughly NGOs. This helps to develop the entrepreneur skill of the women in our country.

Chapter 12

CREDIT SUPPORT TO WOMEN ENTREPRENEURS UNDER SGSY : A CASE STUDY OF TRIPURA

*A.V. Yadappanavar

ABSTRACT

Credit being a critical component in SGSY. Under this programme, banks and other financial institutions are being involved in planning and preparation of projects, activity identification, infrastructure planning as well as capacity building of the women through SGSY. In order to analyse the constraints faced the financial institutions, a study was conducted in Tripura. 12 bank branches and 39 Swarozgaris were selected for detailed analysis. The entrepreneurial activity taken by the Swarozgaris are piggery, dairy, pritry, handicraft bamboo works and tailoring. The study found that most of the commercial banks do not have special field staff to look after SGSY scheme. The rate of interest charged vary from 9.25 to 12 per cent per annum and repayment period ranges from 3-5 years depending upon the kind of activity chosen by SHG members. The study further found that delayed financing has resulted in poor income generation and diversion of funds by the Swarozgaris.

Introduction

Among the various Poverty Alleviation Programmes, SGSY is one such programme in achieving the goals of self-reliance and self-development. Economic development through self-managed activities equips the poor to play their role in more assertive way in the community. Community initiatives in the implementation of such measures with a

* Centre for Women Development, National Institute of Rural Development, Rajendranagar, Hyderabad-500 030.

strong coalition of the poor could therefore make a significant difference. Nation wide study by NABARD has shown that SHGs – bank linkages have produced positive results. It is therefore, necessary that financial institutions harness the full potential of self-help groups for mutual benefits and also integrate them in the process of rural development with synergic affect.

SGSY is continuing to be a credit-cum-subsidy programme. Credit being a critical component in SGSY, the success of the programme depends considerably on the confidence with which banks and other financial institutions lend to the rural poor. Under SGSY, banks and other financial institutions are being involved in planning and preparation of projects, identification of activity clusters, infrastructure planning as well as capacity building of SHGs. Mechanisms have been put in place for closer effective involvement of banks in the selection of beneficiaries, pre-credit activities as well as post-credit monitoring including loan recovery. The programme has been so structured as to develop a close and long-term relationship between the bankers and the swarozgaris. SGSY seeks to promote multiple credits rather than a one-time credit 'injection'. All these measures are designed to improve the performance of the programme not only in terms of higher returns to the swarozgaris but also in better and prompt loan recovery.

Need for the Study

An important issue in the development process relates to the provision and delivery of credit and financial services to the poor so that they emerge out of poverty while taking the meaningful productive and production activities. Credit is also seen as integral component of anti-poverty programme like SGSY. As a result micro finance is equated with credit for micro enterprises. However, some studies by NIRD and elsewhere on various aspects of implementation of SGSY indicated some limitations such as inadequate involvement of bankers in planning, identification of key activities, preparation of project profiles and extending credit support to the swarozgaris etc.

A related important reason for the slow progress of the programme is the sanction and disbursement of loans by Banks. During 2000-01, against the total 13.55 lakh loan applications submitted by the DRDAs, only 7.56 lakh loans were sanctioned and 6.80 lakhs loans disbursed. Similarly during the current financial year upto November 2001, against a total of 8.34 lakh applications submitted to the Banks, only 2.86 lakh loans have been sanctioned and funds have disbursed only to 2.17 lakh cases

Keeping in view the inadequacies and shortcoming mentioned above, there is an imperative needs to understand and critically analyse the constraints faced by the financial institutions and implementing agencies extending credit support to the swarozgaris under SGSY.

Objectives

- To examine the extent of credit dispersed by financial institutions under SGSY Programmes;
- To suggest relevant strategies for effective assistance to swarozgaris.

Methodology

***(a)* Study area :** The study was taken up in two states and one Union Territory spread across three geographic regions. The states selected was Tripura. From the state, two representative districts were selected from each district two blocks, one developed and one backward was selected. The details of field work done in these places are as under:

***(b)* Sampling :** From each district, six bank branches and one Lead Bank was covered. Bank branches include Commercial Banks, Regional Rural Banks and Cooperative Banks, Lead Banks and other financial institutions like WDCs etc. The total sample of 12 bank branches were selected for detailed analysis. Apart from these, officials of implementing agencies such as PDs, APOs of DRDAs, are interviewed to understand their perceptions about the constraints in accessing financial institutions for credit support. The total sample of individual swarozgaris and SHG members covering 39 respondents were interviewed for indepth analysis.

Table 1 : TRIPURA

Sl. No	*District*	*Block*	*Village*	*Economic Activities*
1.	West Tripura	Dukli	Amtoli	Dairy
			Badgarghat	Retail cloth business
			North Jogendranagar	Piggery
		Jrinia	Mohanpur	Handicrafts
			Radhacharan	Tailoring
			Thakurapar	
			Vraddinagar	Dairy
			Uttarchampparam	Piggery
2.	South Tripura	Matabari	Paratia	Fisheries
			Rajarbagh	Grocery & Stationary
			Kunjaben	Poultry
		Bagafa	Baikhora	Mango Nursery
			Girnia	Handicraft/handloom
			Kalashimukh	Bamboo work
		Kakraban	Majjari	Pottery

(c) Analytical framework : Both secondary and primary data was collected. The secondary data was collected at the level of state, district and block about the credit flow from banks. The opinions and perceptions of the officials from DRDA and block level were also obtained through semi-structured interview schedule. Primary data was collected from the selected individual swarozgaris and self help groups to ascertain the problems faced by them in getting loan from banks.

Profiles of Selected Districts

Table-2 : Demographic Features of Selected Districts

Feaures	*West Tripura*	*South Tripura*
Total population	15,30,531	7,62,565
Male	7,83,825	3,91,179
Female	7,46,706	3,71,386
Density	505	243
Literacy %	77.82	70.39%
Sex ratio	953	949

South Tripura

Animal Husbandry and Poultry

As the majority of the cultivators of this district belongs to the category of small and marginal farmers, the government has taken up a number of schemes for the development of livestock and the poultry with dual objective of providing such farmers with cheap animal protein and a supplementary source of income. The main objectives are to increase the supply of animal husbandry inputs to the beneficiaries of the district under different schemes like SGSY. And to the progressive farmers, in the shape of bullocks, fowls, ducks pigs and fodder seeds. The farms also serve as demonstration centres for public which will motivate them to undertake mixed farming. There will be facilities for farmers training also.

Block Profile

Matabari block: (1) Dairy (2)Fishery (3) Betelvine (4) Sericulture (5) Piggery were the key activities approved under SGSY by district level committee. In this block six banks are working they are two branches of SBI, two branches of UBI and two branches of TGB.

Bagafa block: (1) Dairy (2)Betelvine (3) Sericulture (4) Piggery (5)Pisciculture were the key activities approved under SGSY by district level committee. There are seven bank branches operating in Bagafa block five are TGB branches and one each of SBI and UBI banks.

West Tripura

In connection with the study on flow of credit -problems and perception of stakeholders under SGSY Tripura was selected in consultation with officials west and south Tripura district were selected. The profile of the selected district were follows:

Banking

The banking system in the district gives far intensive coverage with 14 commercial banks including Regional Rural Banks and three cooperative banks. As on March 2001 co-operative banks and commercial banks have 112 branches including those of Regional Rural Banks (RRBs) and co-operative banks. All development of bank of the district have been covered by commercial bank branches.

Apart from the commercial banks the cooperatives banks have 23 branches in the district of which, the Tripura State Cooperative Banks Ltd. (TSCB) alone has 20 and Tripura Co-operative Agricultural Rural Development Banks (TCARDB) 2 and Agartala Co-operative Urban Bank (ACUB)-1. While the branches of ACUB is located at Agartala only, TSCB are distributed throughout the district are in all Blocks.

As per instruction of RBI, this new area allocation was effective from 1st April,1989. In compliance with the RBI guidelines vide letter No. RPCD. No. LBS(SAA) DC49/65-90-91 dated 09.11.1990, the BLBC meeting of 10 Blocks were held to introduce the guidelines on (A) preparation of Credit Plan under Service Area Approach (SAA) and (B) monitoring of performance thereunder.

Industry

Industrial scenario of the district is, however, dominated by rural and cottage industries. These industries include handicrafts, tannery, bidi making and carpentry. The major problems confronting the industry sector of the district are poor communication facility.

Animal Husbandry and Poultry

Despite the various schemes undertaken by the government from time to time, there appears to be shortage in the availability of improved quality of milch cows, pigs goats etc. The government to Tripura is also thinking to purchase improved quality breeds of animals from outside the state to meet the growing demand of the state.

Infrastructure

Lack of Railway communication with rest of the country is a major constraint for the growth of the district economy. This has led to high transport cost for all goods. Besides communication, other items of infrastructure are also conspicuous by their low levels of development in the district.

SGSY in Tripura

Position at Tripura SHG-Bank Linkage Programme had not picked up well in Tripura as in other states of the country till 2001-02.

Even as compared with other states in NER, the performance of the programme in the state was very poor. This can be seen from the fact that only 2 SHGs were credit linked during 2001-02 and cumulative linkage position in the state upto 31 March 2002 was only 7 SHGs. However, SHG-Bank Linkage Programme witnessed great leap during 2002-03 in the state with credit linkage of 97 SHGs. The details are given below:

Table-3 : Position of SHG Linkage in Tripura

Year	*No. of SHGs linked*	*Bank loan*
Upto March 2001	5	0.32
2001-02	2	0.01
2002-03	97	6.49
Total	104	6.82

Out of 97 SHGs financed by banks in Tripura during 2002-03, Tripura Grameen Bank financed 93.

Initiatives/Capacity Building

Realizing the need of creating awareness and sensitizing all those involved in the programme, NABARD gave emphasis on capacity building to upscale SHG-Bank Credit Linkage Programme in the state of Tripura on a massive scale. The details of initiatives taken by NABARD for capacity building of various partners and bringing coordination among them are given below:

In addition to the above, NABARD provided faculty support in the training programmes organized by State Government Banks, NYK, NIRD and other institutions on SHGs during the year.

Continuing emphasis on capacity building and initiatives, NABARD has planned number of training programmes for bankers, government officials, SHGs and NGOs in the state during 2003-04. During the month of June 2003, NABARD conducted 9 training programmes of two days duration each for branch managers, field officers.

Table-4: Capacity Building Programmes for Partner Agencies (2002-03)

Particulars	*No. of programme*	*No. of participants*
Bankers – One day sensitization training programme for branch managers	1	23
SHG leaders – One day training programme for SHG leaders	36	1,381
PRIs – Two days training programme for elected women representatives of Panchayat	1	21
NGOs – Two day/one day training programme for animators/volunteers of NGOs	3	150

Training to Bank Officials

The state has a good record of implementing poverty alleviation programmes and this is also true of SGSY and SHGs. The state has formed 793 SHGs as against a target of 620 groups. The funds utilization is to the extent of 90 per cent. SHGs have been formed in the state under other programmes too like the India Rubber Project, special package programme for STs. However, there is reluctance on the part of the banks to provide credit and subsidy to the groups. Further when it is given it is neither adequate nor timely. Such low and poor financing will lead to poor income generation as well as diversion of funds by the swarozgaris, he said. The BPL will not be able to cross the poverty line and the entire objective of the programme will be defeated.

Physical and Financial Progress Under SGSY

In west Tripura district in the year 2002-03 out of a total target of 2896,1723 (59.49%) received credit of 132.09 lakhs, and subsidy of Rs. 75.429 lakhs.

In the year 2003-04 out of a target 324 cases, credit was given 232 individual swarozgaris(71.60%). The credit disbursed was Rs. 14.535 lakhs and the subsidy disbursed was Rs.10.567 lakhs. State Bank of India Dukli has displayed better performance compared to State bank of India Amtoli, Tripura grameen bank Jogendra nagar, and united bank of India Bazarghat.

In case of Jirnia block out of target of 380,155(40.78%) individual swarozgaris received credit of Rs. 13.54 lakhs and a subsidy amount of

Rs.6.99 lakhs. UBI Ranibazar and UBI Jirnnia have displayed better performance compared to TGB Champakanagar and TGB of Khyerpur.

Table-5: Physical and Financial Progress under SGSY Since Inception

Sl.No.	*Items*	*1999-2000*	*2000-2001*	*2001-2002*	*2002-2003*	*Total Average*
A. Financial Progress						
1.	Total Allocation	573.44	1161.23	690.93	533.00	2958.60
2.	Central Allocation	430.08	870.92	618.20	399.75	2218.95
3.	State Allocation	143.36	290.31	172.73	133.25	739.65
4.	Central Releases	488.12	860.44	622.08	599.65	2570.29
	Central Release to Central Allocation	113.50	98.80	120.05	150.01	115.83
5.	State Releases	119.10	360.98	386.43	233.25	1099.76
	% of State Release to State Allocation	83.08	124.34	223.72	175.05	148.69
6.	Opening Balance as on Ist April	323.30	79.71	175.41	10.26	147.17
7.	Misc. Receipt	86.31	19.39	152.26	9.26	66.81
8.	Total Funds Available	1016.83	1320.52	1336.18	852.42	4525.95
9.	Total Funds Utilized	836.58	1231.26	1170.46	975.63	4213.93
	% of Utilization to Funds Available	82.27	93.24	87.60	114.45	94.39
	% of Utilization to Allocation	145.89	93.24	87.60	114.45	151.09
	% of Utilization on Subsidy	77.89	106.03	169.40	183.05	113.94
	% of Utilization on Infrastructure Dev.	9.50	22.39	150.62	166.53	10.53
	% of Utilization on Training/Skill Dev.	3.69	1.19	5.24	4.98	
10.	Total Credit Target	1100.00	1100.00	1.85	4.21	2.74
11.	Total Credit Mobilized	3.69	1171.48	2100.00	1462.07	576.07
	% of Credit Mobilized	1100.00	106.50	1311.96	1626.22	5029.83

Table-6 : Physical and Financial Progress under Self-help Group (SHG)—as on 31.3.2002

District	*No. of Groups formed*	*Gradation Completed*	*No. of SHGs Receiving revolving fund*	*Credit Disbursed (Rupees in Lakhs)*	
				No	*Amt.*
West Tripura	586	216	230	—	—
South Tripura	389	77	70	4	4.00
Total	1409	412	336	5	5.25

Details on the credit given to different categories of swarozgaris in Dukli and Jirnia block and in the district as a whole is given in table. SGSY is basically a subsidy linked credit-oriented program, it goes with saying that adequate and timely flow of subsidy is as much important for its success as the flow of credit itself. Details of number of swarozgaris covered, amount of released as subsidy in the selected blocks and district is given in table. During 2001-02, 246.50 lakhs were disbursed as subsidy to 7062 beneficiaries.

In case of South Tripura district out of a target of 1157 physical achievement was 801 (69.23%) in the year 2002-03 got loan of 151.36 lakhs and subsidy of 51.51 lakhs.

Tripura

Socio-Economic Characteristics of SHG Members

Generally the membership has ranged from 9 to 16 majority of the women are in the age group of 30 to 40 years. All women are married, the average size of family ranged from 2 to 5. The primary occupation of the women is agriculture labour. About 70 percent of them are literate. All of them have their own houses, the family monthly income ranged from Rs.1000 to Rs.1300 a majority of them were drawn from BPL families, reflects the homogeneity of the group.

Interaction with selected SHG members in Dukli and Jirnia Matabari and Bagafa, Kakraban blocks in west and south district of Tripura indicated that member were regular in conducting monthly meetings and in maintenance of records on savings internal lending, repayment etc. .

Groups have selected the economic activities from the identified key activities from the block by SGSY committee. Out of 12 groups two groups each opted for piggery and pottery, three for handicrafts (bamboo products), one each for dairy, fishery, retail cloth selling, mango nursery, poultry and duckery. The project cost ranged from Rs.18,000 to Rs.2,97,000 depending upon the number of members and type of activity.

Table-7: Physical Progress under SGSY in South Tripura

District	*Year*	*Formed during the year*	*Passed Grade-I*	*Passed Grade-II*	*Women SHGs formed*	*No. of women Groups taken to Economic*	*Total No. of groups taken to Economic*	*Members covered under SHGs (not Economic)*	*No. of individual Swarozgaris*	*Total Swaro-zgaris assisted (10+11)*
1	*2*	*3*	*4*	*5*	*6*	*7*	*8*	*9*	*10*	*11*
South Tripura	1999-00	118	38	12	105	27	38	1749	2670	4419
	2000-01	97	44	15	57	35	44	1212	3242	4454
	2001-02	174	112	23	130	91	112	2031	4126	6157
	2002-03	1157	492	7	701	366	492	11700	3076	14776
Upto Nov.	2003-04	1427	58	2	710	32	58	16088	801	16889
	Total	2973	744	59	1701	551	744	32780	13915	46695

Table-8 : Physical Progress under SGSY in West Tripura

Year	*Formed during the year*	*Passed Grade-I*	*Passed Grade-II*	*Women SHGs formed*	*No. of women Groups taken to Economic Activities*	*Total No. of groups taken to Economic Activities*
1	2	3	4	5	6	7
2000-01	126	43				
2001-02						
2002-03	626	NA	NA			129
2003-04						
2004-05	600					

Table-9: Physical Progress under SGSY in West Tripura

Year	*Formed during the year*	*Passed Grade-I*	*Passed Grade-II*	*Women SHGs formed*		*No. of women Groups taken to Economic Activities*	*Total No. of groups taken to Economic Activities*
1	2	3	4	5		6	7
Dukli	1999-00	13	13	9	11	8	9
	2000-2001	10	10	6	8	4	6
	2001-2002	22	13	2	19	12	19
	2002-2003	78	18	Not taken	58	29	45
	2003-latest upto Nov. 03	306	Not taken	— —	202	23 (from the thrift amount)	34
	Total	429	54	17	298	76	113
Jinani	1999-2003	54	12	3	10	10	10
	2003-2004	360	25	-	80	22	22

As per the programme guideline, banks have sanctioned Rs.1.25lakhs as group subsidy and deposited as back end subsidy reserve fund in the name of the group, the repayment duration for the project was 3 to 5 years and the interest rate charged ranged from 11 to 13 per cent. The time taken for sanction and disbursement of loan ranged from months. Most of the group members managed the economic activity individually.

Interactions with bankers and block level officials (RDOs) revealed that the group leaders were managing the economic activities.

Table-10 : Financial Progress in South Tripura

District	*O.B. as on 1.4.03*	*Allocation*			*Release*		*Miscellaneous Receipt*		
		Central	*State*	*Total*	*Central*	*State*	*Interest Accured*	*Return of subsidy*	*Others*
1	2	3	4	5	6	7	8	9	10
South Tripura	22.03	195.08	65.02	260.10	195.08	65.02	1.28	1.48	0

Contd...

Total fund available		*Utilization of Fund*	*Utilization of total fund available (%) (13/12)* 100*	*Utilization of total allocation (%) (13/5)* 100*
Total	*Total fund available (2+6+7+11)*			
11	12	13	14	15
2.76	284.89	252.00	88.46	96.89

Non-Farm Activities

With limited further scope for absorbing burgeoning population in agriculture, Rural Non Farm Sector (RNFS) plays a very important role in economy of Tripura, due to its potential for providing additional income and employment opportunities in rural areas. Apart from traditional activities like handloom and handicrafts, it covers various activities like manufacturing, agro processing, services sector activities. Financing for small road transport operators has emerged as major source for bank finance. Housing is also emerging as important segment of bank finance in state. In addition to refinance support NABARD has undertaken a number of promotional interventions like training cum production centers, ARWIND, MAHIMA, Cluster Development Programme (CDP) and Rural Entrepreneurship Development Programme(REDP)

- Considering the availability of bamboo, there is lot of scope for development of bamboo handicrafts in the State. However, due to absence of adequate organized marketing arrangements for bamboo handicrafts, the artisans are not getting remunerative price. There is a need to focus attention to this area by State Government and other agencies involved.
- Organizing the artisans into industrial cooperative society and provide all infrastructure will give boost to this activity.

- Cluster Approach–the cluster approach envisages the convergence of all schemes and financial resources of various departments relevant to the identified clusters. Directorate of Industries and Directorate of Agriculture (Horticulture) may incorporate the needs of the identified clusters in their plans and make enhanced budgetary provisions for successful implementation of the same. The State has got good potential for establishment of processing industries for pineapples, oranges and Jack fruits. There is an urgent need to identify the prospective entrepreneurs by the Department of Industries/Directorate of Agriculture (Horticulture) in consultation with financing institutions.
- Establishment of RUDSETI type of institutions for imparting technical skill to young entrepreneurs.

Bamboo Work

The group got sanction for the total project cost of Rs. 21052000 for 13 members with repayment period of 3-5 years, and interest rate of 12-13.Bankers have released RS 10000 as first installment. The group has passed first grade in November 2003. Most of the poor women work as wage labour, as main source of income and undertaken production of Bamboo products like Muda, Carpet, File covers, Dustbin, Baskets, purses etc.

The members are undergoing four months training organized at Bagafa block. They will be getting a stipend of Rs. 900 per month. The group has been formed in September 2002 in Kalhimukhi village of Bagafa block. The group consisted of 13 members. The group has started internal lending Seven members have taken loan from the group, out of seven, five members took loan for purchase of (30) pigs and 2 took for medical treatment of their family members. Group also purchased (8) goats for Rs.10,000. The repayment of group accounts to 50.58 per cent, members also sell dressed and undressed chickens at one rate of Rs.120 and Rs.60 per kg respectively. The Tripura grameen bank Baikhare has financed the present SHG under SGSY.

Pottery

Two members have started tea stall in march 2003 taking Rs. 1000 and Rs. 1500 respectively from the group pottery. 10 micro entrepreneurs formed SHG in the year 2001in Majjari village in Kakraban block of south Tripura district. All the members belonged to other bank were caste group. Government block and DRDA promote the group. The group members are saving Rs.30 per month in the initial year now they are saving Rs.100 per member per month as on December 2003. The total amount saved so far is Rs.8000 the balance on the bank as on Dec 2003 was Rs.3905. Group got sanction of Rs.18000 for pottery scheme clay model as per NABARD unit cost for key activities under DSB sector. United bank of India in Kakraban block has financed this group under SGSY. First and second grading of group is being done in June 2002 and September 2003 respectively. Out of 10 member 3 member have taken loan from the group.

Table-11: Purpose-wise Utilisation of Credit by SHG Members

S. No	*Amount*	*Purpose*	*Amount repaid*	*% of Interest*
1.	Rs. 2500	Business	Rs. 1000	2%
2.	Rs. 10,000	Pottery	Rs. 1000	Rs. 100 p.m.
3.	Rs. 3000	Business	Rs. 3000	3%

In the year 2003 this group has done business worth of Rs.50,000 during DWCRA exhibition. The group member have activity participated in pulse polio programme. Total sanitation programme, has helped banks and Panchayat in recovery of loan amount and tax to the tune of Rs.1,66,000. Members explained that they need advanced training on pottery to up grade their skill. All the members also want to start duckery unit as a side business.

Animal Husbandry

In Bagfa block women formed SHG in the year 2001. Out of 10, 6 were scheduled caste and rest belonged to OBC. They started pottery unit, earlier they were doing only household works only, United Bank of Santibazar sanctioned was of Rs. 7500 in Oct. 2003 and DRDA sanctioned subsidy of Rs. 5000, out of which group has repaid Rs. 2000 in Nov. 2003. The group members were saving Rs. 50 per head per month. So far the group has saved Rs. 7500 as on December 2003. The group has passed first grade, out of 10 members 2 members have taken loan of Rs. 800 each for purchase of goats and for mushrooms cultivation and repaid Rs. 400, 500 each. Two members have taken loan of Rs. 1000 for stationary supply and rubber plantation and paid Rs. 200 in Oct. 2003. One member has taken Rs. 900 for fisheries and Rs. 600 is repaid and one member took Rs. 1500 in Nov. 2003 for purchase of goat and returned Rs. 500 as on December 2003.

Piggery

Ten women belonging to SC community started piggery unit under SGSY on 15Th march 2001 in Charipura Sukanta village of Dukli block in west Tripura district. They have taken loan from United Bank of India Badarghat branch for purchase of pigs. The amount of loan taken from bank was Rs.1,72,000 and subsidy released by DRDA was Rs.1,25,000. The sanctioned project cost was Rs.2,97,000. The group was saving Rs.50 per month, each member got a loan of Rs.23,000. The amount has to be repaid in 3 years as per with monthly installment of Rs.650. unit cost fixed by NABARD guidelines for piggery unit is Rs.24,850 (for pig lets). The group purchased 33 pigs from government farms out of which one pig died. The feed required for pigs are purchased once or twice in a month the cost of production is Rs.1700 depending upon the requirements. Pig rearing has helped the group to supplement the income apart from their daily wage.

The group has passed grade I in Aug 2001and grade II in July 2002. Revolving fund received by the group was Rs.32,863 as on Dec 2003. The balance amount of SHG was Rs.1,42,380.

Plantation and Horticulture

The favorable agro-climatic conditions, fertile soils, sub-tropical climate, large hill lands and abundance of rainfall offers immense scope for development of plantation and horticulture sector in Tripura. Mango is grown in 3150 ha. It has also set up number of Orchards and Orchards-cum-Nursery in south Tripura district for the development of horticulture. Arrangements has also been made for supply of grafts and seedlings from these centres to the prospective fruit growers in the District.

Mango Nursery

The group has started in December 2002 group got sanction for Rs7500 for the 10 members all are agricultural labourers. The group passed first grade, Revolving fund is also sanctioned. The group has saved Rs.3700 as on December 2003 per head per member savings are Rs.30 the group composed as in December 2003 was Rs.1731 The group has received 7000 plants of mango, for Rs. 1200 from government nursery. The group wanted to take up some official kind of economic activity in the block so they opted for this. Three members have taken loan from the group. 2 person have taken loan of Rs. 500 each for cultivation, and attending interview and Rs. 50 is being paid monthly and the member has taken Rs. 300 for rickshaw repaid. The interest charged by group is 2 per cent group has also taken 2 goats for Rs. 100. Member spend 2-3 loan for mango nursery. They expect an income of Rs. 32000 from this nursery the member was an agricultural labour in the field for a minimum wage of Rs. 50-60 for 20 days in a month.

Retail Cloth Business

14 members belonging to Badarghat village formed SHG in the year 2000 to do cloth business group got loan sanction for the total project cost of Rs. 3,28,000 with subsidy of Rs. 1,25,000 and revolving fund of Rs. 30,600. The group has saved Rs. 50,400 as on Dec. 2003 with a monthly saving of Rs. 100 per head. The opening balance of the group was Rs. 17,425 in united bank of India of Badarghat branch. The group has kept fixed deposit of Rs.1,90,400 as subsidy was not released by bank so fixed deposit was with drawn on Feb 1st 2003 Rs.1,00,000 was with drawn and on 5th June Rs.60,000 was with drawn as on 2nd June. Rs. 40,000 was with drawn for purchase of cloth and other raw material. Readymade garments worth of Rs.25,000 Rs.30,000 was brought from Calcutta. One of the people from Tripura state government calls tender get to and help these poor women in their business. The member stitch various items like blouse, petty coat, sweater, etc., Group has opted for tailoring because they thought it is convenient and easy in their free time they can attend such work.

Fisheries

Majority of state population is fish eating and from demand side there is good scope for fish production, which is in short supply. At present, fish is imported food for states like Andhra Pradesh. The state has become self sufficient in supply of fish seed and fingerlings. Fisheries sector can play a strategic role in the state economy by contributing towards food and nutritional security and employment generation.

Sixteen women members from Paratia village in Matabari block of south Tripura district formed SHGs in 1998. All the members were S.C in the beginning members were saving Rs.10 per month. After 2 years they enhanced it to Rs. 30. As on 2003 they raised saving to Rs.50 per month, as on December 2003 their saving amount was Rs.3700. Tripura grameen bank of Chandrapur branch financed loan of Rs. 25000 for this SHG. (RF is Rs15000 at the rate of 13 per cent interest per year (DRDA-Rs10, 000 TGB-Rs5, 000). The loan was sanctioned on 24.9.2001 and was released on 9.10.2001. SHG has taken loan on cash credit scheme. In the year 2002-03 the group has earned income of Rs.10000 by sale of fingerlings. The group has taken pond on lease for 3 years at the rate of Rs.10,000 the area of pond belongs to Panchayat on 11.10.2001 as Rs.40,000 of the loan is repaid (Rs. 25,000 on 9.10.2001 and Rs.15,000 is repaid as on 11.10.2001). The balance amount of the group in the bank as on 10.11.2003 was Rs.5455. The group has also earned profit of Rs.2500 per head Rs.50 is profit earned by sale of pigs. Interaction with group members revealed that balance of Rs.15000 credit is outstanding. (Table:23).

Fisheries

There are lot of ponds and tanks owned by Gram Panchayat, Zila Panchayats, and municipalities presently leased out to private parties. However, these ponds and tanks are very shallow and require development for increasing the yield.

Integrated farming technology has to be popularized to ensure increase in income as well as reduce the risk of failure of any one of the component of the farming system.

Socio-Economic Profile of Individual Swarozgaris

The average age of individual swarozgaris is 29.52 on an average there were members in their households. The total population of the 34 households. As far education level 17.64 per cent studied upto primary level and 44.11 per cent were illiterate 14.70 per cent studied upto middle school. 8.82 per cent was studied upto lower primary level. 2.9 per cent went upto high school. The 34 individual swarozgaris 15 (44.11%) were scheduled castes, 5 (20.58%) were from other back ward castes, 5 were Muslims (14.70%) four were belonging to general category (11.76%) and only 3 were Hindus (8.82%) 21 of the 34 swarozgaris (61.76%) did not own any land. 4 (30.76%) owned upto 4 acres and 2 (23.07%) owned land upto 3 acres and owned land upto 2 acres two (15.38%) and one each owned land 18 acres, (7.69%) 4.5 acres, 5 acres. The value of land owned by individual swarozgaris ranged from Rs.8000 to Rs.80,000. The average value being Rs. 24,142.85. The average income received by individual swarozgaris per month was Rs. 557.35.

The main source of loan for majority of individual swarozgaris was from bank loan only. They also saved part of money from this wage income. Few also got a share from husbands wage. While other depended on income derived from sale of bamboo handicrafts, sale of Sarees, clothes, eggs, milk etc. majority of the entrepreneurs purchased raw material monthly. Operational problems faced by individual swarozgaris activity wise is given below:

Piggery

Locational disadvantages: village situated being interior from the block headquarters posed a problem in getting transport, feed and piglets from the district headquarters.

Table-12: Profile of Individual Swarozgaris in South Tripura District

S. No.	*Activity*	*Age*	*Loan*	*Subsidy*	*Income*
1.	Poultry	28	11,244	10,000	400
2.	Poultry	26	11,244	10,000	700
3.	Poultry	34	14,871	6,979	1200
4.	Milch cattle	31	26,570	7,950	900
5.	Milch cattle	40	3,470	7,500	
6.	Milch cattle	46	26,570	7,500	1000
7.	Gro / stationery	32	3,600	7,500	1000
8.	Gro / stationery	28	25,000	10,000	1000
9.	Gro / stationery	37	3,500	7,500	1160
10.	Gro / stationery	36	25,000	10,000	-
11.	Gro / stationery	32	3,600	7,500	400

Due to lack of availability of veterinary facility pigs and piglets died. Doctors charge Rs100 for every visit.

Dairy

- Due to lack of availability of jersey cow one individual swarozgaris opted for poultry:
- UBI has not given passbook to individual swarozgaris in few villages. So swarozgaris are not aware of amount to be repaid per month and no. of installments;
- Swarozgaris earn profit of Rs.1500 per month.

Poultry

- Due to market fluctuation there is no assured income.

Handicraft

- Because of accident of head of the household individual swarozgaris is not regular in repayment.
- Home being too small posed problems for storing goods.

Bamboo Works

- Due to insurgency problem market is closed for bamboos works. Most of good quality bamboos are grown insurgency area.
- Lack of timely and insufficient loan at once.
- High transport cost.

Table-13: Socio-Economic Profile of Individual Swarozgaris

S.No.	*Literacy*	*Activity*	*No. of members*	*Install-ment in months*	*Land in Ha.*	*Value in Rs.*		*Annual*	*Loan*	*Susbidy*	*Amount to be Paid in*	*Rate of interest*
1.	Illiterate	Piggery	3	36	2	80,000	43	10000	-	10,000	650	12.00
2.	8th	Poultry	7	60	2	20,000	32	1,2000	-	7,500	650	12.00
3		Piggery		36	1	10,000	34	3000	19,700	10,000		12.00
4.		Piggery	11	36	4	40000	35	30,000	35,000	10,000	750	12.00
5.	VIII	Grocery	4	36	5	50000	27	1,000	35,000	7,500	750	12.50
6.	VII	Grocery	4	36			30	1000	22,000	7500	392	11.50
7.	VIII	Tailoring		60	4	40000	32	1400	34,000	7500	-	11.00
8.	V	Dairy	5	60	-	-	28	1000	32,000	7,500	750	12.00
9.	3rd	Grocery	5	60	-	-	35	1,200	-	-	-	11.50

Table-14: Block wise Classification of Key Activities Opted by Individual Swarojgrais

Activity	*Dukli*	*Jirnia*	*Matabari*	*Total*
Piggery	3	-	3	6
Poultry	1	-	3	4
Handicraft	4	-	-	4
Tailoring	2	1	-	3
Dairy	1	4	-	5
Grocery	2	1	8	11
Fisheries	-	-	1	1
Total	13	6	15	34

Grocery is the most popular unit chosen by 11 of individual swarozgaris. The second popular activity was piggery unit taken up by 6 individual swarozgaris. Four swarozgaris each opted for handicraft and poultry units. Tailoring was taken by 3 swarozgaris, and only one opted for rearing fish.

Credit Support Under SGSY

There are 223 branches of various financial institutions in the state consisting 92 branches of commercial banks, 86 branches of RRB (Tripura Gramin Bank), 39 branches of Tripura State Cooperative Bank (TSCB), 5 branches of Tripura Cooperative Agriculture And Rural Development Bank (TCARDB) and 1 branch of Urban Cooperative Bank. The branches of commercial banks and RRB in the State accounted for 79.8% of the total bank branches in the state. The short term cooperative structure in the State is 2 tier in nature while long term cooperative structure in the state is unitary in nature.The branch network details are as under:

Table-15: Branch Network

Agency	*No. of Branches*			
	Rural	*SemiUrban*	*Urban*	*Total*
Commercial Banks	48	17	27	92
Tripura Gramin Bank	73	8	5	86
Tripura State Cooperative Bank	19	11	9	39
T.C. Agri & Rural Dev. Bank	4	_	1	5
Urban Cooperative Bank	_	_	1	1
Grand Total	144	36	43	223

Subsidy Adjustment

Release of credit in time and immediate adjustment against the loans account is necessary to replenish the finances of the loaning agencies and reduce interest burden to the swarozgaris. For avoiding delay in disbursement of subsidy the DRDA have been directed to keep the subsidy amount in the participating banks by opening S/B account. The average amount of subsidy per beneficiary was Rs1117 in South Tripura district.

Release of subsidy was lowest in the year 2000-01 and lower in 2001-02, but it has increased considerably in the 2002-03 to the extent of 162.82 lakhs.

Table-16 : Banking (2002-03)

1. No. of banks	Nos.	17
2. No. of branches	Nos.	218
3. Total Deposits (as on Dec, 2002)	Rs. Crores	1,339.88
4. Total Credit (as in Dec, 2000)	Rs. Crores	339.88

Table-17: No. of Swarozgaris under SGSY in West Tripura District

Sl. No	*Name of the Block*	*No. of Swarozgaris assisted under SGSY From 1999-2003*				
		1999-2000	*2000-01*	*2001-02*	*2002-03*	*Grand total*
1.	Jirania	99	436	505	245	1285
2.	Dukli	411	588	650	330	1979
	Total	500	1,024	1155	575	3,264

Table-18: Details of Expenditure under SGSY in West Tripura District

Sl. No	*Items of expenditure*	*1999-2000*	*2000-01*	*2001-02*	*2002-03*	*Total Rs. in lakhs*
1.	Subsidy	322.941	343.574	275.518	323.124	1265.157
2.	Training	6.197	2.300	5.662	7.534	21.693
3.	Revolving fund for SHG		0.855	12.44	11.300	24.595
4.	Infrastructure	6.111	81.647	20.236	13.573	121.567
5.	Other (for DRDA) administration	9.981				9.981
	TOTAL	345.230	428.376	313.856	355.531	1442.993

Sector-wise Disbursement

The flow of ground level credit to priority sector increased from 5708.56 lakhs in 2000-2001 to Rs.8939.29 lakhs in 2001-02 registering a growth of about 56.4 per cent and it further increased to 12283.50 during 2002-03 registering growth of 37.41 per cent .

Broad Sector-wise Flow of Credit to Priority Sector

Broad sector-wise disbursement of credit under priority sector in the state during last two years is shown in the table given below. It shows that flow credit to agriculture came down during 2002-03 in absolute terms. The share of agriculture and allied sector came down 15.62 per cent during 2002-03 from 32.72 per cent during 2001-02. Services sector has emerged as major sector for bank finance as its share in total bank finance went to 66.78 per cent during 2002-03 from, 54.15% during previous year.

Table-19. Broad Sector-wise Flow of Credit

(Rs lakh)

Purpose	*2001-02*	*% of total*	*2002-03*	*% of total*
Agri. & Allied	2924.74	32.72	1918.86	15.62
Industry	1173.99	13.13	2161.71	17.60
Services	4840.56	54.15	8202.93	66.78
Total	8939.29	100.00	12283.50	100.00

The bank wise physical and financial performance of SHG in the selected blocks namely Dukli and Jirnia of west Tripura district is presented in table 46.

During the year 2002-03 DRDA forwarded 620 application under SGSY scheme to the selected banks in Dukli and Jirnia blocks. Among there 39 application are pending with the bank because of paucity of fund and lack of timely release of subsidy by DRDA.

Tripura

Perceptions of Officials of DRDA and Banks

For understanding of the problems experienced by the bankers in implementation of SGSY programme bankers of the selected districts and blocks were interviewed and their views are given below:

Official Perception

- Bankers hesitate unless pursued by block and DRDA in grading of groups.

Table-20: Bank wise Performance of Fund SGSY in West and South Tripura in 2002-03

United bank of India

Block	*Target*	*No. of applications sent to bank*	*No. of loans sanctioned*	*No. of applications disbursed*	*Total subsidy*	*Total loan amount*
Jirina	Ranibazar 8.68	270	302	120 (39.73%)	120 (39.73%)	5.62
Dukli	Badharghat 4.475	125	145	96 (76.8%)	96 (76.8%)	3.971
	Total 13.155	395	427	216	216	9.591
Central Bank of India						
Dukli	Amtoli 16.487	240	240	174 (72.5%)	174 (72.5%)	8.425
Dukli	Dukli 4.85	240	243	59 (0.24)	59 (0.24)	4.7
	Total 21.337	480	483	233	233	13.125
Tripura Grameen Bank						
Dukli	Jogendranagar	45	45			
Jirnia	Champaknagar 0.17	20	22	5 (22.72%)	5 (22.72%)	0.15
Jirnia	Khyerpur 0.5	15	15	5 (33.33%)	5 (33.33%)	0.25
	Total 0.67	80	82	10	10	0.40

- Application is received throughout the year.
- About time taken for processing of applications, officials mentioned that DRDA takes 3-4 months and bank takes 5-6 months.
- Banks hesitate to disburse on various places.
- About release of loan they stated that in maximum cases fast payment is made.
- About release of loan depending upon facility cash or input is given.
- Interest charged is 10.00%
- Problems faced by adhering to service area approach. Due to financial problems of RRB (TGB) some GPS were endorsed to commercial banks as designated branch and tenure has expired but RBI has not yet extended the tenure.

Perception of bankers on SGSY

With regard to grading of groups all the bankers mentioned that grading of SHG is being done in west and south Tripura district by group of people consisting representative from NABARD, DRDA, block level staff (BDO/RDO), NGO, heads of line depts., and official from PRIS. The various problems mentioned by bankers and officials in grading of groups are as follows.

- Hangover of IRDP
- Lack of presence of expert NGOS has affected great deal in group formation
- Lack of sufficient time
- Lack of sufficient training
- Lack of proper maintenance of accounts record due to illiteracy of villagers.
- Irregularities in attending meetings.

Table-21.

S. No.	*Functions*	*Time Spent by bank officials (in days) For processing of applications for disbursement of Loans*			
		DRDA	*BANK*	*DRDA*	*BANK*
1.	Identification of Borrowers	15	15	15	28
2.	Collection of Application/ Verification of Documents	30	32-60	10	1
3.	Pre-sanction Visit	21	15-30	15	2-3
4.	Loan processing	-	42	10-13	15
5.	Post-sanction visit	90-120	-	-	3-4
6.	Monitoring, follow-up and recovery	-	-	-	7

Most commercial banks do not have special field staff to look after SGSY scheme in these branches, the various problems mentioned by bankers about repayment is that swarozgaris lack repayment ethics and they have negative attitudes towards re payment. Low finance by banks and financial crisis among banks are other factors responsible for poor repayment. Some bankers indicated that at times there is a delay in release subsidy from DRDA because as cash credit scheme (CCS) is phase wise so it gets delayed.

Regarding release of loan majority of bankers mentioned that depending upon the kind of scrutiny opted by swarozgaris loan is released phase wise.

With regard to rate of interest majority of bankers mentioned they charge interest between 9.25-12 per cent per annum following RBI guidelines bankers mentioned that as far as SHGs are concerned repayment period ranged between 3-5 years depending upon the kind of activity chosen by SHG members. Few bankers mentioned that villagers located in interior places adoption of service area approach in rural banks has become difficult.

Regarding credit utilization bankers mentioned that respective bank branch, DRDA and block staff peruses the matter for improving credit mobilization following suggestion were given by bankers and officials

- Preparation of project report on key activities at the block level;
- Arrangement of input supply and market tie-up;
- Involvement's of PRIS for collection of revenue
- Check on diversion of funds and better coordination through line departments and joint follow up.

About the implementation of SGSY in west and south Tripura district bankers and officials held the view that scheme should not be target oriented otherwise this defeats the purpose of the scheme

Suggestion for enhancing credit-delivery mechanism under SGSY mentioned by bankers and officials are as follows:

- Subsidy-credit ratio (1:3) as per guidelines may kindly be adhered to.
- Time gap between first phase and second phase disbursement may be deceased.
- Credit delivery as per unit kindly be followed by the bankers.
- Banks may not kindly insist the swarozgaris to repay the loan before implementation of the project.
- Banks may not kindly transfer loan at the respective bank pass book of swarozgaris in lieu of disbursement of loan in favour of swarozgaris

The specific problems and areas of concern in the state are:

- Reluctance on the part of banks
- Inadequate investment
- Poor income generation and diversion of funds
- Declining CD ratio
- Wrong poverty percentage
- Inadequate credit mobilization to primary sector

Observation and Conclusion

Analysis of Performance

- All districts have taken more than the Central allocations.
- All districts have utilised to available funds for more than 100 per cent with minimum in West Tripura (120.06%) and minimum in South Tripura (105.51%).
- The per family investment at the district level varies from Rs. 23086/- in South Tripura to Rs.68709/- in North Tripura.
- As per the state government the poverty ratio in Tripura stands at 66 per cent and not 45 per cent as given by the Planning Commission.
- The per capita investment under SGSY stands at Rs.15,970 as against Rs.25,000 needed.
- Under -financing and delayed financing has resulted in poor income generation and diversion of funds by the swarozgaris.
- The Credit Deposit Ratio that was 49 per cent in 1992-93 declined to 23 per cent in 1999-2000 and further down to 17 per cent in the current year 2003-04.

The state has taken some steps to overcome the constraints in the patch of development. The new vision was brought out as the "Approach to People's Plan in Tripura", a key component of development is "participatory and area based planning". This "Gramoday" programme was launched in February 2000. A ten-year perspective plan is prepared for sectors like self-sufficiency in food production, horticultural development and fisheries. Agriculture and irrigation have been given a pride of place in the plan. The package for the development of scheduled tribes consists of 25 points, which include education, socio-cultural, economic and infrastructure aspects. Similar packages have been evolved for scheduled castes and backward classes. This has given some dividends in the last few years. The state has immense potential for economic development. It has large resources of natural gas and there are several projects in the pipeline for power generation. An opportunity also lies in the form of trade and transit through Bangladesh as well as access to Chittagong port.

Chapter 13

IMPACT OF MICRO FINANCE ON WOMEN EMPOWERMENT: A CASE STUDY

*Dr. K. Thiripura Sundari

**Mr. Raj. Santan

ABSTRACT

Micro finance is the provision of financial services to the poor people. In micro finance system, the Self Help Groups (SHG) played a vital role through the NABARD. Linking of Self Help Groups with banks have evolved as a cost effective and transparent supplementary credit system for reaching the unreached rural poor, the linkage is expected to promote thrift and inculcate credit discipline among the rural poor. Hence, this paper brings out the impact of microfinance on Self Help Groups in Thenkalam Panchayat Union in Tirunelveli District of Tamilnadu State. The study was carried out with 150 micro finance clients from 10 Self Help Groups. Impact is measured as the difference in the magnitude of a given parameter between before and after Self Help Group situations and conclusions are drawn.

Introduction

Micro Finance has, recent times, come to be recognized and accepted as one of the new development paradigms for alleviating poverty through social and economic empowerment of the poor, with focus on empowering women. Self Help Groups have been recognized as a supplementary mechanism for providing credit support to the rural poor in the MICRO FINANCE system.

* Reader in Commerce, Sri Parasakthi College for Women, Courtallum–627 802.

** Research Scholar, M.S. University, Tirunelveli – 627 012

In the Micro Finance system, the Self Help Groups played vital role through the NABARD. It has pioneered the concept and implemented the SHG Bank linkage programme since 1992 for providing easy access of institutional credit to the rural poor.

There have been perceptible and wholesome changes in the living standards of the Self Help Group members in terms of increase in savings and borrowing capacity, income -generating activities, income levels and savings. The corporate mission set by NABARD for reaching micro Finance services to the very poor envisages coverage of one third of the rural poor of the country that is population of about 100 million through one million Self Help Group by the year 2007-08.

Micro-finance means providing very poor families with very small loans (micro credit) to help them engage in productive activities or grow their tiny businesses. Over time, micro finance has come to include a broader range of services (credit, savings, insurance etc.) as we have come to realize that the poor and the very poor that lack access to traditional formal financial institutions, require a variety of financial products.

Hence, against the above background an attempt is made in this paper to explore the impact of Micro Finance on Self-Help Groups. The researcher has chosen Thenkalam Panchayat Union in Tirunelveli district as the area of the study. The Self Help Groups functioning in the study area were taken for analysis and analysis were made in three different angles such as 1. Profile of the groups 2. Assistance received from the banks 3. Performance of the groups and conclusions were drawn.

Description of the Study Area

As per the 2001 census, Thenkalam Panchayat has the total population of 2950 and it includes six small villages namely 1. Puliyan Kottaram 2. Thenkalam Pudur 3. Gandhinagar 4. Nallamalpuram 5. Mela Thenkalam and 6. Kamaraj Nagar. As per 2001 census the Thenkalan Panchayat has 1319 men and 1631 women. The economic activities are agro-based activities, basket making, beedi making, tailoring, carpentry etc.

Methodology

The field studies involved a mixture of qualitative and quantitative research methods. In total, the study drew on data from field interviews with more than 150 micro-finance clients from 10 Self Help Groups in Thenkalam Panchayat. The present study is based on both primary and secondary data.

The reference year for the study is 2004-2005 and all economic parameters for both before and after Self Help Group situations are valued for the reference year. Data on various economic aspects like asset structure, net income, savings, loaning and investment patterns, employment patterns and social aspects such as improvement in self-confidence, communication skills, behavioral changes etc., are collected to assess the impact of the micro-finance system in Thenkalam Panchayat. The primary sources are the responses and views of the animators, representatives and members of the Self Help Groups, and the representatives of NGOs through interviews and well-defined structured interview schedule. The secondary sources are accounts of Self Help Groups in banks as well as books maintained by Self Help Groups. The statistical tools are simple average and percentage. The sampling technique used in this study is convenient sampling. The sample size of the study is 150 SHG members. The study is carried out in Thenkalam Panchayat of Tirunelveli district. Thus this research is a data based descriptive and analytical study.

Analyisis

The study is executed to find whether there is any impact on Self Help Groups who received assistance from various banks under the micro-finance SHG-bank linking programme in Thenkalam Panchayat on various aspects with reference to profile of Self Help Groups, Assistance Received and Performance.

Profile of Self Help Groups

Formal Background

The formal background of Self Help Groups taken for sample has been given in the table no. 1 with reference to the name of the SHG, date of formation and total number of members and Name of the NGO.

Table 1 : Formal background of Self Help Groups

Name of SHG	*Date of formation*	*Total number of members*	*Name of NGO*
Kattu Roja	11-05-96	14	Dew
Sindhu	11-05-96	14	Dew
Thamarai	02-11-97	18	Tss
Anbu	23-06-01	18	Tamilnadu
TamilNadu	24-06-01	14	Tss
Tajmahal	04-08-01	15	Panchayat Office
Malairani	10.01.02	14	Arumbugal
Mullai	01-08-03	17	Arumbugal
Village Upliftment	01-11-03	12	Global
Dr.Muthulakshmi	01-11-03	14	Arumbugal

Source: Secondary Data

Details of Self Help Groups account in Banks

The table gives the details of Self Help Groups account in banks with reference to total saving, interest earned, interest on Bank loan and its balance. It is also possible to cross check the balance to ensure the accuracy of accounts maintained by Self Help Groups.

It is observed that all the Self Help Groups have deposits in banks in the form of savings. They have also earned interest on the deposits in the banks. It is an additional source of income for the Self Help Groups.

It is revealed that the role played by banks is inevitable. The balance of Self Help Groups in banks (i.e.) unutilized amount also earns interest for the SHG. Hence the NPA of the SHG is almost nil. On observing the table, it is understood that every SHG is encouraged enough to maintain high thrift balances in banks as their Self Help Groups accepts the banker as an inevitable partner for their progress.

Table 2 : Details of Self Help Groups Account In Banks

Name of the SHG	*Total savings Rs.*	*Interest earned Rs.*	*Total Amount Rs.*	*Expenses Rs.*	*Interest of Bank Loan Rs.*	*Balance Rs.*
Kattu Roja	41720	19260	60980	6650	44900	9430
Sindhu	41720	20953	62673	6623	45900	10250
Thamarai	21260	10410	31670	1800	28300	1870
Anbu	23100	6051	29157	2350	19700	7101
TamilNadu	22100	2793	24893	1557	15200	8136
Tajmahal	22400	2919	25319	1505	20100	3709
Malairani	9180	745	9925	723	5600	3602
Mullai	10800	4320	11232	230	9500	1502
Village upliftment	10200	593	10793	293	10000	500
Dr. Muthu-lakshmi	9650	600	10750	200	9200	850

Source: Secondary Data

Age Profile of Members

To ascertain the class of age group, which has been actively participating in the Self Help Group activities, the following table is classified on the basis of different age group:

Table 3 : Age profile of members

Age group	*Number of SHG members*	*Percentage*
18-35 years	75	50
36-45 years	54	36
Above 45 years	21	14
Total	150	100

Source: Primary Data

It is observed that 50 per cent of the Self Help Group members belong to the age group of 18-35 years and 14 per cent of the Self Help Group members belong to the group of above 45 years.

Educational Profile

To ascertain the literacy rate the Self Help Group members, the following table has been classified on the basis of educational qualification say below V standard, XII standard and above.

Table 4 : Educational profile

Education	*Number of SHG members*	*Percentage*
Below V Standards	75	50
VI – X Standards	45	30
XI – XII Standards	24	16
Above XII	6	4
Total	150	100

Source: Primary Data

It is observed that 50 per cent of total Self Help Group members have got education less than V standards and only 4 per cent of the total Self Help Group members have got education more than XII standard.

It is revealed that most of Self Help Group members are illiterates. So they are unaware of many of the schemes and policies of government for their empowerment.

Livelihood Profile

The analysis of livelihood profile of SHG members is necessary to find out reason for the poverty, as in some cases their economic activities would not let them to overcome their poverty. The below table classifies the livelihood profile of the Self Help Group members as Own Farms, Wage Labour, Allied Agricultural activities, Handicraft, Household and Personal Services, Manufacturing and Production, Small Business etc.

As per Table 5, 40 per cent of the occupations of the Self Help Group members are dependent on factors like monsoon climate, rainfall, etc. rather than on their skill and talent. The most dominant occupation of Self Help Group members is agriculture and its allied activities. As agriculture depends on rainfall, the income from agriculture is very uncertain. Any change in rainfall will drastically affect the income of Self Help Group members.

Table 5 : Livelihood Profile

Livelihood	*Number of SHG members*	*Percentage*
18-35 years	75	50
Own farms	6	4
Handicraft	6	4
Wage Labour	32	21
Allied Activities (Agriculture)	60	40
Household and Personal Services	15	10
Manufacturing and Production	9	6
Small Business	22	15
Total	150	100

Sources: Primary Data

Analysis of Self Help Groups on the Basis of Assistance Received from Banks

Visits to Groups by Bank Staff

As per NABARD norms, every bank has to send its staff to the Self Help Groups financed by banks regularly say, once in a fortnight especially at the time of disbursal of loans. The following table classifies the visits of bank staff on the basis of period he made visit.

Table 6 : Visits to groups by the bank staff

Period	*Number of Self Help Groups*	*Percentage*
Monthly	5	50
Quarterly	4	40
Occasionally	1	10
Total	10	100

Source: primary Data

As per table 6, the 50 per cent of the total Self Help Groups visited by the bank staff regularly once in a month and 40 per cent of the total Self

Help Groups have visited regularly once in a three months and 10 per cent of the Self Help Groups have visited occasionally.

It is revealed that the bank staff has constant vigil over the activities and performance of Self Help Group to ensure productivity and 100 per cent recovery of loans disbursed. It can also be understood that the bank provide for the effective function of Self Help Group by providing training in maintaining books of accounts, creating awareness regarding various schemes of banks for their upliftment aid availing loans for banks etc. So visits of bank staff is very helpful for the SHG members.

Capacity Building

The capacity building of Self Help Group members through vigorous training plays an important role in future sustainability of Self Help Groups.

The awareness, skill talent, exposure etc., of the Self Help Group members would improve based on the technical support received from the banks, NGO, voluntary agencies, and the number of training attended.

Table 7 : Trainings attended

Type of training attended	*Number of SHG members*	*Percentage of Total in each training*
SHG member training (1 day)	150	100
Animator training (2 days)	36	20
Marketing training (2 days)	54	30
Agricultural training (15 days)	54	30
Skill training (7 days)	41	27

Source: Primary Data

As per the Table 7, all the Self Help Group members have attended the SHG member training for 1 day, On the other hand, the animator training has been attended only by 20 per cent of the total SHG Members, as one or two animators are essential for one Self Help Group at the introducing stage.

On an average, around 25 per cent of the total Self Help Group member have attended different types of training like marketing, training, agricultural training, skill-based training etc. It is a healthy sign for the improvements of Self Help Group members and Self Help Group as well. It provides adequate technical support for the Self Help Group members to maintain books of accounts, providing a new source of income, ability to organize the activities and conduct meetings of the Self Help Group, providing access to new markets etc.

Distribution of Groups by Amount Sanctioned for the First Time

The table 8 classified the Self Help Groups on the basis of amount sanctioned for the first time in the Self Help Group Bank Linkage programme after opening of the savings bank account. The amount is not only in proportion of their savings but also the demand of the Self Help Group is considered within the prescribed limit say 1:2 to the savings of the Self Help Group in the bank. When there is no demand of huge fund, the Self Help Group is given liberty to decide the loan amount.

Table 8 : Distribution of Groups by Amount sanctioned for the first time

Quantum of Amount (In Rs)	*Number of Self Help Groups*	*Percentage*
Below 5000	5	50
5001-10000	3	30
10001-20000	2	20
Above 20000	-	-
Total	10	100

Source: Secondary Data

It is observed that 50 per cent of total Self Help Groups have availed loan between Rs. 5000 and 20 per cent of total Self Help Groups have availed loan between Rs. 10000 and Rs. 20000.

It shows that more earning are mobilized by the Self Help Groups in the initial stage as lending are in proportion to their savings (i.e.) in the ratio of 1:2. Hence, it is understood that most of the Self Help Groups have saved more money in order to avail large amount of loans from banks as shown in the table. By this way, the savings of Self Help Group are being encouraged indirectly.

Distribution of Groups by Amount sanctioned for the Second Time

The table 9 classifies the Self Help Groups on the basis of amount sanctioned for the second time in the Self Help Group Bank Linkage programme. Here, the amount of loan would be sanctioned in the proportion of 1:4 to the saving account. The liberty still lies with the Self Help Group to determine the amount of loan provided it is within the reasonable limits.

As per Table 9, it is observed that 40 per cent of Total Self Help Groups have availed between Rs.10000 and Rs.20000 and 20 per cent of the total Self Help Groups have availed loan above Rs.20000. It shows

Table 9 : Distribution of groups by amount sanctioned for the second time

Quantum of Loan in (Rs.)	*Number of Self Help Groups*	*Percentage*
Below 5000	—	—
5001-10000	4	40
10001-20000	4	40
Above 20000	2	20
Total	10	100

Source: Secondary Data

that the size of the loan availed from the banks have increased over the period of time. It is understood by comparing the previous table. In the previous table, only 20 per cent of Self Help Groups have availed loan between Rs. 10000 and Rs. 20000, whereas now 40 per cent Self Help Groups have availed loan between Rs. 10000 and Rs. 20000. Even percentage of Self Help Groups who have availed loan more than Rs. 20000 has also increased. It can be inferred that the requirement of Self Help Groups members have increased due to the scale of operation they operate. As the size of investment increases, obviously their need for credit would also increase and thereby their income. It also shows that how the Self Help Group members are in need of credit in order to meet their expectations. The other factor should also be considered that is the second linkage (credit) would be given in the ratio of 1:4 to savings whereas in the pervious case, it was 1:2. Anyhow, unless the need arises the Self Help Group would not borrow, as the interest on loan is relatively higher comparing to savings.

Table 10 : Distribution of groups on the basis of insurance policy holders

Type	*Before joining SHG*		*After joining SHG*	
	Number of respondents	*Percentage*	*Number of members*	*Percentage*
Policy holder	3	2	105	70
Non Policy holder	147	98	45	30
Total	150	100	150	100

Source: Primary Data

Insurance Assistance

As most of the SHG members are depended on agriculture, which in turn depend on rainfall for its prosperity, it is unlikely that the SHG members would have regular flow of income. In the times of drought and crisis, the need coverage against these risks at the fair cost. The only solution for this problem is insurance.

As per table 10, 70 per cent of the SHG members have become insurance policy holders under purview of Micro Finance whereas only 2 per cent of the members before joining SHG were policyholders. Hence, Micro Finance provides cover even to the poorest of the poor.

Analysis of Self help Groups on the Basis of Performance

I. Conduct of meeting : Self Help Groups ' have to function in a democratic manner. Regular meeting of group members is one of the activities of the Self Help Groups that ensure effective participation of members. In these meetings, they undertake financial transitions of both collection of savings and disbursement of loans. Meetings are also an occasion for the members to discuss their common problems and other issues that need to be sorted out through the intervention of the group of other members.

II. Frequency of Meetings : Meeting brings members together and help them to express and share their views with each other. By which they learn to know the importance of documents like minutes and they realize the need to act in a transparent and accountable manner. The following table classified the groups based on the frequency of their meetings (i.e.) regular and not regular. Regular meeting means they meet periodically, say weekly.

Table 11 : Frequency of Meetings

Frequency	*Number of Self Help Groups*	*Percentage*
Regular	9	90
Not regular	1	10
Total	10	100

Source: Primary Data

As per the Table 13, it is revealed that 90 per cent of Self Help Groups are conducting meetings periodically say once in fortnight.

Hence, it is ascertained that Self Help Groups are very committed and prompt in organising meeting for the progress of the Self Help Group members. It also helps them to motivate the other Self Help Group members to contribute regularly for savings and finds out the borrower who needs the amount utmost. Constant feedback is made possible in this case. Regular meetings of the members develop a sense of belonging and remind them the objective of the formation of Self Help Group. Regular meeting is a prerequisite for success of any Group/organization. Self Help Group is not an exception to this.

Awareness about objectives and procedures of Self Help Groups

Awareness about objectives and procedures of groups among members is a pre-requisite for success. The following table classifies the awareness as clear and vague based on their ability to enlist their objectives and procedures of the group.

Table 12 : Awareness about objectives and procedures of Self Help Groups

Indicator	*Number of Self Help Group members*	*Percentage of Total*
Clear	90	60
Vague	60	40
Total	150	100

Source: primary data

The above table 12, shows that more than 60 per cent of the Self Help Group members are well aware of the objectives, procedural formalities that are very essential for the accomplishment of the well-laid objectives. Unless the objective is very clear or known, it is not possible to accomplish the objectives. As many are aware of the objectives of the group, it is very certain that the Self Help Group would accomplish its objectives as early as possible.

Record Keeping

Record keeping is necessary to ensure transparency, accountability, accuracy, evidential proof etc. for all the activities of the Self Help Groups . The following table classifies the record keeping of the Self Help Group on the basis of promptness, details and number of records maintained.

Table 13 : Record keeping

Record keeping	*Number of Self Help Groups*	*Percentage*
Good	4	40
Moderate	4	40
Bad	2	20
Total	10	100

Source: Secondary Data

It is observed that 80 per cent of Self Help Group are maintaining all the necessary books which are supposed to be maintained by the Self Help Groups e.g. Resolution register, cash book, loan book, bank passbook, receipt books, members pass book. 40 per cent (Moderate) of Self Help Groups are maintaining all the necessary books but not update in time. i.e. making entries for two, three meeting at a stretch. At the same time 20 per cent of Self Help Group are maintaining the books properly and promptly. As bankers, for availing bank loan, have insisted prompt record keeping, most Self Help Groups have maintained record properly. Regular and prompt record keeping is necessary to ensure accuracy, transparency, accountability and safety. It is essential for effective mobilization of savings, on leading credit and financial management.

Purpose of Loan

Although every member has their own need for credit, the purpose of loan, the duration of the loan, extent of urgency differ from one member to another. It is analysed because genuinely of the need would be assessed on the basis of purpose of loan. The following table classifies the purpose of loan on the basis of assets creation, agriculture etc.

Table 14 : Purpose wise distribution of loan

Purpose	*Number of Self Help Groups members*	*Percentage*
Asset creation	30	20
Agriculture	36	25
Small enterprises	60	40
Education	8	5
Consumption	8	5
Function and activities	8	5
Total	150	100

Source: primary Data

It is observed that 40 per cent of the loans are given to start small enterprises and 5 per cent of the loans are given for functions and activities.

It is understood that encouragement is given for productive and income generating activities like small enterprises, agriculture, assets creating etc. at the same time it has not ignored the genuine, essential and urgent needs like education, consumptions, function and activities etc.

Loan Repayment

The performance and integrity of the SHG could also be revealed through the extent of repayment made for the loan. The table classifies the Self Help Groups on the basis of type of repayment made.

Table 15 : Repayment performance of Self Help Group

Type of repayment	*Number of SHG*	*Percentage*
Prompt	6	60
Delayed	4	40
Total	10	100

Source: Secondary Data

It is observed that 60 per cent of the total Self Help Groups have paid their due on date whereas the other 40 per cent of the total Self Help Groups have also paid due but as a delayed payment (within reasonable period as provided). At the same time no SHG has outstanding balance till date.

It reveals that the Self Help Group has ensured 100 per cent recovery of loans for the banks and it also improves the Non-Performing Assets of the banks. It yields more profits for the banks as banks loans/advances to Self Help Group are refinanced by NABARD for about 90 per cent of advances to Self Help Groups. It proves that Self Help Groups are bankable from the standpoint of banks.

Distribution of Groups by Frequency of Lending

It is essential to know what the Self Help Groups are doing with their common fund and loans received from the banks. Usually, they lend to their members who need money utmost. Hence, the table classifies the groups on the basis of frequency of lending internal loans, to their members.

Table 16 : Distribution of Groups by Frequency of Lending

Period	*Number of SHG*	*Percentage*
Monthly	7	70
Quarterly	2	20
Half yearly	1	10
Total	10	100

Source: Secondary Data

As per table 16, 70 per cent of the Self Help Groups are lending internal loans monthly from the savings of the members and the loans received from the banks.

It shows that most of the Self Help Groups are utilizing the corpus of the Self Help Groups effectively by lending the loans immediately once it is available. Hence, the productivity/utilization of the loans would be improved rather than deposit it in the bank as savings and earn low interest. It is also understood that most of the Self Help Group members are in need of credit regularly say every month. By lending both the members of Self Help Group and the Self Help Group are availing the credit in time and it increases the profitability of the Self Help Group by charging relatively high interest on loan comparing to interest on savings.

Quantum of Thrift

The following table classifies the members of the Self Help Group on the basis of Quantum of Thrift before and after joining the Self Help Group to analyse the impact of Self Help Group on the quantum of thrift among the Self Help Group members, as the Self Help Group promotes and collect thrift regularly.

It is observed that no Self Help Group member has saved money before joining the Self Help Group. At the same time, around 95 per cent of the Self Help Group members have saved around Rs. 1000 as the Self Help Group members have saved around Rs. 1000 at the end of the first year after joining the Self Help Group and around 90 per cent of the Self Help Group members have saved around Rs. 3000 at the end of second year.

Table 17 : Quantum of Thrift after joining SHG

Quantum of Thrift	*Before Joining SHG*		*One Year (After)*		*Two Years (After)*	
	Number of SHG members	*Percentage*	*Number of SHG members*	*Percentage*	*Number of SHG members*	*Percentage*
Below 1000	123	82	142	95	-	-
1001-3000	27	18	8	5	135	90
3001-5000	-	-	-	-	15	10
Total	150	100	150	100	150	100

Source: Primary Data

It is a big surprise to note that the Self Help Group members are able to save such amount (as shown above) after joining the Self Help Group, whereas before joining the Self Help Group, they have saved nothing. It shows that they are in utmost need for a medium to save their income. The thrift is compulsory among the Self Help Group members.

Distribution of Groups on the Basis of Income

The table classifies the Self Help Group members on the basis of income received during its respective years before and after joining the Self Help Group to analyse the impact of Self Help Group on the income earned by the Self Help Group members.

Table 18 : Distribution of SHG members based on the Income

Quantum of Income (in Rs)	*Before Joining SHG*		*After Joining SHG*	
	No. of SHG Members	*Percentage*	*No. of SHG Members*	*Percentage*
Below 5000	120	80	45	30
5001-10000	22	15	90	60
10001-20000	8	5	12	8
Above 20000	0	0	3	2
Total	150	100	150	100

Source: Primary Data

It is observed that 80 per cent of the Self Help Group members are in the income group of Rs. 1001 to Rs. 3000 before joining the Self Help Group, where as the 60 per cent of the Self Help Group members are in the group of Rs. 3001 to 5000. It is revealed that the income of the Self Help Group members have increased relatively after joining Self Help Group. It is because they avail loan or credit in time at the reasonable rate and by availing credit and employed it in the investment (or) productive avenues, as they yield additional income which result in the increase of their total income. It provides notional income by saving the amount of interest on loan which would have been borrowed, from unscrupulous moneylenders at an exorbitant rate of interest in the absence of SHG and its fund. This is how Self Help Groups help to increase the income of the members and thereby their standard of living.

Findings and Conclusion

This study is executed to find out the impact of micro finance (Self Help Group bank linkage programme) on the Self Help Groups by ascertaining the objectives of Self Help Group - bank linkage programme and to check whether the objectives have been fulfilled or not, through the data collected. The analysis of data of this study proves that the objectives of Self Help Group BANK linkage programme have been accomplished in the area of the study to the satisfactory level.

Findings of the study

- The data collected is analysed on three broad factors say profile of Self Help Groups, Micro finance assistance received and performance of Self Help Groups .

Regarding profile of Self Help Groups, the following findings were made

- Majority of the members of the Self Help Groups belong to the age group of 18-35 years as they are physically and mentally able to participate actively in the Self Help Groups activities.
- The number of Self Help Groups have been consistently increasing as they got overwhelming response from the public especially women and they also get more financial assistance from banks, NGOs and governments.
- The Self Help Groups' bank linkage programme mainly funds all the performing and potential Self Help Groups as their own grading sheet based on the norms of NABARD assesses every Self Help Groups .
- The educational profile of members is very poor as they are able to access the educational services.
- The most predominant occupation of the members of Self Help Groups is agriculture and its allied activities. As a result, their flow of income depends on the quantum of rainfall received. In the times of crisis and drought, they suffer more and become poorest of the poor. Some of the SHG members are doing small business.

On the basis of Micro Finance Assistance received by Self Help Groups from banks, the findings are as follows:

- The bank staff often pays visits to the Self Help Groups for effective supervision of performance and their activities.
- They also provide many training opportunities to the SHG members for creating awareness, improve the skills and talents and give access to the new markets and business.
- The Self Help Groups have availed more number of loans from banks by prompt repayment of previous loans and interest.
- The Self Help Groups gain the confidence and goodwill of the bankers and proved that they are bankable. Mostly, the Self Help

Groups get the next loan within a very short period after the repayment of first loan as the banks adopt the method of progressive lending based on its performance repayment.

- The banks also provide insurance cover for the SHG members at a very reasonable rate. Hence the number of policyholders in Self Help Groups has gone up.

Regarding the analysis of Self Help Groups on the basis of performance the following findings were made.

- The majority of the Self Help Groups conduct the meetings very promptly and the attendance of the meetings is also impressive.
- The awareness about the objectives and procedures of Self Help Groups among the members is very high as they are very committed in achieving it.
- They maintain records as they are accountable for all activities carried out by the SHG.
- The loans are lent not only for productive and income-generating activities even for consumption purpose like hospitalization.
- They mobilize thrift (saving) from the members regularly preferably weekly.
- The repayment performance of SHG members is almost 100 per cent which is quite impressive and they also repay the loans in a short interval from the date of availing of loan.
- The Self Help Groups NPA is almost nil. They lend both the savings and loan received from the banks to its members as the credit earn interest (profit for SHG)

Conclusion

The micro finance programme initiated by NABARD is the largest in the world which has helped them access to credit. It can be stated that the prospects of micro finance (SHG-bank linkage programme) would blossom further in the years to come as it has got overwhelming support from the society at large. It is believed that the micro-finance, if utilized properly, provides ample chances to SHG members to develop multifaceted skills with the increase in the annual income and standard of living. It gives the member's exposure to the style of various upliftments in social cultural, economic, political and finally self-esteemed personalities. The bottom line is that micro-finance is the new mantra for poor.

REFERENCES

- Micro credit for macro impact on poverty, Mrs. Indira Misra, National Publishing house. New Delhi, 2004.
- Entrepreneur–Handbook, Tamilnadu Corporation of Development of Women Ltd., 2001.
- Emerging micro-finance innovations, NABARD, 1998.
- Journal of Microfinance, vol-5, No.1, 2003.
- Business India, June 9-12, 2003.
- Bank Quest, vol-74, No.3, July-sept 2003.
- www.tamilnadu women.org
- www.adb.org/microfinance

Chapter 14

OBSERVATION OF SHGS IN MICRO ENTERPRISE ACTIVITIES

*Dr. M. Soundarapandian
*G. Saravanan

ABSTRACT

In India nearly 40 per cent of people live under poverty line and many educated youth remain unemployed. In order to solve the unemployment problem the SGSY (SWARNA JAYANTI GRAM SWAROJGAR YOJANA) Programme was introduced in April 1999. This study attempts to analyse various issues related to micro finance under SGSY. It is also aimed to find out how it helps the poor people, increase their income and ultimately break the vicious circle of poverty under SGSY.

Introduction

In the United States of America there were no micro enterprises programmes before 1980s, but after 1980s a few micro enterprises programmes were introduced since solve the problem unemployment which was not acute in that country. Even though they are capitalist, they introduced micro enterprise programmes so as to absorb excess labour force in organized sector. In India, nearly 40 per cent of people live under poverty line and many educated youth remain unemployed. In order to solve the unemployment problem the SGSY (SWARNA JAYANTI GRAM SWAROJGAR YOJANA) Programme was introduced in April 1999. This programme attempts at establishing large number of micro enterprises in rural area building upon the potential of the rural poor in India have enough skills and competence and if the governmental and

* Professor in R.I.M., G.R.V. Gandhigram.

* Research Scholar, Department of Rural Industries and Management, GRU, Gandhigram.

non-governmental institution extend the right support they can emerge as successful producers of valuable goods and services.

Role of SGSY in Poverty, Unemployment and Micro Enterprises

A large number of studies in India have evidenced that the earlier self-employment programmes like NREP, RLEGP, JRYP AND IRDP, have failed to tackle the problem due to lack of participation, co-ordination, inadequate financial facilities and social and political. Thus, SGSY was introduced. It is in this context the micro enterprises programme like SGSY assumes significances and it is believed that it can provide income to the rural poor on a sustainable basis.

The anti-poverty programmes have been strengthened in successive years and have reduced the magnitude of poverty from 56.44 per cent in 1973-1974 to 37.27 per cent in 1993-94. The number of rural poor has more or less remained static. Thus, the micro finance will help the poor people, increase their income and ultimately break the vicious circle of poverty.

Evidences of Successful SHGs through Micro Enterprises

National Institute of Rural Development conducted a study on Micro Enterprises. Which are developed by SHGs in Tamil Nadu. Kaveri Self Help Groups was formed on 11-1-1999 with 12 members by Sevai Trust. After forming the group members started saving Rs. 25 per week. All the members were trained for two months in mat weaving by the SEVAI Trust. The raw material required for weaving is korai grass. So one acre land was taken for lease for five years.

The rent for land is Rs.5000 per year but income for grass is Rs.7000/- per year. Four members, out of twelve are engaged in cultivating grass for mats. Four members are working in production unit and their wages are Rs.60/- per day. The other four members are engaged in finishing work and earn Rs. 35/- per day. The four members are engaged in finishing work and earn Rs. 35/- per day. The marketing for mats and the maintenance of machinery was undertaken by the NGO.

Vauduriyam SHG was formed in July 2000 with 15 members. The group started with weakly savings of Rs.25/- in January 2000 all the members joined in the training programme conducted by SEVAI. DRDA has provided transport and lunch for six months during the training period. Banama fibre is locally available. They are trained to make bags, file bags, tea mats, table mats, and dolls.

Mrs. Benjamin a French lady and social worker from Bangalore gave the idea and also helping in marketing of the products. She has a shop in Bangalore in addition. SEVAI is arranging to participate in exhibition at Mumbai, Delhi and Chennai with the Tamil Nadu Government support. In Trichy Town poomalai shop supported by DRDA is also purchasing the products. Thus, author was told that each member is getting not less than Rs. 1500/- per month.

Sevai is forming SHGs and starting with thrift and credit activities providing training to the women in tailoring, embroidery type writing, gem cutting, mat weaving and banana fibre, product etc. they also provide employment in the organization and helping in marketing for their products.

The activities like candle making, agarbathi, readymade garments, hollow brick manufacturing, paper making etc, are not having good market. So they are diversifying to other activities.

Strategy of SHGs through Micro Enterprises

The true effectiveness of any activities means the improvement of income, expenditure, savings personal investment and business investment of self help group members after being trained.

To cope with the modern and highly competitive markets, means and ways can be provided to induce technology, to increase production and to attract the customers easily. Modern technology is lacking in the rural area, which can be eliminated by updating them with new technology.

SHGs can be involved in poverty alleviation programme, as their performance in income generation is good they are not only aiming at income earning, but also motivated in savings, this is made compulsory with the repayment itself. Hence, this scheme can be encouraged to mobilize more savings and there by reducing poverty, unemployment and improve their standard of living of the poor and marginalized people.

Micro enterprises train poor to improve entrepreneurial ability and skill to obtain economic independence.

Women employment is possible only through micro enterprises. Many studies evidenced that micro enterprises really contribute to women empowerment and try to reduce gender inequality.

SGSY should be encouraged to take up not only income generating activities, but also activities relating to the social sector through micro enterprises.

Conclusion

Evidence clearly show that micro enterprise helps the poor to come out of poverty, unemployment and increase income generation capacity.

Through micro enterprise it is not only earning income of SHGs but also it helps for generating national income and induce the export of goods and services.

REFERENCE

- Dr. V. Darling Selvi, "Impact of Self Help Group Training", Kissan World, Vol. 32, No. 3. March, 2005, Page No 31-32.
- R. Asokan, "Micro-Enterprises": An Alternative Strategy for Poverty Alleviation", Kissan World, Vol. 32, No. 3. March, 2005, Page No 49-50
- Training Programme on "Management of SGSY with special focus on marketing" 24-29th May, 2004, NIRD, Hydrabad.
- Handbook of SGSY, Dept of Rural Development, Government of India.
- Amal Mandal, "Swarna Jayanti Gram Swarozgar Yojana and self help group" An Assessment, Kurukshetra, Vol. 53, No. 3, January, 2005, Page No. 4-9.

Chapter 15

SUSTAINABLE LIVELIHOOD OF WOMEN : A CASE STUDY OF MANGALORE CITY IN KARNATAKA

*D.P. Angadi
**Jayasheela

ABSTRACT

The major objective of this study is to identify the attitude of women towards sustainable livelihood, given access to resources, assets and other benefits thereof. Primary data was collected from Mangalore city of Karnataka. Spearman correlation analysis was used to find out relationship among variables. Findings and conclusion drawn are presented.

Introduction

Human beings are at the centre of concerns for sustainable development. They are entitled for a healthy, productive life in harmony with nature. Development needs must be fulfilled so as to equitable meet human and environmental needs of present and future generations. In order to achieve equitable development, sustainable livelihood of women protection shall constitute an integral part of the development process.

The term livelihood refers to activities and entitlements by which people make a living, while the concept of sustainable livelihood clearly establishes the linkages among poverty, environment and participation or empowerment. Participatory approaches at the community level clearly highlight gender differences in perceptions regarding livelihood and the differential impact of resource degradation. Sustainability depends on, or stems from livelihood security, much may be defined by an income level, income stability, seasonality of livelihoods and degrees of risk

* Lecturer, Department of Geography, University College, Hampanakatta, Mangalore.
** Reader, Department of Economics, Mangalore University, Mangalagangothri-574199.

involved. Sustainability also depends on processes, which lead to better use of resources.

The important role of women in economic and social development at both community and national level is being increasingly recognized. The spate of conferences, formal declarations and intentions over the past fifteen years suggest that the role of women is changing, and is receiving growing recognition. Yet deeds do not always match words, nor does action necessarily follow from good intentions. A more fundamental issue is that of gender. Attention is also drawn on differences between women and gender issues, and some experiences in which attempts have been made to institute gender focused change. For gender planning, one of the greatest challenges to be overcome is the frequent assumption about gender based division of work within and outside the households.

In the third world countries, women's work usually involves three components;

1. Reproductive work which relates to child bearing and raising, as well as nurturing of all family members to ensure their health and well being.
2. Productive work which involves activity outside the home by both women and men, for payment in cash or kind. Such work can be market based production that result in earning of money. Much of the productive work of women, especially in the rural areas, generates in kind returns that are essential for the well being of the families. In many societies, men dominate market-based economic activity, where as women are more frequently active in non-market based activities.
3. Community managing which involves time allocated for participating in the activities which the local community arranges for the welfare of its members. In many ways, this kind of activity is an extension of the reproductive role. The aim here is to ensure both provision and maintenance of facilities for collective needs, such as water, health care and education. Community managing work is often voluntary and is done during free time. In contrast, men tend to allocate their time to indulge in community politics, often paid, either directly or indirectly by enhanced status and power.

The implication of the multiple roles of women is significant while considering the issues of empowerment, social justice and equity. First the triple role of women means, they are the first to begin working in a day and often the last to finish their work. As a result, there is a little time for self-improvement. Second, much of these productive and community managing activities are invisible in any economic account. Third, the opportunity for monetary income is low. Fourth, the lack of involvement in community politics reinforces a gender bias in many decisions, and opportunities for women are significantly less than that of their male counterpart.

Objectives

- To identify the difficulties and constraints faced by women of the Mangalore city.
- The attitude of women towards a sustainable livelihood, given their access to resources, assets and benefits thereof.
- To analyse the socio economic development of women from various social strata and from several spatial locations within the city.

Methodology

Mangalore city of Karnataka has selected for the purpose of study. The data for the study was collected from both primary (field data) and secondary data in order to understand the status of women and their livelihood in the city and to draw a clear picture of prospective and analytical conclusion. Spearman correlation analysis used to find out relationship among variables.

Respondents Personal and Household Information

Age Distribution

Age distribution of women in Mangalore city indicates that their mean age is 33.5 years, with a standard deviation of 10.57 and a co-efficient of variation of 111.74, which means that there is a wide variation in the age distribution among women. Table 1 indicates that a little more than 29 per cent of them are in the age group of 21-25 years, which means majority of them are adults and capable of doing work. Only 3 per cent of them are less than or equal to 20 years, and nearly 15 per cent each are found to belong to the classes of 26-30 years and 31-35 years. Nearly 30 per cent of them are of middle age, with a distribution of 15.7 per cent in 36-40 years, 7.2 per cent in 41-45 years and 6.8 per cent in 46.50 years. Women with more than 50 years of age account for 7.6 per cent only. There is, however, a progressive decline in their proportions after 50 years.

The women population being studied is generally middle aged as two thirds of them are young, less than 35 years old. Nearly four fifth (78.4% of women) are aged less than 40 years. This also indicates that women are economically active even after 60 years of age.

Table 1: Age Distribution of Women of Mangalore City

Age class	*Percentage*	*Cumulative*
<20	3.0	3.0
21-25	29.3	32.3
26-30	15.3	47.6
31-35	15.1	62.7
36-40	15.7	78.4
41-45	7.2	85.6
46-50	6.8	92.4
51-55	5.1	97.5
56-60	1.4	98.9
61-65	0.4	99.3
66-71	0.7	100.0
Total	100.00	

Educational attainment

Education of women in Mangalore City indicates that they have on an average 11 years of education (possible class 11) with a standard deviation of 4.24 and a co-efficient of variance of 17.99. this means that most (59% of the educated) of them not completed the school final, although nearly 41 per cent of them have collegiate education with professional and technical degrees as well (Table.2). In fact a large number of women have attained professional and technical education. This itself an indication of an urban milieu, which comprises well educated women even though the number of employed may not be large.

Table 2: Educational Attainment of Mangalore City Women.

Years of education	*Percentage*
<3 Primary	4.4
4-5 H. Primary	22.3
6-10 Middle and High	13.4
11-12 Higher Secondary	14.3
13 Diploma	4.3
14 Degree	0.5
15-18 P.G	40.8
	100.0

Family size

Family size of the women households interviewed indicates that their mean family size is nearly 5, with a standard derivation of 2.03 and a co-efficient of variance of 4.13 family of more than half of the women households (53.3%) is medium sized, usually consisting of 4-6 members. Larger families primarily joint or extended, with more than 10 persons constitute 4.3 per cent of the total households. Small families of 3 or less than 3 members account for 23.1 per cent of the households of the city.

Table 3: Family size of the Mangalore city

Family size	*Per cent*
<3 Small	23.1
4-6 Medium	53.3
7-10 Large	19.3
>10 V. large	4.3
	100

The distribution of sizes are indicative of the fact that the family welfare planning is yet to penetrate the urban milieu in Mangalore city. This may even be attributable to the fact that the urban families are mostly medium sized and that the large ones are likely to have relatives who may have come for studies or employment seeking, staying with the families.

Occupational Characteristics of women in Mangalore

Economically Active Persons

There is gender participation in various occupations, most of them city based and are non agricultural. One or two or more persons are economically engaged in some worth while livelihood. Some households (16.2%), however, report of one (7.2%) or two (9%) people engaged in subsidiary occupations, which are by no means regular. Only 10.4 per cent of the households indicate that the subsidiary occupations are also regular, with one person each in 3.2 per cent of the households and two persons each in 7.2 per cent of the households.

Access to Resources

There are always problems in respect of access to resources. More than half of the respondents have indicated to a lack of adequate rest and recreation, while 11.9 per cent have indicated lack of institutional support. Nearly one tenth of the women lack own technical and professional knowledge, while 7.9 per cent of them lack personal resources, especially capital for investment. Nearly 8 per cent of the women of the city report of lack of access to resources, which jeopardizes them from taking relevant investment activities.

Constraints at Work Place

As much as 88 per cent of the women interviewed would like to switch to new a job. One fourth of the women have found constraints regarding transport to work places, while 9 per cent of them have encountered difficulties in getting labour and assistance or help. One twentieth of the respondents have indicated that they have capital constraints in their operations. 4.3 per cent of them have time constraints and 3.6 per cent feel the lack of land, space and /or accommodation. A negligible 2.5 per cent of them feel the constraints in the flow of raw materials. Only 0.8 per cent of them feel a lack of training or human capacity building in regard to their jobs, while 0.4 per cent indicated marketing constraints.

Income of Women households

Income of the households of women in the city (Table 4) reveals that, their mean income is Rs. 11,323 p.m. This average is rather sufficient for an average household of 5 members. Those who have income below Rs.1000 comprise 4.8 per cent and the highest percent is 30.4 where the income is between Rs. 5000 and Rs. 10000. There is 10.6 per cent of women who belong to the category fo Rs. 200 to Rs. 3000 while 10.1 per cent of them belong to Rs. 1000 to 2000 income group. It is evident that about 42 per cent of the households have an income less than Rs. 5000 and 10000. One fourth of the households have reported a monthly income of more than Rs.10,000 and less than Rs. 50,000. Two per cent of households have very good income of more than Rs.50, 000 p.m. On the whole, 5 per cent of the households are very poor, 37.3 per cent of the households are poor and three of them are fairly well off. Yet a majority of women households of the city belongs to the middle class.

Occupational Characteristics of Women

Seventy seven per cent of the women interviewed revealed that their main occupations, are fin jobs (77.4%), they fetch adequate income (52.3%), gives satisfaction (69.9%), and offer better working conditions (74.6%) and the women are proud of their job (79.9%). It appears that women are essentially satisfied with their jobs and the money they bring and also satisfaction they offer. There are indeed some women, but less than one fifth of them, who are not really proud of their jobs.

Table 4: Details od income of the women households

Income	*Percent*
<1,000	4.8
1,001-2,000	10.1
2001-3000	10.6
3001-4000	6.5
4001-5000	10.4
5001-6000	30.4
10001-15000	5.4
15001-20000	8.6
20001-30000	8.0
30001-50000	3.2
50001-75000	0.4
75001-100000	0.8
>10,00,000	0.8
	100.0

For a large majority of women (92.5%), there is a lack of access to resources in their jobs, interviewed complain of a lack of rest and recreation, although only 12.5 per cent of the women feel the lack of own capital for investment even as 6.2 per cent of them considers the lack of own technical or professional knowledge.

The women list a large number of problems encountered by them in their day to day life, primarily in connection with their main occupation. There are by even a cursory count, as many as 100 different, pressing problems, with several minor irritants making life difficult as well.

Years on job

The women in Mangalore city do not remain in a particular job for a long period, that is, most of them hold a job for less than 5 years. Only 19.7 per cent stay in a job for a period of 6-10 years, while 17.2 per cent stay on between 11 and 15 years (Table 5). Those who stay in the same job, for long, comprise 6.8 per cent and they mostly hold permanent jobs. This shows that women of Mangalore city are engaged in different types of jobs.

The above table reveals that, 39 per cent of the women of the city would like to change their jobs (against almost half of the women who would not like to). Of those who wan to start on a new job, 31.5 per cent really want to change while 57.3 per cent do not. Only 32.3 per cent of the women are sure of the opportunities and choices they may have in changing to a new job (against 49 per cent who do not see any opportunities or choices in the present circumstances).

Table 5: Particulars of years on job.

Family size	*Per cent*
< 5	45.0
6-10	19.7
11-15	17.2
16-20	8.0
21-25	3.3
>25	6.8
	100.0

Expenditure and Consumption Patterns

Consumption expenditure is the main item of expenditure in every household. Largest proportion of income is spent on food. On an average, a majority of the rural households spends between Rs. 800 and Rs. 1200 per month on food. In urban areas, the largest proportion of 55 per cent incurs an expenditure of Rs. 500 to Rs. 1500 on food, while 14.4 per cent incurs more than Rs. 1500 per month.

According to women, 0.4 per cent of the households spend Rs. 2000, 1.8 per cent Rs. 2500, 12.2 per cent, Rs. 3000, 0.7 per cent Rs. 3500 and 0.4 per cent Rs.5000/- per month on food. Most of the households therefore spend less than Rs.2000 per month as they cannot afford more than that. Housing is the next largest expenditure, with 0.7 per cent spending Rs. 1000, 0.4 per cent, Rs. 1,500, 0.7 per cent, Rs. 2000 and 1.8 per cent, Rs. 500 each. A large section of the population does not have house of their own. On clothing, the expenditure pattern is the same with 1.4 per cent of the household spend Rs.1000 per month.

Recreation is an important item of expenditure as well. On an average they spend Rs. 300/- per month, also spend on social occasions such as marriages and festivals. Several families in the city have fall in debt due to expenditure on social occasions. The pattern of spending on religious ceremonies more or less confirms to that of the social occasions. It can be inferred from the study that the people of Mangalore city are not very religious or are not one spending lavishly on religious celebrations or otherwise.

Health and education are two important socio-cultural aspects of the region. This expenditure does not occur all the time but most certainly on certain dates and months. However, education and health expenses are negligible because of the various welfare programmes introduced by government.

Savings is a habit that only a few exhibit and among the women 1.1 per cent each save Rs.100, Rs.150 and Rs.200 per month, respectively, whereas only 0.4 per cent each save Rs.250 per month and Rs. 50 per month respectively.

A large proportion of the women respondents feel that making a living is hard. Only 2.2 per cent of them do not feel like that. 13.3 per cent feel it hard; 48.4 per cent feel that making a living is moderately difficult while nearly one fourth of them think it is very hard. One fifth of them feel it is very easy to get into troubles. More than just one third of the people feel it is not easy at all. They revealed that in 80 per cent of the cases getting help/assistance from friends and relatives is very difficult as well.

Women and how they make a living in a city: Relationships among variables.

Table 6 reveals, the correlations between pairs of variable which are statistically significant in terms of probabilities. Only the pairs with high, positively significant relations are retained in the table and the rest have been eliminated to avoid clutter.

Table 6: Women and how they make a living in Mangalore city: Relationships among variables

Independent variable(x)	*Dependent variables(y)*	*Correlations ®*	*Probabilities*
Espm	Famsize	0.544	0.0001xx
Eapt	Famsize	0.413	0.002xx
Education	Income	0.326	0.0001xx
Socreg	Affordcost	0.657	0.0001xx
Soccreg	Howeasy	0.850	0.001xx
Prioccu	Afford cost	0.434	0.0001xx
Eapm	Adultm	0.766	0.0001xx
Prioccu	travel	0.416	0.0001xx

Source: Correlation analysis (spearman). R-values less than 0.400 have been eliminated except in certain cases where they are important in explaining relations.

Households of Mangalore city are male dominated (0.544) than female dominated (0.434). Income and education are dependent (0.326) but is does not have strong correlation with education even if it is positive. Living is affordable (0.657) out of regular subsidiary occupations in which women are engaged. Similarly, it is easy to get into difficulties and problems (0.850) even if women hold regularly subsidiary occupations, and if such dependence is not very strong as the R value indicates weak relations. Cost of travel is affordable (0.434) because of the primary occupation as well as income which it fetches for the household and therefore women could make travel to work. Economically active persons in most households are essentially males as the elations between them is strong at (0.766) as against the weak relations between adult female and economically active persons: (0.376). Travel to work places is dependent on primary occupations of the households (0.416) is also borne out by the correlation.

Conclusion and Recommendations

Life and living are hard, especially in these days of limited opportunities and stiff competition. Women find themselves in a spot because they are often the losers in a competition for occupation, raw materials, capital, time, business investment, resources, capital for investment, institutional support and rest and recreation.

Women are generally engaged in both 'unpaid' as well as 'paid' work and are contributing to development of the society, community and milieu. Their unpaid work is far more important than their paid work. In comparison with the women of India, the socio-economic status of women of Mangalore is no better and is not seems to be any better in the future, as they face same problems, especially economic and social: lack of empowerment, social justice and recognition for their work and contribution. Reality of life around these women is more or less the same as with any women of the Indian households. They get into difficulties and problems as easily as they extricate themselves from them, because of their primary as well as subsidiary occupations. The income that the occupations fetch are not extraordinary but something that affords them food, shelter, clothing, education and health, recreation and welfare reasonably. They could always do betters, but opportunities and choices are limited. Given these socio economic conditions:

- Women of the city must be allowed to choose an alternative employment that would fetch their households higher incomes and better living.
- They should be allowed/provided better utilities, infrastructure and services.

- Their 'unpaid' work at home and their contribution to household economy and development must be explicitly recognized and in accordance a position of respect be accorded to women towards their empowerment as move towards social justice.
- Women's role in socio-economic development must also be recognized and due acceptance must be given to their work and contribution.
- Above all, their equal role with men in responsibility and accountability of the households must also be recognized.

REFERENCES

- Anderson, Mary, B. (editor, among othrs) 1985: Gender Roles in Development – A case book, Kumarian Press.
- Bardhan, Pranab, (eds) 1989: Conversations between economists and Anthropologists-Methodological issues in Measuring Economic Change in Rural India. Oxford University Press, Delhi.
- Boserup, E. 1970: Women's Role in Economic Development. London: George Allen and Unwin.
- Braindotti, R.E. Charkiewicz, S. Hansler and S. Wieringa 1994: Women, the Environment and Sustainable Developmetn: Towards a Theoreticla Synthesis, London: Zed.
- Dankelman, I, and Davidson, J. 1989: Women and Environment in the Third World: Alliance for the Future. London: Earthscan Publications.
- GAP Research of Team 1994: Women's status in the GAP Region and their Integration to the process of development, (Executive Summery), Development Foundation of Turkey, Ankara.
- Ghadially, Rehana, (editor), 1988: Women in Indian Society: a reader, Sage Publications, New Delhi, India
- Guijt. I. and Shah. M. (Eds) 1998: The Myth of community: Gender Issues in Participatory Development, London: Intermediate Technology, Publication.
- Harcourt, W. 1995: Understanding Women, Environment and Development: key terms and concepts, proceedings of the SPPE Serninar on Women – Environment Development, Berne, 31, October.

Chapter 16
WOMEN ENTREPRENEURSHIP : ISSUES AND CONCERNS

Dr. Yathish Kumar

ABSTRACT

Issues pertaining to women entrepreneurs are discussed in this chapter. Two powerful approaches to women empowerment and rural entrepreneurship have emerged during the last decade, viz., (i) information of self-help groups among women and (ii) clusters among similar or mutually related enterprises. The underlying principle in that collective wisdom and strength for common benefits, through cooperation and competition. However, the road to achieve success is not easy for them. There are many obstacles that hinders women entrepreneurship in rural areas – financial constraints, indebtedness, limited marketing net works, social barriers, inadequate access to technology and so on.

Introduction

In most of the developing countries of Africa and Asia, an overwhelming majority of enterprises—more than 90 per cent – are micro, small and medium enterprises (MSMEs). These account for nearly 75 per cent of the gross domestic product against 50 per cent in the rest of the world. They play a very important role in the economic and social life of the people and generate a large number of non-agricultural jobs. They also account for a large proportion of exports, sales and value added. They contribute in a big way to employment creation as well as to the improvement of skills through on-the-job training. Therefore, integrating small enterprises to the economic development is essential in the present era of globalisation.

* Senior Scale Lecturer, Dept. of Commerce, University College, Mangalore-575 001, Karnataka.

Especially in the rural context, micro and small enterprises assume an enhanced significance because nearly 70 per cent of the population in the developing nations is concentrated in rural areas. Research studies and surveys reveal that the growth of agro-based sector has the inherent promise for promotion of rural entrepreneurship. Unless this potential human resource is tapped and translated into creation of viable rural enterprises, the country's economic growth will lag behind in its journey of development. The economic development of a country is the function of the availability of entrepreneurship. If today, some countries like India have remained as developing ones, it is largely because of the dearth of an important input, viz., entrepreneurship. It is true to say that the dearth is not only in the case of male entrepreneurs but it is significant in case of women's participation in the economic development process.

Women comprise nearly half of the national population of any country. Hence, the development of any country is inseparably linked with the status of development of women.

Economic empowerment is one approach to enable women to realise their inherent knowledge, skills and competencies for creation of small business enterprises. There are shining examples from the developing nations those women entrepreneurs who started small and grown to large enterprises. Empowered women will contribute to achieving the national economic and social goals, and take the nation forward.

Experience has shown that promotion of enterprise creation and income generating activities among these women would go a long way in improving their conditions – transform them from 'being alive' to 'living with dignity'. The process will be faster and smoother, if conducive climate is created at policy and implementation level.

Two powerful approaches to women empowerment and rural entrepreneurship have emerged during the last decade: formation of self-help groups (SHGs) especially among women; and clusters among similar or mutually related enterprises. Both these approaches are based on the underlying principle of using collective wisdom and strength for common benefits, through cooperation and competition.

The strategy of SHG formation among women has fetched noticeable results in India and Bangladesh. The states of Karnataka, Andhra Pradesh, Tamilnadu, Goa etc., in India leads in this regard. The SHG approach has proved successful not only in improving the economic conditions through income generation but in creating awareness about health and hygiene, sanitation and cleanliness, environmental protection, importance of education and better response for development schemes.

In most of the countries, women are considered as a focal point and the unifying force in the family. While their contribution to the family and society is considerable, they are subjected to numerous constraints undermining their potentials. They receive only small share in development opportunities and are often excluded from education, better jobs, participation in political system and better health care, decision making, etc. Besides, they suffer from physiological, psychological, social and cultural barriers, which hinders their empowerment. In rural areas, women are preoccupied with mostly household work - including the bearing and rearing of children. Accordingly, the opportunities for improving their conditions are limited.

Hence, what is needed is a favorable environment to maximise their potentials. This encouraging environment should include basic amenities such as better health and nutrition, education and sensitisation to their rights and protection under the law and employment opportunities, etc. Over the decades, various strategies have been adopted to empower rural women with some mixed results. One of the viable strategies, quite often talked about, is the role of enterprise to empower rural women. For example, promotion of rural enterprise makes full use of family labour; requires less capital in production and uses locally available raw material. In addition, family ties and kinship linkages may help in promoting rural enterprises. Thus, enterprise development has been considered, among other factors, a powerful tool to eradicate poverty especially among rural women.

Another advantage of the rural enterprise development is that it provides employment and income generating opportunities to rural women on a sustainable basis and thus multiplying contribution in the national income. Besides, enterprise development offers scope for supplementing family income. Thus, the potential benefits of rural enterprise, among others, include diversification of factors of production and products, value addition, creation of wealth, export earnings and economic self-reliance.

Highlights of the Women Entrepreneurs Development

The First National Conference of Women Entrepreneurs held at New Delhi in 1981 advocated the need for developing women entrepreneurs for the overall development of the country. It called for priority to women in allotment of land, sheds, sanction of power, licensing etc. The Second International Conference of Women Entrepreneurs organized by the National Alliance of Young Entrepreneurs (NAYE) in 1989 in New Delhi also adopted declaration involving women's participation in industry.

The report of the National Commission of Self-employed women and women in the informal sector known as Shram Shakti Report also emphasizes that women possessing skills, education, literacy and a sense of enterprise should be encouraged to take up self-employment programs. It also advocated multi-pronged strategy encompassing not only self-employment opportunities but also a package that contains child-care, introduction of technology to reduce drudgery and overall development of women. The Rashtriya Mahila Kosh (RMK) and the Mahila Samridhi Yojana(MSY) are the relatively new schemes initiated in 1993 for economic empowerment of women. Significant government and local initiatives have been introduced with the intention of stimulating entrepreneurship among women.

One of the most important methods that the Sixth Five Year plan mentioned for doing so is the creation of income-generating activities for women. The government moved a step further in the 7th plan by including a special chapter on Integration of Women Development. In the Industrial policy of 1991, the GOI further stressed the need for conducting special entrepreneurship development programs for women with a view to encourage women to enter industry. Product and process oriented courses enabling women to start small-scale industries are also recommended in the policy statement. Even the Industrial Policy for small scale, cottage and tiny sector 1992 of the country emphasizes the promotion of women entrepreneurship. But probably more needs to be done to ensure that their benefits finally trickle down to the common women and give vent to their latent entrepreneurial talents.

Constraints of Women Entrepreneurship

Promoting entrepreneurship for women will require an even greater reversal of traditional attitudes than the mere creation of jobs for women would. This does not mean that we should wait for societal change to take place first. But it does imply that the programme should go beyond subsidies and credit allocation to attitudinal changes, group formation, training and other support services.

Training in entrepreneurial attitudes should start at the high school level through well-designed courses, which build confidence through behavioral games. This exercise would illustrate practical application of the academic knowledge being imparted regarding management (financial, legal, etc.) of an enterprise. This curriculum should include simple project work designed to give hands on experience of assessing the marketability of a commodity or a service. EDI Ahmedabad appears to be running a programme on these lines in Gujarat, which could be, replicated elsewhere. While making this compulsory for girls at the high school level, however, care must be taken to ensure quality and the syllabus should be reviewed continuously on the basis of the feedback received using professional inputs.

Training in Skills

Skill development is being done in women's polytechnics and industrial training institutes. Under various schemes like the World Bank sponsored programme to upgrade polytechnics, separate institutes have been set up for women. From the inception these should have 100 per cent quality hostel facilities with adequate security arrangements, as this is a major cause for poor occupancy and parental disinclination to send their daughters to such institutes. Under no pretext should institutes set up exclusively for women be converted to men's institutes. The course design should keep in mind the special needs of women, such as their preference to work from their homes, which would enable them to fulfill their household responsibilities. This should not, however, result in mechanically restricting them to low technology linked skills traditionally believed to be suitable for women. Several hi-tech functions with substantial value addition and good profitability could also be undertaken within homes and the courses should be imaginatively and innovatively designed.

The common practice of selecting occupations for women is that women are only supplementary income providers and, therefore, do not require a full day's wage for a full day's work has resulted in their large-scale exploitation. Activities in which women are trained should focus on their marketability and profitability, and not be routinely restricted to making pickles and garments. A high power and professionally involved committee must constantly review the courses and the curriculum on the basis of evaluation studies and market developments. In addition to skill development, these institutes should also provide practical management inputs.

Appropriate training is still the key to a successful programme to develop entrepreneurship among women. There are funds available from several sources; finding effective trainers is the greater problem. NGOs like RUDSET in Karnataka have succeeded in achieving reasonably high success levels, but others including governmental bodies have still not reached these levels. Continuous monitoring and improvement of training programmes should eventually spread the cult of entrepreneurship among young women.

All this can be achieved in a training environment, especially one in which the woman is distanced from the normal restrictive family environment and is taught to recognise her own psychological needs and express them. To encourage more passive women entrepreneurs whose men folk run businesses in their names, and to actively involve the women in their businesses, one must aim at covering all the women who claim to run 'women's enterprises' in training programmes. Repeated exposure to women who are successfully managing enterprises might encourage some women who are passive now to involve themselves to a greater extent in the enterprises to which they have lent their name.

The availability of finance and other facilities like industrial sheds and land for women entrepreneurs is often constrained by restrictions that do not account for practical realities. Funding is not often available for activities in which women are predominantly involved. The field of marketing provides an example. Women of all income levels are engaged in marketing activity from vegetable vending to the sale of more sophisticated items. There is no effective institutional channel to make money available for this activity.

A look at the various schemes available reveals that under the Integrated Rural Development Programme (IRDP), finance is not denied for setting up a shop, and the Prime Minister's Rozgar Yojana (PMRY) extends assistance for trading activity including simple trade finance. IRDP is confined to rural areas and PMRY covers urban areas. Both schemes are limited to persons with very low-income levels.

Some schemes have tried to get around this problem by offering working capital assistance if it is supported by group formation through NGOs, banks or government. This, however, is limited to very low-income groups. That is, a woman or any small business has no access to institutionalised trade finance and must operate only through very expensive informal channels. Yet it is perfectly possible to extend the usual institutional interest rates to this area by taking suitable collateral (after all, the alternative is for loanees to pay exorbitant rates to private moneylenders) or by progressively building up collateral from earnings over time and by initially working in regional clusters to facilitate operations. The effort could yield growth in accounts and deposits and other businesses too. Any move to make banks and institutions enter this area is likely to benefit women more than men.

Inclination to Women

Infrastructure to set up industries is provided in the form of industrial plots and sheds by state run agencies. Apart from allotting units to women entrepreneurs on priority basis, it is desirable to provide amenities particularly required by them in industrial areas.

Both women entrepreneurs and workers seek easy mobility and closeness to homes and childcare facilities. Regular internal bus services are essential in industrial areas. Common crèches run with the involvement of NGOs and industrial area associations must be compulsorily provided as a part of common amenities, since the legal requirement of each unit to provide such facilities is circumvented by keeping the number of women employees below the prescribed limit.

As regards allotting sheds or land on priority basis or at concessional rates, in the case of women, the scope for misuse is much higher than in the case of any other disadvantaged group. For this reason, one must be cautious about making special allotments especially in highly sought after areas. If such a scheme is inevitable, precautionary measures should be built in screening committees to evaluate whether the beneficiary is indeed going to be in full charge of the enterprise. (Men should under no circumstances be permitted to appear or represent women before the committee). Training in running an enterprise in quality-approved institutions should be insisted upon as a precondition for such priority allottees. This certainly encourages the mushrooming of training institutions for women entrepreneurs as a profitable sideline by unqualified and uncommitted persons. The same conditions could be applied to judge eligibility for special investment subsidies or margin money facilities being extended for women.

Financing Difficulties

Credit is available for women through a plethora of schemes but there are still bottlenecks and gaps. The multiplicity of schemes is not adequately listed nor is there networking among agencies. As a result, clients approaching one institution are not made aware of the best option for their requirements. A closely integrated data bank into which all concerned agencies are plugged is a real need. The Karnataka Women's Corporation has plans to set up a resource centre, which apart from acting as a data bank, will also provide counselling and prepare research and evaluation studies.

The greatest constraint is that availability of funds is very low since the schemes operate solely through banks, which are extremely reluctant to extend trade-related finance to small customers because of the risks and operational costs. State finance corporations and financing institutions are not permitted by statute to extend purely trade related finance not linked to asset creation. Women's development corporations, however, are fully aware of the significant presence of women in this area but have only a catalytic role in financing.

Group financing is being extended through banks operating with NABARD refinance, under the IRDP and the training and production centre programme implemented mainly through Mahila Samajas of the Karnataka Women's Development Corporation. Group formation has proved remarkably successful in empowering women and introducing them to income generating activity, animators and introducing them to income generating activity through bank loans. Such schemes need intensive monitoring and effort at the micro-level and are difficult to replicate.

A widely utilised scheme was the Small Industries Development Bank of India (SIDBI)'s Mahila Udyam Nidhi which covers projects up to Rs 10 lakh and provides 15 percent margin money and a service charge of 1 percent (the promoters' contribution is only 10 percent). This has been supplanted by the liberalised National Equity Fund scheme, which covers entrepreneurs, where the margin money component has been fixed at 25 percent. A lower promoter's contribution is not desirable, as it will reduce the entrepreneur's commitment to the success of the enterprise. In any case, for loans up to Rs 50,000, no promoter's contributions are being insisted upon.

For larger loans, no margin money assistance is generally available and women entrepreneurs have to follow norms applicable to others, that is to provide between 17 and 25 per cent of the cost of fixed assets out of own resources.

The same situation applies in the case of collateral. There is a justified widespread demand for a waiver or reduction of collateral for women entrepreneurs because of the above difficulties. This has two implications. A generalised system of exemption of collateral for women entrepreneurs will definitely result in a proliferation of "women's" enterprises to take advantage of the facility. And bankers will find the open-ended benefit risky and tend to restrict financing under this scheme. This would be counterproductive. One practice, though not very satisfactory, that has been introduced in the Karnataka State Financial Corporation is again a screening approach through a committee of representatives from concerned agencies to ensure that the beneficiary is indeed capable of running the project and is genuinely in need of relaxation of this condition. But larger coverage is possible only with the backing of a special fund created for the purpose, as done by Women's World Banking for example.

In the area of guarantees, several humiliating habits have become ingrained in financial institutions and banks. They tend to depend on male members accompanying women entrepreneurs for finalising projects proposed by women and almost invariably insist on guarantees from males in the family.

The second condition will not necessarily affect women alone since it is well-known that assets are very rare held in the names of women. Repeated gender sensitisation programmes should be held to train financiers to treat women with dignity and respect as persons in their own right.

Confidence in Marketing

A major area of difficulty for women entrepreneurs is marketing. Several initiatives have been put in place to remedy this defect. At the initial stages women prefer to be locked into programmes, which ensure almost total marketing support, since they seldom have the time or the confidence to seek out and develop markets. Even when they are otherwise in control of an enterprise, they often depend on males of the family in this area. Marketing means mobility and confidence in dealing with the external world, both of which women have been discouraged from developing by social conditioning. Women's development corporations try to hold frequent exhibitions and set up marketing outlets to provide space for the display of products made by women. Some NGOs have marketing vans and even organize exhibitions. However, such arrangements are not adequately publicised and quality control is inadequate with no arrangement for adaptation to market requirements or consumer tastes.

The long-term strategy should in any case be to inculcate marketing skills in women entrepreneurs to enable them to produce for the market. This means that a market survey to select the product should be made part of all training and advice given to expose enterprises to markets and make them responsive to them. Professional marketing expertise is essential to identify marketing channels for the products made by women entrepreneurs. Industrial estates could also provide marketing outlets for the display and sale of products made by women.

Unfamiliarity with the external world and lack of ease in moving around in it greatly hamper women when it comes to dealing with a multiplicity of agencies in setting up or running a business. It is here that, despite professional competence and training, women are forced to turn to men for assistance.

An experiment that was tried out in the Karnataka State Financial Corporation has received positive feedback. A Women Entrepreneur's Guidance Cell set up to handle the various problems of women entrepreneurs working directly under top management has proved a focal point for monitoring and assisting projects run by women. Similar cells in the District Industries Centres and Single Window Agencies could be extremely useful in assisting women. But they must on no account degenerate into routine departments and should be staffed with the most committed trained personnel and given continuing and total support by the head of the office.

A final area of concern in the case of women entrepreneurs is stagnation in their growth. This is due to various reasons like the demands of household duties, mobility problems and the need to expand space and staff. It is also often due to psychological causes like lack of self-confidence and fear of success (women who succeed often face hostility and resentment within their family circles). The necessary managerial and technical skills are also lacking, which is a barrier to the growth of women's businesses. Training and counseling on a large scale of existing successful women entrepreneurs who seem to have plateau is a necessity.

Surprisingly, very little attention is being paid to this requirement by any agency, governmental or voluntary. Counseling through the aid of committed NGOs, psychologists, managerial experts and technical personnel could result in the development of appropriate strategies and enable growth

Conclusion

For a woman to become successful entrepreneur, she needs access to capital, technical and managerial know-how and market. However, the road to achieve success is not easy for women entrepreneurs. There are many obstacles that hinder women entrepreneurship in rural areas, influencing both the extent and form of entrepreneurial activity and its prospects for sustainability. Such obstacles include financial constraints, indebtedness, limited marketing networks, local demand and social barriers, inadequate access to technology, etc. In fact, mobilizing financial resources has been extremely difficult for women entrepreneurs as the financial institutions are unwilling to extend credit to women due to the fact that women have little or no collateral. Marketing is another area where women entrepreneurs face tough competition as rural products, quite often, is unable to compete with urban based technologically intensive products. Globalisation has also set new market trends by allowing transnational corporations in domestic market thus further jeopardizing entrepreneurial activities.

Rural entrepreneurs do not have updated information about changing market trends, which again negatively affect their business potentials.

Moreover, inability to keep pace with recent advances in technology as well as high cost in acquiring new technologies has further constrained their initiatives.

Several NGOs are contributing to entrepreneurship development in the country. NAYE has been engaged in protecting and developing women entrepreneurs in the country. World Assembly of Small and Medium Entrepreneurs (WASME), Xavier Institute for Social Studies, Self-Employed Women Association (SEWA) of Ahmedabad, 'Y' self employment of Culcutta, Association of Women Entrepreneurs Of Karnataka (AWAKE) and Rural Development and Self Employment Training Institute (RUDSET) based in Karnataka have proved as an effective agent in developing entrepreneurship both in urban and rural areas of the country. The government agencies engaged in this activity strengthened the NGOs by cooperating and collaborating with them to encourage entrepreneurs among the less-known target groups.

REFERENCES

1. Anita,H.S and Laxmisha,A.S 1999. "Women Entrepreneurship in India", Southern Economist, pp. 11-13.
2. Banerjee, M and Talukadar, R.K 1997. "Women Entrepreneurs in Assam: A Profile", Productivity, Vol.37, No. 4, pp. 679-684.
3. Manimekali, N and Rajeswari, G 2000. "Nature of Women Entrepreneurship in Thiruchirapalli" SEDME, Vol.27, No.2, pp. 68-81
4. Murugaiah, V. and Vishvas Radhika 2006. " Entrepreneurial Initiative among Women A case Study of Davangere",SEDME, Vol.33, no.2 June 2006, pp. 79-90.

Chapter 17

EMPOWERMENT OF WOMEN THROUGH ENTREPRENEURSHIP : AN EMPIRICAL STUDY

*Dr. G. Vijayalakshmi
**B. Prajeetha

ABSTRACT

The present study is concerned with only those women entrepreneurs who own as well as operate their business in Madurai. The women entrepreneurs dealing with tailoring unit, beauty parlour, computer centre and boutique shops are selected 120 samples were selected purposively. The data was collected in 2005. The data was analysed with the help of simple statistical test, namely chi-square test, Garrett's Ranking technique and 't' test. The study found that there is a significant contribution by entrepreneurs towards empower-ment of women. Self interest is the prime cause for starting all the business enterprises. In general, the respondents with higher qualification enter into innovative type of enterprises. The entrepreneurs who engaged in computer centres earn more income. Majority of the innovators are high income earners and most of the imitators belong to low income group. The study suggest that entrepreneurial awareness camp at the college level should be organised in order to motivate the women to enter in enterprise activities.

Introduction

A nation's march towards progress and prosperity will remain a dream and its aspiration unfulfilled and unrealised, till women actually

* Reader in Home Science, Gandhigram Rural University, Gandhigram.
** M. Phil Scholar in Home Science, Gandhigram Rural University, Gandhigram.

participate in the development process. The position of women in a society is an index of its degree of civilisation. Emancipation of women is one of the generators of economic development and progress.

The status of women is intimately connected with its economic position which depends on opportunities for participation in economic activities. Absence of adequate opportunities for women to take part in the process of development because of social handicaps present obstacles in the path of economic and social progress. The orientation of the society towards equal role for women in the country's development paves the way for advancement not only of women but the country as a whole.

Employment gives economic status to women and this paves the way for social status. Entrepreneurship provides total independence. When proper education and environment are assured, the social taboos can be removed and the women force can be used as a good human resource potential for the development of the nation.

Empowerment and entrepreneurship complement each other. While successful entrepreneurship can lead to empowerment, empowerment enables the entrepreneur to be motivated enough to accomplish the set goals. Rural women need support, counselling and training to become empowered. Empowerment enables an entrepreneur to think independently and make her own perception and judgement.

According to the Government of India, a women entrepreneur is defined as "an enterprise owned and controlled by women and having a minimum financial interest of 51 per cent of the capital and giving at least 51 per cent of employment to women. (Shreegouri V.Savadi, 2001)

The concept of women entrepreneurs is heterogeneous.

(*a*) There are women in whose name the business is registered but for all practical purposes run by men.

(*b*) Business is registered in the name of women but run jointly, women playing a subsidiary role.

(*c*) Units registered in the name of women who manage themselves by getting counselling from other family members.

Women who own and run the units independently by themselves. The present study is concerned with only those women entrepreneurs who own as well as operate their business.

Empowerment

Empowerment in its simplest form means the manifestation of the redistribution of power that challenges patriarchal ideology and the male dominance. (Chandra and Shanta Kohli, 2000)

Keller and Mbewe (1991) describe empowerment as a process whereby women become able to organise themselves to increase their own, self-reliance to assert their independent right to make choices and to control resources which will assist in challenging and eliminating their own subordination.

According to Pramila Kapur, "Women's empowerment could be considered as a process in which women gain greater share of control over resources-material, human and intellectual like knowledge, information ideas and financial resources like money and control over decision making in the home, community, society and nation and to gain power. (Shyam Sundar *et al.,* 2002)

Empowerment according to P.K.B. Nayar is "an aid to help women to achieve equality with men or at least to reduce gender gap considerably". (Shanthi K., 2001)

Empowerment of women is one of the major objectives of the Ninth plan. The strategy is to adopt an integrated approach towards empowering women in all fronts like social, economic, political and legal. The Government of India also has prepared a National Policy for the empowerment of women in 1996 which recommends adoption of this policy along with Gender Development Index. (Suguna, 2002)

Tongue specifies the different levels of women empowerment viz. welfare, access, conscientisation, participation and control. (Anandavalli Mahadevan, 1999).

Pilot Study

The researcher conducted a pilot study in order to ensure validity, reliability, flexibility and acceptability. The objective of the pilot study was to identify the important enterprises run by women entrepreneurs. For this purpose a formal discussion with the officials of the District Industries Centre, Madurai, Centre for Entrepreneur Development of Tamil Nadu, Madurai was conducted. A well structured questionnaire was framed and pretested with twenty different entrepreneurs in different fields such as Tailoring unit, Beauty Parlour, Computer Centre and Boutique shops.

Schedule

The schedule has 10 distinct parts. The first part deals with personal particulars and the second part about the enterprises. The third and fourth parts deal with the psychological and personality factors respectively. The fifth part deals with the personnel. The sixth one deals with the education and training undergone by the respondents. The seventh part deals with investment and returns.The eighth and ninth part deal with the availability of raw materials and marketing facility. The last part deals with empowerment aspect of women.

Sampling Design

The population consists of all the women entrepreneurs dealing with Tailoring unit, Beauty Parlour, Computer Centre and Boutique shops in Madurai. The following criteria were used to select business units for study.

(*i*) The unit should be owned and managed by women.

(*ii*) The unit should have been started before the year 2000.

(*iii*) The unit should be an ongoing one.

The sample frame is based on the list of women entrepreneurs collected from the office of DIC of Madurai. The sample size is 120 covering four important fields such as Tailoring (including textile shops), Beauty Parlours, Computer Centres and Boutique shops-each representing 30 samples.

The sampling technique adopted for the study is the purposive sampling. In this procedure, it is assumed that with good judgement one can hand pick the cases to be included in the sample and thus develop samples that are satisfactory in relation to one's needs. The cases that are judged to be typical of the population in which one is interested are picked on the assumption that errors of judgement in the selection will tend to counter balance each other Objective basis for making the judgements is an essential point to be considered.

Period of study

The data collection was undertaken for three months from August to October 2005.

Hypothesis

1. There is no significant difference in empowerment between before and after starting business.
2. There is no significant difference between education level of respondents and income.
3. There is no significant difference between nature of entrepreneurs and income level.
4. There is no significant difference between social status and income of entrepreneurs.

Statistical tools used

The data collected for the study have been suitably classified and tabulated for the purpose of analysis. The following statistical tools have been applied for interpretation of data,

(*i*) Percentage analysis

(*ii*) Chi square test

(*iii*) Garrett's Ranking Technique

(*iv*) 't' Test

Entrepreneurship and Empowerment

Hypothesis No: 1 : There is no significant difference in empowerment of women entrepreneurs before and after starting their business.

The empowerment of women in this study has been analysed under four aspects-individual, family, economic and social. The following table deals with entrepreneurship and empowerment.

Individual aspect	*Before*	*After*	*% of improvement*
Self confidence	32	58	81.25
Problem solving ability	72	90	25.00
Health consciousness	60	68	13.33
Overall	164	216	31.7

Family aspect	*Before*	*After*	*% of improvement*
Decision making ability	45	68	51.11
Meeting demands of children	48	72	50.00
Overall	93	140	50.53

Economic aspect	*Before*	*After*	*% of improvement*
Better economic status	36	60	66.66
Better quality of life	42	66	57.14
Overall	78	126	61.53

Social aspect	*Before*	*After*	*% of improvement*
Attending social function	56	72	28.57
Able to meet other people	40	48	20.00
Overall	96	120	25

The greatest improvement in empowerment is found in economic aspects by 61.5 per cent and the least in social aspects by 25 per cent.

With in economic aspect there is improvement in family status by 66.6 per cent and in quality of life by 57.1 per cent. Similarly in individual aspects highest improvement of 81.2 per cent is found in gaining self confidence and the least in health consciousness at 13.3 per cent. In family aspect, decision making ability and meeting demands of children find equal improvement of 51.1 per cent and 50 percent respectively.

The mean level of empowerment before starting enterprise was 47.9 and after becoming entrepreneurs it went up to 66.9. For rigorous testing of the difference in empowerment before and after becoming entrepreneurs, the |t| test has been under taken.

Table value at (8 – 1) difference is 2.31. Since the calculated value is greater than table value (8.14>2.31) the hypothesis is rejected. So the inference is that there is close relation between entrepreneurship and empowerment. In other words, there is significant contribution by entrepreneurship towards empowerment.

Hypothesis No: 2. There is no significant difference between education level and income.

Income slab/ Social level	*Low*	*Medium*	*High*	*Total*	*Chi-Square Value*
HSC	18	4	1	23	
UG	12	16	9	37	5
PG	11	12	6	29	
Overall	51	41	28	120	

Since the calculated value is greater than the table value (19.942> 11.020) at difference 5, it may be inferred that difference in education level accounted for the difference in level of income among the respondents.

Hypothesis No: 3 : There is no significant difference between nature of entrepreneurs and income level.

Income slab/ Social level	*Low*	*Medium*	*High*	*Total*	*Chi-Square Value*
Innovative	9	20	22	51	
Imitative	40	13	5	58	36.4
Forced	2	8	1	11	
Overall	51	41	28	120	

Since the computed value is greater than the table value (36.4 > 5.99 at 5% level of significance) it may be inferred that the difference in nature of entrepreneurs accounted for difference in income level.

Hypothesis No: 4 : There is no significant difference between social status and income level

Income slab/ Social level	*Low*	*Medium*	*High*	*Total*	*Chi-Square Value*
FC	11	8	6	25	
BC	32	26	18	76	
MBC	6	6	4	16	0.23
SC, ST	2	1	—	3	
Overall	51	41	28	120	

Since the computed value is less than the table value (0.23< 7.815), the hypothesis is accepted i.e. there is no relation between social status and income level.

Findings of the Study

(*a*) Personal Details

1. Most of the respondents belong to middle age i.e. 30–40. The representation of women above 40 years is high in tailoring units and low in beauty parlours.
2. Majority of the respondents have higher education and among them computer centres are run by those with technical education.
3. The unmarried are a minority and most of the married live together with their families. The cases of widows, separated and divorced constituted 15 per cent of the total.
4. The order of communities is BC which is majority followed by forward community, MBC and then SC, ST.
5. The Hindus are the majority followed by Christians and Muslims.
6. Majority of the respondents belong to nuclear families in all business enterprises except computer centres where half of the respondents belong to joint family. In all cases extended families constitute the minority.
7. Most of the women entrepreneurs under the present study have started their enterprises only after their marriage. So the starting of business is closely related to family support or economic necessity of family. Among those who have started business

enterprise after marriage, a large number comes under tailoring business.

(*b*) Details about Enterprises

1. A greater proportion of women entrepreneurs belong to imitative type. A slightly smaller proportion of respondents are innovative type. Among the different enterprises, large number of innovative entrepreneurs are found in computer centres.Forced type of entrepreneurs are found largely in boutique shops.
2. Self interest is the prime cause for starting all the business enterprises. Bank officials play a vital role in motivating the entrepreneurs of boutique shops and computer centres next only to self interest.
3. The analysis on reasons for choosing the present enterprises shows that ease of entry is the important reason under tailoring and boutique shops while the expectation of high returns is the reason for starting beauty parlours.
4. In general there is less involvement of family members in the selection of enterprises by the respondents. Within the respondents, involvement of family members has been high in computer centres and tailoring units. Naturally there is independent decision by greater number of respondents running beauty parlours and boutique shops.
5. Regarding the occupational hazards associated with the business, majority of the respondents owning tailoring units expressed of suffering from occupational hazards. The incidence of occupational hazards was low in beauty parlours. Those running computer centres also complained about back pain.

(*c*) Training and Finance

1. Formal training has been undergone by majority of respondents running computer centres followed by beauty parlours. The owners of beauty parlours have qualified as certificate or diploma holders in beautician courses. Boutique shops do not require any formal training. Two third of tailoring units are owned by those without formal training since they employed as labour those with training in tailoring.
2. Capital is not a botheration for 30 per cent of the respondents and they used own funds only, where as 70 per cent depended on borrowed capital either partly or wholly. The proportion of respondents depending exclusively on borrowed capital is high among tailoring units.

3. Among those who borrowed capital, the major source of borrowing is banks. Within this group, greater proportions of entrepreneurs running boutique shops (75%) were using bank funds. Among those who depended on private sources for borrowing, the tailoring units constitute the largest group.
4. Majority of the borrowers from banks have expressed dissatisfaction over bank loans. The level of dissatisfaction is the highest more particularly with regard to the security aspect (66.1%) followed by loan procedure (61%) and loan adequacy (54.2%). The interest component is satisfactory for large number of respondents since the banks charge a lower interest rate following the cheap money policy adopted by the Reserve Bank of India. How ever the charging of lower interest rate alone is not beneficial if the other practical aspects of loan procedure, loan amount and collateral security norms are not satisfactorily framed.
5. The respondents faced many problems of which raw materials, labour, finance and marketing were taken for analysis. The tailoring units were mainly confronted with the labour shortage since the labour turn over was very high. Finance especially for working capital is the major problem for others. Difficulty in procurement of materials is felt mostly under boutique shops and beauty parlours.

(*d*) Nature of Entrepreneurs

1. The interrelationship between educational level and nature of entrepreneurs shows that respondents with higher qualification i.e. PG and Technical were mostly of innovative type. The category of forced entrepreneurs was more prevalent among those with higher secondary qualification.
2. Religion wise innovators and imitators were equally distributed among Hindus and Christians. There were no innovators among Muslims. The percentage of forced entrepreneurs was high among Muslims.
3. On the basis of social status, majority of the forward class and backward class entrepreneurs (48% and 50%) were innovative while most backward class and scheduled caste entrepreneurs were imitative (87.5% and 67.7%)

(*e*) Income Level

1. A high proportion of high income group i.e. earning an average monthly net income of more than Rs.20,000 belong to computer

centres. High percentage of low income group belongs to beauty parlours. A major proportion of medium income group are found in tailoring units and boutique shops.

2. On the basis of education, the large proportion of low income group belongs to those with low educational standards. Entrepreneurs with technical qualification constitute greater proportion of high income group.
3. On the basis of social status, SC, ST groups are largely found in low income group. Among all the groups, the proportion of low income groups is greater compared to others.
4. Majority of innovators are high income earners and most of the imitators belong to low income group.

Garrett's Ranking

1. The results of Garrett Ranking technique over the reasons for starting the particular unit are as follows (mean scores within brackets)
    - To earn more money (63.14)
    - To secure socio economic status (59.61)
    - To be independent (51.30)
    - To keep oneself busy (46.67)
    - Failure to get a job (24.57)
    - Success story of entrepreneurs (20.15)
    - Out of necessity (19.24)
2. The result of Garrett Ranking technique to analyse the views of entrepreneurs about qualities required to attain success are as follows.
    - Self confidence (66.68)
    - Risk taking ability (52.87)
    - Innovation (52.60)
    - Training and Experience (42.86)
    - Dynamism (42.12)
    - Education (33.26)

Empowerment

1. There is vast improvement in empowerment of women in economic aspect and least in social aspect.

2. Entrepreneurship has helped most in building self confidence in the minds of entrepreneurs.

Chi-square test results

1. Difference in education level accounted for difference in income level.
2. Difference in nature of entrepreneurs also accounted for difference in income level.
3. There is no relation between social status and income level.

Result of Test

There is significant contribution by entrepreneurship towards empowerment.

Suggestions

1. Most of the entrepreneurs have started their business only after marriage. Hence entrepreneurial awareness camps may be organised at the college level in order to motivate them to enter enterprise soon after their studies.
2. Most of the entrepreneurs are of imitative type. Hence the guidance by institutions like DIC, CED and MADITSSIA will help them to become innovative entrepreneurs.
3. There is discontentment among the respondents over bank finance as regards the tangible security required, cumbersome loan procedure and inadequate loan amount. If the Government is really interested in promoting women entrepreneurship, the security norms are to be relaxed, loan procedure is to be simplified and loan amount is to be hiked.
4. The problems in procurement of raw material and finance can be solved through institutional support.
5. Since the entrepreneurs with technical education prove to be high income earners, technical skill can be imparted to potential entrepreneurs even at the college level.

Conclusion

To sum up, the women entrepreneurs have succeeded in generating adequate income and also gained self confidence. Liberal and concessional credit along with relevant training will go a long way in motivating more women to join the ranks of entrepreneurs. The entrepreneurial traits are to be taught to the students as a part of the curriculum to make them learn the management strategies which are indispensable for survival in the modern day competitive business world.

REFERENCES

1. Chandra and Shanta Kohli, (2000), Women and Empowerment, Indian Journal of Public Administration, Vol. XLII No. 3, pp. 12-16.
2. Shreegouri V.Savadi, Women Entrepreneurs in India: Scope and Opportunities, Southern Economist, Vol. 40 No. 8, pp. 17-20.
3. Dimensions of Women's Environment, Social Welfare, Vol. 49, No. 5, pp. 10-17.
4. Suguna.B, Aug 2001, Planning for Economic Empowerment of Women, Social Welfare, Vol. 48 No. 5, pp. 31-34.
5. Suguna. B, Dec. 2001, Women's Empowerment: Concept and Framework, Social Welfare, Vol. 48 No. 5, pp. 3-7.
6. Suguna.B, Aug 2002, Strategies for Empowerment of Rural Women, Social Welfare,Vol. 49 No. 5, pp. 3-6.
7. Anandavalli Mahadevan, 28, April 1999, Women, Work and Employment – A Futuristic Analysis, Seminar on Empowerment of Women Labour, Madurai Kamaraj University.

Chapter 18

WOMEN ENTREPRENEURS IN JHARKHAND : AN OVERVIEW

*Dr. Kiran Mishra

ABSTRACT

The chapter traces the scope for developing women entrepreneurs in Jharkhand, which was bifurcated from Bihar. Six years ago Jharkhand is visualized as a land of immense scope and promise. The high literacy rate, abundant natural resources, the flood of educational institutions may influence women to enter into entrepreneurship activities. In addition, the other factors like women's capacity to take risk, preference for independence, higher social stratum, professional skill may also help the women entrepreneurs to flourish in the state. Although the women have a lot of avenues, but a huge number of women entrepreneurs are engaged in the field of education, namely schools and cowling centers than other activities. Few involved in private nursing homes, beauty parlour and computer centre. According to observation the tribal women and settler women will have a bright future than the other women in the state.

Introduction

In India, women were given equal status since the Vedic times. We have instances of many women who were no less than their male counterparts, in any respect. During the middle ages, when India was subjected to foreign invasions and rules, the situation changed drastically. Upto the eighteenth century, there were some rays of hope but the nineteenth century became the darkest period for women. The evils of parda-system, child-marriage, female-infanticide and male-chauvinism put

* Department of English, Ranchi Women's College, Ranchi Jharkhand.

them behind the four walls of home and destroyed completely all prospects of their education and knowledge. Sati-pratha did not grant women even the right to live after the death of her husband.

Although the British rule in India was indifferent to education in India yet the reform movements started by Ishwar Chandra Vidyasagar, Pandit Ramabhai, Swami Vivekanand, Maharshi Karve, Swami Dayanand Saraswati and Raja Ram Mohan Roy, through Arya Samaj, Brahmo Samaj, Ram Krishna Mission, Theosophical Society, tried to restore the status of women. Yet the result was dismal. Education was the privilege of a very small minority. It is Gandhijee's freedom movement that gave a boost to restoring the status of women in India. At the call of Gandhijee, women broke all boundaries and came out of their houses to work in the freedom movement. The several years that the movement took taught them to face the outer world and their extraordinary participation in the movement proved their worth and raised automatically their status in the society. "There was no suffragette movement in India", says K. M. Panikkar in his essay 'The Awakening of Women', "no feminism, for the share of women in the battle of freedom gave them their position of equality without their having to fight for it separately". The emergence of the 'new women' has changed the ageold concept about them, which was,

"Man for the field women for the hearth
Man for the sword and for needle she
Man with the head and woman with the heart
Man to command and woman to obey".

(Alfred Lord Tennyson : *The Princess*.)

In today's world where melieus and priorities are changing fast, entrepreneurial endeavour has gained sanctions. Many have braved themselves to lake risks as entrepreneurs and proved themselves successful. In this enterprising sphere, woman are nowhere behind men. Education of women laid the foundation for the emancipation and empowerment of women. Other operative forces behind this change of scenario are:

1. Equal constitutional rights of women as independent individuals to have her will in matters of education, marriage and property etc.
2. Government policies and schemes for their development.
3. Change in social outlook towards them.

In all these, education plays the pivotal role. Without education and awareness, the rights and preferences, given to them, are redundant and just paper-work. The awareness of the rights and women's stand in the society, have freed women from some of the subversive bondages.

Jharkhand is a nature-nurtured state of India which was only six years ago a part of Bihar. It is a land of immense scope and promise. In Jharkhand, women-education has gained momentum. More and more women are coming out of universities and technical institutions, every year. The formal and non-formal education and the programmes like 'Sarv Shiksha Abhiyan' etc. have prompted each and every child, both male and female, to come out and join schools. There is a flood of educated or at least, literate women in Jharkhand. These educated women are looking for jobs which were scarce only a few years ago but now in big cities, many of them find jobs in public and private sectors. Still there are some who are unable to find jobs that suits them. They then, look for self-employment. Earlier there was some hesitancy in them, in choosing the path of entrepreneurship but nowadays, they have started preferring entrepreneurship to office-jobs. Many factors have given rise to this inclination towards entrepreneurship, such as:

1. Her capacity to take risk : A woman who is well-equipped with skills such as education, training, managerial skills, is much more sure of herself in minimizing the risk factor.

2. Her preference for independence; Many women do not like to work as slaves, doing office-jobs, where there is though less uncertainty but where they suffer gender-descrimination, male-chauvinism and sometimes sexual abuses etc. Entrepreneurship safeguards them from all this, to a great extent.

3. Her social and family condition: If a woman belongs to a high social stratum, she is less subjected to hardships but a woman belonging to the lower social stratum, is likely to be subjected to greater hardships, in opening up a business for herself. Moreover, family matters much in her venturing into the world of entrepreneurship. If the family is over-critical, much of her energy will be lost in protecting hereself. Moreover, if the family nurturing is thus that promotes in her self-confidence and less of bias, she will see things in the right perspective. A balanced personality from the professional point of view, is helpful in this endeavour.

4. Her professional skill in a particular field: Skilled entrepreneurs such as doctors, lawyers, architects, beauticians, tailors etc. have benefits over others for their skills guarantee their success, all the more.

Entrepreneurship is flourishing in Jharkhand. One of the main reasons behind this, besides education, is family-planning. It has given woman time. These days women insist on having not more than two children. As soon as the children grow up to be able to go to school, a woman has plenty of time to do something else. If she is skilled in any particular field, and if she has need and urge to do something, she doesn't like to sit idle. In schools and colleges also, there is much emphasis on vocational training to help students acquire some skills besides their general curriculum. Computer training and beautician course are gaining popularity besides other courses like nutrition-and-dietitian course, soft-toy-making course etc. Classes of spoken-English and personality-development are also in vogue which prepare the ground work for entrepreneurship. The capacity to speak in English is a must these days, for potential success in life.

Broadly speaking, the population of Jharkhand comprises three communities—the tribal, the sadaan and the settler. The state government has a number of schemes for the development of women in Jharkhand. Under these schemes, the development of women, especially of the tribal women, has gained momentum. There is a great upsurge of awareness in them towards education and well-being. The tribal women are even more active than men. With the new-found facilities, empowerment and awakening, they are no less active in taking the light of knowledge to their sisters, living in far-off places. Moreover, they have proved their worth in games and sports too and many of them have gained national and international fame as sports women. A wide vista of avenues lies open for them and there is also a tremendous verve visible in them. A vivacity and eagerness to reach out hands towards success in life is visible but in lower strata of the tribal community, there is still much to be done. Many of the families are still in the primitive stage, where ignorance and helplessness loom large .The traditional pattern of living is prevalent. The greatest harm is wrought by the practice of haria-drinking (Haria is a local wine made of cooked rice fermentation). Haria is in vogue among the people of lower sections of all communities but the tribals are more prone to it as it is encluded in their traditional ceremonies of all kinds, be it a ceremony of birth, death or marriage. As a result, their development is stunted. The poverty-striken girls and woman do come out in search of work to sustain themselves but they find only the work of house-maids or labourers on building-construction sites.

So far as entrepreneurship among the enterprising and progressive tribal woman is concerned, the prospects are bright. Many of them have ventured into this field. They are hard working and have the intrinsic motivation and also have the capacity to make their voices heard in the corridors of power.

Besides having the essential qualities of courage, hard work and intrinsic motivation, these women are also striving towards achieving business and managerial skills. However, this awareness is limited only to a handful of women. Most of them do not have the needed skill and perheps do not consider it vital. A. G. Matani in his essay "Encourageng Entrepreneurship as a Profession" has very rightly said that behavioural skills and knowledge to understand people, are also among the prerequisites of entrepreneurial endeavour. Mr. Matani lists various other skills besides the technical, such as: economic business skills, evaluative skills, implementing skills and also the conceptional skills to evaluate global realties, as essential for an entrepreneur, if she wants to carry out his project on a large scale.

Without proper education and training entrepreneurship is difficult even for men what to talk of women. In the absence of such skills, as mentioned by Mr. Matani, the women entrepreneurs of Jharkhand have resorted to enterprises on a lower scale, such as: owning beauty parlours, boutiques, tailoring and xeroxing shop, hotels etc. Selling fruits and vegetables is common among the poor and uneducated women. Though the examples of driving autorikshaws are scarce but one or two women are reported to be doing that also. Some women are engaged in door to door service, providing useful household items at the door. Many have chosen particular places or institutions to sell their goods. There they get several customers at one place. This is convenient for them as well as for their customers.

A huge number of women entrepreneurs are engaged in the field of education. They are running private schools and coaching centres and some of them have carved a niche in this field. Children from neighbouring states also come and join their schools. In so doing, these private educational centres are doing a great job. Because of them, there is an inflow of money in the state,. While others are just putting the state money into circulation, they are the source of generation of money. Moreover, this profession is flourishing well as for a woman it is very convenient to have her workplace and home at one place.

Private nursing homes owned by lady doctors, are common enough sights. There are lady architects and lawyers as well who are skilled entrepreneurs like lady doctors. These women do not merely find self-employment, they give employment to others also and help in the well-being of the state. There are women who participate actively in state politics.

There are women-societies, working as anciliaries to government organisations. There is one such society in Itky, a place not very for from

Ranchi, the capital of Jharkhand, which is run by Muslim women. It is associated with "State Tassar Institute". Boreya, an adjacent village of Ranchi, has a women society that works for the cause of women. It also lends money, contributed by its members, to needy people of the village, on reduced interest rates.

Another category is of women who are entrepreneurs in a different way. They do not have their independent profession. They have come out to help their husbands or family members in their enterprises. Their helping hands have wrought growth and increase in income. Seen from this point of view, women are born entrepreneurs. By working at home and looking after the household, they have been helping their male-counterparts to earn. Their share of work towards generating family income is thus, undeniable.

Studies , however, point to the fact that the role of women in entrepreneurial sphere is limited. "According to a study on the empowerment of women in the workplace, women constitute just 6 per cent of India's work force. The study, conducted by the confederation of Indian Industry (C.I.I.), says the number further skewed as you climb the ladder." ("*Still miles to go* – an article published in Employment News). There is thus, much to be done, women have still miles to go.

Moreover, there is a general indictment against women, working independently that their work, after sometime, becomes so engrossing and demanding that it takes them away from home. Once they have tasted success, there is no coming back. They become workcoholic, shrewd and loose all their innocence, soft-feelings and sometimes their character. A report in the Employment News, quoting an article titled "Don't Marry Career Women", published in Forbes in August, says that you shouldn't marry professional women because they "are more likely to get divorced, more likely to cheat, less likely to have children, and if they do have kids, they are more likely to be unhappy about it." The unkindest cut, says the writer, is: "Even your house will be dirtier." And the gospel of Forbes is:

"Stay at home, young ladies."

Perhaps the picture is not so dark in India but the western-wave is so great, that the time is not much off-hand when it will sweep away everything that we proudly call, Indian. We should think of a way out. If it is a must that women should prosper, it is also a must that they should maintain balance and preserve family values.

With all these thoughts hovering in my mind, I went in search of women who as entrepreneurs, have made some mark. It was raining one day when I opened the tinted-glass door of a beauty parlour. Mrs. Pratima

Gupta, the owner of the Modern Beauty Parlour, was there busy with her customers but warm and hospitable as ever. My silence for a moment perhaps communicated to her that I had come with a special purpose. She was quick to perceive and quick to settle the matter that as it was a Sunday, she won't be treating any more customers, she could soon join me. I waited but not very long. Born and brought up in Hilsa, Bihar, she got married when she was only in ninth class. Still she graduated with high second class in Botany Hons. from S. U. College, Hilsa. Amidst hardships, as her father and also her husband were not in a position to support her much, financially, she decided to make the ends of life meet, on her own. By that time two children were born to her. Somehow she managed to be trained as a beautician and started her own parlour in a rented room, in Ranchi, nineteen years after her marriage and after nearly twenty-five years of her marriage, she is well-settled and satisfied with a house of her own and all the four children – three daughters and a son, really faring well. In the mean time, her husband Mr. Janardan Prasad Gupta, who had constantly been a source of encouragement and help, also got a government job.

It is worth mentioning that Mrs. Gupta is a daring, hardworking lady. She is by nature a lady of strong determination. She loathes dependence and believes in doing her work by herself. She gets up everyday at four A.M., herself cooks meals for the family, goes to the parlour at ten and works their till eight or nine p.m. except on Sundays. She comes back home, which is nearby and does cooking for the night with the help of her daughters, makes preparations for the next day and then her hectic day ends. Inspite of her busy schedule, no regret, no irritation finds place in her facial expression & behaviour. The only point of regret is that she is unable to give ther family freshly-cooked food but that is something that her family understandably bears with her. Besides being a working woman, she is a home-maker, a loving and caring wife and mother. Her relationships with her in-laws and other relatives and also her staff, have always been congenial. There is something very sweet yet practical in her. Her balanced behaviour saves her from untoward problems. Mrs. Gupta belongs to the settler business community of Jharkhand. It is perhaps her background that installed in her the needed intrinsic motivation and professionalism. She is so confident that she says, she can go to any corner of India and settle there with her profession. However, she likes working in the cosmopolitan culture of Jharkhand. She is cautious too about the materials used in her parlour and cares to use standard cosmetic-items. She wants to visit renowned beauty parlours of big cities, to gain knowledge of recent advancements in this field.

Another thing she would like to have, is some sort of device like a raised chair with attachments to keep things in, so that ladies like her can be saved from standing all the time in the parlour.

Sita Swansi is another woman enterpreneur who belongs to the tribal community. She got married when she just passed school final, to Karmu Swansi who was at that time unemployed but now he is a government employee. Sita has two sons who are studying, she proudly said, in a Mission school. She has taken all care that her children do well at school.Sita has seen the low and high of life. She now seems to be quite sync with the time.She is hard working.With a very supportive family, her personality got the opportunity for its full flowering.She is a graduate and owns a xerox shop – *Devi Xerox* ,in the court premises.The shop is sanctioned by the Bar Association . Besides that, she is associated with various women-societies and self-help groups. She is secretary and founder person of *Diya Seva Sansthan* and general secretary of *Mahila Samiti* . She works for the awakening of tribal women towards health and education. Once she had contested for an MLA seat from a reserved constituency of Jharkhand. She is fully devoted to the cause of tribal women. She knows that the government is doing everything possible for their upliftment but because of the traditional habit of liquor – drinking and the inability to have a control over themselves, the tribal women are unable to reap the full benefit of the facilities provided by the government. Most of the women, living in remote areas do not even know of such schemes. Awareness is missing not only in tribal women. Even the non-tribal women, living in cities, show regrettable ignorance towards the schemes of the government. Women like Pratima Gupta also, are ignorant and even show a reluctance to utilize the benefits of the schemes, perhaps because of the lengthy and tortuous process of getting things done from government offices.

Anyway, women like Sita Swansi, are doing a great job spreading awareness among women. She has a great propensity towards social work. She has declined government jobs, offered to her twice because of the great devotion towards her community. Moreover, due to her outgoing, independent nature, she finds entrepreneurship more suitable for her. Now, she is enjoying her success in life and says that a women who was a non-entity a few years back, is now the owner of a four-wheeler and is soon going to have a house too. This is a success-story of a woman who is up and doing.

In Pratima Gupta and Sita Swansi, we have examples of women-entrepreneurs who stood to face the challenges of life on their own accord. In Usha Pandey, we see a woman-entrepreneur who has a keen inner urge to do something. Sitting idle is something, she abhors. She is an M.Sc., B.Ed. and belongs to a family which is well off. Her husband Dr. K. K. Pandey, is a renowned Pathologist of the town. Besides being very good at house-keeping, she is amiable, a good wife and mother of two sons. Both of them are engineers. Usha has ample time as her children have grown up and are working away from home. A very good thing about Usha is that she knows the importance of time and does not believe in whiling it away. Thus, she joined her husband's 'collection centre', where she works supervising and managing things. Her work does not require any specific skill but the managerial skill, required in this venture, is in ample measure in her. She easily establishes a good rapport with people around her and takes good care of the people employed in the centre. How much she earns, is of little importance to her. She is satisfied with the feeling that she is a helping hand in earning for the family. The fact of the matter is that since the time she joined the centre, the graph of income shows a steady increase.

The women-entrepreneurs have proved that there is "a source of immense untapped power in the womanhood of India." (K. M. Panikkar, 'The Awakening of Women'). It can most advantageously be turned to the growth of the country. Gandhijee had realized this from the very first days of his movement. There is no doubt that the women of India, who had so long been shut up in seclusion, can shoulder actively, the responsibilites not only of their own families but also of the country. The spirit of active interest in public life that Gandhian movement initiated in women, should be kept alive. This spirit, that taught women to shake off delicateness and unnecessary inhibitions, is forever required in a woman to win the battle of life. The intrinsic motivation for entrepreneurial enterprise also comes from the spirit which has strong will-power and determination, which is not disheartened easily and which does not shrink from hard work. Among the women of Jharkhand, the tribal and the settler women possess these qualities and perhaps because of this they are far ahead of the sadaan women.

Chapter 19

ECONOMICS OF WOMEN MICRO ENTERPRISES—A CASE STUDY OF VISAKHAPATNAM CITY

*Dr. B. Padma Narayan
Dr. B.V. Suryanarayana

ABSTRACT

This chapter attempts to examine the economics of women micro enterprises, income generating potentiality, and the problems and constraints faced by the micro women entrepreneurs. Primary data was collected from 150 women micro entrepreneurs in Visakhapatnam city during 2006. Personal interview method was followed to collect the primary data in order to assess the determinants of net income regression analysis was employed. The regression analysis brought out the picture that the time spent on the activity that in micro enterprise has a positive relation with the net income the stable enterprises are getting more income than the mobile enterprises; the amount of fixed capital is having positive sign to the enterprises and enterprises run outside the house premises are earning more income than the enterprises functioning within the household premises. The study suggests that financial assistance to meet out fixed and working capital needs and neet impart managerial skills and to provide proper guidance at the initial stage of the enterprise.

Introduction

It is a well-known fact that the adverse effects of industrialization and mechanization pushed female persons into more exploitative and

* Faculty Associate, GITAM Institute of Foreign Trade, GITAM Campus, Rushikonda, Visakhapatnam-45.

** Associate Professor, Department of Statistics, Andhra University, Visakhapatnam—3.

invisible occupations of the unorganised sectors. In India, more than 90 per cent of women workers are engaged in unorganised sectors. Within this sector, agriculture plays a major role. Relatively, more information is available about this sector than the non-agricultural sector. Particularly, to know about the urban informal sector where industry, trade and services play a dominant role, one should rely upon the micro level studies conducted at various cities. Studies conducted in Delhi, Calcutta, Chennai and Ranchi by Mujumdar, Menefee Singh, Wiebe, Vandem Bogaest, Lubell and others showed that the urban poor women are at a greater disadvantage with respect to education, income and employment when compared to the rural poor women (Alfred de Souza, 1988). Their participation in the unorganized sector particularly in the urban areas is increasing and it is higher than their participation ratio in the economy as a whole (C.A. Grown and J. Sebstad, 1989). As a result of this, a section of urban women have emerged as potential entrepreneurs. Among SSI entrepreneurs, only 9 per cent constitute women who still hold traditional business like garments, food, leather, interior decoration and handicrafts (Gouri V. Savadi, 2001). The segment of SSI entrepreneurs is insignificant when compared to the medium and micro level enterprises.

Women entrepreneurs can be grouped into three categories. The first group consists of women with educational and professional qualification, who take the initiative and manage the business. These women, due to their education, skills and the opportunities open to them, are in a superior position and have an edge over others to set up and manage the unit. The second group of women constitutes those who do not possess any formal education and training, but have certain skills required setting up small scale units which are developed practically. Such women choose the line of activity with which they are familiar and which is easy for them to organize. These women require certain amount of assistance and special privileges to overcome reluctance of financial institutions to provide support, lack of information, formalities required to be completed in starting the venture etc. The third group of women entrepreneurs those who work in cities, slums with lower means of livelihood. These women mostly belong to the economically backward sections. The ventures they run are tiny or micro enterprises. They require the support of the government in meeting, acquiring finance at concessional rates of interest, purchasing of their products by government at preferential prices and the same mode (N. Sarnagharan and Resia Beagam, 1995). The important factors that have great effect on productivity and raising income of the women informal micro entrepreneurs are availability of resources for working capital requirements, tools and equipment, the ability to buy raw materials in bulk and improvements to the work place (URBAN EDGE, 1988).

A study conducted by NIUA examined the determinants of income levels of the women workers in the informal sector. The Study enlightened the fact that the monthly returns of the workers not only vary across different types of activities but also within the same activity. These variations can be attributed to the duration of work done/availability of work, regional variations in prices and wages, the nature and quality of goods and services and the scale of operations (NIUA, 1991). Lack of managerial skills, apathy, sense of fear and insecurity towards the concept of entrepreneurship, high degree of illiteracy, outdated customs and traditions were some of the hindrances in the way of entrepreneurship development as well as their potentiality to prove themselves as successful enterprises (Harinarayana Rao 1991). Promotion of women entrepreneurship is far behind due to lack of financial assistance, family and community support, ignorance of the opportunities, lack of motivation, shyness, inhibitions, preference for the traditional occupations etc (Raghavulu 2003). Generally, women entrepreneurs seem to gravitate towards industries with low investment and technology barriers. The dependency on their limited personal finance compels the women entrepreneurs to start tiny industries, using obsolete technology. Women, by and large, are bound by their domestic and child care responsibilities and therefore, choice of industry, the location of units and their area of operation cannot be of their individual taste. This results in lack of mobility amongst women entrepreneurs (Jyotsna Sethi, 1994). Selection of the enterprise is mainly based on their familiarity with the activity ranging from food processing to hi-tech computers. The problems faced by women entrepreneurs were not because they were women but because of their attitude towards entrepreneurial career and their social-cultural value system (Krishna Kumar and G. L. K. Durga, 2000).

The traditional occupations like fish vending enterprises were dominated by the women both in number and generating income than men (Rathakrishnan and Sellammalle 1999). The amount of investment, literacy level and time spent on economic activity by the self-employed are the significant variables in determining the income of the self-employed women workers (Ratna Kumari, 1994). The economic constraints are quite common among women entrepreneurs. They lack the knowledge about various managerial aspects of enterprises. They are also not well known about various programmes and institutions aimed at developing Women Entrepreneurs (Anju Gupta, Inderjeet Khanna 1997). Apart from these aspects, family help and support have an impact on maintaining the enterprise successfully (Aravinta and Renuka 2001). With respect to the motivation and perception of women entrepreneurs' financial return was a very strong motive not only to start but also to carry on with the enterprise but there exists the differences in their perception about the degree of success (Beena and Sushma, 2003) .

Research studies on women micro-entrepreneurs are few in number. Most of the literature on women entrepreneurs is focused on the small scale units. Little attention is paid to micro enterprises, in general, and micro enterprises run by women in particular. Generally, the available studies on the women workers in the unorganized sector analyzes the socio economic conditions of micro entrepreneurs and the problems and constraints faced by them along with other categories of workers in the unorganized sector. Due proper is not paid in the studies to analyze the processing of micro enterprises. Hence, there is a need to conduct an in-depth study of the financial matters of micro enterprises and their working needs, specific to women micro entrepreneurs. This will enable to formulate separate policies that could help women micro entrepreneurs, to supplement their family income which is necessary for their survival. In this context, the present paper attempts to examine the economics of women micro enterprises, to assess the income generating potentiality of the women micro enterprises and to document the nature of problems and constraints that they face in holding the enterprises.

Methodology

The study is based on the primary data collected from randomly selected 150 women micro entrepreneurs in Visakhapatnam city during May and June, 2006. The various activities of the selected women micro enterprises are presented in Table 1. Data is obtained from the micro entrepreneurs through canvassing well-structured interview schedule among the selected women and by adopting personal interview method. A minimum of three visits were made for each entrepreneur to observe the functioning and working procedures and processes because of the non-maintenance of records about account or transaction details on paper. The income generating potentiality of the activity is assessed by measuring the net Income generated by the enterprises. Net income from the activity is calculated as:

1. Total monthly expenses.
   - (*a*) Cost of material Rs. ____________
   - (*b*) Cost of maintenance & repair Rs. ____________
   - (*c*) Amount paid on wages for hired labour Rs. ____________

(*d*) Interest on total investment Rs. ____________

Rs. ____________ (*i*)

2. Total Revenue (per month)

(*a*) Through sales Rs. ____________

(*b*) Through service charges Rs. ____________

Rs. ____________ (*ii*)

Net Income (p.m.) = Total Revenue - Total Expenses

(ii) _ (i)

While calculating the total expenses, the cost of own labour is not included. In economic theory, the cost of production includes rent on land, interest on capital, wages paid to the labour and profit to the organisation. The economic activities considered for this Study are micro enterprises, which are mostly single-person-operated activities. The amount of profit or the surplus can be interpreted as the remuneration got to the own labour of the entrepreneur which implies that a net zero income from the enterprise indicates zero imputed value of female labour.

The following regression equation is used for assessing the determinants of net income function of the enterprises

$$Y = a + b_1 C + b_2 H + b_3 PE + b_4 D_1 + b_5 D_2 + b_6 D_3$$

Where Y = Net income

C = Amount of fixed capital

H = No. of hours spent per day

PE = Period of Existence

D_1 = Location of the enterprise

D_2 = Caste

D_3 = Mode of operation

a and b_i (where $i = 1, 2, 3, 4, 5, 6$) are parameters to be estimated.

Characteristics and Economics of the Sample Women Micro Enterprises

Some of the characteristics of the micro enterprises run by women are presented here, in order to understand the operational aspects of the enterprises. To examine the economics of the micro enterprises, factors like range and average amount of fixed capital, average and frequency of replenishment of working capital, sources of purchases, mode of purchases and sales were estmated.

Period of Existence of the Women Micro Enterprises

The period of existence specifies the capacity of that enterprise to sustain in the market. The longer the period, the greater will be its' survival, if not being in process. The distribution of the women micro enterprises according to the period of existence is presented in Table 1. The percentage of micro enterprises which are having four years and more period of existence are less. Upto a period of two years, they are able to survive but beyond that, the chances of their survival get reduced. The high competitive nature of the urban sector for these micro enterprises makes their existence as difficult.

Place/Location and Mode of Operation of the Women Micro Enterprises

The place where the enterprise is located will also influence the competency and longer existence of that enterprise. The preference, as well as the requirement for the place for operation depends upon the nature of the enterprise. The activities like Tailoring and Typing or Job Works, and Xerox Machines are of stable nature, which can be set up within or nearby the house premises. If they are established nearby the commercial areas they may be very successful. Under Food processing, enterprises like Papad Making can be taken up as home based activity, but needs commercial place for marketing. In case of small Tiffin or Tea Making, they should be located at nearby commercial places. Some type of enterprises which are carried out on wheel carts are of mobile nature and need a proper fixed market place to sustain over longer years. Broadly, the sample micro enterprises are classified as three categories like located within or nearby the house premises, Outside-stable and Outside-mobile.

It is clear from Table 2 that nearly 57 per cent of enterprises are located in the house premises which are backed by the women's preference. Outside-mobile enterprises are 24 per cent where as 19 per cent are of outside-stable nature. However, the enterprises which are small, both in physical size and financial size can be accommodated in house or nearby the house premises. Women prefer to have within or nearby the house premises. But this preference of the women towards the location has its implications on the competitive strength of the enterprise. In case of the outside-house enterprises, some problems mentioned by women like health and pressure of domestic work have their own implications to increase the scale of operations of women micro enterprises.

Source of Finance for Investment of the Women Micro Enterprises

The average amount of the investment from different sources is presented in Table 3. It can be seen from the table that the major source of investment is through borrowings from money lenders which accounts around 44 per cent. The assistance from bank is only around 30 per cent of the total investment. The remaining amount for investment is either from own funds or borrowings from friends or relatives. This clearly indicates the need for special attention to meet the capital needs of the women micro entrepreneurs. Special provisions should be made to provide the financial assistance for women micro enterprises, so that their reliance on money lender for investment will be reduced. This increases the net income from the enterprises by reducing the interest payment charges which in turn reflects its viability.

Amount of Fixed Capital Invested in Women Micro Enterprises

The amount of fixed capital invested for the activity influences the permanent status of the units of micro enterprises. For example, vegetable vending at a stable place having a fixed structure like "KIOSK" will provide permanency for the unit, rather than selling vegetables carrying head load where less fixed capital is invested. Table 4 presents the details of fixed capital investment. The amount of fixed capital range from a minimum of Rs. 3000/- to Rs. 11000/-. The minimum and maximum amounts are needed as fixed capital depends upon the nature of enterprise. For example, the enterprises like Xerox machines, Tailoring etc need more amount of fixed capital than the other categories.

Amount of Working Capital and Frequency of Replenishment of the Women Micro Enterprises

The amount of working capital and frequency of replenishment of women micro enterprises indicates the level of operations of the unit, as well as total turnover of the unit. Table 5 and Table 6 present the average amount of working capital and its frequency of replenishment. The average amount of working capital is the highest in enterprises like fruit vending, vegetable vending and Xerox machines etc. The difference lies in the frequency of replenishment, according to the durability of the items. Around 65 percent of enterprises function on the basis of daily investment of the working capital. The enterprises which are working with weekly investment are very meagre. The funds available for the investment on working capital, seriously limit their level of operation as well as their profitability. They are unable to gain the benefits of economies of scale. If some mechanism, like supplementary loans on monthly repayment basis by the banks at lower interest rates for the good running enterprises can be developed, it will definitely benefit the micro enterprises in the urban informal sector.

Sources and Mode of Purchases of the Women Micro Enterprises

The Sources of purchase of goods/ raw material which are needed for the business of the enterprise are important as the cost of raw materials or goods form a major part of the cost of operations. Table 7 provides details of the sources of purchases. Around 50 per cent of entrepreneurs make their purchases from the whole-sale dealers and another 22 per cent of the units make their purchases from retailer/mediatory men. 28 per cent of entrepreneurs purchase both from whole-sale dealers and retailer/ mediatory men. Their purchases are mainly influenced by the credit facility provided by the seller i.e., goods available against the credit. If the purchases are on credit basis, the prices will carry a premium. This is primarily due to lack of adequate amount working capital on hand. The information presented in Table 8 clearly indicates this point.

Mode of Sales of the Women Micro Enterprises

The details of the mode of sales are presented in Table 9. When the sales are observed, as many as 73 percent of the units have to depend on both cash and credit sales and in their opinion, credit sales are inevitable to maintain the customers in the localised micro enterprises. But it has negative impact on the capacity of rotation of working capital, and in turn, limits the turnover and the level of profits.

Determinants, Measurement and the Expected Signs of the Co-efficients of Net Income Function of Micro Enterprises

Variables considered in the equation are examined below:

The Net Income (Y) from the activity is defined as the difference between total revenue and total expenses. It is calculated per month. The net monthly income in rupees is taken as the dependent variable.

The first independent variable considered, is the 'Amount of Fixed Capital' (AFC) invested on the enterprise which is the first important factor determining the scale of operations. The expected sign of the coefficient of the variable is positive. This implies that an increase in the amount of capital increases Y and vice versa.

The second independent variable considered, is 'Time spent on activity per day' (NOH). Generally, in this type of micro enterprises, the activity is conducted throughout the year. Therefore, it is the time spent on the activity, rather than the number of days worked on that activity which influences the income. Particularly, in case of women entrepreneurs, the time constraint due to domestic activities is more. Therefore, the time that they are able to spend will have an impact on the net income of the enterprise. It is also expected to be positively associated with Y.

The third explanatory variable considered is the 'Period of Existence of the Enterprise' (PE). It is expected to be positively correlated with Y. The longer the period of existence, efficient will be the management, and in turn, higher will be the returns. It is considered in terms of years.

The fourth variable considered, is the 'location of the enterprise'. It is also an important variable in determining the income from the enterprise. It is defined as 'within the house premises' and ' outside the house premises'. It is a dummy variable for which the value zero '0' is given for the enterprises conducted 'within the house premises' and one '1' for the enterprises conducted 'outside the house premises'. The assumption here is that, enterprises conducted outside the house i.e., at some business places will have more operational area and demand for their activity than the enterprises conducted within the house premises whose demand is extended only to the street level. It is denoted by 'D_1' in the equation.

The next explanatory variable, is the caste dummy variable. It takes the value of zero '0' for the reserved castes viz., backward and scheduled castes, and one '1' for other castes. Theoretically, forward caste people are more enterprising and they can manage the business more efficiently than others. But, most of the micro enterprises are traditionally, caste determined ones. For example, vegetable vending and fruit vending is dominated by some caste known as ' Relli', fish vending is dominated by 'Jalary', and pottery is the traditional occupation of 'Kummari'. Therefore, caste has a significant influence on the skills or experience of the worker, which makes them more enterprising. It is denoted by 'D_2' in the equation.

The last explanatory variable is the mode of operation of the activity of the enterprise. The value zero '0' is given for the enterprises which are conducted in 'mobile' manner and one '1' for the enterprises which are conducted in 'stable' manner.

Results of the Net Income Function for Micro Enterprise

The estimated values of the parameters of the net income function along with the values of 't' and `R^2 are presented in Table 10. Out of the six explanatory variables, three variables turned out as significant with the explanatory power of 36 per cent variation. The time spent on the activity has a positive relation with the net income from the enterprise. Incase the mode of operation, the negative sign of the regression co-efficient indicates that stable enterprises are getting more income than the mobile enterprises. The amount of Fixed Capital is having positive sign but the coefficient value is very small. These three explanatory variables are statistically significant. Even though, the other variables are statistically insignificant, the results indicate some interesting trends. Particularly, the caste dummy variable has a negative sign which indicates that urban informal sector is becoming more competitive day by day with expanding variety of modern occupations by blurring the boundaries of traditional occupations dominated by the caste system. Surprisingly, the period of existence turned out as negatively associated with net income. Even though, these enterprises are able to continue for longer time, they may not be turning out competent with the changing scenario which determines the net income of the enterprise. The variable location has got negative sign indicating that enterprises run outside the house premises are earning more income than the enterprises functioning within the household premises.

Problems and Constraints

Generally, it is felt that women entrepreneurs face lots of personal, financial and family problems and social, family, and time constraints, etc. Table 11 presents the response of the sample women micro entrepreneurs' about the problems and constraints they face. Some respondents are indifferent that they can't say either 'yes' or 'no' to the specific issue. The problems like capital needs, raw material problems, marketing problems, production problems, information problems are general to the micro enterprises. These problems when faced by women take additional dimensions.

It could be observed from the table that insufficiency of loan amount to start the enterprise is the major constraint. Demand and supply fluctuations of the product of the enterprise are problems reported by women which in turn reflect the inconsistency of income. Time constraint due to domestic responsibilities and health problems are the major ones which women feel in carrying out the enterprise. Women need more help from family members so that they can better utilize their potentiality in developing their skills as well as their families.

Findings

The existing policies and programmes should be strengthened and intensified to provide the financial assistance for women micro enterprises to meet both the fixed and working capital needs. If some mechanism like supplementary loans on weekly repayment basis by the banks at lower interest rates for the good running enterprises can be developed, it will definitely benefit the women micro enterprises in the urban informal sector. The analysis of these reasons reveals that generally, female depend on other male members of the family for the help and guidance necessary for conducting the enterprise. Some times, dependency on others due to lack of own managerial skills makes the enterprises liable to loss and finally, hampers the existence of the enterprise itself. So, there is a need to impart managerial skills and provide proper guidance, at least in the initial stage of the units. Most of the vending enterprises are conducted by carrying heavy loads on head and walking long distances. In turn, this leads to health problems. Lack of proper work place is also an important factor for the failure of the activities. So, providing proper work places like shopping complexes, giving priority for female in allotting them is necessary. Another important reason is the burden of household responsibilities or work that includes both child rearing and domestic work. By creating cretches or balwadies, to some extent, child rearing responsibilities or workload can be reduced. But the help of the other family members alone can reduce the burden of domestic work as the improved and sophisticated devices of domestic work can't be afforded by poor families to reduce the burden. One more important reason is the easy opinion towards the female enterprises. At times of urgency, the amount invested on the female enterprises is diverted for the other needs leading to the financial inefficiency of the enterprises. Therefore, the casual attitude of the family members towards the female enterprises should be changed. The attitude towards the women enterprises should change at the family level, as well as in the society.

APPENDIX

Table–1 : Distribution of the Micro Enterprises according to Period of Existence

Period of Existence (years)	*No. of Enterprises*	*Percentage*
One and below	42	28.00
Two	46	30.67
Three	36	24.00
Four and above	26	17.33
Total	150	100.00

Table–2 : Location & Mode of Operation-Wise Distribution of the Micro Enterprises

Place / Location (years)	*No. of Enterprises*	*Percentage*
Within or around house premises	86	57.33
Outside-mobile	36	24.00
Outside-stable	28	18.67
Total	150	100.00

Table–3 : Average Amount of Investment by Source of Finance

Source of Investment	*Average Amount (in Rs.)*	*Percentage*
Money lenders	3245	43.89
Banks	2156	29.16
Own Funds	722	9.76
Friends & Relatives	1271	17.19
Total	7394	100.00

Table–4 : Range and Average Amount of Fixed Capital

Fixed Capital	*Amount (in Rs.)*
Minimum	3000
Maximum	15500
Average	7394

Table–5 : Average Amount of Working Capital

Working Capital	*Amount (in Rs.)*
Minimum	50
Maximum	1000
Average	485

Table–6 : Frequency of Replenishment of Working Capital

Frequency of Replenishment	*No. of Units*	*Percentage*
Daily	97	64.67
Weekly	42	28.00
Monthly	11	7.33
Total	150	100.00

Table–7 : Number of Units by Sources of Purchase

Sources of Purchase	*No. of Units*	*Percentage*
Wholesale Dealer	74	49.33
Mediatory men /Retailer	33	22.00
Both	43	28.67
Total	150	100.00

Table–8 : Number of Units by Mode of purchase

Mode of Purchase	*No. of Units*	*Percentage*
Cash	64	42.67
Credit	63	42.00
Both	23	15.33
Total	150	100.00

Table 9 : Number of Units by Mode of Sales

Mode of Sales	*No. of Units*	*Percentage*
Cash	41	27.33
Credit	79	52.67
Both	30	20.00
Total	150	100.00

Table–10 : Estimated Values of the Explanatory Variables for the Net Income Function

Explanatory variable	*Total*
Constant	389.561
Amount of fixed capital used (AFC)	0.005* (2.36513)
Time spent on activity per day (NOH)	36.257* (4.62499)
Period of Existence (PE)	-2.772 (-0.809)
Location of the enterprise (D_1)	-121.6 (-0.502)
Caste of the entrepreneur (D_2)	-4.43 (-0.476)
Mode of Operation (D_3)	-4.468* (-2.476)
R^2	0.36244

Figures in vaule parenthesis indicate the't' values

Table 11 : Problems and Constraints of Women Micro Entrepreneurs

S. No.	*Type of Problem / Constraint*	*Neutral*	*Yes*	*No*	*Total*
1.	Insufficiency of Capital	10 (6.67)	75 (50.00)	65 (43.33)	150 (100.00)
2.	Seasonal Fluctuations	50 (33.33)	65 (43.33)	35 (23.33)	150 (100.00)
3.	Demand and Supply Fluctuations	10 (6.67)	90 (60.00)	40 (26.67)	150 (100.00)
4.	Personal Health Problems	25 (16.67)	65 (13.33)	60 (40.00)	150 (100.00)
5.	Social/Gender Constraints	5 (3.33)	25 (16.67)	120 (80.00)	150 (100.00)
6.	Time Constraint	9 (6.00)	75 (50.00)	66 (44.00)	150 (100.00)
7.	Support from Family members	10 (6.67)	40 (26.67)	100 (66.67)	150 (100.00)
8.	Bad Habits among Family Members	8 (5.33)	80 (53.33)	62 (41.33)	150 (100.00)
9.	Diversion of Funds	6 (4.00)	100 (66.67)	44 (29.33)	150 (100.00)

REFERENCES

- Alfred de Souza (1988): "The challenge of urban poverty: An introduction " in *THE INDIAN CITY (poverty, ecology and urban development)*, Alfred de Souza ed., Manohar Publications, New Delhi, p. XVII.
- Anju Gupta and Inderjeet Khanna (1997): "Constraints Analysis of Women Entrepreneurs", *SEDME*, December, Vol. XXIV, No. 4, pp. 49-54
- B. Ratna Kumari (1994): *Self Employed Women in the Unorganised Sector in Visakhapatnam City*, Project Report, Centre for Women Studies, Andhra University, Visakhapatnam.
- C. Beena and B. Sushma (2003): "Women Entrepreneurs Managing Petty Business: A Study from Motivational Perspective", *Southern Economist*, May 15, pp. 5-8.
- C. Harinarayana Rao (1991): "Promotion of Women Entrepreneurship: A Brief Comment", SEDME, Vo. XVIII, No. 2, pp. 21-27.
- C.A. Grown and J. Sebstad (1989): "Introduction: Towards wider perspective on women's employment", *World Development*, Vol. 17, No. 7, Pergaman Press, p. 938.

- Gouri V. Savadi (2001): "Women Entrepreneurs in India: Scope and Opportunities", *Southern Economist,* August 15, pp.17-20.
- Jyotsna Sethi (1994): "Women Entrepreneurship in India: A Brief Comment", *SEDME,* Vol. XXI, No. 4, pp. 69-73.
- L.Rathakrishnan and B.Sellammalle (2001): "Micro-Women Entrepreneurs and Socio-Economic Empowerment: A Study", *Southern Economist*, Vol. 40, No. 8, pp. 14-16
- M.V.Raghavulu (2003): "Women Entrepreneurship in backward Areas", *SEDME*, Vol. XXX, No. 4, pp. 43-52
- N. Sarnagharan and Resia Beagam (1995): *Women Entrepreneurship – Institutional Support and Problems*, Discovery Publishing House, New Delhi, pp. 15-16.
- National Institute of Urban Affairs (1991): *Women in the Urban Informal Sector* Research study series, Number 49, NIUA, New Delhi, p. 134.
- URBAN EDGE (1988): *Issues & Innovations*, Vol. 12, No. 1, January/ February, p. 4.

Chapter 20
EMPOWERMENT OF WOMEN ENTREPRENEURSHIP IN VISAKHAPATNAM CITY

*Dr. B. Ratna Kumari
**Ms. Zilani Begum
***Ms. M. Anitha

ABSTRACT

The chapter examines the growth of women entrepreneurship in greater Visakhapatnam city in Andhra Pradesh. The major objective is the study the factors which contribute income and employment generation through women entrepreneurship. The primary data was collected from 50 multi-stratified random samples. The study found that the respondents who live in joint family enjoy the support of family and able to concentrate more on their occupation and earn more.

Introduction

Women entrepreneurs may be defined as the women or a group of women who initiate, organize and operate a business enterprise. However such innovators are rarely sound in the under-developed countries, the enterprises for these people may be small and unimpressive when judged by standards of the developed countries. But the high propensity to imitate can set in motion of the chain reaction which leads to cumulative progress. Thus, in the Indian context, entrepreneur is an adopter and imitator than a true innovator.

* Presently working as Associate Professor Dr. Durgabai Deshmukh Centre for women studies, Andhra University.

** Research Scholar, Dept. of Applied Economics, Andhra University.

*** Research Scholar, Dept. of Applied Economics, Andhra University.

According to the government of India, a women entrepreneur is defined as "an enterprise owned and controlled by women and having a minimum financial interest of 51 per cent of the capital and giving at least 51 per cent of the employment generated in the enterprises to women".

Enterprises set up by women should be provided with incentives and support on the basis of their ownership and management characteristic and not linked with employment of women. Word 'entrepreneurship' broadly stands for self-employment. It mainly involves identification of opportunities within the economic system. It involves assumptions of risks and responsibility in designing and executing a business strategy of starting a new business venture. Entrepreneurs are skilled organizers of various activities such as identifying the needs for various products or services, originating or generating ideas on how to provide the desire products or services, evolution of well through out ideas and present a business enterprise opportunity, and finally, a plan of action to translate idea into a commercially viable proposition. Entrepreneurship has been attracting more and more attention of policy makers, academicians and business practitioners since early nineties. The main reason behind this is that the creation of new enterprises has a great potential to contribute to a balanced and accelerated economic growth and creation of employment opportunities.

In India, entrepreneurship has been dominated by male governed economy, where the role of women as entrepreneurs has been negligible. However, in the recent past women entrepreneurs has been playing an increasingly important role in promoting growth and economic development of country's economy (1). Women's entrepreneurship is also gaining increasing importance in public policy circulars. National governments and international organizations are coming to realize that promoting women economic development through women entrepreneurs plays a critical role in economic growth, particularly at the grass roots level. First and foremost, it enhances the tempo of the economic growth provides greater prosperity to the small scale entrepreneurs and their workers. Moreover, it directly provides employment and economic independence to women and improves their social, educational and health status. Vast majority of the population of India still lives in rural areas and depend for their economic sustenance on agricultural and allied economic activities. Although much has been written about aspects of women empowerment and entrepreneurship in Indian, not very much has been done when it comes to quantify the extent of women's business ownership and their contribution to economic growth. Relationship of economic activity among women to a country's economic growth shows that there is a distant and strong correlation between women's entrepreneurship and GDP growth (2).

The limited availability of reliable and valid data is one of the key obstacles to understand the specific challenges to women's entrepreneurship and their impact on economic growth. Sex-disaggregated statistics and sex-based policy analysis have become more widespread in recent years; still non-availability of sufficient data makes it difficult to assess the quantum of women's contribution in economic development, particularly in urban areas(3).

Need of the Study

The present study is aimed at analyzing women participation in the informal sector of Visakhapatnam city, Andhra Pradesh on the East-Coast of India. The study observes that most of the working women folk in the urban informal sector are engaged in vegetable vending, fruit vending, fish vending, trading, manufacture and service sectors. Kailasa and Yarada the two hill ranges with a maximum height of 1663 inches and 1179 inches respectively. The two ranges are separated from each other by intermediate low and with few scattered hills. Rest is tidal basin on the south-west while a narrow beach of 30 to 200 meters width lie on the east. Such natural features along with the favourable infrastructural facilities have facilitated the location and rapid growth of a number of industries such as Bharat Heavy Plate and Vessels Ltd.(BHPV), Coromandel Fertilizers Ltd... Hindustan polymers, Hindustan petroleum corporation Ltd, Eastern Naval command, Port Trust, etc. in the city. The other big industry which has national importance is the Visakhapatnam Steel Project which is also Government established. There are 33 major and medium industries also established in this "City of Destiny" the name was given by former Prime Minister Late smt. INDIRA GANDHI. It has occupied the second place in industrialization in the entire state. Thus, Visakhapatnam urban Agglomeration consists of greater Visakha Municipalities, Gajuwaka (old Gajuwaka) and Gopalapatnam Panchayats. In order to explain the socio-economic and working conditions women entrepreneurship in greater Visakhapatnam city.

Objectives

The present study examines the growth of women entrepreneurship in Greater Visakhapatnam city in Andhra Pradesh. It studies inter alia, the educational background , community to which they belong, motivation to initiate to entrepreneurial career, and their problems. It is also further observe that the trend income and employment generating capacity and the constraints of women entrepreneurship.

The objectives of the study are as follows:

(1) to define the term women entrepreneurs and relevance(a) conducive environment for women empowerment in Visakhapatnam city.

(2) To study the socio- demographic profile of the women entrepreneurs in grteater Visakhapatnam city.

(3) To observe the factors which contribute income and employment generation of the women entrepreneurs.

(4) To find out the reasons for their success.

(5) To suggest policy and implications to create of their growth with economic development.

Research Methodology

The study is based on primary and secondary data. This data has been collected from multi-stratisfied random sample. 50 Women entrepreneurs are selected with the help of a detailed Questionnaire. The greater visakha is situated among big industries like Steel plant, HPCL, Visakha port trust, shipyard and other industries. So, many women were migrated from rural areas of Visakhapatnam district and a number of women have been engaged with in self employment, hence there is a activity need to find out the status of women entrepreneurs especially Muslim women entrepreneurs in the City.

The study has been taken data from secondary sources i.e. from the reports Andhra Pradesh minority Commission and District Industries Centre (DIC) in greater Visakhapatnam city.

The study has used the percentage method to find out the above objectives.

Present Status of Women and Entrepreneurs in India

Having realized the importance and role played by women in the nation's development, in the sixth five year plan, a special chapter on women's development has been included". The objective of women entrepreneurship movement is to give representation to women in the field of small industry development with a view of uplifting their status in the economic and social fields. Due to the growth of industrialization, urbanization education and democratic system in the country, the traditional bound Indian society is now undergoing a change and women are now seeking gainful employment in several fields in an extreme level. Still it can't be said that the women entrepreneurship movement has taken in the ground and it is felt that the movement is still in transition period.

Women Entrepreneurs in Large and Medium Sector

In this, women with educational and professional qualifications take initiative and business as well as men. A women entrepreneur who has received managerial skill, training and educational qualification usually lead the medium level and other opportunities which are available to them are in a high position and have a competitive edge over others.

Women Entrepreneurs in Small-scale Units

The women entrepreneurs who do not have any education or any formal training in management but have developed skills, and manage small units. For this they choose the product which is familiar to them like garments, weaving, and handicrafts. Some have ventured into engineering electronics, chemicals and pharmaceuticals, surgical instruments, furniture and pottery because of their family background or other assistance.

The third category

This type of entrepreneurs are working in cities and slums to help women with lower means of livelihood. Some of the service motivated organization like minority commission, District Industries Centre, Schedule Corporation and Backward Corporation help economically backward sections. They need government support in marketing as well as getting finance at a concessional rate for their products. Preferential purchasing policy of Government helps such institutions to manufacture and sell the same to the Government items like files, chalk, stationary act.

In a country like India, social value system and cultural tradition exercise a strong hold in the mass mind. Any innovation to succeed in our society needs to be acceptable to our value systems and socio-cultural tradition. Further, in our country where vast majority of the population is more concerned about making both ends meet, entrepreneurial activity can achieve sustainability only when policy planners devise strategies for tackling women entrepreneurship in an integrated manner by providing due support and encouragement at societal and governmental levels. When it comes to define the rationale for women entrepreneurship, there are two important arguments. First the economic argument which focuses on utilization of human resources forming around 50 per cent of the population without overburdening the employment market. Second the social argument which deals with development of self-esteem and a sense of the 'self' for creation of an entrepreneurial socially transcending the gender divide.

The census commission of India and the national sample survey organization (NSSO) are the two main sources of data on women's employment. The human development report of 1990 also highlights that much of work that women do is 'invisible' in national accounting and censuses, in spite of its obvious productive and social criteria. The reason is that women are heavily involved in small-scale agricultural informal sector mind household activities, areas where tangible data lacking for any worth while input to strategic planning. In India, women constitute about 48 per cent of the population but their participation in quantifiable economic activity is around 34 per cent. The effect of this economic inequality is mirrored in the social scenario, where a small percentage of population is becoming more and more prosperous and about two-third of the population still remains poor and untouched on technological progress (4).

The female total entrepreneurial activity (TEA) index measures the percentage of women in the labour force who are either activity involved in starting new business or who have been owning or managing a business for less than 42 months. The UN report on TEA shows ratio of 1.52 women entrepreneurs which is the ratio based on men to the insignificant women entrepreneurs between age group of 16-64 years per 100 adults, clearly signifying the insignificant women entrepreneurial activity as compared to men (5).

Almost half the population of our country comprises of women, while business owned and operated by them constitute less tan 5 per cent. Out of the total women workforce in India in the organized sector, 58 per cent were in the public, and 42 per cent in the private sector. This a data comprises of both urban and rural women put together. Globally, the unorganized sector has been growing much faster than the organized sector. In this sector, there are no defined or regulated conditions for work or employment. The percentage of self-employed women is higher in own account enterprises (Oases) as compared to those in other establishment or business centers. The persistence of female-male gaps in human development offers a challenge and an opportunity to the developing countries to accelerate their economic and social progress by investing more on women.

In an environment of globalization and an era of liberalization, the impact of globalization in all sectors of economic development is visible in a variety of ways like technological change, 'flexibilisation' of the workforce opening of new markets, changing social norms, growing pressures on resources and so on, thus creating a favorable environment for more and more entrepreneurial activities for urban women. The status of women in India has been changing due to growing industrialization and urbanization, spatial mobility and social legislation. During the 1970s, the decade of the urbanization, women's years, and efforts to promote self-employment among women received greater attention from the government and private agencies. The new industrial policy of the government of India has laid great emphasis on the need for conducting special entrepreneurial training programmes for women to enable them to start their own ventures. Against the above backdrop, an attempt has been made in this paper to focus on the various issues and challenges in regard to urban women entrepreneurship.

Urban Women Entrepreneurship

Women's entrepreneurship needs to be studied separately for two main reasons. The first reason is that importance of women's entrepreneurship has been only recently recognized during the last decade as an untapped source of economic growth. Women entrepreneurs' creative solutions to business related problems as regards administration, supervision and other organizational related issues. A part from the tacit assumption that women are failing and indecisive, women entrepreneurs encounter many problems in their efforts to develop the enterprise they have established. The main problems faced by the women entrepreneurs may be analyzed as follows.

A part from the tacit assumption that women are failing and indecisive, women entrepreneurs encounter many problems in their efforts to develop the enterprise they have established. The main problems faced by women entrepreneurs may be analyzed as follows.

Problems

(1) Shortage of finance
(2) Inefficient arrangements for marketing and sale
(3) Shortage of raw materials
(4) Shift competition
(5) High cost of production
(6) Low mobility
(7) Family responsibilities
(8) Social attitudes
(9) Low ability to bear risk
(10) Educational and training
(11) Enterprise networking
(12) Gender differences

Occupation pattern

Table 1 explains that the respondents belong to a variety of occupational background of 20 per cent of the respondents belong to food processing units, 14 per cent belong to tents materials supplies, 12 per cent belong to watch shops and 10 per cent belongs to each watches and fancy toys and the remaining 44 per cent of the respondents belong to fancy and kirana and other business respectively on the whole, out of the total women entrepreneurs, the food processing units have occupied a major role, because of change in the food habits of the consumers in Visakhapatnam city.

Table–1 : Respondent's Occupation

Activities	*No. of Entrepreneurs*	*Percentage*
Cloth business	3	6
Fancyskirana	4	8
Mike setlighting	3	6
S.T.D shops	3	6
Fancy toys	5	10
Photo colour Lab	1	2
Wheel chairs walk sticks	2	4
Dental X-ray	1	2
Watches	6	12
Tents materials supplies	7	14
Book stationary	5	10
Food processing units	10	20
Total	50	100

Religion Pattern

According to Table-2 majority (40%) of the women entrepreneurs belong to Hinduism, 34 per cent belong to Islam and 26 per cent belong to Christianity.

Table-2 : Religion pattern of women entrepreneurs In Visakhapatnam city

Religion	*No.of Entrepreneurs*	*Percentage*
Hinduism	20	40
Christianity	13	26
Islam	17	34
Total	50	100

Martial status

Table 3 explains that the martial status of the respondents out of the total entrepreneurs 60 per cent belong to the married, 20 per cent belong to the widows, 14 per cent belong to the unmarried and 6 per cent belong to the Divorced respondents

Table – 3 : Martial Status of the Respondents

Martial Status	*No. of entrepreneurs*	*Percentage*
Un-married	7	14
Married	30	60
Widows	10	20
Divorced	3	6
Total	50	100

Family Pattern

Table 3 explains the family pattern of women entrepreneurs in Visakhapatnam city. Out of the total entrepreneurs 60 per cent of the respondents belong to Nuclear while 40 per cent belong to joint family. This is evident from the above table that 40 per cent of women entrepreneurs are enjoying the family support and leaving the burden of joint family.

Table-4 : Family pattern of women entrepreneurs in Visakhapatnam city

Family Type	*No. of Entrepreneurs*	*Percentage*
Nuclear	30	60
Joint	20	40
Total	50	100

Age Pattern

It is evident from table -5 that out of the total women entrepreneurs 40 per cent belong to the age group of 20-30 years, 30 per cent belong to the age group of 31-40 year, 20 per cent belong to the age group of 41-50 years and 10 per cent belong to the age group of 51-60 above years. On the whole the young women entrepreneurs are in interested establish in a with than the elders due to their resistance to keep with uncertainty, risk bearing and competition from others under the globalization process.

Table–5 : Age-Wise Distribution of Respondents

Age group	*No. of entrepreneurs*	*Percentage*
20-30	20	40
31-40	15	30
41-50	10	20
51-60 (above)	5	10
Total	50	100

Educational Status of the Respondents

The greater the educated the more the entrepreneurship activities in the country. Table-6 explains that out of total respondents 24 per cent belong to secondary education (6th-10th classes), 20 per cent belong to intermediate education (10 plus), 16 per cent each belong to postgraduate and primary education. On the whole 10 per cent of the respondents are non-illiterate. It is evident from table-5 that the post graduate women are to start up a unit on their own.

Table – 6 : Educational Status of the Respondent

Educational Status	*No. of Entrepreneurs*	*Percentage*
Illiterate	5	10
Primary Education(0-5)	8	16
Secondary Education(6-10)	12	24
Intermediate	10	20
Degree	5	10
Post Graduate	8	16
Professional Degree	2	4
Total	50	100

Income pattern

It is evident from the table -6 that out of the total women entrepreneurs 24 per cent belong to the monthly income at to Rs. 4100-5000, 16 per cent belong to monthly income of Rs. 5100-6000 to 7100-8000, 14 per cent belong to the income of Rs. 8100-9000 and 12 per cent belong to income of Rs. 3000-4000 to 6100-7000 and low income respondents 6 per cent

Table – 7 : Income of the Respondents

Average Income	*No. of entrepreneurs*	*Percentage*
3000-4000	6	12
4100-5000	12	24
5100-6000	8	16
6100-7000	6	12
7100-8000	8	16
8100-9000	7	14
9000-above	3	6
Total	50	100

Investment pattern

It is evident from table 8 that out of the total women entrepreneurs invested of 24 per cent belong to the investment of Rs. 9100-10,000, 20 per cent belong to investment range of 5700-8000, 16 per cent belong to the 8100-9000 amount invested. 6 per cent belong to the highest amount invested.

Table-8 : Investment of the Respondent

Investment Rs. Per annum	*No. of Entrepreneurs*	*Percentage*
5700-8000	10	20
8100-9000	8	16
9100-10,000	12	24
10,000-50,000	11	22
50,000-1,00,000	6	12
1,10,000-1,50,000	3	6
Total	50	100

Suggestions

1. In order to overcome the problem, women should be made aware of loans, schemes and programmes launched for them by the government.
2. This can be done through training programmes. Women entrepreneurship programmes need focus on important dimensions like strategies for finance, marketing, and facilitating the growth of network. This will help building confidence and make women economically more productive.

3. Women entrepreneurs should be equipped with entrepreneurial skills and modern management practices. Modern technologies to overcome the problems related to production and marketing. This will impact positively on the overall development of the women entrepreneurs.

Conclusion

It may be concluded that entrepreneurship among women requires a congenial entrepreneurial climate which motivates and facilitates them to take up entrepreneurial career.

REFERENCES

1. Syal P., Dhameja S.K. (2003) Entrepreneurship – Key to Women Empowerment, Science Tech Enterpreneur.

   [http://www.techno-preneur.net/new-timeis/Science TechMag/june03/ juneindex.htm].
2. Ray D., The role of entrepreneurship in economic development, Journal of development planning, Vol.No.18, page No.3.
3. Women's entrepreneurship : Issues & Policies, Promoting Entrepreneurship and Innovative SMEs in a Global Economy, 2nd Organization for Economic Co-Operation And Development ('OECD), Conference of Ministers Responsible For Small And Medium–Sized Enterprises (SMEs), Istanbul, Turkey, 3-5 June, 2004.
4. National Commossion on Labor, Second Report, Chapter IX, Ministry of Labor, Government of India, 2003.
5. Maria M., Arenius P., Women in Entrepreneurship, The Entrepreneurial Advantage of Nations : First Annual Global Entrepreneurship Symposium, United Nations Headquarters, April 29, 2003.

Chapter 21
CAPACITY BUILDING OF WOMEN THROUGH TINY INDUSTRIES

***L. Rathakrishnan**

There is no occasion for women to consider themselves subordinate or inferior to men.

–M.K. Gandhi

ABSTRACT

The chapter presents the socio-economic background of the women entrepreneurs in the rural and urban areas of Dindigul district. It has also covered the factors, which motivated the women to undertake enterprise activities. The study also gives an overview of the problems faced by the women entrepreneurs in undertaking their micro-business activities in the study area. Primary data was collected from 43 women entrepreneurs in 2005. It is found that majority of them falls under the category of first generation entrepreneurs and they concentrate only one unit. Family support was the main reason for success of the entrepreneurs. Finance is the limiting factor for their progress. Proper guidance based on scientific inputs, suitable products ideas, product identification, market survey and project formulations should be given to women entrepreneurs for their sustainability.

Introduction

The development of a nation can be measured by the progress of its women folk. All through the ages, women have contributed immensely to the enrichment of culture and progress of civilisation without getting due recognition for their contribution. It is only in the last couple of

* Reader in Rural Industries and Management, Gandhigram Rural University, Gandhigram–624 302.

decades that there is a growing awareness that human development is likely to make a quantum leap only if substantial investment is made in improving the status of women. Human progress will be sustainable only if mutually reinforcing effects of the status of women on employment, poverty and environment deterioration is appreciated and consciously attended to.

In India, about 50 per cent of total population constitutes women. But women workers constitute only 16 per cent of the total population. Out of this 16 per cent, 80 per cent remain engaged in unorganised sectors. Entrepreneurship among women is a recent phenomenon. Women entrepreneurs may be defined as a women who initiate, organize and run a business enterprise. In terms of schumpeterian concept of innovative entrepreneurs, women innovate, imitate or adopt a business activity are called "women entrepreneurs".

Statement of the Study

Mass poverty and widespread unemployment are the two most pervasive problems faced by the third world countries. India is no exception from this. India is a land of villages with 77 per cent of her population lives in village and majority of them are poor. The causes of poverty are many and well known. However, some of the important reasons can be identified as: uneven distribution of resources; rapid growth of population, low productivity, high dependency on agriculture and high rate of illiteracy. The culmination of all these factors is reflated through low income and large unemployment.

On the other hand there in a discrimination based on sex. In India, women are still confined to four walls of home, children and family rituals. In a male chauvinist society, women are not treated on par with their male counterparts. They are victims of social discrimination and prejudice. Women are not taught to bring the best, on par with man.

In this scenario, self employment is the only way to solve the problem of unemployment. Self employment can be achieved through the promotion of entrepreneurship and that too of women entrepreneurship. Because majority of the women living in the rural areas are illiterate, malnourished, and unemployed.

Keeping this idea in mind, the present study has analysed the socio-economic background of the women entrepreneur in the rural and urban areas of Dindigul District. It has also covered the factors which have motivated them to undertake these activities. The study also gives an overview of the problems faced by the women entrepreneurs in undertaking their micro business activities in the study area.

Objective of the Study

The major objectives of the study are:

(*i*) To study the socio- economic background of women entrepreneurs in the rural and urban areas of Dindigul District.

(*ii*) To analyse the factors that motivated the women entrepreneurs to start new ventures, and

(*iii*) To outline the constraints faced by the women entrepreneurs in the selected area.

Materials and Methods

The present study is mainly focused on the development of women entrepreneurs' right from their socio-economic background and the motivation factors that led them to undertake entrepreneurship activities and also the problems faced by them in their filed. Primary data was collected in January 2005 from 43 women entrepreneurs. Simple random sampling technique was used to select the respondents.

The following criteria have been applied for the selection of women entrepreneurs for the study. They are:

(*i*) The women entrepreneurs should have actually contributed to the capital of the enterprises.

(*ii*) The women entrepreneurs should be the real owner of the enterprises and

(*iii*) The women entrepreneurs should be actively participating in the proper functioning of the enterprise.

For data collection an interview schedule was prepared covering profile of women entrepreneurs, the family size the reasons for starting the business, the nature of the enterprises other details about the enterprise like its location, investment pattern and also the expenditure pattern.

Interpretation & Discussion

The study has covered a total of 43 women entrepreneurs of various categories, namely petty shop units (10), tailoring shop units (10), hotel units (10), vegetable shop units (8) and beauty parlour units (5).

Table shows the age of the respondents. The age category ranges from 18 to 50 years. Only 19 per cent of the respondents are falling in the age of above 50 years. The hotel industry people are found to be occupying their job even after 50 years. Nevertheless 40 per cent of tailoring sectors are found in the age category between 18-25 years.

SOCIO–ECONOMIC BACKGROUND

(*a*) Age of the Respondents

Table – 1 : Age of the Respondents

Sl.No.	*Respondents Category*	*Age of the Respondents*			*Total*
		18-25	*25-50*	*Above 50*	
1.	Petty shop	2 (20)	6 (60)	2 (20)	10 (100)
2.	Tailoring	4 (40)	5 (50)	1 (10)	10 (100)
3.	Hotel	1 (10)	5 (50)	4 (40)	10 (100)
4.	Vegetable	3 (38)	4 (50)	1 (12)	8 (100)
5.	Beauty parlour	-	5 (100)	-	5 (100)
	Total	10 (23)	25 (58)	8 (19)	43 (100)

Source: Primary data collected from the field in the month of January 2005.
Note: Figures in parentheses represents percentages.

(*b*) Religion and Caste of the Respondents

The selected respondents are following Hindu, Muslim and Christian religion. It is found that 84 per cent of the respondents are falling in Hindu religion and 14 per cent are following Christianity religion and a fraction of the respondents have adopted Muslim religion. All beauty parlour units and 90 per cent of the Tailoring units and hotel units falling in the category of Hindu religion.

The respondents are from two castes namely backward caste and most backward caste. In this study, majority of the respondents belongs to backward caste (93 per cent) compared to most backward caste (7 per cent).

(*c*) Place of Entrepreneurial Activity

All most, all hotel units, petty shop units and tailoring shop units are concentrated in the villages whereas majority of the vegetable shop units and beauty parlour units are concentrated in the town.

(*d*) Educational attainment of the Respondents

The education particulars of the respondents are divided into six categories, namely primary, middle, high school, higher secondary, graduation and illiterate.

Table-2 : Religion and Caste of the Respondents

Sl.No	*Respondents category*	*Religion*			*Total*	*Caste*	
		Hindu	*Muslim*	*Christian*		*BC*	*MBC*
1.	Petty shop	7 (70)	-	3 (30)	10 (100)	10 (100)	-
2.	Tailoring	9 (90)	-	1 (10)	10 (100)	9 (100)	1 (10)
3.	Hotel	9 (90)	-	1 (10)	10 (100)	9 (90)	1 (10)
4.	Vegetable	6 (75)	1 (12.5)	1 (12.5)	8 (100)	8 (100)	-
5.	Beauty parlour	5 (100)	-	-	5 (100)	4 (80)	1 (20)
	Total	36 (84)	1 (2)	6 (14)	43 (100)	40 (93)	3 (7)

Source: Primary data collected from the field in the month of January 2005.
Note: Figures in parentheses represents percentages. Here 'BC' refers to backward Class and 'MBC' refers to Most Backward class.

It is found that 91 per cent of the respondents are literate, studied from primary to college level. A large number of respondents (81 per cent) have studied upto High School (Economic and Social problem cause low level educational attainment). It is pathetic to note that four respondents were illiterate from the category of petty shop, hotel, vegetable and beauty parlour units.

Table-3 : Educational Qualification of the Respondents

Sl.No	*Respondents Category*	*Education Qualification*						*Total*
		Illi	*P.*	*M.*	*H.S*	*H.Sec*	*G*	
1.	Petty shop	1 (10)	4 (40)	2 (20)	3 (30)	-	-	10 (100)
2.	Tailoring	-	1 (10)	2 (20)	6 (60)	1 (10)	-	10 (100)
3.	Hotel	1 (10)	2 (20)	6 (60)	1 (10)	1 (10)	1 (10)	10 (100)
4.	Vegetable	1 (12.5)	2 (25)	3 (37.5)	2 (25)	-	-	8 (100)
5.	Beauty parlour	1 (20)	-	-	3 (60)	-	1 (20)	5 (100)
	Total	4 (9)	9 (20)	11 (26)	15 (35)	2 (5)	2 (5)	43 (100)

Source: Primary data collected from the field in the month of January 2005.
Note: Figures in parentheses represents percentages. Here 'Illi' refers to Illiterates, P-primary, 'M' – Middle ' H.S' – High school. 'H.Sec- Higher Secondary and 'G'- Graduation.

(*e*) Family size of the Respondents

It is observed from the study that majority of the respondents (52 per cent) have a family size, less than 5 members. It shows that as the family size increases the demand also increases, which has compelled the respondents to undertake self employment.

Table-4 : Family Size of the Respondents

Sl.No	*Respondents Category*	*Size of the family*			*Total*
		Less than 3	*3-4*	*More than 5*	
1.	Petty shop	1 (10)	4 (40)	5 (50)	10 (100)
2.	Tailoring	-	4 (40)	6 (60)	10 (100)
3.	Hotel	1 (10)	4 (40)	5 (50)	10 (100)
4.	Vegetable	-	4 (50)	4 (50)	8 (100)
5.	Beauty parlour	-	4 (80)	1 (20)	5 (100)
	Total	2 (5)	20 (47)	21 (48)	43 (100)

Source: Primary data collected from field in the month of January 2005.
Note: Figures in parentheses represents percentages

(*f*) Year of establishment of the Enterpris

In order to understand the experience of the entrepreneurs, a question was asked about the year of establishment. Although women were doing some business since 1960 in the study area, 76 per cent of them have started their units only after 1991. This shows that new economic policy opened the eyes of the aspiring and challenging women entrepreneurs.

(*g*) Reasons for Establishing the Enterprise

Four reasons attribute for stating an enterprise. They are respondents' poverty which forced them to start some economic activity. Self-confidence and motivation of family members is another inducing agent; Training received or technical education obtained had been an instrument for starting a new venture; and the respondents self-esteem like easy to handle or manage is yet another attributing factor for establishing micro industrial activity.

Table-5 : Reasons for Establishing Enterprises

Sl.No	*Respondents Category*	*Reasons*				*Total*
		Poverty situation	*Easy to manage*	*Self confidence*	*Training*	
1.	Petty shop	4 (10)	3 (30)	3 (30)	-	10 (100)
2.	Tailoring	2 (20)	-	4 (40)	4 (40)	10 (100)
3.	Hotel	2 (20)	-	4 (40)	4 (40)	10 (100)
4.	Vegetable	4 (50)	1 (12)	3 (40)	-	8 (100)
5.	Beauty parlour	3 (60)	-	2 (40)	-	5 (100)
	Total	15 (35)	8 (19)	14 (32)	6 (14)	43 (100)

Source: Primary data collected from field in the month of January 2005.
Note: Figures in parentheses represents percentages.

Self confidence (32 per cent) and poverty (35 per cent) situations are the major motivating factor for establishing small enterprises in the study area. Training received on tailoring, beauty parlour, and hotel management are the other interesting factors for starting enterprise in the study area. It is found from the study that even without any background training one can start industry and can run successfully. Entrepreneurs can do well if they have self confidence, motivation and some inducement from the Government side.

(*h*) Previous Employment Details of the Respondents

The study indicates that 60 per cent of the respondents in petty shop unit, have previous employment experience just as they have worked in sweet stalls, tea shops, and tailoring units. But in respect to other respondents, namely in tailoring unit, hotel unit, vegetable unit and beauty parlour they have no previous experience in handling the unit. The study clearly shows that majority of the respondents have no previous experience and they are newly emerged entrepreneurs.

(*i*) Type of Training Required by the Respondents

It is observed from study that more than 50 per cent of the respondents in all the categories desired to have training in all the fields, namely training in administration, production management, sales and marketing, which shows that training is very much essential for a successful entrepreneurship.

Table-6 : Types of training required by the Respondents

Sl.No	*Respondents Category*	*Type of Training*					*Total*
		Adminis-tration	*Production Management*	*Sales*	*Marketing*	*All*	
1.	Petty shop	-	-	1 (10)	3 (30)	6 (60)	10 (100)
2.	Tailoring	-	-	1 (10)	-	9 (90)	10 (100)
3.	Hotel	1 (10)	1 (10)	2 (20)	1 (10)	5 (50)	10 (100)
4.	Vegetable	-	-	1 (12.5)	6 (75)	1 (12.5)	8 (100)
5.	Beauty parlour	-	1 (20)	-	1 (20)	3 (60)	5 (100)
	Total	1 (10)	2 (4.7)	5 (12)	11 (25)	24 (56)	43 (100)

Source: Primary data collected from the field in the month of January, 2005.
Note: Figures in parentheses represents percentages.

(*j*) Satisfaction with the Occupation and Willingness to Continue

Majority of the respondents in all the categories are satisfied with their present occupation except one case in the petty shop unit due to competition from the neighbouring shop.

All the respondents in the selected categories are very much willing to continue in the present occupation due to their family support and future prospects of the enterprises.

Details about the Enterprises

(*k*) Ownership and Rent Payment of the Enterprise

Units selected for the study are micro enterprises owned by the women entrepreneurs and there is only sole proprietorship was found or in other words no partnership was noticed in the study area.

Table –7 explains rent payment details of the respondents. It is found from the table that 65 per cent of the respondents operate their industrial activities in their own building. 35 per cent of the entrepreneurs run their business in rented building and 40 per cent of the beauty parlour, hotel industry, and tailoring unit run in rented buildings. The rent amount varies from place to place and industry. It ranges from Rs.1000 to 10,000/- per year. As the beauty parlours are located in cities, that too in prime place 20 per cent of the tiny entrepreneurs pay even above Rs. 10000/- per year. The rent payment data indicates two eventuality, namely (*i*) the demand for the particular industry is high in the market by and by possibility for high return; (*ii*) the higher payment of rent may escalate the price of the particular product. In the process this will increase the cost of production of the particular trade.

Table-7 : Rent payment Details

Sl.No	*Represent Category*	*Own Building*	*Rent (in Rs. / Year)*			*Total*
			1000-5000	*5000-10000*	*Above 10000*	
1.	Petty shop	7 (70)	1 (10)	1 (10)	1 (10)	10 (100)
2.	Tailoring	6 (60)	1 (10)	2 (20)	1 (10)	10 (100)
3.	Hotel	6 (60)	1 (10)	2 (20)	1 (10)	8 (100)
4.	Vegetable	6 (60)	1 (12.5)	-	1 (20)	8 (100)
5.	Beauty parlour	3 (60)	-	1 (20)	1 (20)	5 (100)
	Total	28 (65)	4 (9)	6 (14)	5 (12)	43 (100)

Source: Primary data collected from the field in the month of January 2005.
Note: Figures in parentheses represents percentages.

(*l*) Employment Details

The employment potentials of the women owned and women operated industries is shown in Table- 8. Although the industries, by nature is tiny but its potential is giving employment to women folk is huge. The five industrial activities providers employment to the magnitude of 70 people. On an average, each industry gives employment opportunity to 14 labourers per year. The women enterprises not only gives employment to the women alone but also for the men folk. 16 per cent of the workers are male members. As the industries are tiny in nature, mostly family members themselves (96 per cent) engaged in the unit. Of the five units, the hotel industry had generated large employment (36 per cent), followed by petty shop (21 per cent) and vegetable unit (19 per cent).

Table–8 : Employment Potentials of Tiny industries

Sl.No	*Respondents category*	*Level of Employment*						*Total in all*	*per cent*
		Hired		*Own*		*Total*			
		Male	*Female*	*Male*	*Female*	*Male*	*Female*		
1.	Petty shop	-	-	5	10	5	10	15	21
2.	Tailoring	-	-	-	10	-	10	10	14
3.	Hotel	-	3	4	18	4	21	25	36
4.	Vegetable	-	-	2	11	2	11	13	19
5.	Beauty parlour	-	-	-	7	-	7	7	10
	Total	-	3	11	56	11	59	70	100

Source: Primary data collected from the field in the month of January 2005.

As these units are owned by women entrepreneurs the number of women employees are more than that of male employees. In some cases there is no male employee engaged in the operation which clearly shows that it is the enterprise run by women.

(*m*) Investment pattern

The investment pattern of the selected enterprises are shown in Table 9. The women entrepreneurs have invested from Rs. 5000/- to Rs. 20000/-. About 70 per cent of the respondents have invested upto Rs. 10,000/- and 21 per cent of the respondents had invested far exceeding Rs. 20,000/-, some times upto Rs. 45000/-. All tailoring unit and hotel industrialists have invested only to the tune of Rs. 10,000/-. A majority of beauty parlour 80 per cent and 40 per cent of petty shop unit had invested more than Rs. 20,000/-. As beauty parlours need high interior decoration and costly equipment, majority of them had invested beyond Rs.20,000/-.

(*n*) Financial Aspects

Capital is important for any industrial activity. As such for this tiny enterprise also, money is needed. Whatever may be the tiny activity they need money. In addition to their own savings, the entrepreneurs have a number of opportunities to avail financial support, namely commercial bank, co-operative bank, non-banking financial institutions and money lenders. The selected respondents in the study area have received money from co-operative banks and money lenders. It's pathetic to note that none have approached commercial banks for financial assistance. Interestingly 81 per cent of the respondents have never availed money from government sources. These 81 per cent industrialist invested in their enterprises on

Table 9 : Investment Pattern

Sl.No	Respondents Category	Investment in Rs.			Total
		Less than 10,000	10,000–20,000	Above 20,000	
1.	Petty shop	6 (60)	-	4 (40)	10 (100)
2.	Tailoring	10 (100)	-	-	10 (100)
3.	Hotel	10 (100)	-	-	10 (100)
4.	Vegetable	4 (50)	3 (37.5)	1 (12.5)	8 (100)
5.	Beauty parlour	-	1 (20)	4 (80)	5 (100)
	Total	30 (70)	4 (9)	9 (21)	43 (100)

Source: Primary data collected from the field in the month of January 2005.
Note: Figures in parentheses represents percentages.

Table-10 : Sources of Finance

Sl.No	Respondents Category	Source of Finance			Total
		Own Savings	Money lenders	Co-operative Banks	
1.	Petty shop	9 (90)	-	1 (10)	10 (100)
2.	Tailoring	8 (80)	1 (10)	1 (10)	10 (100)
3.	Hotel	7 (70)	3 (30)	-	10 (100)
4.	Vegetable	7 (88)	1 (12)	-	8 (100)
5.	Beauty parlour	4 (88)	1 (12)	-	5 (100)
	Total	35 (81)	6 (14)	2 (5)	43 (100)

Source: Primary data colleted from the field in the month of January 2005.
Note: Figures in parentheses represents percentages.

their own savings. Nearly 90 per cent of petty shop owners, vegetable unit and beauty parlour unit and 80 per cent of tailoring unit and 70 per cent of hotel unit have invested from their own savings. 30 per cent of hotel industry owners have received finance from money lenders. Only one respondent in each category have received money from co-operative banks. Thus, it's very clear from the table that the role of Government or semi- government financial institution in funding the tiny enterprise is almost nil.

(*o*) Manufacturing Improvement

The study reveals that majority of the respondents (53 per cent) in all the units have registered an improvement in their production and sales during the study period.

(*p*) Share of respondents contribution to the Family Income

The share of respondents contribution to the family income is an indicator of an economic improvement and progress of a particular enterprise. Higher the enterprise contribution to the family, more will be the prosperity of the particular trade. Of the five tiny industrial entrepreneurs identified and interviewed, vegetable and petty shop unit members have contributed more than 70 per cent of their income to run the family. The hotel industry and beauty parlour units have contributed 50 per cent of the family income. Tailoring units have contributed least, namely only 34 per cent of the family income. Thus the petty shops and vegetable units have high scope for prosperity and brightness. But women engaged in tailoring units have less scope as compared to other enterprises. The highest share of family income of particular enterprise attribute a fact that the petty shop and vegetable unit of particular enterprise attribute a fact that the petty shop and vegetable unit give regular income and have higher demand in the market, where as the demand for tailoring unit is seasonal, hence low contribution to family income.

Table 11 : Share of Respondents Contribution to the Family Income

Sl.No	*Respondents Category*	*Total Income of the Family*	*Contribution by the respondents*	*per cent share of the Respondents*
1.	Petty shop	2,68,360	2,07,360	77.27
2.	Tailoring	5,93,800	2,00,800	33.82
3.	Hotel	3,36,400	1,80,400	53.63
4.	Vegetable	2,64,000	1,88,000	72.21
5.	Beauty parlour	1,50,800	82,800	54.91

Source: Primary data colleted from the field in the month of January 2005.

(q) Problems Faced by the Respondents

Due to good management, the units run by the women entrepreneurs are doing well. Till date no respondent has experienced any major problem. But some respondents experienced some general problems in the study area, namely (*i*) competition from the neighboring units; (*ii*) problems of procurement of raw materials; (*iii*) lack of training & skills; (*iv*) problems created by anti-social elements; (*v*) problem of marketing; (*vi*) problems in obtaining credit, and persistent dependence on men folk for the successful running of their endeavour.

(r) Technical Advise from the respondents to the new incubators

All the respondents felt that if a woman entrepreneur wants to start business of her own then she needs some pre-requisite qualification like. (*i*) the location of the unit should be in a main area, (*ii*) the quality of the products should be good, (*iii*) proper training is very essential, and above all (*iv*) customer satisfaction should be taken care of all. If these things were kept in mind then women can run their units successfully.

(s) Expenditure Pattern

The expenditure pattern of the respondents is shown in Table 12. Although 70 per cent of the respondents have invested upto Rs. 10,000/- but only 12 per cent of the respondents spent less than Rs. 10,000/- . This shows that there is no relation existed between investment and expenditure and the entrepreneurs level of earning.

Table 12 : Expenditure pattern

Sl.No	*Respondents Category*	*Expenditure*				*Total*
		Less than 10,000	*10,000- 25,000*	*25,000- 40,000*	*Above 40,000*	
1.	Petty shop	3 (30)	5 (50)	2 (20)	-	10 (100)
2.	Tailoring	-	1 (10)	3 (30)	6 (60)	10 (100)
3.	Hotel	1 (10)	4 (40)	4 (40)	1 (10)	10 (100)
4.	Vegetable	-	4 (50)	1 (12.5)	3 (37.5)	8 (100)
5.	Beauty parlour	1 (20)	8 (20)	3 (60)	-	5 (100)
	Total	5 (12)	15 (35)	13 (30)	10 (23)	43 (100)

Source: Primary data collected from the field in the month of January 2005.
Note: Figures in parentheses represents percentages.

Table 12 depicts that 65 per cent of the respondents spent from Rs.10,000/- to Rs. 40,000/- per year. About 23 per cent spent more than Rs. 40,000/- per year. Among the industrial category the tailoring unit entrepreneurs (60 per cent) and vegetable unit entrepreneurs spent more than Rs. 40,000/- per year than any other respondents. 30 per cent of the petty shop owners spent least amount (Rs. 10,000/-)

(*t*) Savings of the Respondents

The savings patter of the respondents is shown in Table 13. Saving habit indicates the performance of entrepreneurs in their enterprises. The enterprises, which run efficiently and profitably earn more income, hence savings. Ratio is also high as such, the tiny industrial entrepreneurs of our study area also save money from their income. Almost all respondents have a habit of saving money, whether it is a small amount or big amount. The women entrepreneurs save money from Rs. 5000/- to Rs. 25,000/- per year. However a majority (60 per cent) of them have saved Rs. 5000/ - per year. More than 40 per cent of the tailoring unit women entrepreneurs save upto Rs. 25,000/- This indicates that the women occupying in tailoring are efficient and manage to save whatever earnings they have. The beauty parlour owners save less than Rs. 50,000/-.

Table 13 : Savings pattern of the Respondents

Sl.No	*Respondents Category*	*Saving in Rs./ Year*			*Total*
		Less than 5,000	*5,000-15,000*	*15,000-25,000*	
1.	Petty shop	1 (100)	7 (70)	2 (20)	10 (100)
2.	Tailoring	-	6 (60)	4 (40)	10 (100)
3.	Hotel	3 (30)	5 (50)	2 (20)	10 (100)
4.	Vegetable	1 (12.5)	7 (87.5)	-	8 (100)
5.	Beauty parlour	4 (80)	1 (20)	-	5 (100)
	Total	9 (21)	26 (60)	8 (19)	43 (100)

Source: Primary data collected from the field in the month of January 2005.
Note: Figures in parentheses represents percentages.

Discussion

The study has brought out the relationship between various factors that has influenced the women to carry out an economic activity to survive and achieve something in life. It is felt that educational status in fact, influences their socio-economic development as it accelerates the social status attainment, and also provides exposure to new and innovative ideas of wider choice of economic and social concern and off-familial commitment and proving thus to be the conditioning factors which limit their fear in the path of entrepreneurship.

It is observed from the study that majority of the respondents are new to their respective endeavor and are coming under the category of first generation entrepreneurs.

As this study of small enterprises owned by the women entrepreneurs, there are no branches and also due to lack of finance, resources and manpower they are not in a position to own another unit and so, they are only concentrating in one unit.

It is also observed from the study that after starting the unit by the respondents, no one has incurred any loss till date. The reason for their success is the full support and co-operation received from their family members and also good rapport with their customers as all know that consumer satisfaction is the mantra or secret of success.

According to the respondents there is a bright prospect for their unit. The only limiting factor is finance, if it is made available to them, they can easily modernise their unit and as a result their business will shine like anything in the future.

Policy Suggestions

1. There is a need to re-examine the educational structure and the entrepreneurial development with respect to women by the Government.
2. The effects of cultural and economic bias against the education and training of girls and women now require extra measures in order to compensate for past neglect and to enhance the productive capacities of the women.
3. We must establish special recruitment, training and extension programmes of development agencies at all levels, including professional fields from which women have been traditionally excluded.
4. The women folk should be given proper information regarding the avenues for revenue and other credit facilities, financial incentives and above all subsidies.

5. The government should lend a helping hand in the form of providing raw materials and marketing facilities to the women entrepreneurs in order to avoid the problem of procurement and brokers and middle men.
6. Proper guidance based on scientific inputs, suitable product ideas, product identification, market-survey and project formulations should be given in order to have an effective sustainable development and technology transfer for the women entrepreneurs.

Conclusion

To conclude, it may be pointed out that women entrepreneurs have the capacity and potentiality to develop and control an enterprise of their own. The only prerequisite is, they should be given proper guidance and encouragement in the form of moral support from their own family members as well as from the society, Government and other institution. Given such situation, the women entrepreneurs can show their business capability not only in India but also in the global arena.

REFERENCES

1. Khanka, S.S., "*Entrepreneurial Development*", S.Chand & Company Ltd., New Delhi, 2003.
2. Manimekalai. M., and R. Ganesan, "Global Women Entrepreneurs Profile: An analysis", *Southern Economist*, July 15, 2001.
3. Sunder, K., J.Gupta, and Syzil Ali, "Women Entrepreneurship in India", *Jagriti,* April 1, 2002.

Chapter 22

EMPOWERMENT OF WOMEN THROUGH INFORMATION AND COMMUNICATION TECHNOLOGY : BARRIERS IN DEVELOPING COUNTRIES

*Dr. U. Arabi

ABSTRACT

This chapter gives an account of I.T enabled business opportunities that could help women empowerment. As per the prediction, more profitable opportunities exist for women's small scale enterprises in business-to-business and business-to-government markets. I.T. enabled communication business offer much promise for women Grameen phone in Bangladesh, Teleboutiques in Senegal and Morocco and Phone shops in Ghana are few to quote. But availability of credit education, skills, and training, access to technologies and foreign languages are some of the constraints the women entrepreneurs may encounter. The author also gives some suggestive measures to overcome all those problems.

Introduction

Communication is indispensable for all endeavours to bring about a societal change. The emergence of Information Communication Technology (ICT) has enabled to collaborate, interact and disseminate information in a fast pace which has brought a greater impact on society. The ICT is a diverse set of technological tools and resources to create, disseminate, store, bring value-addition and manage information. In fact Internet Technology has redefined the way we communicate, live, work

* Reader, Department of Studies & Research in Economics, Mangalore University, Mangalgangothri, Karnataka-574 199.

and conduct our business. Traditionally the organizations which operated in a face-to-face context are now increasingly engaged in virtual communications supported by a wide range of ICT including e-mail, teleconferencing, mobile technology, videoconference etc. ICT makes the role of time and distance less significant in organizing business and production related activities. Thus the role of ICT and e-commerce in driving the global economy is now widely recognized.

ICT and the Internet reach many people, have a wide geographical coverage and are efficient in terms of time and cost. They facilitate access to markets, commercial information, new processing technologies and knowledge. But do women have equal access to these new technologies and the Internet? Does e-commerce enhance business opportunities for women, especially in the developing countries? What are some of the promising new employment opportunities for women in the ICT sector, or does it replicate patterns of segregation elsewhere in the job market? These are some of the issues largely posing, as the barriers in entering the women in to ICT sector require policy measures in the developing economy.

In the developing world the use of ICT and e-commerce is attractive to women owning small enterprises and these female entrepreneurs are now able to use ICT to identify new business opportunities or communicate with potential clients. New IT business run by women have emerged along the models of teleboutiques or telecentres of Senegal and Morocco, phone shops in Ghana, Internet cafes or kiosks in Thailand and Malaysia, and the Grameen Phone in Bangladesh. The Grameen Phone in Bangladesh has been cited as a successful example of women entrepreneurship, where financing from the Grameen Bank allowed women to buy cell-phones and provide mobile pay phone services in their shops or local markets at a mutually agreed mark-up with Grameen Telecom. These IT-enabled business have the advantages of low capital and skills requirements. The ICT industry has been the principal contributor to increase the real standard of living of people in the industrialized world five-fold. Apart from telephone services, women's handicrafts business also be developed using business-to-consumer (B2C) e-commerce. B2C endeavours have been found in South Asia, Latin America, Africa and the Middle East in the areas of clothing, bakery, gifts and other handmade products. Using the Internet, women are able to tap into new markets while saving time and money otherwise spend on travelling or selling in the local markets. For small home-based business the Internet offers information and networking opportunities that could make these endeavours profitable rather than marginal. The ability of women to earn income at home while raises a family – with the technology to communicate inexpensively with customers around the world, and handle accounting and order processing online – is adding to the attraction of the Internet for women business owners.

As a result of the technology, a high proportion of jobs outsourced by big firms are going to women. Women therefore can work from anywhere and at anytime and raise that extra income to become more financially independent and empowered. Recently companies like Ford and General Electric have moved their back-end operations to Asia and employ a large number of women workers having basic information technology and data management skills. New areas of employment such as tele-marketing, medical transcription etc. have also opened up tremendous job opportunities for women. These jobs are definitely under-paid and fall at the lower segment of ICT jobs; nevertheless, they are opening up avenues where none existed before. Significantly, the process of initiating knowledge networking by itself creates jobs in developing countries and a number of women get employed in such jobs. Thus, women over time have learnt the advantages offered by ICT and its potential in opening up windows to the outside world. This has put them in a greater control over the activities performed by them by laying the foundation for entrepreneurship development.

Information Technology (IT) Revolution – A Tool for Empowerment

Technology is the non-linear tool available to humanity, which can affect fundamental changes in the ground rules of economic competitiveness. Technology consists of stages like research and development, technology transfer, technology absorption and production of products or systems with the desired performance, quality, and cost-effectiveness. In the case of India, progress in technology, particularly indigenous design, is the thrust area to enable India to become competitive with other countries. Hence technology empowers the nation. (Abdul Kalam, 2006). Information technology (IT) has become a potent force in transforming social, economic, and political life globally. Without its incorporation into the information age, there is little chance for countries or regions to develop. More and more concern is being shown on the impact of those left on the other side of the digital divide – the division between the information “haves” and “have nots.” Most women within developing countries are in the deepest part of the divide – further removed from the information age than the men. It is imperative to ensure that women in developing countries understand the significance of these technologies and use them. If not, they will become further marginalized from the mainstream of their countries and of the world. It is essential that gender issues be considered early in the process of the introduction of information technology in developing countries and not as a corrective measure afterwards. It can be an important tool in meeting women's basic needs and can provide the access to resources to lead women out of poverty.

IT can offer significant opportunities for virtually all girls and women in developing countries, including poor women living in rural areas. However, their ability to take advantage of these opportunities is contingent upon conducive policies; an enabling environment in their countries to extend communications infrastructure to where women live, and increased educational levels. In other words, the ITC can be a viable sector through which the empowerment of larger women population could be envisaged. The empowerment process is one where women find time and space of their own, and had begun to re-examine their lives critically and collectively. They enable women to look at old problems in new ways, analyze their environment and situation, recognize their strength, alter their self-image, access new kinds of information and knowledge, acquire new skills and initiate action aimed at gaining greater control over resources of various kinds. In a way, the term empowerment is often used to describe a process whereby the powerless or dis-empowered people gain a greater share of control of resources and decision-making.

As far as the women empowerment is concerned, it is about gaining autonomy and control over one's life, which includes many dimensions such as, economic, social and political. Comprehensively, "women empowerment is a state of being that reflects a certain level of critical consciousness about external realities and an awareness about their internal though construction and belief systems that affect their well being in terms of gender justice; as well as the determination to use their physical, intellectual, emotional and spiritual resources to protect their lives and sustain values that guarantee gender equity at personal, social, economic, political and institutional level". The single most resource that liberates people from poverty and empowers them is "knowledge". At this juncture, it is essential to see the possibilities of women's empowerment through 'knowledge'. And this knowledge is passed by Information Technology. The need to use information technology in empowering women can be understood in two fold manner. Access to information is the key for economic, social and political empowerment of women. So far no other technology claimed to have given the instant, uncensored, practically feasible, economically viable information to the women folk than the information technology. The IT poses new forms of learning, education, health services, livelihood options, governance mechanisms and e-commerce options which would lead to the ultimate goal, i.e., women's empowerment. Hence the use of IT will be a necessary condition, if not sufficient one for the women's empowerment.

The second reason why IT should be used for women's empowerment is something to do with the digital dive between the information "have" and "have not". Women within developing countries like India are in the deepest part of the digital divide. The gender gap in the digital divide is perhaps the most neglected issue in recent times. If access and use of information technology is directly linked to social and economic development, then it is imperative to ensure that women in India, understand the significance of IT and use them. If not, lack of access to information technology becomes a significant factor in the further marginalisation of women from the economic, social and political mainstream of our society. This necessitates the condition whereby women have to make use of information technology, not only for getting them empowered but also for avoiding further marginalization.

Following the Okinawa Summit in August 2000, the Group of Eight nations set up a Digital Opportunities Taskforce to work on ways on eliminating the divide. Moreover, the United Nations places access to information technology as the third most important issue facing women globally, after poverty and violence against women. Although women in developing countries have had little contact yet with the new technologies, it is clear that there are many opportunities to improve the lives of women and their families. The options offered by information technology have to be seized deliberately because the cost of not doing so is very high. The technology is not a panacea for women's problems in developing countries, since IT can bring threats and challenges along with opportunities. In general, IT offers many new possibilities that offer women in developing countries a lifeline for economic, social and political empowerment.

Economic and Political Empowerment through IT

The new information economy offers many possibilities for new IT-enabled business that women could establish or in which they could work. Women's handicrafts can find niche markets, but marketing and management skills are needed, and supply and delivery problems must be addressed. Some successful developing country e-business have targeted their Diaspora markets and taken advantage of local delivery. More profitable opportunities exist for women's small-scale enterprises in business-to-business and business-to-government markets.

Women farmers could greatly increase productivity using ICT to assist them in their current economic activities, including farming, trade, and entrepreneurship, to obtain information on improved technologies in agricultural inputs, weather and markets and disseminate information about their business. For instance, School girls from the local communities who generally learn computer skills rapidly could be trained to serve as information intermediaries for the older women.

IT-enabled communications business offer much promise for women entrepreneurs, following the model of Grameen Phone in Bangladesh, teleboutiques in Senegal and Morocco, and phone shops in Ghana. Given high demand, low capital and skills requirements, these businesses are within the reach of many women in developing countries, if their country has the necessary enabling environment permitting the establishment of such business. Availability of credit, particularly in the form of micro credit, is a necessity for women to enter such business. For employment in core sector information technology jobs, women in developing countries need to acquire the necessary training to move into more technical, better-paying, cognitively oriented jobs. While degrees in science and technology are the entry tickets to the higher end of using and producing information technology, women can master many aspects of computer use and maintenance with much less training, with much of it available outside the formal education system.

Political empowerment still remains a distant dream for Indian women. Information technology can contribute to the political empowerment of women as tools for networking women to perform social and political advocacy, to strengthen women's participation in the political process, to educate, and to disseminate indigenous knowledge. IT is particularly useful in increasing the transparency and accountability of government.

Gender Difference in IT Education and training

Women in developing countries do not yet find it easy to obtain suitable jobs or income-generating work in the fields of network management, web design or software development, because they are not equipped with the necessary skills. The explanation does not necessarily lie in discrimination against women in centres of education and training in developing countries. In developing as well as in developed countries, there are difficulties in attracting and retaining women in ICT training and education. An example used by Taggart and O'Gara (2000) from the experience of Cisco's international Networking Academy Program (CNAP) provides some answer to why women's participation in IT training has been minimal. Female enrolment in IT courses is lower in both U.K and Philippines countries. However, in the Philippines, where employment and career prospects are more limited than in the United Kingdom, opportunities for overseas work depict a higher proportion of women graduating in ICT. While women lack behind their male counterparts in ICT enrolment, they are ahead of male in terms of the number of computer graduates.

Given the scenario of a prevailing IT skills shortage and the increasing trend towards business activities and corporate functions becoming IT-based, another manifestation of the gender digital divide is the lack of adequate representation of women in the higher echelons of IT-related jobs. Few women are actual producers of information technology as Internet content providers, web designers, software programmers or computer trouble shooters (Hafkin and Taggart, 2001). In the United States, female comprises a minority in mid to upper-level IT-related jobs, notwithstanding the fact that 50 per cent of Internet users in the country are women (Taggart and O'Gara, 2000). For instance, only 9 per cent of engineers, 28.5 per cent of computer programmers and 26.9 per cent of systems analysts in the United States are female. Women, however, reportedly constitute the majority (85 percent) of data entry workers. Moreover, there are gender disparities in the salaries between men and women in IT in the United States. According to Taggart and O'Gara, women in IT career jobs earn 67 per cent of what their male counterparts earn. It is to be expected that this disparity would be much wider in developing countries. According to them women trainees in an ICT school in Brazil, enrol work in word processing courses that would prepare them for support and secretarial positions. In contrast, the networking or programming courses are predominantly attended by their male counterparts, who would thus obviously be equipped for higher-paying jobs and more remunerative career paths of IT are not sufficient indicators of equitable participation of women in the information society. Instead, what should be looked is how women use at the Internet and what skills they are equipped with, as these would determine their role in and contribution to the digital economy. In order to meet the impending skill shortages in critical areas, women must therefore be prepared for careers at all levels of the ICT sector, from data entry to software design, network management and IT entrepreneurship. In considering how ICTs and the Internet could benefit women economically and socially, policy-makers should think beyond women selling their crafts via the web, to women selling their skills as website designers, network managers or IT service consultants.

Access to Internet Technologies

Recently many researchers and policy makers have expressed concern that inequality in access to Internet technology will increase the existing polarity between countries as well as between groups within a country. In such a digital divide, gender issues will receive greater attention. However access to infrastructure alone, in the absence of access to market and skills will not enhance participation in e-commerce. Human resource development issues that focus on technical and marketing skills should perhaps feature as prominently as infrastructure in a policy framework. The cost of infrastructure, however, is likely to remain a major issue for both women and men, particularly in the poorer countries. In Bangladesh, for example, the cost of a computer equals nearly two years' salary for a professional person, and a modem costs more than a cow (Mitter, 2001). The collective use of telephone and Internet facilities to some extent of assistance, or might help, traditionally disadvantaged groups, such as women, to overcome the challenges of infrastructure constraints. The use of cyber kiosks and Internet cafes are examples of collective use facilities that come from the market-oriented private sector. Tele centres present possibilities of collective use with subsidies and support from donor agencies and the public sector. Concerns about bandwidth are often overlooked in the discussion of collective use. To conduct e-commerce in a sustainable and efficient way, it is not enough to have connectivity – the right amount of bandwidth is also needed. Developing countries generally lag behind the developed ones in a dramatic way in terms of access to bandwidth. According to the ITU (2002), there is an uneven distribution of bandwidths among countries – for example, the 400,000 citizens of Luxembourg between them have more international Internet bandwidth than Africa's 760 million citizens. Given their position in the economy and in society in the poorer parts of the world, it is likely that woman more than men will have problems in having access to adequate bandwidth necessary for conducting e-commerce. This is an issue that policy makers should be concerned with. Some preliminary indicators provided by Hafkin and Taggart (2001) show that of the total number of Internet users in 2000, women accounted for 22 per cent in Asia, 38 per cent in Latin America and 6 per cent in the Middle East.

Most women Internet users in almost all developing countries are not representative of women in the country as a whole, but rather are part of small, urban educated elite. In many developing countries, less than one percent of the population male or female – has Internet access. By regions, women are 22 percent of all Internet users in Asia, 38 percent of those in Latin America, and six percent of Middle Eastern users. No regional figures by sex are available for Africa. E-mail is the major information technology application that women's organizations and individual women in developing countries use. But, time constraints as well as bandwidth limitations make Web use difficult for women. Few women are producers of information technology, whether as Internet content providers, programmers, designers, inventors, or fixers of computers. In addition, women are also conspicuously absent from decision making structures in information technology in developing countries.

Of the more than 300 million people connected to the Web worldwide, only 3.2 million or just over one percent live in Southeast Asia. Globally, UNDP reports that more than three quarters of Internet users live in high income countries which contain 14% of the world's population. Asia as a region has a reasonable presence in the map of internet users and it may have a more impressive record in the future. The International Data Corporation reported that 90% of Internet usage is located in industrialized countries, where about 60% are already dominated by the USA and Canada. However, with an annual growth rate of 38% by 2005 the forecast is that US would fall to third place in terms of Internet usage, trailing behind Asia-Pacific, which would capture 27% of the market and Europe, which would garner more than 30%. However, aggregate statistics on the rapid deployment of telecommunication infrastructure and facilities within Asia and the Pacific are misleading. The region is vast and diverse with heights and depths in terms of ICT. For example, apart from spectacular progress made in China, Singapore, Taiwan, South Korea, and Japan, the rest of the Asia-Pacific countries are languishing. At the present rate of development, Bhutan, for example, would take until 2050 to achieve the tele-density that Singapore has today. The International Telecommunication Union reports that fewer than two in ten thousand Cambodians and Vietnamese use the Internet, while nearly four out of every ten Singaporeans use the Internet (See Figure 1). In the context of inter and intra-regional inequalities which exist in access to internet technologies and this digital divide is also found within a country. For example, among India's 1.4 million Internet connections, more than 1.3 million are in the five states of Delhi, Karnataka, Maharashtra, Tamil Nadu and Gujarat.

Even in these states, women as well as men in the rural and in semi-urban areas are generally excluded from the opportunities of the digital economy. Prospects for women in rural areas need to be evaluated in the light of this inequality. Desagregation of Internet usage by sex, even in urban areas, is difficult to obtain and available data is unreliable and not comparable with other countries. However, even if the figures are not reliable, the numbers of women Internet users are certain to be miniscule and insignificant. In most countries aggregated statistics show an insignificant proportion of Internet access for the entire population (See Figure 1).

Figure-1: Internet Users per 10, 0 00 people

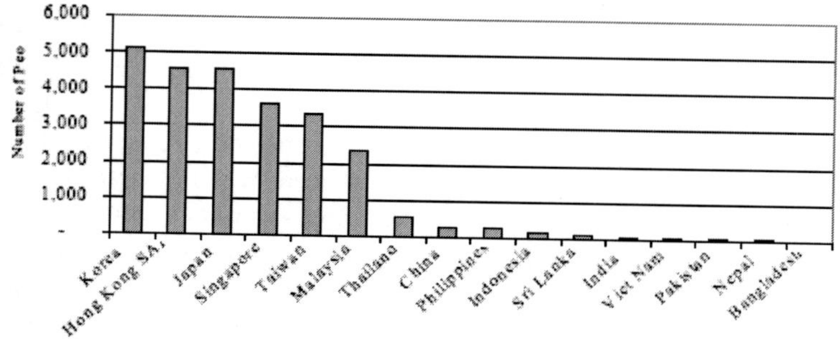

Source: World Telecommunication Development Report 2002, ITU

The ITU recently released some statistics on female internet usage in its Telecommunications Outlook, see Figure- 2. However, there is no information regarding, whether women use internet for trade or business.

Figure-2: Total Internet users and female internet users

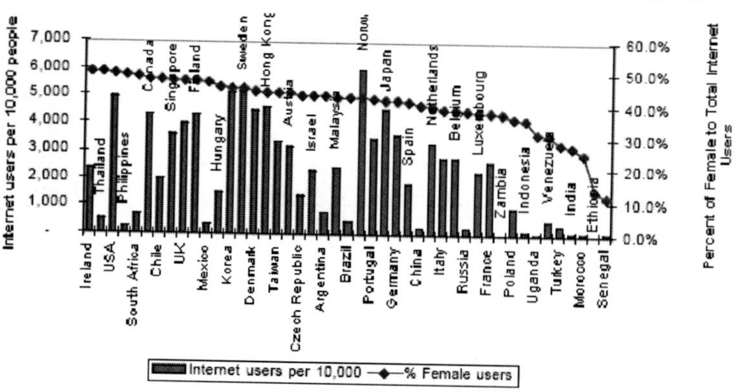

Source: ITU, 2002.

There are some signs that the gender gap is narrowing in certain countries. In the US and Canada, women have recently overtaken men in their use of the Internet at 51 per cent, while in Singapore, Chile, Hong Kong, Iceland and Thailand the percentage of women users has increased in the last few years to between 47 and 49 per cent. In several countries, such as China, South Africa and the Scandinavian countries, the percentage of women users is at or over 40%. But even in countries with a high use of ICT, women users are often greatly outnumbered by men. For example, in India, male Internet users outnumber women 77:23.31.

It should also be remembered that in developing countries where women's representation is high, users represent a very small elite, often less than 1 percent of the population.32 Women's participation in the IT sector is also low. In the US, where women have the greatest representation as Internet users, their participation in IT-related employment lags far behind men. According to UNIFEM, women hold 9 percent of mid- to upper-level IT related jobs in engineering and make up 28.5 percent of computer programmers and 26.9 per cent of system analysts. Only among data entry workers do they form the majority at 85 percent. Research carried out for Cisco Systems in the UK found that even if the number of women in the computer networking industry in Western Europe doubles by 2004 to 94,000 women, they would still constitute only just over 7 percent of the workforce.33

Nevertheless, in some developing countries, computer science is seen as more appropriate for women. Kandaswamy noted that in India there is a comparatively strong participation of women in the IT and software industry as well as other technology careers. The enrolment of women in technical institutions has increased in the last 20 years from just 5 per cent to 45 per cent. 90,000 women engineers graduate in the ICT fields from colleges in the 4 southern states each year, and in fact it is seen as a more feminine field than other engineering disciplines. This is in contrast to the US and Canada, where enrolment of women in computer science has been decreasing for several years. The reasons for the increased participation of women in the IT sector in some developing countries are not entirely clear. Some factors could include socio -cultural attitudes which allow or promote women's participation in S&T and IT; (in the case of India) a national strategy to promote an IT workforce as well as national information society; and nature of the national education system.

Barriers to Women's Participation in the IT Sector

Despite the great potential for job creation and development, only those who can afford the new technologies, and have the skills to use them, will benefit, while the poor risk being marginalized. Given that women make up the large majority of the poor worldwide, any strategy to increase their participation in the digital economy would increase national capacity and help raise the national standard of living. The large majority of women in developing countries are "employed" by the informal economy (street vendors or women working at home on, for example handicrafts and sewing). Reaching these women will be the major challenge for policy makers trying to bridge the digital – and particularly the gender digital – divide. Among the key barriers faced by women are access to education, skills and training, access to the technologies themselves (both hardware and connectivity) and other constraints such as those related to knowledge of foreign languages (i.e. access to Internet content) or lack of financial resources to acquire access.

Women experience low rates of access to information and communication technologies for a number of reasons, ranging from socio-cultural attitudes and preconceptions about women's interaction (or lack of) with technology to a lack of understanding of the resource and situational obstacles experienced by women. Specific barriers include literacy and education, domestic responsibilities, training, language, time, cost, and the value to women of the information carried by ICT. Research and analysis on the effects of development on women, specifically development technologies, has found that gender biases exist in determining who receives technologies and who receives the education, credit and other resources for technologies. A series of constraints to women's use of technologies and their participation in the knowledge society follow from or exacerbate the results of gender misperceptions framing ICT implementation. In general, women are more likely to lack basic literacy and computer skills. Girls are less likely than boys to enroll in maths and computer science courses. Socio-cultural barriers to the education of girls and women in science, maths and technology further restrict their interaction with technology as well as their entrance into S&T fields

Internet Language

One of the most important impediments to women's engaging in ICT-enabled employment possibilities is often geared to the life cycle and aspirations of men. Women, particularly of childbearing age, find it difficult to cope with the training given either by employers or by private sector institutions. The drop-out rate for women even in the high-skilled software services sector has been alarming, even in areas where there is a need for trained personnel (Arun and Arun, 2002; Ng, 2001).

The dominance of English as the language of the Internet represents a serious problem for the majority of the world's population, which does not speak English. Women without access to formal schooling that allows them to learn foreign languages are again marginalized, but so are men in countries or regions where English is not "the" language, such as Latin America, the Middle East, French-speaking Africa and Eastern Europe. According to Hafkin and Taggart (2001), language was among the main barriers to Internet usage that women cited in their response to the Association for Progressive Communications (APC) Women's Networking Survey in 1996. Even where women do have equal access to formal schooling, they may need to receive additional training in foreign language skills, for which time and resources will be scarce.

Hafkin and Taggart (2001) also noted that "even users with basic proficiency in English experience discomfort that discourages Internet use when using other than their native language". They cited a technical training programme conducted in Mexico, which discovered that users with a low English proficiency level were reluctant to access online help centres simply because it was in English.

Education, Skills and Training

The gender digital divide is usually greater in countries where women have less access to education than men. According to the UN, in 2000 women made up nearly 2/3 of the world's 876 million illiterates. Hence, in countries where girls are excluded from the basic education system or prevented from continuing beyond primary school levels, they are also excluded from gaining access to the new technologies and learning how to use them (given that an increasing number of countries use their basic education system to improve digital literacy and enhance access to ICT); they are also excluded from acquiring foreign languages, another essential prerequisite for effectively using many new ICT and the Internet. Even where women do have access to basic education, few women pursue careers in IT professions. In both developed and developing countries (with a few exceptions such as the Philippines) there are difficulties in attracting and retaining women in IT training and education. Hence, for women to move into high-skilled IT employment, efforts need to be made to increase the number of female in IT training.

Education is considered to be by far the most important policy intervention to improve the ability of girls and women in developing countries to participate in the information society. The key strategy would be to focus attention in generating demand for IT education from the women themselves through awareness programmes. Exposing girls to computers and the Internet at early stages should be initiated by governments, particularly education ministries, before gender stereotypes start to influence female attitudes. In a number of developing countries such as Thailand, Malaysia, South Korea and Taiwan, governments have started incorporating ICTs in the educational agenda, specifically in equipping primary and secondary schools with computers and other basic infrastructure needed to access the Internet. These could be useful measures to enhance digital literacy and stimulate the use of ICT among girls at early stages.

Availability of Finance

Apart from access to infrastructure and education (skills), lack of capital is the other key obstacle facing woman (especially women entrepreneurs) wishing to engage in e-commerce and e-business. To start ICT-enabled business or to employ ICT tools to enhance existing business, women will need capital from special financial institutions in developing countries that lend specifically to women entrepreneurs who have no collateral, and who work mostly in the informal sector. The most likely source of the necessary financial capital could be micro credit schemes that specifically target women because of high take-up and repayment experiences and social dividends reaped from lending to them (Hafkin and Taggart, 2001). In this sense, ICT-enabled business are no different from other traditional micro enterprises in which women in developing countries are engaged. They both involve light-based manufacturing, trade, or service activities; employ about five people or less, mostly family members; have low barriers to market entry; are home-based; and require less professional experience and knowledge than those of their male partners. The only differentiating factor is the use of new technologies. The micro finance or micro credit programmes are aimed at empowering women beyond just the setting up or expansion of micro enterprises. Specifically, micro credit schemes increase women's income levels and their economic independence, enhance their autonomy over household decisions about expenditure, promote positive attitudes to women's social and political roles in communities, and provide them with information and support networks to protect their individual and collective interests at the local and macro levels. The outreach of the world's largest micro credit schemes shows a varied performance ranging from a 100 per cent outreach in countries such as India, Malaysia, Bangladesh and Mali to less than 50 per cent in Uganda, Nigeria, Ethiopia, Nepal and France (see table 8 for a detailed description of the 34 largest micro finance schemes). These schemes could be useful entry points for policy makers in a programme aimed at facilitating women's opportunities in ICT related business. As described by Hafkin and Taggart (2001), among the two million borrowers of the Grameen Bank, who received wireless phones as an in-kind loan to village phone operators, 75 per cent are women. The operators resell the mobile phone service to fellow villagers, earning an average annual income of $300 as against the national average per capita income of $286. About 90 per cent of the women operators are married and have no formal education. The phone business can be managed simultaneously with another business or while doing household chores. The major advantages of this type of ICT-enabled enterprise are the minimal educational requirements (just some basic mechanical aptitude), and the small capital needed, enough to be supported by micro credit schemes. There are positive externalities also in accelerating rural development where telecommunication density is sparse. Another successful example of ICT-enabling business with a micro financing component is the use of smart cards by Indian women milk collectors in Rajasthan. The smart cards were used to record the quality, fat content and sales of milk to distributors and served as their bankbook, thereby empowering them to make spending decisions and increasing their profits while eliminating the middlemen (called *dhudhwala).*

Access to Technologies and Foreign Languages

In most countries, the typical Internet surfer used to be male, young (in particular in the developing countries), well educated and well off. This stereotype is changing, in some countries rapidly, in others slowly. While five years ago there was a significant gap between male and female users, with men accounting for the large majority of Internet users, women are catching up quickly in most developed and some developing countries, where growth rates of female Internet users are steeper than those of male users.

In the United States, most European, and some Asian countries, female Internet users have surpassed the 40 per cent mark, rapidly evening up the gender split. In Latin America, while only four years ago 75 per cent of Internet users were male, today the split is about 60 (male) to 40 (female). In some Asian countries, such as India or Indonesia, female Internet users account for ¼ to 1/3 of all Internet users. In Africa, the female shares of Internet users range from 37.5 per cent (Zambia) to 12 per cent (Senegal) and probably less in some of the poorer LDCs. In the Middle East and Arab countries shares of women Internet users are the smallest at the global level. In general, the gender digital divide is bigger in countries where women have less access to education than men (as is the case in many poor countries) and in those that for cultural or religious reasons discriminate against women. Here, women are still a small minority on the Internet.

Since women mainly access the Internet from home, and less from work, they need to have a PC and an Internet connection at home. This is only possible if costs for PCs and Internet access are low. In many developing countries, however, PCs and Internet connections are expensive and few households can thus afford to pay for them. This affects women more than men who may have access through their jobs or public places. Public entities that offer Internet access, such as schools, universities, Internet cafes and community centres are also often less accessible to women, who are often excluded from basic and higher education and who may for cultural and religious reasons have less access to public places.

The dominance of English as the language of the Internet has led to the exclusion of a majority of the world's population who does not speak English. Women without access to formal schooling that allows them to learn foreign languages are again marginalized, but so are men in countries or regions where English is not 'the' language such as Latin America, the Middle East, Francophone Africa, and Eastern Europe. Language has been cited by women as being one of the top barriers to Internet usage.

While the predominance of English is a threat to social inclusion of women in the digital economy, the increasing trend towards multilingual content also provides a digital opportunity in terms of language translation in software development and in web design in native languages.

The other implication of the predominance of English as the Internet language is the close correlation between outsourcing and English proficiency. The two top outsourcing markets, the United States and the United Kingdom are both English-speaking, hence those developing countries that would want to tap these markets would have to learn English. Companies that outsource normally list English proficiency as among the requirements aside from possessing an array of IT talent. This invokes some policy implications for improving schooling and literacy of women where a second language – English – should be learned.

Other Factors

Women's high representation in low-paid, non-formal sector employment militates against this form of access Domestic and reproductive responsibilities: Another important restriction for women is their domestic responsibilities, including daycare, childbearing and subsistence activities. Women's double and triple roles in the family and community mean that around the world their workday is consistently longer than that of men's, by two hours or more. As a result, time is a precious resource for women, and a major constraint to the use of ICT by women. They are less likely to have free time to use or learn to use the Internet. Any systems or activities meant to improve their lives and increase their empowerment must be perceived to save time or increase their efficiency, and be made available at flexible hours. Cultural attitudes and practices can preclude both opportunities for use of ICTs as well as training in their use, in restricting or prohibiting women's interaction with men in public and, in some areas; preclude women's travel outside the home. Additionally, in many cultures women and girls are considered to be less capable of understanding scientific and technical concepts.

In developing countries in Asia and Sub-Saharan Africa, women tend to outnumber men in rural areas; a result of male migration to urban centres for employment. Internet access is less available in rural areas as a result of lack of reliable infrastructure (electricity and phone lines) and the cost of setting up and maintaining equipment. Public and community access sites (including tele-centres and cyber cafes) can be a solution, but the few evaluations done to date indicate that women do not have the same rates of access as men. Public access is sometimes located in an environment where women do not feel comfortable or in locations women have difficulty traveling to. Cyber cafés, for example, often have a predominantly male customer base and tend not to provide a separate space for women. The natural geographical features-such as vast expanse of land area, scattered islands, and difficult terrain have combined with the intrinsic urban bias in development denying the benefits of technology to a vast majority of women in countries like India, Nepal, Indonesia and the Philippines

Strategies to Overcome Barriers

- The majority of women who have access today do so from research institutions, governments and some businesses. Access among poorer and rural classes is currently non-existent, but is critical for any developing country like India. A technical mix of transmission of old ICT"s with new ICT's combining networks, fax, telephones, radio, Television, computer communications and even WWW connectivity and connects them to larger off-line or low-tech dissemination networks should be made available. Information can be locally distributed by downloading from the Internet by a communications centre or NGO, through verbal interaction and education. Access needs to differentiate from connectivity and the government needs to engender the process so that it is not left to the individual women to make the access. Further interventions are needed to make connectivity accessible to the grassroots' women.
- Specific government commitments to gender equality set the stage for the adoption of transformative strategies that aim at ensuring that women's development priorities and needs are considered in all policy areas, including the many areas where ICT policy is relevant (e.g., gender equality, rural development, education, health and telecommunications universal access policy, among others). Thus governments needs to take this issue of women empowerment through ICT's as a priority issue and frame necessary policies in consultation with NGO's, grassroot workers, women themselves apart from ICT's specialists. This policy should be able to address issues like urban – rural bias, literacy levels, etc.

- There is a need to use a rights-based approach to ICT policy development, where everyone has the right to affordable access to ICTs. Only then we can work toward securing universal access to ICTs, and consequently promote and facilitate the use of ICTs for women's empowerment.
- Information about newer ICT's (computers & networking) can be disseminated through a proven effective dissemination medium like the radio, TV, street theatre, CD - ROMS and even music. The experience of the Zambia Association for Research and Development (ZARD), which downloaded information on the Fourth UN World Conference on Women and distributed it regionally, including to local libraries, is an example of the success of this kind of distribution system. One of the challenges in a system such as this, however, is filtering of information which naturally occurs as a result of the choice of the downloader concerning which information is important enough to distribute. This could be resolved by frequent consultation with the receptor groups. Another challenge is to produce content that is interesting to the viewer. Unless women perceive it to be useful and one that will add value to their daily lives, women will not come forward to attend these programmes as time is premium to her.
- Promote the enrolment of women in ICT programmes by providing incentives such as scholarships and awareness-raising activities.
- Language access must be addressed as a serious barrier to gender equity on the international ICT policy level. Language options have to be taken as a political issue, an issue that must be in the centre of policy decisions.
- ICT policy must rest on the understanding that technology must be adapted to fit the needs of women. The key issue is that the technologies should be adapted to suit women rather than that women should be asked to adapt to suit the technologies. Most policymakers are proceeding on the second premise. If they can be encouraged to think and act in terms of the first premise then we will ensure that ICTs become more "women-friendly" in terms of cost, access, applicability in different fields, etc.

There is a need to explore many more useful models of participation of the private sector in social development projects in order to reduce costs and make ICT accessible to women.

Suggestive Measures

1. Women's access to technology and training is a basic requirement for their participation in the global information economy. A focused and timely effort to provide women and girls with IT education and skills can enable them to compete successfully in the global information economy and play a leadership role in its development. Women must act as leaders in its development and as agents of change, using technology to accelerate their empowerment. If pursued thoughtfully and strategically, IT can position women as global leaders in the mainstream of those seeking development solutions in the information age
2. Training Programs may be designed specifically for women in IT so as to have a deep insight into the technology
3. Lower cost and maintenance networking technology may be explored and made available for women's usage
4. Better policies favouring women in IT field may be devised
5. Mentorship programs should be organized to connect women support for learning in appropriate settings where women are comfortable and safe, promotion of new initiatives to explore the possibilities of communication technologies; the capacity for women to access the internet and learning through their local women's centres, recognition and support for the women leaders in the community who can organize and build momentum for women's internet learning.
6. There is need for a support in the use of the internet as;
   (*a*) An awareness tool: to promote our issues, and support informational resources

   (*b*) A form of media: to develop ways of getting our voices out, extend electronic networking, women's radio online, communication inter-activities and

   (*c*) A way to engage in policy issues with the government; to prepare for civic participation, e-democracy, online consultations.
7. Measures need to be taken to ensure that women and women's organizations will be consulted by government on policy issues. At the same time there is a need to facilitate the development of women's capacity in understanding the technology and online consultation.

8. Collaboration amongst organization, sharing information and strategizing together enhanced by online capabilities-are important factors in effective participation on policy issues.
9. Building community online and learning from each other key to women's use of the internet for equality.
10. Participation in electronic networking can create a sense of learning together with women's organizations with similar goals which is a vital factor in building an empowerment environment

Conclusion

Government policies and programmes to facilitate support networking and career development for women in IT and telecommunications are inevitable in the digital divide era. IT jobs that are cerebrally – rather than physically-challenging, demands creativity, flexibility, teamwork and multi-tasking - all qualities at which women excel naturally in their everyday lives. ICT could moreover, enhance rural productivity. Access to market information via communication networks could help farmers make judicious and timely decision. ICT can provide access to rural finance, a facility indispensable for most entrepreneurs who are unable to undertake projects because of lack of information about credit facilities and methods.

More workshops and training programs need to be in place to address the digital divide, which is evident because of the lack of access women have to both the opportunity and accessibility to IT. The mainstreaming of gender in the socioeconomic development of the country, on the whole, needs to be addressed. This must be achieved in the areas of research, training, public education, access to credit, and sensitization. The educational level of the female has an impact on family health and nutrition, agricultural production, and fertility. Yet, there is a wide gender gap in education, which must be bridged. This can be enhanced through technology education. In sum, it is not technology that creates and perpetuates the digital divide that keeps women in low-paid, low-status jobs. Rather, the lack of training, cultural nuances, and stereotyping does so irrespective of the level of technology available.

Equitable access to ICT technology and the autonomy to receive and produce the information relevant to their concerns and perspectives are therefore critical issues for women. Women should be empowered by enhancing their skills, knowledge and access to information technology. This will strengthen their ability to combat negative portrayals of women internationally and to challenge instances of abuse of power of an increasingly important industry. Women therefore need to be involved in decision making regarding the development of the new technologies in order to participate fully in their growth and impact. The priority themes like supporting electronic networks, promoting strategic use of information and communication technologies among partner communities, developing information content and tools, lobbying and advocacy etc. thus have to be given an emphasis.

REFERENCES

1. Abdul Kalam (2006), "Technology Empowers the Nation", Productivity News, Vol. 44, No. 3, May-June, 2006, pp. 3
2. Arabi.U, (2005a), "Impact of "IT" on Women's work: Policy Implications on Employment in Developing World," Sedme, Vol, 32, No. 3, Sept., pp. 7-24
3. Arabi.U, (2005b), "Empowerment of Women in Information and Communication Technology (ICT)-Enabled Services; Opportunities and Challenges," The Asian Economic Review, Vol. 47, Dec., 2005, pp. 465-485
4. UNCTAD, (2002), E-Commerce and Development Report, United Nations, Newyork
5. UNCTAD,(2004), E-Commerce and Development Report, UN, Newyork, pp. 1-24

Chapter 23

ENTERPRISE AMONG FARM WOMEN IN INDIA AND UNDERSTANDING THEIR CONSTRAINTS : AN EXPLORATION OF NSSO'S HOUSEHOLD DATA

*Dr. Nilabja Ghosh

ABSTRACT

Women in agricultural households are doubly distressed. Despite hard work and high work participation, they suffer the deprivations that have become a lot to their gender and in addition, they encounter the vicissitudes of their households as agriculture presents indifferent performance and mounting pressure on India's limited land resources. The success of Indian economy in the post-reforms economic scenario rests with the enterprise and industry of the people. Diversification of farmwomen from traditional crop based agriculture to high valued agricultural and allied activities and enterprises with emerging prospect merit considerable attention in the current context. While advocating enterprise, it is important to remember the restraints faced by women in work participation imposed largely by the society and developmental shortfalls of the rural economies. This paper discusses the problems of women in agriculture and then analyses household survey data from NSSO to study the status of entrepreneurial activities among these women belonging to Indian farm households. The study identifies the industries of enterprise through the secondary data and the profile

* Institute of Economics Growth, University of Delhi Enclave, Delhi-110007, Ph. 91-11-2766-7424, Fax: 27667410, E-mal: nila@iegindia.org; nilabjag@yahoo.com.

of the enterprises and entrepreneurs. Further, the study also examines their dispersion across the states and state wise entrepreneurial tendencies and finds that the tendencies and choices are associated with various development indicators of the state with profound implications for gender. (210)

Introduction

In the days of liberalization India has achieved unprecedented high growth rates through the enterprise and industry of the people. However development of the country requires that the growth be 'inclusive' so that all sections of the population participate in the growth process and benefit from it. Women who make up half of human community are largely left behind in this development. A division of labor that had evolved in historical times and is of little relevance now essentially defines women's place and role in society. Despite demonstrations of women's success in various walks of life and most notably as entrepreneurs and managers in even India's corporate sector, large sections of women still live under the shadow of traditional social norms and resultantly suffer much more poverty, violence, subjugation and insecurity than men. Above all they remain as underutilized human resources.

Women in agricultural households are doubly distressed. Agriculture is the dominant sector in India in terms of livelihood and the rural sector that houses the agriculture accounts for 72 per cent of India's population. Farm households drawing support from agriculture either through cultivation or labour supply make up 65 per cent of the rural households. Women belonging to such households suffer the deprivations that have become a destiny to their gender and in addition, encounter the vicissitudes of their households as agriculture presents indifferent performance and mounting pressure on India's limited land resources. Diversification to high valued agricultural and allied activities and other enterprises have now become indispensable as a route to development in rural sector. Farm women participate relatively more in economic as well as semi-commercial activities although society and they themselves often do not recognize their contributions. The problems of farm women and the issue of diversifying them from traditional crop based agriculture to enterprises with emerging prospect merit considerable attention in the current context. Promoting enterprises among women from agricultural household is a way to empower them, to ameliorate the economic conditions of farm households and also to build up valuable productive assets under female ownership paving the way to a more gender balanced future when both men and women operate the enterprises of success. This paper uses NSSO's nation wide household survey data to examine the status of the women workers and entrepreneurs who come from farm household

Silent Distress

There has been no big revolution, in fact no hue and cry worth reporting made by the women from agriculture of the sector that supports about 60 per cent of Indian population. Yet academic discourses of researchers have gradually unraveled the silent distress that has become the destiny of nearly 50 per cent of Indian's women population for being born or linked to rural farm households. Work participation among rural women is known to be high at least compared to urban women but even this is not captured fully by our official surveys. They combine economic work on fields, animal sheds and village commons with household chores and the blurred distinction makes their contribution appear invisible. The women's own perceptions become 'adaptive' to social assessments Hirway and Roy (1999) and they are likely to report themselves as housewives even when they are no less 'farmers' by participation. Even as non-workers they perform a range of work for home that would be priced in a typically urban household. The poor amenities in most rural households, lack of cooking gas, electric connection, tapped water and sewerage mostly adds to women's burden of work for their household leaving little time and energy for income earning pursuits in contrast to the urban women. Above all the urban bias in the development that took place in Indian economy over the decades created little opportunity for rural people and especially the women to integrate into the modern economy.

A large number of rural households are poor and sometimes have little access to land. More than 80 per cent of the holdings belong either to the landless or to small farmers with no more than 2 hectares of land. For, survival women offer themselves as casual labour to neighboring farms. While men migrate to towns for earning, women suffer immobility due to household's responsibilities and lack of living facilities in towns. This possibly creates a relative abundance of female labour in rural markets. Women are hired for arduous, injurious and monotonous work and command discriminatingly lower wage rates (Kaur and Goyal, 1996, Sudha Rani et al, 1990). There are evidences that women suffer more deprivation and food insecurity than the man who are deemed as bread earners. Yet research has also shown that women's earnings can be more beneficial for the nutrition and health of the children (Kumar, 1978, Gulati, 1978) as men tend to spend on personal consumption such as alcohol. In case of death or illness of the male earner, or abandonment or sickness the responsibility falls on the women to support a household, increasing their distress and the children's vulnerability. The customary inheritance norm for land in India also makes women's status totally contingent on the land holding of the father or husband (Agarwal, 1994).

Yet growth or affluence of the household under the given social structure is no guarantee for betterment of women's conditions. Increasing affluence in agrarian families or increase in male earning is associated with women's withdrawal from the labour market and reduced labour supply (Bardhan, 1978; Dasgupta and Goldar, 2005), also inevitably increasing dependence and social subjugation. Unhappily, there is an apprehension that economic growth can lead to 'intensification of gender bias' (Dreze and Sen, 2003).

Agriculture has been growing at a lower rate compared to industry and services. The emergence of new prospective sectors and high growth rate of economy have now motivated the rural population to move from agriculture for higher income occupations. In a growing economies facing globalisation, men in rural labour force are found to move away from villages to urban areas with new opportunities while women stay back confined to agriculture in the process 'feminizing' agriculture. In India, there is a slight diversion of female workforce between 1993-94 and 19900 (table 1) but comparing 1987-88 and 1999-00 the share of male workforce fell while that of female rose in agriculture to reach 84 per cent.

Table 1: Employment in Usual Status of Women in India

Workers	*Rural*	*Urban*	*Rural*	*Urban*	*Rural*	*Urban*
Time	*1987-88*		*199394*		*1999-00*	
%Workers (PS+SS)	32.3	15.2	32.8	15.5	29.9	13.9
%Workers (PS)	24.5	11.8	23.4	12.1	23.1	11.7
%Unemployed (PS-adj)	2.4	6.2	0.9	6.1	1.0	5.7
%Undermployed (PS)	36.2	28.4	33.7	23.4	32.4	20.9
%Agriculture	82.5	21.8	84.7	19.3	84.1	14.6

Source: Employment and Unemployment Situation in India 1999-2000, NSSO.

Objectives, Data, Concepts and plan of paper

The issue of farmwomen's entrepreneurial activities can be only viewed in the broader context of the issues impinging on agricultural development and gender. The gender issues itself is a subject of a long debate involving academicians, activists and policy makers and often reflecting extreme and conflicting view points. At the same time agriculture has itself created a set of constraints and opportunities, which more often than not become significant for the male and female members of such households overriding mainstream gender issues viewed in isolation. Development aspects that transcend economic performance are also inextricably linked not only with entrepreneurial possibilities at all levels and for all citizens but also with gender. Lack of socio-economic development more often has proved greater obstacles for women than men and constraints generated by underdevelopment are unfortunately likely to be confused with gender constraints per se.

This paper examines the data provided by NSSO'S household survey to study the tendencies of entrepreneurship among farmwomen and its linkage with development through a cross-state analysis. Specifically the study will attempt to address the following concerns related to farmwomen workers:

(1) The occupational pattern and tendency for entrepreneurship among farmwomen.

(2) The broad categories of enterprises indulged in by farmwomen.

(3) Spatial dispersion of the enterprises and states accounting for larger share of entrepreneurs.

(4) The main socio-economic characteristics of the entrepreneurs.

(5) Possible association between women's entrepreneurship and the states' status with respect to gender relevant economic and social conditions of development relating to income infrastructure, health including reproductive health, awareness and household status of women.

This paper uses statistics obtained from analysis of unit level from National Sample Survey Organisation (NSSO)'s 55th Round household survey on Employment for 1999-00 comprising over three lakh rural household members responding to questionnaire slated as Schedule 10. We have made our specifications of various categories using the concepts employed by NSSO in the data. The different estimates are obtained by using weights as provided by NSSO. Because of its size of the survey, the data may be suffering to a degree of inadequate capturing of women's commercial and semi-commercial activities that micro level surveys could be more appropriate for. Nevertheless NSSO data is considered as the largest of its kind and most scientifically designed survey with uniformity of design and comparability across the country.

Farm households: Farm households are specified as households categorised by NSSO as *types* Agricultural labour and Self-employed in agriculture, which are essentially the type of work from which the households derived maximum income in the 365 days preceding the survey. Unless mentioned otherwise Usual Principal status employment is considered. Since the broad categorization made by NSSO relates to rural and urban sectors we used unit level data to isolate the farm households for our analysis.

Entrepreneurs: Workers are engaged in various activities signifying a range of income possibilities and security implications. We have specified Entrepreneurs as constituted of two status categories: (1) Own Account Workers comprising of those members who are self-employed in household enterprises with or without partner(s) and helpers but hiring no labor and (2) Employers who hire labor. Apart from entrepreneurs, members could work as unpaid family help, salaried/regular employee and casual wage labourers.

Industries: To identify the industry in which the member works National Industrial Classification (NIC1998)'s 5-digit and 3 digit codings provided by NSSO are interpreted. Specifically, agricultural and manufacturing entrepreneurs are focused on.

Gender, Agriculture and Policy

Gender, as an issue, remained to disturb human society from times immemorial and yet women in most societies and most parts of history stagnated at an inferior position. Worse, mainstream philosophers and theoreticians hardly addressed questions on intra-household domains such as why women stayed deprived of livelihood, esteem, education and skill. Majority of the thinkers being males, the gender bias was inevitable although a handful of them did confer some attention to women's position in society (Mill, Engels and Condorcet). The assumption of a unitary household prevented gender from entering the domain of conventional economic analysis for years (Sen, 2006) but many modern day thinkers now work with frameworks that have a space for gender. The capability approach of Sen (2006) and Nussbaum (1995) and measurements of human well-being of Narayanan, (2000) and Alkire and Black (1997) are some of these influential strains of thought. The capability approach has inspired the international community to set the goals of human development and gender development. In a second line of action the so-called feminists and activists have for long played a meaningful part in facilitating women's entry into economic life. The feminist movement had a significant role in changing laws of inheritance and in modifying working conditions in women's favour initiated in the west but finally affecting life all over the world. Some of their contributions relating to maternity, abortion and harassment in work place directly addressed the concerns of working women. In recent literature, powerful voices of feminism inspired writers are raised, rejecting the 'biology as destiny' argument for women's capabilities and the 'private public' gender demarcation (Fleur-Lobban and Billson, 2005) drawing from numerous examples of women's success even in fields traditionally occupied by men. The scholars contended that the reproductive role of women cannot account for life long differentiation (Verma, 1995) between the genders.

Men and women have rarely enjoyed equality in any society. In India tradition has ordained that women take care of households, a valuable service that is overlooked in all accounting protocols and mostly underestimated for that reason. Paradoxically, women in agriculture participate significantly in economic life too, mostly in a semi-commercial ambience and in close conjunction with household duties. Yet, sharing the social perceptions these women mostly accord themselves the status of housewives while as breadwinners and farmers the men enjoy more importance. Despite hard work the women are deprived of money income, esteem and security. A large number of farmwomen do considerable work as unpaid family help on family farms and enterprises. It is sometimes believed though without enough evidence that women initiated agriculture in a landmark contribution to human civilization. Some sociologists thought that women enjoyed much more prominence and independence in historical times but agrarian civilization brought their downfall.

In India, however a larger share than the self employed are women from landless or small holding household, who hire out their labour to other farms. In either capacity woman are allotted work that is repetitive, arduous and even injurious. They are manual operations and require little skill or decision power. This is society's decision that women are incapable of skill, decision or machine use. Further, even when men move out of the village in search if earning, because of household responsibilities women stay back and work in near by farms. This abundance and their lack of skill both contribute to low wages that are both unequal and discriminatory.

Further, Indian society illustrates the historical existence as well as a wide spatial variation in the patriarchal norms. The male dominated household structure where the men earn for family sustenance and women either work indoors or in own farm is widely noted by critics. The system confers a social prestige on a family from women's staying out of market. Although this is more common among the higher castes and classes, the practice is emulated by the others too encouraged by the unenviable state of rural market for female labour. Patriarchal norms are found to be stronger in many north Indian states and regardless of economic conditions, maladies like demographic backwardness, prevalence of violence and anti-female bias (Dreze and Sen,2003) have come in the way of women's work participation in many states of northern and central India.

Along with the tradition bound social norms and the women's spontaneous adaptation to them, the Indian government also have some complicity in maintaining the status quo of women's social position. The five year plans that guided India's progress and development started with an extremely narrow vision and till about the Sixth Plan, treated the household as the basic unit of development and implicitly went along with the preconceived idea that men were the only potential earning members of households. Women's issues however were gradually taken up in development but they were viewed more as targets of welfare than development, as bearer of children than as human resources of the country. Nevertheless, though directed at controlling population, welfare measures relating to women's education and reproductive (and child) health had valuable benefits for women's development as well. The international conference on women in Mexico in 1975 and international resolves had profound impact on India's planning approach as reflected in subsequent plans but emphasis on women's empowerment and employment, even seeking to channel one third of plan resources for development programmers for women's benefit. The tenth plan also treats women's empowerment as an issue of special significance.

Why Entrepreneurship may be Promoted

Based on the given background a number of reasons may be given why farmwomen's enterprise could be important.

(1) In a gender-neutral context, there is an urgent need for employment generation in the rural sector. Decelerating and slower growth of rural employment relative to urban, slowing pace of urbanization, gaps between income in agriculture and non-agriculture and between organized and unorganized sectors within the non-agricultural sectors are features that prophesy persistence of poverty and indicate that GDP growth may be by-passing a vast majority of the people (Sen and Jha, 2005) The result has been the prescription and initiation of an all India public works programme (NREG) in which 100 days of employment is guaranteed to a household. Although the NREG has attractive features like creation of rural assets and infrastructure and in-built gender concerns, such wage

employment of a casual nature may not escape the ills and discriminations of an open market of rural labour. The targeted scheme is for unskilled labour with low wage, is likely to face social stigma and is susceptible to monitor by the local powerful. Above all, it is inconsistent with the current spirit of fiscal restraints, enterprise, aspirations and free economy and is not a long term solution.

(2) Salaried employment has a small place among farm people especially the women. In particular not even 4 per cent of rural female workers are regular employees as compared to 38 per cent among urban female (NSSO, 1999-00). The recent growth process in the liberalized regime has been described as jobless growth (RIS, 2006.) It has created jobs for skilled and educated workers in modern service sectors but has done little for the vast majority of the unskilled or semi-skilled that find abundance in rural India.

Points number (1) and (2) provide some rationale why there is reason to explore the enterprise option to create self-employment and build up assets in keeping with the modern economy rather than depend on land. In other words diversification from agriculture is important for both men and women workers also implying transfer of productive assets to rural people and women that would be the engines of growth in a coming years.

(3) Women, further have several concerns to draw attention. First and foremost, government policies must attempt to integrate the neglected half of society into mainstream economy by enabling them to engage in economic or gainful activity as distinct from household and non-market activity and contribute to economic development (Dandekar, 1982). While men have a role in sharing the women's household burden, economic incentive in the form of income opportunity is itself a motivation for the men to be more cooperative and reject the age-old division of labour that goes against women. Women's success in various occupations and scientific and technological achievement in recent times making most jobs less intensive of physical strength provide further rational for their inclusion.

(4) Closely associated with the division of labour and women's economic participation is the issue of women empowerment. For many centuries women have been allotted only domestic duties, shielded from public life and market challenges and denied skills

and higher learning and access to income. The lack of monetary income whether they do or do not contribute in economic activities have generated underestimation of their worth in society and in their own eyes. In many cases women suffer denials and subjugation, even violence at home and in many others a patronization that keeps them powerless too. Empowerment through various means such as access to income would bring an internal opposition to the existing order whereby improvement in self-esteem, confidence communication and awareness would help in building up leadership and women's agency. The Indian governance system now allocates one third of the seats in local governments to women and looks forward to greater participation in state and national government.

(5) Women's earning possibilities have been found to have important benefits for household and children. Not only is the overall household income enhanced pulling up the living standards but also there are evidences that women spend more on family's and children's food and welfare than men. Women's economic activity will possibly act as insurance for agricultural risk and at the same time improve women's status at home.

(6) Women contribute significantly to household wellbeing but are likely to suffer more poverty and are vulnerable to greater insecurity from desertion, accident and widowhood. In a land scarce country land distribution could hardly be a solution and in times of technological progress and marker led growth capability advancement should mean much beyond possession of land.

(7) Women from poorer households and households with no or little land often hire themselves out as casual labour in discriminating and poor terms, which in turn discourages women from participating once their male kin's earnings increase An alternative employment market offering a reasonable minimum earring could be a way to turn rural labour market in favour of women.

(8) Feminists have minimized the working difference between men and women. Whether we go with such an extreme view or not, there is ample reason to believe the differences due to the reproductive role have come down. Scientific development in abating women's special difficulties, the gradual fall in statistics total fertility rate (TFR) and infant mortality ratio (IMR) and the awareness about birth control measures are some of them.

Nevertheless, reality shows that women prioritize childcare and household management, functions that are partly natural but transitory and partly made a burden by social and governmental forces and failures. Enterprises, particularly drawing on local resources could require less mobility, be more consistent with women's way of life and confer greater benefit through linkages on rural economy under given conditions.

Constraints on Entrepreneurship: A view of Indian States

We have noted that farmwomen as entrepreneurs face compounded constraints generated by the occupation in agriculture, their rural residence and their gender roles. In profound interrelation among these aspects, there are important ways in which the general development status of a spatial unit can be particularly relevant for women, their pursuit of income earning activities and enterprise. In the current practice of job specialisation in society women are allotted duties directly for the consumption in households. Women currently spend considerable time in household chores that not only include cooking food, caring for family members and washing and drying activities but also arranging for water and fuel (Table A1). Unless earning opportunities grow it may not be realistic to expect a significant change in the division of labour among the households as things are. It is also useful to remember that among the rural households yet more than 90 per cent do not use LPG as cooking fuel and a large 64 per cent gather firewood for the purpose, this time consuming task being left mostly to women. Again, more than 30 per cent of rural households have no access to water in premises by taps or even hand pumps and it is predominantly the women who fetch water, often from a considerable distance and in competition with other women in semi-arid areas that suffer from water scarcity. Nearly 80 per cent have no bathroom in the house. Electricity is not only an important input for industry such as manufacturing but also in domestic life, making many household operations mechanized and hence swift, efficient and easier, releasing time for income earning. Although most villages are electrified, more than 44 per cent households do not have electricity connection. Women are particularly dependent on good infrastructure combined with law and order and safety for an active life. Unfortunately, the biological constraint on women becomes clear in this matter if one considers the fear of rape, harassment and trafficking. The credit delivery system, like the public extension system, also historically overlooked women, implicitly assuming men's superiority in credit use and it is now more and more realized that the simple effort at diversion of a quantum of credit to women entrepreneurs through Self Help Groups or otherwise could be gainful as also benefit the same households even while raising the esteem the women can command at home.

Yet as entrepreneurs, women's enterprises can also like any other enterprise depend on demand and supply linkages of development and the standard of infrastructure. The rural areas particularly fall back in economic development and infrastructure and certain states are more advances in these respects than others. Such attributes draw investment from organized sector and further benefits but there are signs the spatial dispersion of growth performance across Indian states has worsened after reforms (Bhattacharya and Shaktivel, 2003).

Tables A2.1 and A2.2 provide statistics on different groups of indicators bearing on development and women's position for 21 major states and state groups in India for which information is available. The states are considered in their pre-bifurcation states so that Bihar includes Jharkhand, Madhya Pradesh includes Chhattisgarh and Uttar Pradesh includes Uttaranchal. The data covers a wide spectrum of aspects and are therefore collected from various sources namely Census for demographic variables, CSO for economic, NFHS2 for social and domestic. NSSO and other official sources are resorted to where necessary. Wherever data are reported for the bifurcated states weighted averages are taken using the populations as weights. The period of indicators is the range 1998-2001.

The first table presents some general macro indicators comprising per capita income, sex ratio, urbanisation, poverty, literacy and social and demographic variables. Maharashtra, Punjab and Gujarat are among the highest in income followed by Karnataka and Kerala. Maharashtra and Gujarat are also highly urbanised states. Poverty is highest in Orissa. Kerala known for migration as also women's position leads in sex ratio and also in female headed households though other migration prone states like Himachal and Meghalaya, Mizoram and Nagaland goup (Megh-Miz-Nag) in north east have high incidence. Similarly literacy is also high in Kerala and Himachal. Total fertility rate and infant mortality rate are higher in Uttar Pradesh, Rajasthan and Madhya Pradesh.

The interest in this study is to capture the association that women's enterprise bears with different dimensions of development. The multiple variables indicating development status of any state show variety and intuitively reflect interrelation with wide overlaps between different dimensions of development. Based on this understanding we have attempted to calculate composite indicators for the different dimensions using the method of Principal components analysis (PCA). For each indicator, relevant variables of development are taken up and after examining the correlations among them the constituent variables are selected. In particular variables showing negative correlations are omitted. The variables are appropriately manipulated for consistency of expected association. For example along with per capita income, the inverse of poverty level (in other words, above poverty line) is desirable for the common indicator. The PCA generated scores are used for ranking the states and sorting for presentation in Tables A2.2. Punjab, Maharashtra, Gujarat and Tamilnadu are states that far best in economic and infrastructure-based indicators while for most social dimensions Kerala and Himachal Pradesh rank at the top. In public safety however Kerala comes down in rank but since the indicator is built on crime statistics that are reported rather than perpetrated (but may have been suppressed) this ranking is not above doubt.

The Profile of a Farm Household and Industries of Enterprise from NSSO Data

Figure 1 portrays the occupation profiles of women. More than 26% of the women in farm households are workers and another 16 per cent also contribute indirectly by free services for home consumption.

It may be more pertinent to look at the participation of workable age more than 15years referred as 'adult' age rather than include children who in principle should not be in workforce. The remaining analysis is done over women above 15 years age.

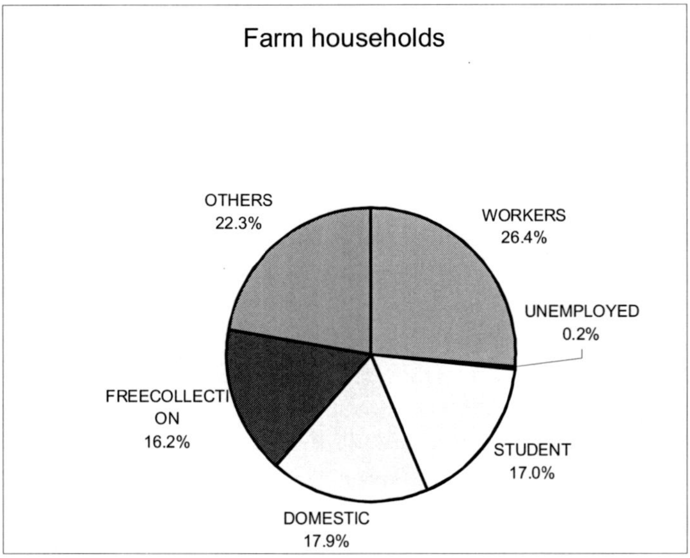

Table 2 : Economic Profile of farm Women in India

Not Literate (% Population)	71.2
Not beyond Primary (% Population)	86.8
Principal status Workforce (% Population)	40.3
Entrepreneur including crop cultivation (%Principal status Workforce)	9.7
Entrepreneur excluding Crop cultivation (%Principal status Workforce)	3.5
Entrepreneur excluding Crop cultivation and Tobacco (% Principal status Workforce)	3.0

Source: Computed.

As is well known within agriculture in India, cultivation of crops both food crops and cash crops constitute the bulk of farmers' activities. These crops cover cereals, pulses, oilseeds, cotton, tobacco, sugarcane, rubber and similar other cash crops. In fact these activities account for respectively 88 per cent and 63 per cent of total workforce and entrepreneurs among the farmwomen. Since diversification is a main objective of current employment policy and a focus in this paper we need to specify entrepreneurs by the relevant industries of activity. One way of defining enterprise could be to exclude agriculture or primary sector as a whole and consider only manufacturing and services. Yet, agricultural in its broader form cannot be disregarded for studying the ventures of rural people nor will it be relevant to do so. Specifically, here we include the so called 'high value products' of agricultural diversification in the basket of enterprises. Tobacco is taken as a category separate from manufacturing for analytical convenience. Among the industries three groups of activities are found with women's presence.

Agricultural (Agri): Growing roots, tubers, cones, forage plants etc., fruits and vegetables; seeds, nursery products, spices, nuts, animals and fishery; agro-services, Forestry, forest services and collection. Manufacturing (Mnfg): Food processing; Textiles; Leather; Wood; Paper.

Tobacco: Tobacco (Bidi) manufacture and collecting Tendu leaves.

Trade: Retail Trade

Services: Hotel; health; recreation; education; washing, hairdressing etc., finance and real estate.

Entrep: All Enterprises (adjusted for agriculture)

Entrep-adj: All enterprises Entrep except Tobacco

Figure 2 illustrates the share of theses industries in farmwomen's work participation and enterprise. Some activities draw women's enterprise disproportionately more than work participation such as agriculture (mainly animal husbandry), tobacco, retail trade, food processing and textile in manufacturing and services group consisting of washing, dry-cleaning, tailoring, hairdressing etc. Trading is confined to retailing and there is no place for wholesale trade. In crop cultivation in the specified group of agricultural enterprises, however like in the case of traditional cultivation of food and cash crops women's role does not seem to be mostly entrepreneurial. Similarly, education service is another area in which the share in enterprise is less than the share in workforce. The composite groups in each of the industries agricultural enterprises, tobacco, manufacturing, retail and services as specified above however claim more share among women entrepreneurs compared to share among women workers. Further, within the manufacturing group the specific activities found preferred by women entrepreneurs are identified on the basis of the NIC coding. These activities are found to be food processing, textile works, bidi making, crafts and perfumery (see listing in Appendix 1).

Figure 2: Industry shares

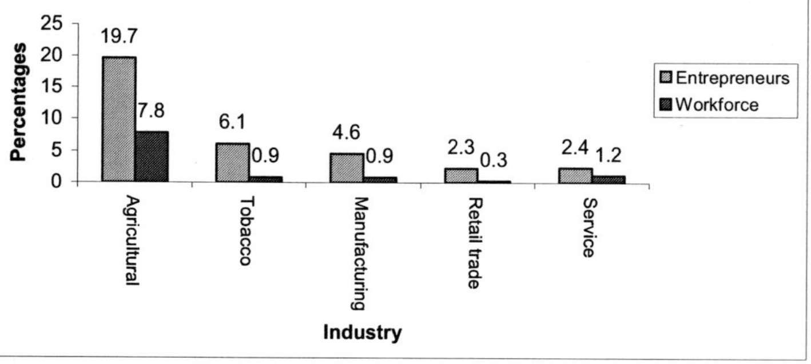

Bidi making is a dominant manufacturing enterprise. Bidi industry spanning most states in India may be as old as 119 years (since 1887) in India. The flexibility of a home-based avenue of earning possibly attracts women (and even children). The pitiable conditions of working in this industry, a subject of several studies (SEWA 1997, Sekhar S., 2004 Verma,2005) as also the decreasing production and consumption of beedi/ tobacco, known to cause 3 million deaths per year in the world and facing curbs from government policies, raise the need for suitable alternative livelihood for women.

Profile of Entrepreneurs

A comparison between the profiles of entrepreneurs in the industries of engagement (except tobacco) is given in Table 3. The MPCE capturing economic well-being of the households is highest among agricultural and least among manufacturing enterprises. Land ownership, another indicator of economic condition of rural people is also least among the manufacturing and highest at 1.4 hectares only for agricultural. More than 41 per cent of the manufacturing entrepreneurs belong to backward castes while this share is 35 per cent for services, 38 per cent for trade and only 28 per cent for agricultural entrepreneurs. Surprisingly, with all the handicaps, the manufacturers seem to be more educated than the others, 14 per cent of them having more than primary level education. This is followed by Services with 12 per cent and trade with 9 per cent and among the agricultural entrepreneurs only 7 per cent are educated beyond primary. However the manufacturing organization is far from modern. Very few of the women keep written accounts or hire labour and only 2.5 per cent use electricity.

Table 3: Socio-economic attributes of women workers and Entrepreneurs from Farm households

Attributes	*Agricultural*	*Manufacturing*	*Services*	*Retail trade*
Household characteristics				
MPCE (Rs)	499	398.8	419.3	445.3
Land owned (hectares)	1.4	0.77	0.97	0.54
SC/ST (%Households)	28	41.3	35.2	37.8
Member not beyond primary education (%)	92.8	86.2	88.2	91.1
Keep accounts	na	0.1	5.5	6.8
Employ hired labour		0.8	0	0
Electricity use	na	2.5	na	na

Source: Computed

State Wise Picture

We also take a look at the state wise picture considering 22 states which includes Meghaya, Mizoram and Nagaland grouped into one (M-M-N). Table 4 gives the top twelve states for each of the groups namely All entrepreneurs (Entrep), All entrepreneurs excluding tobacco (Entrep-adj), agricultural (Agri) and manufacturing (Mnfg), Trade and Services. The dispersion or concentration of farmwomen entrepreneurs across all states is measured. The share of the top twelve states in total number of entreprenurs in the country obtained from the survey data is provided in the table. Also dispersion indices based on Hirschman-Herfindahl (HH) method based on all the 22 states are worked out and presented. The dispersion index DISP intuitively gives the probability of obtaining the same state in two random picks of the worker or entrepreneur.

$$DISP = 1 - \Sigma (E_i/E_T)^2$$

Where E is the number of women entrepreneurs and subscripts i and T stand for the state i and total of states respectively.

The top twelve states account for 93 per cent or more of the entrepreneurs in each case and 99 per cent in case of services. Correspondingly, the value of DISP index is high above 90 per cent suggesting an even dispersion of women entrepreneurship (or lack of it) across India through varied conditions but the dispersion is less for agriculture than manufacturing and is also low for trade and least for services. Manufacturing seems to be the enterprise most dispersed in the country. Considering entrepreneurship as a whole, inclusion or exclusion of tobacco manufacturing makes a small difference with Madhya Pradesh moving out of the list and M-M-N joining it if tobacco is excluded. Tamil Nadu, Uttar Pradesh, Gujarat and Andhra are the first four states. The eastern states West Bengal, Orissa and Bihar and southern states Tamil Nadu, Andhra, Karnataka and Keral are all among the states as also Maharashtra, Gujarat and Rajasthan. There is a small change for the group of agricultural enterprises in which Punjab comes in. In manufacturing the eastern states have highest three places and even Assam enters the list. The southern states are retained and Maharashtra also comes in. In trade and services southern states rank high and Punjab and Haryana join ranks in Trade and Punjab in Services. Notably, eastern states West Bengal, Orissa and Bihar and southern states Andhra, Tamil Nadu, Karnataka and Kerala are found in all the lists except for Orissa in Agricultural enterprises and Kerala in Trade.

While the state populations influence their shares, the tendencies of taking up entrepreneurship by farmwomen are better captured by the shares in workforce. The work participation rate (WPR) of the farmwomen and the share of entrepreneurs in workforce are worked out in Table 5 and we rank the states by these tendencies. There is some contrast that comes out. The developed north Indian states- Punjab and Haryana record lowest WPR of farmwomen but rank high among the tendency towards enterprise, specifically in agricultural enterprises. In fact, agricultural appears as a strong influence on Enterp-adj with states in north and western India like Punjab, Haryana, Gujarat and Rajasthan faring higher, southern states and West Bengal in the middle and some of the Himalayan states among the lowest. However, M-M-N in north-east is a leader in agricultural enterprises and Manipur in manufacturing.

Table 4: First Twelve States ranked by Entrepreneurship

Rank	*Entrep*	*Entrep-adj*	*Agri*	*Mnfg*	*Trade*	*Services*
1	Tamilnadu	Tamilnadu	Gujarat	WestBengal	TamilNadu	Andhra
2	UttarPradesh	Gujarat	Tamilnadu	Orissa	Andhra	Karnataka
3	Gujarat	UttarPradesh	UttarPradesh	Bihar	UttarPradesh	UttarPradesh
4	Andhra	Andhra	Rajasthan	TamilNadu	Bihar	Orissa
5	WestBengal	Rajasthan	Andhra	Karnataka	Gujarat	Maharashtra
6	Rajasthan	Karnataka	Karnataka	Andhra	WestBengal	Tamilnadu
7	Karnataka	WestBengal	Kerala	Uttar Pradesh	Maharashtra	West Bengal
8	Bihar	Bihar	Maharashtra	Rajasthan	Madhya Pradesh	Kerala
9	Kerala	Maharashtra	M-M-N	Madhya Pradesh	Haryana	Assam
10	Maharashtra	Kerala	WestBengal	Kerala	Orissa	Bihar
11	Orissa	Orissa	Bihar	Maharashtra	Karnataka	Punjab
12	Madhya Pradesh	M-M-N	Punjab	Assam	Punjab	M-M-N
Share %	94.4	93.4	96.2	94.9	92.7	99.4
DISP	90.51	90.06	87.6	90.34	88.69	79.23

Women Entrepreneurship and State Development

Like any other economic activity, women's enterprise would be likely to be linked with general economic development of the states through demand and supply linkages and with the infrastructural facilities of the state. In particular women, because of conventional household duties are more strongly linked with aspects of infrastructure, household amenities, health and awareness. Due to biological reasons and social backwardness women's integration in economic life could be additionally related to fertility rate and public safety.

To examine the linkage among various aspects of enterprise and development we have computed correlation coefficients (Pearson's) and tabulated them in Table 6 and 7. Constrained by data availability we considered only 21 states excluding Tripura. On the one side we have considered women's participation in enterprise and also work as variables Worker, Entrep, Entrep-adj, Agri, Mnfg, Trade and Services. On the other side we considered the development related variables. These include certain broad macro variables as given in Table A2.1 as also composite indicators of economic development, infrastructure, awareness, health, safety and household position of women as in Tables A2.2. The data sources, construction and implications of the variables are explained in Appendix 2.

Table 5: State ranks in Work participation and Entrepreneurship of Farmwomen

Rank	*Worker*	*Entrep.*	*Entrep-adj.*	*Agri.*	*Mnfg.*
1	Andhra	Punjab	Punjab	Punjab	Manipur
2	Maharashtra	Kerala	Manipur	Meg-Miz-Nag	J&K
3	Meg-Miz-Nag	Manipur	Meg-Miz-Nag	Kerala	West Bengal
4	Tamilnadu	Meg-Miz-Nag	Kerala	Gujarat	Orissa
5	Madhya Pradesh	West Bengal	Haryana	Rajasthan	Tripura
6	Karnataka	Haryana	Gujarat	Haryana	Kerala
7	Gujarat	Tamilnadu	Rajasthan	Tamilnadu	Assam
8	Arunachal	Gujarat	Tamilnadu	Himachal	Bihar
9	Rajasthan	Rajasthan	West Bengal	Uttar Pradesh	Rajasthan
10	Sikkim	Uttar Pradesh	Himachal	West Bengal	Tamilnadu
11	Himachal	Himachal	Uttar Pradesh	Sikkim	Karnataka
12	Orissa	Orissa	Tripura	Karnataka	Himachal
13	Bihar	Tripura	J&K	Andhra	Uttar Pradesh
14	Manipur	Karnataka	Orissa	Orissa	Andhra
15	Uttar Pradesh	J&K	Sikkim	Maharashtra	Meg-Miz-Nag
16	Kerala	Bihar	Assam	Bihar	Maharashtra
17	West Bengal	Sikkim	Andhra	Assam	Madhya Pradesh
18	Assam	Assam	Karnataka	J&K	Gujarat
19	Tripura	Andhra	Bihar	Tripura	Sikkim
20	J&K	Maharashtra	Maharashtra	Manipur	Punjab
21	Haryana	Madhya Pradesh	Madhya Pradesh	Madhya Pradesh	Haryana
22	Punjab	Arunachal	Arunachal	Arunachal	Arunachal
Max	68.3	23.3	23.3	19.0	9.2
Min	4.0	0.1	0.1	0	0

In brief, the reasons for expectations for possible association are as follows:

Per capita income (NSDP): Demand for products will be higher and procurement of produced inputs easier.

Diversification: The tendency of the state as a whole to diversify away from agriculture may have a bearing to women's enterprise which is also diversification.

Urbanisation: The share of urban population in the state affects the taste and demeand patterns of the consumers.

Roads: Transportation facility will facilitate marketing of products, procurement of materials and availing training.

Electricity and power: Help in mechanisation and operation of enterprises as well as lighten the load of household jobs that compete for time and effort.

Literacy and schooling: Exposure to print medium of information and awareness.

Other communication media: For continuous and easy flow of information even for the non-schooled and illiterate. They are a source of awareness of competition and the world affairs.

Household Amenities: Easier and faster workload at home and more time for productive activities.

Health facilities: Helps to maintain good health for regular economic activities and less time taken for taking care of the ill at home.

Public safety: Incidences of crime, especially directed at women such as rape and abduction inhibits women's free mobility and confidence for public interactions and also over time may reinforce social restraints on women's movements.

Household position: A position of subservience and lack of independence renders women's participation a subject of decision of male and elder members rather than choice and opportunity.

Although above are some of the ways in which the development indicators can influence women's participation, the associations are actually profound and often with two-way causality. For example, women's superior position at home may encourage economic activity and enterprise among them but at the same time such economic independence or access to earn money income can also empower women and gain status at home. We have opted for a correlation analysis rather than regression because of following two reasons:

(1) There cannot be any presupposition that any of the two side variables is non-stochastic, in fact both the development and participation indicators are random and inter-dependent and

(2) The number of observations is limited by the number of states.

The magnitudes of the coefficients are an indication of the strength of association but the coefficients are also tested for significance. Entrepreneurship adjusted for tobacco is significantly correlated with NSDP and literacy. Literacy and NSDP are positively correlated with WPR but the coefficients are not significant and literacy shows a low value less than 0.1 value. Urbansiation is significant influence for work participation and enterprise with tobacco. The more urbanised states have more jobs for women. The same is true for agricultural enterprises, understandably as demand for the 'high value' agro-products are more in demand by urban people. Manufacturing is inversely related to urbanisation perhaps reflecting the existence of superior products from organised sector and also in line with the profile of the manufacturing units. Fertility rates have expected negative correlation with all but Worker and manufacturing but the coefficients are low and insignificant barring services. Incidences of rape, a heineous crime against women is negative in all the cases though significant for workers as a whole and trade (which might involve some movement).

Considering the composite indicator for the economic dimension Entrep, ntrep-adj and Agri are positively and significantly correlated in that order with the coefficient highest for agricultural at 0.571 while correlation with worker is found insignificant and manufacturing having a negative though insignificant correlation. The case is same for infrastructure but here Sevices also show significant correlation and the negative correlation with manufacturing becomes significant. The dimension Awareness bears negative correlation in no case and is significant for Entrep, Entrep-adj, Agri, Trade. Among the industries, Trade has the highest correlation coefficient with this information indicator. Poor health facilities once again yields negative correlations in most cases, specifically in agricultural enterprises but the relation is found reverse for worker as whole and manufacturing. Poor public safety, in which rape is a component, also indicates negative relation in all cases, the highest value obtained for trade but insignificant in all cases. The lack of significance in this case need not be informative as the incidents are only as reported and not at actuals. Household amenities have positive associations in most of the cases. The coefficient is not significant with Worker and is negative with manufacturing. Similar association is indicated in case of Poor household position.

Despite the variety the correlations across states seem to suggest that (1) most development indicators are positively associated with enterprise (2) Agricultural entrepreneurship are also associated with progressiveness of the states but not manufacturing as it could be an outcome of distress

(3) Work participation as a whole is associated positively with some of the development indicators but the relations are not strong. Only urbanisation of the state and its public safety are important associates.

The correlation analysis undoubtedly is a call for the lacking states to strengthen their overall economic development and incentives, infrastructure, their rural social infrastructure for health, education and communication, their law enforcement and rural amenities. The analysis also seems to suggest an advantage in agricultural enterprise for women and this is justifiable also for recent emphases on diversification and the overall integration with agriculture, which needs a serious overhaul. However, the case for manufacturing is a matter of concern. As summarised in the Appendix the enterprises in which women manufacturers are involved also show substantial potentials and have even export advantage at the national level and with remarkable participation from organised sector. Yet the women who are involved seem to be participating only where development is lacking and are able to operate at primitive levels of organisation. Moreover the coverage of activities is narrow and traditional and there is no reason given the congenial ambience why women cannot diversify into other prospective areas of manufacturing and services. There is a serious need to look at this aspect particularly these women come from relatively less developed states and from less endowed households. The initiatives shown by these women notwithstanding their disadvantages certainly deserve greater opportunities of success. Drawing the corporate sector involvement through proper training, information and contracts, outsourcing and tie-ups could be possible strategies for the goal.

Table 6: Correlation coefficients (Pearson's) between Economic Participation and Macro variables

Indicators	*NSDP*	*URB*	*TFR*	*Literacy*	*Rape*	*IMR*
Worker	0.340	0.448*	0.011	0.048	-0.431*	0.047
Entrep.	0.516**	0.379*	-0.318	0.524**	-0.289	-0.481*
Entrep-adj.	0.541**	0.357	-0.262	0.471*	-0.256	-0.417*
Agri.	0.691**	0.457*	-0.233	0.454*	-0.209	-0.254
Mnfg.	-0.336	-0.66	0.073	-0.001	-0.107	-0.255
Trade	0.268	-0.174	-0.254	0.321	-0.417*	-0.44*
Services	0.310	0.173	-0.391*	0.219	-0.184	0.085

Note for Tables 6 and 7: One tailed tests conducted * Significant at 0.05 **Significant at 0.01.

Women are performing and excelling in various fields including business. There is no reason why women should be suppressed into a life of poor esteem, subjugation and economic dependence especially in agricultural sector in which women do actually contribute substantially in terms of economic work. Development of enterprises in agro-related or other industries could be a way to empower women, release them from discriminations of labour market and society and build up capabilities consistent with modern life. At the same time enterprises as self-employment could be more in consonance with women's way of life.

Table 7. Correlation coefficients (Pearson's) between Economic Participation and Development indicators

Indicators	*Economic*	*Infrastructure*	*Awareness*	*Poor Health*	*Poor Safety*	*Amenities*	*Poor Position*
Worker	0.335	0.284	0.020	0.123	-0.234	0.011	-0.227
Entrep.	0.443*	0.585*	0.547**	-0.633**	-0.361	0.506**	-0.404**
Entrep-adj.	0.457*	0.632**	0.521**	-0.589**	-0.311	0.573**	-0.393*
Agri.	0.579**	0.797**	0.408*	-0.577**	-0.152	0.620**	-0.441*
Mnfg.	-0.263	-0.380*	0.183	0.064	-0.223	-0.202	0.192
Trade	0.260	0.271	0.428*	-0.446*	-0.327	0.509**	-0.348
Services	0.292	0.509**	0.246	-0.381*	-0.312	0.347	-0.218

Concluding Remarks

This paper examines nation wide data of women in agricultural households and finds them involved in a limited array of industries and to a small degree in enterprises. Enterprises are more likely to be in agricultural activities and for that reason the states leading in agriculture and agro-enterprises stand out women enterprises although they fall back in work participation. Women enterprises are found to be linked to the development status of states in respect of various social and economic dimensions. The manufacturing enterprises show signs of being distress driven and call for attention in view of their prospects.

Appendix–1

Activities of Farm women Manufacturing Enterprise

Food processing1:

Flour milling, Dal milling, Rice milling, Processing and grinding grains, vegetable milling, flour of meal of dried leguminous vegetables of roots and tubers of edible nuts, breakfast foods by swelling and roasting cereal grains, starch and sago products, glucose syrup, gluten, corn oil, animal feed, bakery products, sugar, gur, khandsari, cocoa, chocolate, confectionary, sweetmeats, macaroni, noodles, tea, coffee, edible nuts, malted and infant foods, spices, papads, vitaminised high protein flour, dried dal and cereals.

Manufacture of Beverages (non-alcoholic)

Tobacco: Bidi,

Textlie: Preparation, spinning and weaving of cotton fibre, of silk fibre, wool, other animal hair, manmade fibres,

Durries, druggets, rugs, carpets, rugs, coverings of jute, mesta, coir, other floor coverings of textiles, sunhemp, cordage, rope, tine, netting, thread, jute rope and cordage, coir rope and cordage, mesta, nets.

Embroidery, laces, fringes, zari, ornamental trimmings, linolium, mantles, canvas goods, sanitary towels and tampons, metallised yarns, gimped yarn, rubber rubber, water proof textiles, knitted, crocheted fabrics of cotton, woolen and synthetic substances. Textile garments and accessories, raincoats, sheetings, hats, caps of waterproof textiles, leather apparels.

Crafts: Basketry, grain bins, bamboo and reeds, wooden containers, canes, rattan, bamboo willow, grass, leaves, wooden, industrial goods, cork products, bamboo and cane articles and fixtures thatching from reeds, grass, broom sticks, wooden agricultural implement, shopping bags and ornamental boxes, costume articles, trays, table-lamps, fancy baskets, table mats, vessel holders.

Perfumery: Agarbatti and other perfumed burning mateials, perfumes, toilet preparations, matches.

Appendix–2

The following sub-sections give the details of the variables considered, the constituent variables used to arrive at the composite indicator and the proportion of variance accounted for. Economic Variables used for the purpose of studying enterprise cover per capita income, diversification from agriculture and inequality indicated by poverty.

Variables in this dimension:

PCNSDP-Per capita Net State Domestic Product (Central Statistical Organisation) 1999-00

SHAREAG-Share of Agriculture sectors in Gross domestic Product (Central Statistical Organisation) 1999-00.

BPL-Share of population below poverty line (Planning Commission 1999)

Variables for PCA

(1) PCNSDP

(2) APL= 1-BPL

(3) SHARENAG=1-SHAREAG

% Variance=63

Infrastructure

Variables deflated by population in the indicator:

SROAD-Surfaced road length per capita in Km as of (Statistical Abstract of India) 1999.

POWER-Installed capacity in 000KW per capita in 2002-3 (Statistical Abstract of India).

LOAN-Loans per capita disbursed by Cooperative Banks 1998-99 (Statistical Abstract of India).

Variables for PCA

(1) SRAOD

(2) POWER

(3) LOAN

%Variance=63.5.

Public Safety

Variables in Dimension (deflated by population):

CRIME-Number of persons arrested for any crime per capita (statistical Abstract)2001.

RAPE-Rate of rape reported ( )2000

ABDUC-Rate of abductions reported ( )2000.

Variables for PCA:

(1) CRIME

(2) RAPE

(3) ABDUC

%Variance=47.5

Awareness

Media related information relate to ever married women between ages 15-59 who are exposed to the media presuming the information reflects the general level of exposure of women of working age in the respective states.

Variables in dimension:

FLIT-Female literacy rate (Census) 2001

MEDSCH-Median years of schooling (1998) NFHS2

NEWSPAP-Proportion of women exposed to newspaper (1998) NFHS2

TELEV-Proportion of women exposed to television (1998) NFHS2

RADIO-Proportion of women exposed to radio (1998) NFHS2

Variables for PCA:

(1) FLIT

(2) MEDSCH

(3) NEWSPAP

(4) TELEV

(5) RADIO

%Variance=75.5

Health

Variables in Dimension:

TFR -Total Fertility rate for rural sector based on 2001 (Census) data. TFR is defined to be the number of IMR-Infant Mortality Rate for rural sector based on 2001 (Census) data. IMR is defined to beCHMR-Child mortality Rate for rural sector based on 2001 (Census) data. CHMR is defined to beMORBTB-Tuberculosis incidence per one lakh rural population (NFHS2) 1998.MORBMAL-Malaria incidence per one lakh rural population (NFHS2) 1998. HFAC-Adequacy of health care facility as average waiting time in the facility (NFHS2) 1998.

%Variance=52.6

Household Amenities

Variables in Dimension:

POWER-Proportion of households having access to electricity (Census) 2001.

WATER-Proportion of households having access to water in premises from tap or hand pump (Census) 2001.

BATH-Proportion of households having bathroom in house (Census) 2001.

GAS-Proportion of households using cooking gas (LPG) (Census) 2001.

Variables for PCA:

(1) POWER

(2) WATER

(3) BATH

(4) GAS

%Variance=64.0.

Women's Position at home

Variables in Dimension:

LITF-Share of women who are literates (Census) 2001 from 100.

NODEC-Proportion of women not involved in household decisions (NFHS2) 1998.

MISHUS-Proportion of women reporting mistreatment from husband (NFHS2) 1998.

MISLAW-Proportion of women reporting mistreatment from in-laws (NFHS2) 1998.

PERMIS -Proportion of women having to take permission to visit market (NFHS2) 1998.

Variables for PCA:

(1) NLITF=1-LITF

(2) NODEC

(3) MISHUS

(4) MISLAW

(5) PERMIS

%Variance=53.8.

REFERENCES

- Bardhan Pranab (1978) "Some Employment and Unemployment Characteristics of Rural Women", *Economic and Political Weekly* March 1978.
- Kaur Satnam and S.K. Goyal (1996) "A Study of Wage Discrimination against Women Agricultural Labourers", *Agricultural Situation in India,* Vol.53 No.4, July.
- Kumar S.K. (1978) *Role of Household Economy in Child Nutrition at low Incomes, Occasional Paper No. 95,* Department of Agricultural Economics, Cornell University.
- Engels F. (1984, 1972) *Origin of the family private property and the state* (ed.) E.B. Leacock international Publishers
- Hirway Indira and Anil Kumar Roy (1999) "Women in Rural Economy: The Case of India" in *Indian Journal of Agricultural Economics* , Vol 54 No 3.

- Gulati L., (1978) "Profile of Female Agricultural Labour", *Economic and Political Weekly* (Review of Agriculture) 13(12) 25 March.
- Agarwal Bina (1994) A *Field of one's own*, Cambridge
- Agarwal Bina (1984) "Role of Women and HYV Rice Technology", *Economic and Political Weekly* 19(13) 31 March.
- Bhattacharya B.B and S. Shakthivel (2003) "Regional Disparities in Growth: A comparison of Pre and Post reform Period" *Discussion Paper* 73/2003 Institute of Economic Growth.
- Engels F. (1984, 1972) *Origin of the family private property and the state* (ed.) E.B. Leacock international Publishers
- Dasgupta Purnamita and Bishwanath Goldar (2005) *Female Labour Supply in Rural India: An Econometric Analysis,* Institute of Economic Growth *Working Paper Non. E/265/2005.*
- Sen Amartya (2006) "Gender and Cooperative Conflicts" in Bina Agarwal, Jane Humphries and Ingrid Robeyns (ed) *Capabilities, Freedom and Equality*, Oxford.
- Dreze Jean And Amrtya Sen (2003) *India: Development and Participation*, Oxford.
- Narrayan, D. et al (2000) *Voices of the poor : Crying out for change*, New York Oxford.
- Alkire Sabina and Rufus Black (1997) "A Practical reasoning theory of Development Eethics: Functioning and Capabilities approach" *Journal of International Development 9*(2)
- Sen Amartya (2006) "Development as Capability Expansion" in Bina Agarwal, Jane Humphries and Ingrid Robeyns (ed) *Capabilities, Freedom and Equality*, Oxford.
- Nussbaum Martha C. (1995) "Human Capabilities, Female Human Beings" in Nussbaum Martha and Jonathan Glover (ed) *Women, Culture and Development* edited by Martha Nussbaum and Jonathan Glover, Oxford 1995
- Carolyn Fleur-Lobban and Janet Mancini Billson (2005), "A critique of social change Theories" in Billson Janet Mancini and Carolyn Fleur-Lobban (ed) *Female Well-Being*, Zed Books, London.
- Verma Roop Rekha (1995), 'Femininity, equality and personhood in Women', *Culture and Development* edited by Martha Nussbaum and Jonathan Glover, Oxford
- Dandekar V.M., (1982), "Integration of women in economic development" *Economic and Political Weekly* October 30.
- Sen Abhijit and Praveen Jha (2005) 'Rural Employment: Patterns and Trends from National Sample Survey' in Rohini Nayyar and Alakh N. Sharma (ed) *Rural Transformation in India*, Institute of Human Development, Delhi.

- Kundu Amitabh, Niranjan Sarangi and Bal Paritosh Das (2005) 'Economic Growth, Poverty and Non-farm Employment: An analysis of Rural-urban Inter-linkages' in Rohini Nayyar and Alakh N. Sharma (ed) *Rural Transformation in India*, Institute of Human Development, Delhi.
- National Sample Survey Organisation, Government of India (2001) *Employment and Unemployment Situation in India 1999-2000 Part I* and II.
- Research and Information System for Developing counties RIS(2006) *Towards Employment oriented Export Strategy: Some Explorations* Report.
- Sudha Rani P., V.T. Raju, P. Raghuram and G. Munaswami Naidu *(1990) Wage Differentials and Factors Governing Employment of Women in Agriculture" Agricultural Situation in India* Vol. 45 No.4., July.
- Government of India (1991, 2001) *Census (Housing Tables).*
- *International Institute of Population Sciences (1998-99) India: National family Health Survey (NFHS-2).*
- Government of India (various) *Statistical Abstract of India.*
- Institute of Applied manpower Research IAMR (2004) *India Yearbook Manpower Profile.*

APPENDIX TABLES

Table A1:Time spent per Week in hours

	Male	*Female*
Cooking	0.52	14.93
Cleaning household	0.21	4.55
Cleaning Utensils	0.10	3.39
Washing and mending clothes	0.18	2.71
Shopping	0.59	0.64
Pet care	0.03	0.04
Care of sick and elderly	0.04	0.19
Care of guests	0.03	0.04
Care of children	0.32	3.16
Accompanying children	0.08	0.09
Supervising children	.28	0.78
Teaching children	0.16	0.19

Source: Women and Men in India 2000

Table A 2.1 : Some Macro Indicators of Development in States

STATE	PCNSDP (RS) AT CONSTANT PRICE	SEX RATIO (PER 1000 MALE)	URBAN (%POPULATION)	BPL (%POPULATION) %	FEMALE HEADED Household	LITERACY RATE (%)	TOTAL FERTILITY RATE	INFANT MORTALITY RATE
Andhra	9445	978	27.0	11.1	12.1	61	2.3	66
Arunachal	8521	893	20.0	40.0	7.3	55	2.7	63
Assam	5785	935	13.0	40.0	8.4	64	2.4	70
Bihar	4245	924	12.9	44.3	9.6	49	3.6	73
Gujarat	13490	920	37.0	13.2	9.0	70	3.0	63
Haryana	13308	861	29.0	8.3	8.1	69	3.1	57
Himachal	11051	968	10.0	7.9	22.0	77	2.2	34
J&kashmir	7385	892	25.0	4.0	6.5	55	3.0	65
Karnataka	10912	965	34.0	17.4	13.9	67	2.3	52
Kerala	10178	1058	26.0	9.4	25.1	91	2.1	16
Madhyapradesh	7849	937	25.2	37.1	6.0	64	3.6	86
Maharashtra	15186	922	42.0	23.7	9.8	77	2.7	44
Manipur	6873	978	24.0	40.0	9.3	69	3.4	37
Megh-miz-nag	8875	938	24.2	40.0	14.4	69	4.4	62
Orissa	5735	972	15.0	48.0	9.3	64	2.5	81
Punjab	14698	876	34.0	6.4	9.5	70	2.4	57
Rajasthan	8550	921	23.0	13.7	8.5	61	4.1	80
Sikkim	10250	875	11.0	40.0	9.2	70	2.9	44
Tamilnadu	12144	987	44.0	20.6	15.0	74	2.2	48
Uttar Pradesh	5787	901	21.0	31.2	9.7	58	4.3	87
West Bengal	9320	934	28.0	31.8	7.8	69	2.5	49
India	93852	933	28.0	27.1	10.4	65.4	3.07	67.6

Sources: NFHS-2, Manpower

Table A 2.2 : Ranking by Scores of States with respect to different dimensions of Development

Rank	*Economic Indicators*	*Infrastructure*	*Public safety*	*Awareness*	*Health*	*Position*	*Amenities*
1.	Maharashta	Punjab	Manipur	Kerala	Kerala	Kerala	Punjab
2.	Gujarat	MahaRashta	Sikkim	Himachal	Himachal	Tamilnadu	Himachal
3.	Tamilnadu	TamilNadu	WestBengal	Manipur	Punjab	Himachal	Haryana
4.	Himachal	Gujarat	Punjab	Punjab	Tamilnadu	Punjab	Maharashtra
5.	Haryana	Haryana	Karnataka	Tamilnadu	Karnataka	Megh-Miz-Nag	Sikkim
6.	Kerala	Himachal	UttarPradesh	Maharashta	Maharashta	Sikkim	Kerala
7.	Punjab	Karnataka	Andrapradesh	Karnataka	WestBengal	Gujarat	Karnataka
8.	Andra	Kerala	MMN	Megh-Miz-Nag	Haryana	Maharashtra	Andhra Pradesh
9.	Karnataka	Andhra	Bihar	Sikkim	J&Kashmir	Haryana	Gujarat
10.	Rajasthan	Orissa	Tamilnadu	Gujarat	Assam	Arunachal	J&Kashmir
11.	J&Kashmir	Arunachal	Gujarat	Haryana	Sikkim	Karnataka	Tamilnadu
12.	Sikkim	Sikkim	Maharashta	WestBengal	Gujarat	Assam	Arunachal
13.	WestBengal	MadhyaPradesh	Orissa	Andhra	Andhra	Manipur	Manipur
14.	Megh-Miz-Nag	Rajasthan	Haryana	Assam	Manipur	WestBengal	Rajasthan
15.	Madhya Pradesh	Megh-Miz-Nag	Himachal	J&Kashmir	Orissa	Andhra Pradesh	Madhya Pradesh
16.	Manipur	J&Kashmir	Kerala	Arunachal	Rajasthan	Rajasthan	UttarPradesh
17.	Arunchal	WestBengal	Arunchal	MadhyaPradesh	Bihar	Madhya Pradesh	West Bengal
18.	Uttar Pradesh	UttarPradesh	Assam	Orissa	UttarPradesh	Orissa	Assam
19.	Assam	Manipur	J.Kashmir	UttarPradesh	Arunachal	UttarPradesh	Megh-Miz-Nag
20.	Orissa	Assam	Rajasthan	Rajasthan	MadhyaPradesh	Bihar	Bihar
21.	Bihar	Bihar	Madhya Pradesh	Bihar	Megh-Miz-Nag	J&Kashmir	Orissa

Note: Based on computed Scores.

Chapter 24

CORRELATES TOWARDS EMANCIPATION OF WOMEN ENTREPRENEURSHIP : A DIAGNOSTIC STUDY ON WOMEN ENTREPRENEURS IN FOOD PROCESSING ENTERPRISES

*Dr. R. Ganesan

ABSTRACT

The food processing industry sector in India was one of the largest in terms of production, consumption, export and growth prospects, and women being the traditional forerunners in food processing in household as a whole draws a major attention in this sector. Women entrepreneurship was not considerably high in India in comparison with other developing countries and developed countries, although it started much before than other countries. The Government envisaged measures to empower them for instance, trade related entrepreneurship assistance development (TREAD) for women was designed to empower women economically through the development of their entrepreneurial skills by eliminating constraints faced by them. It included assistance in form of loans, trade related training, trade information, counselling, and extension activities relating to product and market development. Thus, in spite of 'fundamental rights' 'equal status' 'tread', and other measures, women entrepreneur-ship was lagging behind, because the basic three concepts of

* Research Coordinator, Centre for Research & Consultancy, Sree Saraswathi Thyagaraja College, Pollachi Taluk, Coimbatore District-641107
E-mail: draganesan.nfed@rediffmail.com

entrepreneur, environment and support system were not integrated. However, several factors, which affected women entrepreneurship in India, were lack of appropriate finances, education and training, and favourable societal attitudes and familial problems. In addition to that, personality characteristics of the entrepreneur played a crucial role in establishing and maintaining any enterprising activity, thus in entrepreneurial growth. The individual's personality traits and characteristics account for the entrepreneurial manifestations and psychosocial dispositions in any entrepreneurship development activity, especially, in the context of emancipating entrepreneurial base more so in inter-relating entrepreneurial success. The effects of social variables, like education, experience, family could confound the output leading to poor entrepreneurial success. This made crucial to understand the psychosocial profile of women entrepreneurs, which could designate appropriate interventions in terms of policies and programmes exclusively in the case of women entrepreneurs in food processing enterprises. Thus, the present study attempted to assess the inter-relationships, nature and degree of psychosocial profile correlates with socio-background of women entrepreneurs.

Genesis of Entrepreneurship in India

In the post independence era, the Government of India envisaged a policy that has to synchronize and harmonize the twin considerations of rapid growth coupled with removal of wide spread poverty and unemployment, in order to fulfill the aspirations of the millions of Indians in terms of providing them a standard of living as desired in a welfare state. The plan objective of 'economic growth with social justice' was kept in view while formulating the strategy of economic development. Development and growth of industries was adopted as one of the pillars of Economic Policy as India had been primarily an agriculture-based economy before attaining independence. The strategy adopted for industrial development, endeavoured to strike a balance between the complementary role to be played by the large and small segments of the industry. Thus, development of small-scale industries sector was considered essential as it could fulfill the twin requirement of providing large-scale employment with low investments in labour-abundant for a capital-scarce oriented country. After then the small-scale sector was well realized and emerged as dynamic and vibrant sector of Indian economy.

The SSIs being labour intensive had the positive implications of equity, flexibility, and capability to contribute to decentralization, promotion of entrepreneurship, optimum utilization of local resources and talents, etc. The seven Industrial Policy Resolutions (1948, 1956, 1977, 1980, 1990, 1991, and 1998) adopted by the successive Government's at the centre aimed at promoting industrial growth and facilitating its rapid development. The Government of India measures varied from time to time, which included policy of reservation, revision of investment ceilings, modernization, technological up gradation, marketing assistance, fiscal incentives, etc. Thus, the emerging economic scenario in the changed liberalized and competitive economic environment had necessitated structural and fundamental changes in policy framework put in to place for the development of this vital sector of economy. The process of liberalization and market reforms had created wide-ranging opportunities for the development of SSIs. At the same time, changing world scenario had grown up new challenges to the very existence of this sector so that it could adapt itself to the changed environment and faced the challenges boldly and effectively. Even before the 4th Industrial Policy (1980) it was realized that agricultural development was crucial to India's overall progress and this can be achieved by intensifying the agricultural and allied activities as well as by diversification and commercialization of agricultural products. Hence, a strong and effective food processing sector played a significant role in diversification of agricultural activities, improving value addition of agricultural produce, increasing employment opportunities, and thereby creating surplus for export of agro food products. This required policies and plans for improvement of food-processing infrastructure including up gradation of technology and enforcement of quality standards, and activating domestic market. A separate Ministry of Food Processing Industries was set up in 1988 to give an impetus to the development of small-scale sectors coming into its fold. Consequently, the focus shifted to facilitate entrepreneurship in rural as well as urban areas on traditional and non-traditional products. In this context, women entrepreneurship is perceived to participate more so in the food processing sectors, the reason being women had expertise over cooking, processing etc. which was an added advantage for them to go for a traditional enterprising activity with some modernization through which they can generate income and raise their livelihood.

Gender and Entrepreneurship

Psychologists, sociologists, and economists define entrepreneurship according to their discipline. According to Gupta and Khanka (2000), entrepreneurship was the process of identifying opportunities in the market place, marshalling the resources required to pursue these opportunities and investing the resources to exploit the opportunities for long-term gains. It involved creating wealth by bringing together resources in new ways to start and operate an enterprise. However, for the present study entrepreneurship was defined as a multi-dimensional practice through an economic return oriented action, which incorporated and integrated the application of psychology, sociology, economics, and management skills, to run an enterprise and to make desired profit out of calculated risk in a conducive environment and choice, thereby becoming *persono-economic* in nature, achieving self-sufficiency, and self-sustainability levels in practice. Thus, an enterprise meant the following in modern era of entrepreneurship development : Profit making, return on investment, en-cashing opportunity, business sense, organized working, cost for every thing, management of time, calculated risks, planning, hard/smart work, and cycling of cash.

Concept of Entrepreneurship

The subtle but effective manifestation of gender phenomenon was reflected in the size of enterprise, product line, growth, composition and management. The feminine psyche, social and economic, educational, financial and legal limiting factors also contributed to the gender status in the entrepreneurship today, although studies compared men and women in terms of personality and behaviour dimensions more or less did not find any substantial difference between sexes. Traditionally, it has been a practice in India by which the selective fruits and vegetables are primarily processed and used for daily consumption and at off-seasons. But, it had not been a practice in those days to make it into an economic activity. It was by late 70s where women's population has been anchored for income generating activities with their traditional processing knowledge and skills, which enhanced their participation and at the same time tapped the workforce into economic returns to become self-sustainable and raising nation's economy. Economic development in India, with realization of women entrepreneurism triggered only in early 1980s. It was the period where a lot of social change occurred due to economic transition in the history of India and women entrepreneurs were created as an interface to bring out social change and economic development through their participation in sustaining the economy of the nation. Almost 9% of the women entrepreneurs are found in small-scale industries (Savadi 2001). The most common and vital enterprising activity for women in rural and urban areas was food processing.

Some studies highlighted the scenarios of their existence in small-scale sectors like one study by Agarwal (1995) stated that in Britain, women entrepreneurs constitute 9 per cent. In West Germany, women run 20 per cent out of three million enterprises, in United States, women run 20 per cent out of all small businesses. The percentage of women in working force in Russia is 41.5, West Germany 33.2, Japan 39.1, and United States 24.6 per cent. As against this, while about 52.5 per cent of the total numbers of males were gainfully employed in India, the corresponding per cent of women was only 12. He further stated that out of 1.8 million small-scale units, those owned by women were not more than 0.15 million i.e., about 8 per cent only. Out of this, 25.5 per cent of women entrepreneurs were involved in manufacturing food products, 16.11 per cent in chemical units, 14.15 per cent in textile units, 9.14 per cent in engineering sector and 5 per cent in plastic and rubber units. Thus, the proportion of women in food processing enterprises was more as compared to other non-traditional enterprises in India. But, the socio-cultural background of our country was patriarchal in nature, wherein women were traditionally and still kept in a view of house keeping resources rather income generating resources.

At this point, the differences among income-generating activities, self-employment and entrepreneurship should be mentioned so as to clarify and identify the problems and prospect of women entrepreneurs. A rigorous study on the problems and prospects found that system lag and 4-Es (Entrepreneur-Entrepreneurship-Enterprise-Environment), role-conflict, training methodology and andro-centrism are the problems of women entrepreneurs which curtail the growing prospects to become vibrant entrepreneurs Ganesan, Kaur, & Maheshwari (2001 & 2002). Income generating activities were often part-time and was practiced for raising additional income and did not tend to be self-sufficient, while self-employment referred to full time involvement in one's occupation, in which one may or may not have to take any risk to mobilize inputs and other resources to organize total production or to market the product and services. Contrast to these two, entrepreneurship involved strong sense of complex business skills and was mainly market and profit oriented. It involved management of other personnel. All entrepreneurs were self-employed and income generating persons, but all self-employed and income generating persons were not entrepreneurs.

In continuation of the gender perspective in entrepreneurship the relationship among enterprise, entrepreneurship and women could always be crucial, because of the socially sanctioned gender stereotyping and socio-cultural background of gender relationship. Entrepreneurship is the medium through which women can become economically independent, gain empowerment, social recognition, and status and gain equality. One of the most important things that a woman needed, in order to be a successful entrepreneur, was society's commitment to become empowered.

Issues & Perspective of Indian Women Entrepreneurship

Women entrepreneurship was not considerably high in India in comparison with other developing countries and developed countries, although it started much before than other countries. The Government envisaged measures to empower them e.g. trade related entrepreneurship assistance development (TREAD) for women was designed to empower women economically through the development of their entrepreneurial skills by eliminating constraints faced by them. It included assistance in form of loans, trade related training, trade information, counselling, and extension activities relating to product and market development. Thus, in spite of 'fundamental rights' 'equal status' 'tread', and other measures, women entrepreneurship was lagging behind, because the basic three concepts of entrepreneur, environment and support system were not integrated. Moreover, there were several other factors affecting women entrepreneurship, such as,

(*i*) Financial e.g. lack of inheritance rights leading to non-availability of collateral and thus blocked access to capital, low exposure to business and other decision making issues, less exposure to investment and saving issues, etc.

(*ii*) Education and training e.g. low levels of education, lack of training opportunities, poor accessibility to training programmes in terms of cost-effectiveness and training component, poor vocational training and poor emphasis on the concept of entrepreneurship in the regular study curriculum, etc.

(*iii*) Societal attitudes e.g. lack of social support, gender role stereotyping, gender inequality, lack of social recognition and society's confidence, etc.

(*iv*) Familial e.g. role conflict due to dual responsibility, family's low socio-economic status and lack of support for taking loan, lack of role models, etc. and,

(*v*) Personal e.g. lack of killer instinct, poor risk-taking behaviour, poor market survey, low decision making ability, attitudes to be satisfied with little male dependence etc.

Moreover, personality characteristics of the entrepreneur played a crucial role in establishing and maintaining any enterprising activity, and act as a catalyst for entrepreneurial growth. The individual's personality traits and characteristics account for the entrepreneurial manifestations in any entrepreneurship development activities especially in predicting entrepreneurial success Chattopadhay and Ghosh (2002). The effects of social variables, like education, experience, family could confound the output leading to poor entrepreneurial success. This made crucial to understand the psychosocial profile correlates of women entrepreneurs, which could designate appropriate interventions in terms of policies and programmes. The present study attempted to find the correlates of certain psychosocial variables over socio-background variables. Following assumption was initially made with corresponding hypothesis in accordance with the core objective.

Assumption

A number of psychological (psychosocial cum entrepreneurial) and background (socio-background) variables facilitate women entrepreneurs' to a more extent towards their success and sustenance in their enterprises. Social category, parental education, occupation, and family's financial status had direct and significant positive impact on women entrepreneurs' perceptions. Similarly, keeping the socio-cultural context of India in view, age of start-up and years of experience in the enterprise for women also played important role for survival in the field and locus of control perceptions. Thus, it was assumed that these psychosocial cum entrepreneurial and socio-background variables might have a definite pattern of correlations and hence, assuming relationships among these psychosocial cum entrepreneurial and socio-background variables was justified.

Objective

To investigate the interrelationships, nature and degree of correlation exist between psychosocial and psycho-entrepreneurial with socio-background variables.

Hypothesis

There is a significant correlation between psychosocial cum entrepreneurial and socio-background variables.

METHOD OF STUDY

Selection of the Area

The sampling has been done through two non-governmental organizations (MOOWES & AWAKE), which have common objectives in women empowerment through entrepreneurship training and marketing. The entire list of women entrepreneurs in food processing enterprises has been obtained.

Sample Size

The total universe was 78 and out of the total, only 32 entrepreneurs responded and included for the present research study. The women entrepreneurs in food processing enterprises involved in preparation of jams, jellies, pickles, papads, squashes, bakeries were considered through a purposive random technique, which comprised of respondents from two metropolitan cities namely Chennai (N=16) and Bangalore (N=16) equally divided numerically. The women were between the age group of 30-60 years and a majority of them were graduates and married.

Profile of the Study Area

The present study has been carried out in two non-governmental organizations in Chennai and Bangalore (two different metropolitan cities in India) named MOOWES and AWAKE respectively working for women entrepreneurship development.

(a) Moowes : Marketing Organization of Women Entrepreneurs, founded in 1990 with 12 members at Chennai. Activities of this organization included firstly, sharing their views and the difficulties while running their enterprises by forming networks amongst the women entrepreneurs, secondly, assisting women in the field of marketing by face-to-face contacts with the customers and thereby gaining confidence within the women entrepreneurs, and lastly, conducting periodic training programmes for women on various aspects required for running a business successfully and develop their entrepreneurial skills.

(b) Awake : Association for Women Entrepreneurs of Karnataka was founded in December 1983 comprising 500 members at Bangalore with an aim to empower women economically through entrepreneurship development. Activities of this organization primarily included counseling, entrepreneurship awareness programmes (EAP), entrepreneurship development programmes (EDP), trainers training programmes (TTP), development agency/NGO sensitization programmes and follow-up programmes.

Sampling Procedure

All the sample of this present study had been contacted through these two NGOs, as they were registered members of these organizations for marketing their products, sharing their technical know-how skills, seeking suggestions, and informal inputs for running the start-ups. The interview schedule was extended to the selected sample in two phases, i.e., Chennai and Bangalore entrepreneurs. The total span of data collection took almost six months in both the cities inclusive of identifying the women entrepreneurs in food processing enterprises, approaching them, convincing them for the interviews, selecting the sample among them, personally interviewing and extending interview schedule.

Variables and Tools

In the present study there are two categories of variables, i.e., socio-background, and psychosocial cum psycho-entrepreneurial.

(a) Socio-background variables

(*i*) Age (A)

(*ii*) Education (E)

(*iii*) Social category (C)

(*iv*) Year(s) of experience in running the enterprise (Y)

(*v*) Family income (FI)

(*vi*) Membership in associations (MA)

(*vii*) Entrepreneurship and technical training (ETT)

(*viii*) Place of enterprise (P)

(b) Psychosocial Variables

(*i*) Locus of control (LOC)

(*ii*) Perceptions of Self-Achievements (POA)

(*iii*) Perceptions of Success (POS)

(c) Psycho-Entrepreneurial Variables

(*i*) Conceptual understanding of entrepreneurship (COU)

(*ii*) Entrepreneurship awareness/technical know-how (EAT)

However, the present study clubbed the above two variables into psychosocial cum psycho-entrepreneurial variables to make discussion more comprehensive and compact (these two variables were related towards women entrepreneurship due to self? environment nature) the sample distribution amongst these variables were indicated in table-2.

Operational Definitions

Locus of Control (LOC): Locus of control is a learned behaviour where in which the individuals attribute responsibility for events or to factors within themselves and within their control or to factors outside their control Rotter (1954; 1966; and 1972). Locus of Control scale by Rao (1985), consisting of 20-paired statements (inventory) has been selected according to the nature of the present study and 10 inventories were used. High score (greater than 3.0) indicated that entrepreneurs are more inclined towards internality. Low score (less than 1.0) indicated that entrepreneurs were more inclined towards externality and medium score (1.0-3.0) indicates that entrepreneurs tending towards internality (i.e., they will be internal with time; range (<1.0->3.0).

Perceptions of Self-Achievements (POA): The perceptions of the self-achievements of women entrepreneurs comprised of six self-devised questions about their accomplishment perceptions with appropriate responses and administered for the present study scored in a four-point scale (range 6-24).

Perceptions of Success (POS): The perceptions of success of women entrepreneurs comprised of the self-rating towards their functioning of their enterprises comprised of six self-devised questions about their success perceptions with appropriate responses and administered for the present study scored in a four-point scale (range 6-24).

Psycho-entrepreneurial Variables: This section included conceptual understanding of entrepreneurship, entrepreneurship awareness and technical know-how skills for their entrepreneurial career.

Conceptual understanding of entrepreneurship (COU): Conceptual understanding of entrepreneurship may be defined as the level of understanding of basic qualities more precisely the personality traits in entrepreneurship for performing an entrepreneurial activity or the entrepreneurial pre-requisites essential for an individual in emerging as an entrepreneur. Conceptual understanding of entrepreneurship schedule had been modified from a training manual (training programme in entrepreneurship, developed by Entrepreneurship Development Institute of India, Ahmedabad in collaboration with Entrepreneurship Development Cell, Indian Institute of Technology, Delhi (1988)), which consisted of 11 questions modified according to the requirements of the present study by the researcher with appropriate five responses on five-point scale. The higher the score indicates that higher conceptual understanding (range 11-55). High score is '5' and low score is '1' against each response. The total part consists of eleven questions the maximum score being '55' and minimum score being '11' (range 11-55), indicating the higher the score better the conceptual understanding of entrepreneurship.

Entrepreneurship awareness and technical know-how skills (EAT): Entrepreneurship awareness here refers to the basic management skills (marketing, training, human resource and finance) and technical know-how refers to the knowledge and awareness on preservation and quality control techniques required for the nature of the enterprising activity more precisely food processing enterprise. It is a total measure through scoring the responses and finding the entrepreneurs' entrepreneurship awareness and technical know-how skills. Entrepreneurship and technical know-how skills schedule had been developed by the researcher individually containing 20 questions on five-point scale consisting of 20 questions with a five-point scale, i.e., strongly agree........., strongly disagree. The higher the score indicates higher entrepreneurship awareness and technical know-how skills (range 20-100). The high score is '5' and the low score is '1' for each response. The total part consists of twenty questions; hence the maximum score being '100' and the minimum score being '20' (range 20-100). Higher score indicates better entrepreneurship awareness and technical know-how skills.

Statistical Analysis

To correlate women belonging to having psychosocial cum psycho-entrepreneurial scores on socio-backgrounds, Pearson's correlation coefficient's ('r') test analysis were carried out using Statistical Package for Social Sciences (SPSS-10.0). The psychosocial cum psycho-entrepreneurial variables (Locus of Control, Perception of Success, Perception about Self-Achievements, Conceptual Understanding of Entrepreneurship and Entrepreneurship Awareness and Technical Know-how Skills) were scored and socio-background variables (Age, Education, Social Category, Year's of experience, Family Income, Membership in associations, Entrepreneurship and technical training, and Place of enterprise) were coded and analyzed in the present study.

Results

As can be seen from the above table-3, age ($r = 0.41$, $p < 0.05$), social category ($r = - 0.45$, $p < .01$) and entrepreneurship and technical training ($r = 0.37$, $p < 0.05$) correlated significantly with locus of control of women entrepreneurs and it was seen out of sample distribution across different socio-background variables (see table-1) wherein age is grouped and majority of the women entrepreneurs (56.25 per cent) lie within the age-group of 30-44 years and remaining (43.75 per cent) fall under the elderly age-group (45-59 years) this showed that increase in age enhanced internal locus of control of women entrepreneurs.

From the table-1 it is evident that majority of the women entrepreneurs hail from general class (75 per cent) in terms of social category ($r = - 0.38$, $p < .05$), and fall under the low family income ($r = - 0.37$, $p < .05$) group (68.75 per cent) and having memberships (71.87 per cent) in associations ($r = - 0.54$, $p < .01$) correlated significantly and inversely with conceptual understanding of entrepreneurship of women entrepreneurs. Thus, it was revealed that higher the social category, family income and membership in associations lower were the conceptual understanding of entrepreneurship for the women in food processing enterprises.

It is seen from table-1 that experience and place of enterprise wherein women equally distributed (50 per cent) respectively. Also from table -3 one can see that perceptions of success correlated significantly with years of experience ($r = 0.36$, $p < .05$). This indicated that years of experience in running the enterprise enabled the women entrepreneur to have high perceptions of success.

Perceptions about/of self-achievements correlated with place of enterprise significantly, ($r = 0.50$, $p < .01$) which clearly indicated that a perfect significant relationship exists between the place of the enterprise and the achievement perceptions, especially in the metros wherein women entrepreneurs have to sustain with their enterprises.

Education did not show any significant relationship with any of the psychosocial cum psycho-entrepreneurial variables.

Discussions

There would be significant correlation between background and psychosocial variables.

Results revealed that significant correlations existed between psychosocial variables and background variables. It was found that locus of control, conceptual understanding of entrepreneurship, entrepreneurship awareness and technical know-how skills, perceptions of success, and perceptions of self-achievements correlated significantly with age, social category, years of experience, family income, membership in associations, entrepreneurship and technical training, place of enterprise. Thus, the hypothesis has been partially accepted. Correlations between Psychosocial cum Psycho-entrepreneurial variables and Socio-Background Variables were discussed below with the background support of some relevant **psychological Theory.**

The findings revealed that locus of control had significant positive correlation with age and entrepreneurial training while it had significant negative correlation with social category. This indicated that an increase in age and entrepreneurship and technical training of women entrepreneurs also increased their internal perception of locus of control. This finding could be explained in terms of social maturity and its relationship with age, stress perception and coping styles. With age persons' social maturity and experience increased tremendously hence, her appraisal of a problem, coping mechanisms and perception of social support became more refined. This could directly have an impact on her ability to manipulate events in her favour, thus, changing her perception of events in terms of controllability or uncontrollability. However, the role of age in locus of control was not significant, in the study conducted by Box, Watts & Hisrich (1994) which attributed to factors like sample characteristics, particularly the age and size of the sample, but significant with a study by Ganesan, Kaur, Maheswari & Satapathy ($r < 0.37$, $p < .05$); 2003)) where they justified that those who were fall under elderly age-group due to their experience in this line developed an external orientation towards their success or failure which in turn kept them with high internality. Moreover, it implies that woman's increase in age-wise experience in a particular line developed more perceptions on internal locus of control. The finding of more internal locus of control among women who had more entrepreneurship and technical training was quite expected.

Training programme in this area generally included components on important psychological processes with specific parameters operating on an individual's (woman) entrepreneurial behaviour and performance. In addition to that, these also included all components related to entrepreneurial activities such as marketing, finance, demand supply etc. Social contacts, role model impact, etc., also increased significantly during training programmes. Thus, these factors might have a positive effect on a person's feeling of things under her control or not, hence could positively affect her internal perception of control.

Locus of control and conceptual understanding had significant inverse correlation with social category and family income, which implied that those women, who had more internal locus of control and conceptual understanding belonged to lower socio-economic category of society and those who had more clarity about the principles of entrepreneurship, were having lower family income. This finding was very encouraging for women belonging to lower socio-economic strata or backward caste prevalent in an Indian society, both for their status upliftment and for the growth of Indian developing economy. This could be due to the fact that once women from this section of the society started some new adventurous venture for making money, social recognition, economically in par status with men (independent sustenance) and self-satisfaction, they had already broken the existing social norms and pattern of coming out from home to participate finance related matters. Hence, they had less inhibition to face family as well as social role conflict. They had started recognizing their abilities and behaviour followed by believing in self, which perhaps fostered their internal perceptions of control.

The discussion gives direction to a further research on control perceptions, as it is exploratory in nature. Similarly, this might also have affected their conceptual understanding, being the beginners (nascent and first generation entrepreneurs) they had faced all obstacles but still continued to stand by with their determination to run the enterprise. The number of problems they faced and difficulty to solve them perhaps enhanced their conceptual understanding of entrepreneurship. The finding of women's perception of success increased with year of experience in running the enterprises. This was supported by one such study conducted by Box, Beisel & Watts (1995) which revealed experience directly influenced person's management skills of solving daily hassles which, has a causality effect in handling the enterprise. This also fostered the growth of the enterprise (both in terms of investment and profit) and thereby women's perception of their success in the enterprising activities. Women's perceptions of self-achievements had significant and positive correlations with place of enterprise, which revealed that self-achievements increased with urbanization of the place e.g., the entrepreneurial potentialities of a metropolitan city. Perhaps in a more advanced metropolitan city factors such as, availability of resources, easy marketing, more number of consumers, easy transport, plenty of financial support, training programmes on skill development, and other aspects of entrepreneurship, etc. which might have helped them to have higher perceptions about self-achievements from their enterprising activity. Above all, women status itself could be a major factor in more advanced metro cities, which might have affected women's perception about their self in terms of achievement and thereby from their entrepreneurial venture.

This finding can also be explained by the help of Maslow's need hierarchy theory (1954) and McClelland's theory on need for achievement (1961; 1962). Maslow's theory of motivation was based on the principles of deficiency stated that a deprived need motivated person's behaviour, and principles of progression advocated that higher order needs became activated only when the lower level needs were perceived as reasonably satisfied. Therefore, women entrepreneurs were motivated by higher order needs like social, ego and self-actualization needs, which were accomplished more in an advanced and modernized metro city. Similarly, McClelland suggested that, entrepreneurs had high 'need for achievement' in general. This theory could be further extended to the extent that when resources (infrastructure, raw material, transport, market, finance, social, etc.) were more accessible and easily approachable, need for achievement could be stronger, hence, in the present study place of enterprise correlated positively with perceptions of achievement. As pointed out by Devi & Latha (2000), the product related problems of the food processing industries were power-cut, non-availability of raw materials, high raw material price, labour, unbranded product in market, poor packaging materials, etc., which perhaps were not so acute in technologically more advanced metro cities. Education has not drawn any relationship with psychosocial cum psycho-entrepreneurial variables, perhaps metro entrepreneurs are well aware about the system of survival wherein education has least importance despite their graduation status.

Conclusion, Limitation, Implication and Suggestion

It is apparent from the present study that socio-background variables, viz., age, social category, entrepreneurship and technical training, membership in associations, family income, year of experience, place of enterprise do play vital roles in having determining relationships negatively and positively accordingly with psychosocial cum psycho-entrepreneurial variables viz., locus of control, perceptions of success, perceptions about self-achievements, conceptual understanding of entrepreneurship and entrepreneurship and technical know-how skills. Surprisingly, education has no correlations with any psychosocial cum psycho-entrepreneurial variables. However, more number of researches with a larger sample should be done in this area will not only widen the scope of generalization of the present findings but also reveal positivistic results in accordance with the current hypothesis thereby strengthening the inter-relationships within the proposed variables in the present study, which may further enrich the occurrence of psychological dispositions amongst corresponding variable specifications.

The study is limited to 32 women entrepreneurs in accordance with time, and concentrated only on married urban women entrepreneurs running food-processing start-ups lying under small sectors. The implication of the findings could be more appropriate for designing the training methodology, curriculum on entrepreneurship, programmes pertaining for tapping women to become entrepreneurs, identification of/ pre-determination potential entrepreneurs through persono-economic attributions, needs to be gendered were highlighted accordingly in lieu with the findings. Moreover, it had also given limelight into the avenues of further research on developing inventory based on perception lines which interface as a crucial parameter and factor to theorists, practitioners, facilitators, psychologists, social scientists, and other inter-disciplinary academicians involved in women entrepreneurship development.

Similar research can be extended to rural women involved in food processing, which might fact-find and decipher some more attributes untapped in the context of women entrepreneurship developmental avenues and support the advance trends in entrepreneurship research. Future researchers could concentrate on the relationships not only on psychosocial cum psycho-entrepreneurial with socio-background variables but also make an attempt to get the information of economic variables to stratify the success, achievements in terms of functioning / production, scale of operation, annual sales turn over, profit and loss etc. which can give substantiate the perceptional parameters on economic cum financial grounds.

Table 1 : Sample Distribution across Different Socio-Background Variables

Age Group	Respondents (f)	**Percentage**
30 – 44	18	56.25
45 – 59	14	43.75
Education	Respondents (f)	**Percentage**
Graduates	23	71.87
Non-Graduates	9	28.13
Social Category	Respondents (f)	**Percentage**
General	24	75.00
Backward Class	8	25.00
Years of experience	Respondents (f)	**Percentage**
1 – 4 years	16	50.00
5 years and above	16	50.00
Family Income	Respondents (f)	**Percentage**
Up to Rs. 4500	22	68.75
Rs. 4501-10000	10	31.25
Membership in Associations	Respondents (f)	**Percentage**
Yes	23	71.87
No	9	28.13
Entrepreneurship and Technical Training	Respondents (f)	**Percentage**
Yes	24	75.00
No	8	25.00
Place of Enterprise	Respondents (f)	**Percentage**
Chennai	16	50.00
Banglaore	16	50.00

N= 32, Respondents (f) – Respondent Frequency/Number of Respondents

Table 2 : Sample Distribution across Different Psychosocial and Psycho-entrepreneurial Variables

Psychosocial Variables

Locus of Control	Respondents (f)	**Percentage**
< 1.0 External	1	3.13
1.0 – 3.0 Internal	31	86.87
> 3.0 Highly Internal	-	0.00
Perceptions of Self-Achievements	***Respondents (f)***	**Percentage**
6-12 (Low)	-	0.00
13-19 (Medium)	30	93.75
19 and above (High)	2	6.25
Perceptions of Success	***Respondents (f)***	**Percentage**
6-12 (Low)	1	3.13
13-19 (Medium)	31	96.87
19 and above (High)	-	0.00
Psycho-entrepreneurial Variables		
Conceptual Understanding of Entrepreneurship	***Respondents (f)***	**Percentage**
11-25 (Low)	-	0.00
26-40 (Medium)	4	12.50
41-55 (High)	28	87.50
Entrepreneurship Awareness and Technical Know-how	***Respondents (f)***	**Percentage**
Less than 40 (Poor)	-	0.00
41 –60 (Low)	-	0.00
61-80 (Medium)	28	87.50
81-100 (High)	4	12.50

N= 32, Respondents (f) – Respondent Frequency/Number of Respondents

Table 3

Correlation between selective psychosocial cum entrepreneurial and socio-background variables

SB / *PSE*	*A*	*E*	*C*	*Y*	*FI*	*MA*	*ETTT*	*P*
LOC	0.41*	0.09	-O.45**	-0.23	-0.19	0.23	0.37*	0.03
COU	-0.07	0.28	-0.38*	0.04	-0.37*	-0.54**	-0.08	0.23
EAT	0.04	-0.23	0.15	0.25	-0.34	-0.18	-0.16	-0.23
POS	0.13	0.11	0.33	0.36*	0.08	0.05	0.14	-0.03
POA	0.32	0.03	-0.03	0.15	0.28	0.15	0.01	0.50**

N=32; *- Significant at 0.05 level ($p < .05$); **- Significant at 0.01 level ($p < .01$)
SB- Socio-Background Variables; PSE-Psychosocial cum Psycho-Entrepreneurial Variables

REFERENCES

1. Gupta, C. B., & Khanka, S. S. (2000). Entrepreneurship and Small Business Management (ed.), Sultan Chand Publishers: New Delhi: pp. 110-1.11.
2. Maslow, A. H. (1954). Motivation and Personality, Harper and Row, New York: 81.
3. McClelland, D. C. (1961), The Achieving Society, Princeton, Van Nostrand.
4. Rao, T. V. (1985). Locus of Control Test: Developing Human Resources, reproduced Goodstein, L. D. and William, J. (Pfeiffer edn.), San Diego, California University Associates.
5. Rotter, J. B. (1954). Social Learning and Clinical Psychology, Eaglewood Cliffs, N.N. Prentice Hall.
6. Rotter, J. B., Chance, E. J., and Phares, E. J. (1972). Application of a Social Learning Theory of Personality, New York; Holt, Rinehart and Winston.
7. Entrepreneurship Development Institute of India (EDI) & Entrepreneurship Development Cell, Indian Institute of Technology, Delhi, Entrepreneurship Development Institute of India Publication, (1988). Training Manual in Entrepreneurship. Ahmedabad, India.
8. Agarwal, C. (1995). Entrepreneurship Development amongst Women, North Eastern Women Entrepreneurs Association (NEWEA) Souvenir, Guwahati: pp. 3-4.
9. Box, T. M., Biesel, J. L., & Watts, L. R. (1995). Thai Entrepreneurs: An Empirical Investigation of Individual Differences, Background and Scanning Behaviour, Academy of Entrepreneurship Journal, Vol. 1, No. 1: pp. 18-25.
10. Box, T. M., Watts, L. R., & Hisrich, R. D. (1994). An Empirical Study of the Correlates of Employment Growth in the Tulsa MSA and Rural East Texas, Journal of Business Venturing, Vol. 9, No. 3: pp. 261-270.
11. Chattopadhyay, R., & Ghosh, A. (2002). Predicting Entrepreneurial Success: A Socio-psychological Study, The Journal of Entrepreneurship, Vol. 11, No. 1: pp. 21-31.
12. Devi, A., & Latha, K. M. (2000). Problems Related to Food Processing Industries in Selected Districts in Kerala, Journal of Avinashilingam Institute for Home Science and Higher Education for Women-Deemed University, Vol. 10, No. 3: pp. 139-145.
13. Ganesan, R., Kaur, D., & Maheshwari, R. C. (2000). Issues in Women Entrepreneurship. Fourth Biennial Conference on Current Trends in Entrepreneurship Research at Entrepreneurship Development Institute of India (EDI), Ahmedabad, Gujarat, India, Nov 8th-10th '2000. (In Proceedings)

14. Ganesan, R., Kaur, D., & Maheshwari, R. C. (2002). Women Entrepreneurs - Problems and Prospects, The Journal of Entrepreneurship, Vol. 11, No. 1: 55-93.

15. Ganesan, R., Kaur, D., Maheshwari, R.C. & Satapathy Sujata. (2003). Demographic Correlates of Background Variables with Locus of Control and Perceived Ladder of Success and Success Rate – A Study on Women Entrepreneurs, International Journal of Entrepreneurship, Vol. 7: 1-16.

16. McClelland, D. C. (1962), Business Drive and National Achievement, Harvard Business Review, Vol. 40, No. 4: 99-112.

17. Rotter, J. B. (1966). Generalized Expectancies for Internal Versus External Locus of Control of Reinforcement, Psychological monographs, No. 80: 1-28.

18. Savadi, S. V. (2001). Women Entrepreneurs in India: Scope and Opportunities, Southern Economist: 17-20.

Chapter 25

WOMEN PARTICIPATION IN DAIRY ENTREPRENEURSHIP A CASE STUDY IN KURNOOL DISTRICT OF ANDHRA PRADESH

Dr. I. Narendra Kumar*, Prof. G. Chandrasekar Rao, Prof. V.K. Reddy***, Dr. V.B. Naidu*****

"WHEN WOMAN MOVES FORWARD, THE FAMILY MOVES, THE VILLAGE MOVES AND THE NATION MOVES"

—JAWAHARLAL NEHRU

ABSTRACT

Dairying is regarded as one of the important activities that could supplement the income of the small rural families. Dairying may be suitable for women as they contribute milk production and animal husbandry. In Kurnool district of Andhra Pradesh, women are engaged in dairy business and dairy enterprise, which provides supplementary income to the family. Hence, a study was conducted in order to analyse the role of women in dairy entrepreneurship and its impact on the family 300 respondents interviewed randomly. It is found that family status has improved considerably as the diary entrepreneurs income substitute family income. They have

* Academic Consultant, Dept. of Econometrics, S.V. University, Tirupati-2, Andhra Pradesh.

** Principal, S.V.U. College of Arts, S.V. University, Tirupati-2, Andhra Pradesh.

*** Professor, Dept. of Econometrics, S.V. University, Tirupati-2, Andhra Pradesh.

**** Associate Processor, Dept. of Econometrics, S.V. University, Tirupati-2 Andhra Pradesh.

added value to the family as well. They have complemented wealth improvement also by means of bringing T.V. C.D, gold, cloth, purchase of house and so on. Even the women dairy entrepreneurs have decided to buy milk animals, improve feeding practices and go for collecting milk from outside. For further improvement the study suggest that the women dairy entrepreneurs need education and advanced training on dairy industry.

Introduction

India is one such Third World country, which is characterised by poverty and unemployment. According to 2001 census 36 per cent of the population is living below poverty line. Further, a huge share of developmental benefits is going in favour of a small section of the society, who has high socio-economic status. This has been resulting in the widening of income and wealth disparities. Consequently, the intensity of poverty has been rising and as a result, high incidence of poverty has been falling on women.

Rural women are mostly engaged in the farms as agricultural labourers. They face the problems of job insecurity and exploitation on par with the male workers. In addition, they are subjected to wage discrimination and the nature of work assigned to them is usually drudgery in nature. They are also subjected to sexual exploitation at the work place. In the homes they are expected to do all the domestic chores. Therefore, the rural women in lower strata of society need urgent and special attention.

Generally, it can be stated that the status of any section of population in a society is closely connected with its economic position. Therefore, many people are of the opinion that the economic dependence is the main cause for the inferior place of women in the society. Jawaharlal Nehru once observed that the freedom depends on economic conditions even more than political. If a woman is not economically free and self-earning, she will have to depend on her husband or some one else and dependents are never free. Therefore, any measure to provide them an opportunity to earn independent income assumes significance in liberating women.

Further, the poor people in rural areas either have no assets or have low productivity assets, which would not allow them to get more income. They are mostly unskilled labourers and do not have regular full time jobs. Even those who get some work are paid very low wages. In these conditions most of the women in rural areas, where 77 per cent of the female population lives, were forced to participate in economic activity to meet necessities of their family. This has further weakened the bargaining power of rural work force in general and women workers in particular. In these conditions, the creation of productive employment opportunities in the rural areas is required to provide necessary economic base and to improve living conditions of the rural people, in general and rural women in particular. In India as elsewhere in the third world, women are dairy farmers. The research studies revealed that women are major contributory to milk production and Animal Husbandry.

Dubey says that women have been playing a vital role in the households since ages. In rural areas where agriculture is the prominent activity, agro-based industries like food preservation, bakery, dairy, poultry are taken up by women[1]. Dairying as an Agro Based Industry is playing a significant role in the rural economy of Andhra Pradesh. The industry being highly rural oriented is a vital source for additional income and employment to small farmers and landless labourers. Andhra Pradesh has made noteworthy strides in organising milk production and in diversification of their products manufactured for local as well as national markets.

Women in rural areas are primarily engaged in various chores connected with the dairy industry. To ensure clean and quality milk production, participation of women in dairy activities is necessary. Women, who occupy half of the world population status, perform two-thirds of world work. Dairy development has been planned to change the rural structure in favour of the weaker sections of the society and especially rural women.[2] A major share of important roles performed in day-to-day activities of dairying has unanimously been accepted by or assigned to the female of the family. Agricultural labourers and marginal and small farmers who practice what can be termed as subsistence production consists of women maintaining small number of milk animals on a precarious feed base of gathered green fodder, grazing and dry fodder obtained as by-products from either a small land-base or as partial payments for wage labour. Interms of labour input, it generally depends more on the status of the women within the family, whether mother, mother-in-law, widow or divorcee or on the caste of the family than on the asset holding of the households.

Adman made an analysis of the value of women economic role. The work on an average ten to fourteen hours a day on seed and grain storage and preservation, post-harvest rice processing, vegetable and fruit-growing, poultry-raising, live-stock care, food processing, household manufacture, building maintenance and repair and fuel and water gathering. Attention is drawn to the lack of appreciation generally given to women contribution, leading to their neglect in policy formulation. Modernisation efforts involving traditional female activities are aimed at men so that women do not have the opportunity to acquire new skills that could raise their productivity.[3]

Athreya dairy farming can help rural women gain an economic asset, secure an equitable income and raise their productivity levels. Although women labour inputs into live-stock maintenance and dairy production vary to some degree by region, age or caste, generally speaking all cleaning, washing, feeding, watering and milking of animals is performed by women and female children of the family.[4]

National Commission of Agriculture reported that Dairy Enterprise is a suitable means for increasing the incomes of rural masses, specially small and landless labourer and marginal farmer households. Operation Flood is the major dairy programme in India today, aimed at extending the benefits of marketing and modern processing to the small producers who are scattered and disorganised.[5]

Dairying is regarded as one of the important activities that could supplement the income of small rural families. Hence promotion of dairying has been recognised as an enterprise which is suitable to be run by women. One of the important factors responsible for placing so much emphasis on dairying as a measure to improve the condition of rural women is the impression that dairying fits well with the farm level infrastructure. Keeping milk animals has never been considered as a separate occupation from Agriculture in our country.

A dairy holding can be compared with a production enterprise where the milk animal is a machine; the raw material is the feed, fodder and the final consumer product is milk. It depends on the proper care and efficient management of the milk animals. The feeds and other resources determine how efficient the produce will be. The management depends upon the intimate knowledge and understanding of the system. Even under unorganised rural situation, improved cattle can produce higher milk.

A major share of important roles performed in day-to-day activities of dairying has unanimously been accepted or assigned to the female of the family. Women are also the major contributors to milk production and animal husbandry. Such female members have less knowledge about scientific know-how and are handicapped in securing such information from various available sources due to many reasons. Unfortunately, the existing training in different aspects of agriculture and particularly in dairying is male biased. They are supposed to communicate with their wives. However, this assumption has been found untrue.

Andhra Pradesh is predominantly an agricultural state with a good potential for milk production. As per 2001 census in milk production Andhra Pradesh was fifth position in India. In Andhra Pradesh the milk production level is 54.60 lakh tonnes in 2005 in terms of anticipated milk production.

Kurnool is the Rayalaseema region, which is dry and arid. A very high percentage, approximately 65 per cent of rural population engaged in milk production. The average monthly milk production in Kurnool district procurement of milk to about 647.60 lakhs litres and hardly 78.10 lakh litres are sold in the district. Women attend to the agriculture in most parts of Kurnool district mostly. Quite a good number of jobs like management of live-stock, feeding and milking of the animals, cleaning of cattle sheds, scratching grass from the fields, chaffing of fodder, filling of manure pits, preparation of milk products etc., are carried out by women.

In cognisance of the above facts, it is felt essential to develop a specific knowledge-base about the role of women in Dairy Entrepreneurship **(DES)**, particularly in Kurnool District, in which most of the women are engaged in dairy business and dairy enterprise provides supplementary income to their families. For some families income from the dairy is the main source, to meet the family expenditure. This might lead to the improvement of the economic and social position of rural women in the family and in the community at large. The present investigation, the main objective is to study the role of women in dairy entrepreneurship and its impact on the family. And to compare the roles of ‘at home’ and ‘mobile’ women entrepreneurs in dairy entrepreneurship.

The district is administratively divided three divisions and from each division one mandal is selected namely Kosigi, Mahanandi and Midthur. From each mandal a sample 100 women are selected. The total sample, there is 300. The present study is by an exclusive interview. Schedule has been preferred and canvassed for the collection of data.

The results are discussed in the concepts like profile of women dairy entrepreneurs, the role of women in dairy entrepreneurship development and the role of women in the utilization of earnings from dairy are discussed keeping in view the objectives of the study. Profile of the dairy women entrepreneurs was studied along the lines of educational status, type of family, occupational status, economic status, land holdings and status of dairy entrepreneurship in DES.

Educational Status

Based on the existing educational status of the women, they were divided into three groups. Viz., illiterates, primary and secondary. The following Table-1 are explain in this case.

Table-1 : Educational Status of the Respondents

Educational level	*Home*	*Mobile*	*Total*
Illiterates	74 (47.43)	62 (43.05)	136 (45.33)
Primary	53 (33.97)	56 (38.88)	109 (36.33)
Secondary	29 (18.58)	26 (18.05)	55 (18.33)
Total	156	144	300

Source : Field Data

The data in Table-1 denote that majority (45.33 per cent) of the women dairy entrepreneurs were illiterates as against 36.33 per cent of them who had primary education. A low 18.33 per cent of the women respondents had secondary education. Similar trend was observed both among 'at home' and 'mobile' women DES. Nearly 45.33 per cent of women DES in both groups were illiterates. It was observed that illiterate group of women are experiencing illiteracy as a problem in maintaining accounts related to dairy business. Hence illiteracy is a handicap for the promotion of women dairy entrepreneurship.

Type of Family

The type of family viz., joint and nuclear was studied as a factor influencing the DES among rural women. The data related to type of family is presented in Table-2.

Table-2 : Types of the Family of the Respondents

Type of family	*Home*	*Mobile*	*Total*
Joint	45 (28.84)	38 (26.38)	83 (27.66)
Nuclear	111 (71.15)	106 (73.61)	217 (72.33)
Total	156	144	300

Source : Field Data

Table-2 shows that 72.33 per cent of women surveyed, belonged to nuclear families. Similarly high per cent of women were living in nuclear families among both 'at home' (71.15 per cent) and 'mobile' (73.61 per cent) women DES. A very few 28.84 per cent women belonged to joint families among 'at home' women DES. Now-a-days nuclear families are preferred in place of joint families and also the conditions are forcing them to do so. This situation is a serious handicap to the management of DES by women who need assistance from others in the family.

Occupational Level

The occupational level of the women DES is categorised into three groups viz., Dairy in combination with Agriculture labour, farmers and business. All the women DES are engaged in dairy in combination with other work. The data in the following Table-3 are explained.

Table-3 : Occupational Status of the Respondents

Occupational level	*Home*	*Mobile*	*Total*
Agriculture labour and dairy	64 (41.02)	51 (35.41)	115 (38.33)
Farmer and dairy	58 (37.18)	45 (31.25)	103 (34.33)
Business and dairy	34 (21.79)	48 (33.33)	82 (27.33)
Total	156	144	300

Source : Field Data

Table-3 indicate that a high (38.33) per cent of them were engaged in a combination of occupations viz., Agriculture labour and dairy. The combination that comes next in order was farmer and dairy in 34.33 per cent of the women were engaged, and 27.33 per cent of women is business and dairy. This 21.79 per cent and 33.33 per cent women DES who belong to 'at home' and 'mobile' the occupation 41.02 per cent and 35.31 per cent of women DES who belong to 'at home' and 'mobile' group were engaged in Agriculture labour and dairy. The remaining occupation is farmers and dairy is 37.18 per cent, 31.25 per cent women DES belongs at home and mobile. The finding it is clear that 41.02 per cent at 'home' group were engaged in traditional occupations of Agriculture labour and dairy.

Land Holding

Land possession of women DES is presented in Table-4. Based on the possession of land holding, the women DES were categorised into three groups viz., small farmers (0 - 2.5 acres), medium farmers (2.5 – 7.5 acres) and large farmers (more than 7.5 acres).

Table-4

Land Holding of the Respondents

Size of the farmers	*Home*	*Mobile*	*Total*
Small farmer	58 (37.18)	65 (45.13)	123 (41.00)
Medium farmer	66 (42.30)	53 (36.80)	119 (39.66)
Large farmers	32 (20.51)	26 (18.05)	58 (19.33)
Total	156	144	300

Source : Field Data

Table-4 reveal that majority of 'at home' (42.3 per cent) and 'mobile' (45.13 per cent) groups belonged to small farmers and medium farmers. In small farmer categories of 'at home' 37.18 per cent women DES belonged to the small farmers and 20.51 per cent large farmers group. In mobile group 36.8 per cent medium farmer 18.05 per cent large farmer group. Totally 41 per cent is small farmers, 39.66 per cent and 19.33 per cent medium and large farmers group.

Economic Status

Based on the income level of the family, the respondents were divided into three groups, viz., low (below Rs.10,000/-), middle (Rs.10,000/- to 20,000/-) and high (Rs.20,000/- and above).

Table-5
Economic Status of the Respondents

Economic level	*Home*	*Mobile*	*Total*
Low	64 (41.02)	71 (49.3)	135 (45)
Middle	58 (37.17)	45 (31.25)	103 (34.33)
High	34 (21.79)	28 (19.44)	62 (20.66)
Total	156	144	300

Source : Field Data

From the Table-5 shows that 45 per cent respondents belonged to low income level. The remaining were distributed over low (34.33 per cent) and high (20.66 per cent) income groups. 'At home' group of women DES distributed over different economic groups indicate that quite a number of them belonged to low (41.02 per cent) and middle (37.17 per cent) and high (11.79 per cent) income groups. Among the 'mobile' group women DES, majority of them belonged to low 49.3 per cent, middle 31.25 per cent and high 19.44 per cent income groups.

Status of Dairy Entrepreneurship

Status of DES of the women was studied in the light of their income from dairy, years of experience are discussed in Table-6. Based on the years of experience in DES, the respondents were grouped into three categories i.e., 1-5, 5-10 and 10 and above years of experience.

Table-6
Income and Experience Status of Dairy Entrepreneurship

Items	*Home*	*Mobile*	*Total*
Years of Experience			
a) 1 – 5 years	56 (35.89)	78 (54.16)	134 (44.66)
b) 5 – 10 years	74 (47.44)	52 (36.11)	126 (42)
c) 10 and above	26 (16.66)	14 (9.72)	40 (13.33)
Income Through Dairy			
a) Low	61 (39.1)	64 (44.44)	125 (41.66)
b) Middle	56 (35.89)	48 (33.33)	104 (34.66)
c) High	39 (25)	32 (22.22)	71 (23.66)
Total	156	144	300

Source : Field Data

The data in Table-6 reveal that most (35.89 per cent) 'at home' and 'mobile' 54.16 per cent women fell into the first category viz., 1-5 years of experience, and there followed by 'at home' 47.44 and 36.11 per cent and 'mobile' women who had 5-10 years of experience and 16.66 per cent and 9.72 per cent women DES 10 and above years exercise in 'home' and 'mobile' category. Based on the income from dairy, women DES were grouped into three groups viz., low (below Rs.2500), middle (Rs.2500 – 5000) and high (Rs.5000 and above). From the data it is clear that majority (39.1 per cent) 'at home' women DES belonged to low income group 35.89 per cent of middle income group and 25 per cent in high income group. In contrast to this 44.44 per cent of 'mobile' women DES belonged to low income group 33.33 per cent of them to middle income group and 22.22 per cent in high income group. From the overall picture it is clear that 41.66 per cent of women DES belonged to low income group, 34.66 per cent middle income group and 23.66 per cent high income group. From the results it is clear that more 'mobile' DES were receiving more money as compared to at 'home' women DES.

Table-7

Impact of Dairy Entrepreneurship on Family Status of the Respondents

Items	*Home*	*Mobile*	*Total*
Purchased T.V. and CD Player	26 (16.66)	21 (14.58)	47 (15.66)
Purchased clothes	45 (28.84)	38 (26.38)	83 (27.66)
Payment of loans	37 (23.71)	33 (22.91)	70 (23.33)
Taken good food	48 (30.76)	52 (36.11)	100 (33.33)
Total	156	144	300

Source : Field Data

Table-7 represents the details about the change in the status of family of women DES. All the DES in both 'at home' and 'mobile' groups agreed that there is a change in their family status after starting DES. The reason for this appears to be as the income of the family increases it is certain that there will be change in certain aspects of the status of the family.

All DES of both 'at home' and 'mobile' used the income from dairies that is a continuous source of income, to buy clothes for and take good food on special occasions. DES gives regular-income monthly or weekly, thus it helps to meet the daily demands of the family easily. Take good food was also made from the dairy income by majority of women DES 33.33 per cent and at home 30.76 per cent and 36.11 per cent at home and mobile DES. Among the two types of DES, considerable number of women DES both in 'at home' 16.66 per cent and 'mobile' 14.58 per cent groups bought equipment like T.V, and CD Players, etc., from the dairy income. Most of 'at home' 28.84 per cent and 'mobile' 26.38 per cent women DES were purchasing clothes through dairy income. The payment of loans 23.71 per cent and 22.91 per cent women DES at home and mobile. The most of DES were utilising the income from DES for both permanent assets as well as daily expenditure.

Table-8

Impact of Dairy Entrepreneurship on Family Expenditure of the Respondents

Items	*Home*	*Mobile*	*Total*
Education for children	26 (16.66)	21 (14.58)	47 (15.66)
Purchasing of gold and others	31 (19.87)	28 (19.44)	59 (19.66)
Purchase house	12 (7.69)	8 (5.56)	20 (6.66)
Purchased clothes	51 (32.69)	39 (27.08)	90 (30)
Daily family budget	36 (23.07)	48 (33.33)	84 (28)
Total	156	144	300

Source : Field Data

Table-8 shows the impact of DES on the family expenditure. All the women DES both in 'at home' and 'mobile' groups agreed that DES is helped to their families in one way or the other. The reason is very simple. DES, being their main or additional source of income that is continuous source of income during off seasons; in particular, it definitely helps their families. All the women DES in both 'at home' and 'mobile' groups reported that they were using the income obtained from DES for buying clothes, 30 per cent and for daily expenditure 28 per cent of the family. Another use of income from dairy as reported by DES was for purchasing of gold (19.66 per cent). From the finding it appears that women DES realised the need for educating the children and as such they are showing interest in educating their children.

15.66 per cent of the DES were also utilizing the dairy income for education for children and 6.66 per cent purchase the houses from daily income. Among the two categories, some 16.66 per cent of the DES from 'at home' group and 14.58 per cent from 'mobile' group were found to be education for children from dairy income. And some families 19.87 per cent of 'at home' group and 19.44 per cent of 'mobile' group women DES were for purchasing gold and others. Some purchase of house 7.69 and 5.56 of the DES from 'at home' and at 'mobile' group. The DES impact the purchasing cloths and daily family budget 32.69 per cent, 27.08 per cent, 23.07 per cent and 33.33 per cent at house and mobile groups.

Table-9

Future Plans of Dairy Entrepreneurship of the Respondents

Items	*Home*	*Mobile*	*Total*
Taking loans for purchasing more milk animals	63 (40.38)	42 (29.16)	105 (35)
Collection of more milk	42 (26.92)	57 (39.58)	99 (33)
Improving feeding practices	51 (32.69)	45 (31.25)	96 (32)
Total	156	144	300

Source : Field Data

Table-9 gives the details about future plans and for improving DES and also the person who suggested these futures plans. From the data, majority 35 per cent of women DES had the idea of buying animals by taking loans to improve DES. Only 32 per cent of them were having the idea of using improved feeding practices and 33 per cent of them were interested in collecting more milk.

Among the two groups, most (40.38 per cent) of the women DES in 'at home' group were having the idea of taking loans for purchasing the milk cattle collection of more milk and improving feed practices (26.92 per cent and 32.69 per cent). But in 'mobile' group 29.16 per cent of the women were interested in taking loans and purchasing more milch animals and the 39.58 per cent were interested in collecting more milk and 31.25 per cent improving feed practices, which is a risk-less job. The loan facility to all and improving the DES. Majority of the respondents felt that buying more milch animals by taking loans will help them in improving the DES. Majority of these respondents feit that buying more milch animals by taking loans help them in improving the DES.

Dairy entrepreneurship seems to be a major enterprise in the rural areas. Impact of DES on their families is definite and positive in the aspects of food, health, clothing and children's education. Some of the rural women DES expressed that they are literally living on dairies, otherwise it is very difficult to survive during off seasons, with uncertain rainfall, in particular. Even though, women DES are managing DES, they are facing many constraints that can be avoided through education and training. Because, most of the women DES were facing illiteracy as a serious handicap in managing money matters in DES.

Though the status of women has increased to a certain extent, due to DES, it is not up to the level of their satisfaction. Economic independence in family budgeting are denied to majority of women, though their involvement in DES is high. In order to improve the condition of DES in their families, there is an urgent need to bring about changes in their role regarding certain aspects of DES. The co-operative venture it needs sensitive approaches to deal with them for achieving appreciable returns.

SUGGESTIONS

- ➢ An exploratory study can be planned to assess and manage the problems of dairy entrepreneurship with special reference to women.
- ➢ Identify the factors responsible for successful and unsuccessful dairy entrepreneurship.

- Development of a tool to identify the characteristics of successful dairy entrepreneurs.
- The research can be planned in consultation with a government agency to improve the dairy entrepreneurship in certain selected rural areas.

REFERENCES

1. Dubey.V.K., Pandey.K.N., Kaur.J., **Reaching Rural Women**, Interaction National Council of Development Communication, Varsha, 1987.
2. Martychan.,Mitra.M., Athreya .G., Dholakia.A., **Indian Women-A study of their Role in Dairy Movement**, Vikas Publishing House Pvt.Ltd., New Delhi, 1986.
3. Adman.S.R., **Social Changes and Rural Women: Possibilities of Participation** paper presented at the seminar on the Project of Woman in Social – Economics Development in Bangladesh, Dacca, 1978.
4. *Op. cit.,* 1986.
5. National Commission on Agriculture Report, New Delhi, 1971.
6. District Hand book, Chief Planning office, Kurnool, 2005.
7. Mandal Hand Book, Chief Planning office, Kurnool, 2005.

Chapter 26
FISHERWOMEN AND ENTREPRENEURSHIP

*Arpita Sharma

ABSTRACT

Issues of fisherwomen in entrepreneurship development are discussed in this chapter. Although women are playing a major role in fisheries sector, but they are not recognized. Entrepreneurial activities undertaken by fisherwomen are a sort of small scale family business but still different from strict family business structure. Two case studies are discussed, one is from the private sector and the other from the public sector. These case studies have brought the picture that fishing entrepreneurship brings additional source of income, confident of tackling challenges, a better quality of life, a motivation on value added products making, developing positive attitude, and actively involving social welfare activities. These case analysis brought out one important conclusion that there are a number of avenues and scope for the women to involve in fisheries enterprises. The study concludes that there is a need to train and equip women to play a larger role as entrepreneurs for which they require capacity development and support in terms of better infrastructural support, markets and finance facilities.

* Senior Scientist, Central Institute of Fisheries Education, Deemed University, Indian Council of Agricultural Research, Seven Bungalows, Versova, Mumbai - 400 061
Email: arpita_sharma@yahoo.com, a.sharma@cife.in

Introduction

The word entrepreneur is derived from the French verb 'Entreprendre'. It means to undertake. In the early 16th century, the French who organized and led military expeditions were referred to as entrepreneurs. The term 'entrepreneur' was applied to business, initially by the French economist Cantillon in the 18th century; to designate a dealer who purchases the means of production for combination into marketable products. Another French person J.B. Say expanded Cantilllon's idea and conceptualized the entrepreneur as an organizer of the business firm central to its distributive and production function. The leading economists of all schools, including Karl Marx have emphasized the contribution of the entrepreneurs to the development of economics.

The term entrepreneur in the modern sense came into usage in the late 18th century with the advent of industrial revolution in England. The entrepreneur is often thought of as the risk taker. The term entrepreneur is subject to a number of definitions. One may define entrepreneur as a person who specializes in taking judgemental decisions about the coordination of scarce resources, discovers new ideas of business and manages the entire operations to exploit the market opportunity.

The term 'entrepreneurship' is often used interchangeably with 'entrepreneur'. Entrepreneurship refers to a process and not a person. It is the outcome of result of continuous inspiration of a person to start her own enterprise. It is the exploitation of the opportunity, readiness to take risks and to face competitive market conditions. The business proposition which involves risks is known as venture. Hence, it can be described that an entrepreneur is a person who establishes a venture. Entrepreneur is a person who discovers new ideas and business opportunities, brings together funds to establish a business, organizes and manges its operations in order to provide economic goods and services to the public.

A successful entrepreneur recognizes the commercial potential of a product or service, designs operating policies in marketing, production, product development and the organizational structure. An entrepreneur is usually expected to perform the following functions

- Assumption of risk
- Business decision
- Managerial functions
- Function of innovation

Opinions are likely to differ about whether given individual has entrepreneurial activity. Some people may overestimate a person's ability and others underestimate it. This means that the identification of an entrepreneur is itself a judgemental activity.

Why entrepreneurship

With entrepreneurship, money is often the initial reward sought. There may be different reasons ranging from wealth creation, variety, control or power etc. Though, not only compensation in its own right, money is often an indicator of other kind of rewards. People get to manage their own wealth. As a women entrepreneur she is responsible for managing the financial resources of her units in the organization, she must assume the responsibilities that go with managing her own financial assets.

Money is often uses as a measure of other specters of life. Prestige and recognition may be by product of income, but they may also be signed out for rewards for their skill, intellect, competence and effectiveness. With money, recognition and increasing prestige comes an accumulation of power. The power base may be positions, but it, it is also a reflection of the enterprise. Effectiveness in management, although difficult to describe is easily recognized.

Research has shown that the percentage of female entrepreneurs still remains low in relation to that of male entrepreneurs and to the percentage of women in the population. The creative and entrepreneurial potential of women is a latent source of economic growth and new jobs, and should be encouraged.

Gender, work and entrepreneurship

It is assumed and reported in literature that in past it was an exclusive privilege of men to take up economic activities and women to manage homes. However, this can be argued on the premise that the interpretation itself that 'women are in the private sphere' and the 'men are in the public sphere' is wrong. The fact is that women go in the public sphere whenever the family wants them to go. In reality the private and the public sphere do not really apply, what really apply is that family controls what women should do. Moreover, women have always worked. The reality is that their work has not been recognized as economic activity. With this context, the definition of work and economic activities needs to be redefined.

The encouraging part is that have literature on women's now we work, over time, space and occupational categories. Many of the characteristics of women's work are documented and in the Indian context we are familiar with the inferior technology, low productivity and low reward in activities performed by women. As also the burdens imposed by their multiple roles as producers and reproducers.

But the standard sources of information about women's activities performed by women present a fractured image of all the work that women actually do. Data systems are particularly weak on women's work.

In 1981, the Bengal census authorities were told that women are not to be entered as employed unless they are engaged in special work of a distinctly definite character. It is thus not difficult to imagine the extent of under reporting that is peculiar to women's economic activity when it is filtered through definitions that emphasize exclusion. (Mukherjee, 2000). The important question is that a century later and after much advocacy for reform in the counting of women's work is the scenario very different? The invisibility seems to be a constant in women's lives.

It is seldom realized that the wide spread practice of arbitrarily defining women's work has very serious consequences. On one hand it systematically understates women's contribution in productive activity and on the other hand it indirectly justifies the gender based wage differentials been where women and men are engaged in the same kind of work.

Elaborating it a little further, to the issue of male migration to the urban areas it is important to emphasis that the responsibility of sustaining links of urban labour is primarily borne by women members of the family. It is their continued presence in the rural homestead that serves to protect whatever frail rights and status the male had in the village and it is the continued supply of the female family labour that ensures unbroken agricultural cycles. In effect, the male workforce can retain its urban profile largely because women hold the rural buffer in place. This work of women is an important element in sustenance of industrial labour but invisible.

As regards to entrepreneurship, the traditional social system is showing substantial changes. Today women in trade and industry have proved more successful than men. Women continue to move into the stream of economic activities and have taken up the responsibility of doing variety of jobs in a big way. Women seek opportunities to move into such projects which can generate self employment. Still there are several problems and limitations which prevent a large number of potential women entrepreneur from entering into a business venture. It is estimated that while women constitute 50 per cent of our population, the proportion of enterprises set up and run by women are just 1 per cent.

But only because of the sex differential of ownership and management of a business, one cannot label a person of a particular sex as entrepreneur. It is reported that an enterprise owned and administered by women having minimum financial interest of 51 per cent of the share capital and giving at least 50 per cent of the employment generated in the enterprise to women are considered as enterprise run by women entrepreneur.

It is assumed that the intention of this definition is good but it can be argued that this is limiting in nature. The first part of the definition which states that enterprise owned and administered by a women having minimum financial interest of 51 per cent of the share capital seems to be worthy. But, the second part of the definition that at least 50 per cent of the employment generated in the enterprise is for women is very limiting in nature and has to be seen in the context whether there are similar conditions for men too.

Fisherwomen and entrepreneurship

This section is started by an old and famous quote of Lao Tzu: *"Give a man a fish and you feed him for a day. Teach a man to fish and you feed him for a lifetime."*

So, can we say that accordingly the man was taught to fish and women took up the pre-harvest and post-harvest activities? Was any training provided to women for undertaking these activities like the man was taught to fish? It is another matter, though often overlooked that in many parts of India and some other Asian countries women do fish and it is reported that 'women do not fish' is a myth (Williams et al. 1998) but due to some reasons or the other there is a very clear exclusion of women form the capture fisheries activities in the literature, planning and policies.

Women in the fisheries sector are everywhere. They are there in pre-harvest, harvest, post-harvest sectors of capture fisheries, in aquaculture, marketing, processing, resource management and as students, researchers, scientists, teachers, change agents/NGO's etc. In fact, they are everywhere. Degree of visibility of women's participation in fishery activities may vary from country to country and within country from region to region.

Fisheries sector has often been mistakenly viewed as mainly male dominated and only the post harvest activities as being female dominated. Whether women have made some inroads into technical and higher level occupations in fisheries is to be questioned but there is an increasing feminization of some of the jobs. (Sharma, 2004)

Feminist work has made us rethink women's contributions to fishery development. One needs to move away from the traditional concept of work, which sees work in terms of male activities to an inclusive emphasis on women's activities. Rejecting the notion that work is neutral, this perspective understands work and gender as socially defined.

Women are productive and efficient when they have access to the right technologies and opportunities. In the era of globalization, it is particularly important to ensure women participate in the new process, namely entrepreneurship since they are often marginalized because of inadequate infrastructure and societal bias.

Without going into the critique of the literature reported as regards to the gender specific roles in the fisheries sector what needs to be emphasized here is that fisheries and the related activities performed by fisherwomen in India have since time immemorial existed as small business development in almost all the states. It is mainly concerned with the economic objective and this has been traditionally done to earn livelihood.

Entrepreneurial activities undertaken by fisherwomen are a sort of small scale family business but still different from strict family business structure. For example, the work of fish marketing which is a century old system has managed on the basis of conventions and beliefs. The style of management is undertaken by the fisherwomen herself or in few cases by the family members. This work does not show a tendency towards diffusion between ownership and control. Here ownership and control go hand in hand. It is controlled, managed and financed by fisherwomen themselves or in few cases family members. There are cases where women enjoy full authority in this entrepreneurial activity. This follows age old traditions and techniques of management. It usually does not employ any modern techniques of management like long range planning. The issue is that whether proper managerial efficiency exists or not. Whatever be the case, fisherwomen herself assumes all business and risks and stands to the event of failure of business or the profits of business.

The work performed by fisherwomen will come under the classification of agriculture and allied industries sector. There is a very good scope and potential in the agricultural sector for entrepreneurial activity. Government also provides different support for this.

Constraints as regards to entrepreneurship development of fisherwomen

It is reported that running a business can be more difficult for women, because they have more family responsibilities and face discrimination. At some point, though, women need access to financing, or their business can't grow. But it's not just finance but life's circumstances that can make opening and running a business difficult for women. "Women carry double burdens," "They're the providers of home and family environment. There are many difficulties due to these roles." There are inherent strengths too when a women takes entrepreneurship like "When women tend to start businesses, they start smaller, grow slower and reinvest everything, but, "They have a more realistic growth plan. It grows in a steady way.

The issues fisherwomen face as regards to entrepreneurship development are presented in table 1. The various issues and problems faced by fisherwomen are presented under different heads. An attempt has been done to list the confronting issues of fisherwomen as regards to entrepreneurship. But, still there are a number of micro issues which affect them.

Table 1: Issues of Fisherwomen in Entrepreneurship Development

Particulars	*Market*	*Finance*	*Management and education*	*Family/ Society*
Hygiene, quality control	Competition with large scale	Inadequacy of finance	Lack of training facilities finance in management, technical and other skills	Family responsibilities
Problem of raw materials	Hardship in marketing outlets	Delayed payments	Lack of education	Male dominant society
Cold storages	Inflation, demand recession	Inadequate Credit control	Deficiency in management	Lack of networks
Transport	Weak competitive positions	Awareness	Less self confidence	
Maintenance	Low sales value	Less risk bearing capacity	Lack of information and expertise	
Poor location, landing centres	Less value addition	Less savings	Less awareness	

Research has shown that women face a number of difficulties in establishing and maintaining business. Although most of these difficulties are common to both genders, in many cases they tend to be more significant for female entrepreneurs. This is due to factors such as a poor business environment, the choice of business types and sectors, information gaps, lack of contacts and access to networking, gender discrimination and stereotypes, weak and inflexible supply of childcare facilities, difficulties in reconciling business and family obligations.

These may be limiting for fisherwomen but it is also well documented that they can be taught to recognize and assess risk in decision making. They can be trained to expand and maximize their potential to make major contributions to organizations. Despite the obstacles, women still want to own their own business. Positive examples of entrepreneurship in fishing community do exist. Although, they may be lacking in large budgets, corporate sponsors, and high media profile of mainstream programs.

Case Studies

Some successful Indian cases are documented in literature like All Women Pisciculture Co-operative, Manipur, Adivasi Mahila Machua Samiti, Bastar, Chattisgarh, Carp spawn rearing by women and fish farming as a livelihood activity for coastal fisherwomen have also been undertaken. In the recent times there have been initiatives for new model of entrepreneurship for fisherwomen, which has tried to integrate and link business development and community development. In this chapter we discuss two case studies. One is from the private sector and the other from the public sector.

Shree Fish Suppliers, a self-help group, Mumbai

This is an example of a private company Taj Group to transform a group of ordinary Mumbai fisherwomen into a collective business enterprise as part of the company's community initiative for building livelihoods.

This is a case study of Shree Fish Suppliers, a self-help group based in a fishing village in Mahim, a suburb of Mumbai. They supply fish to three Taj Group hotels in Mumbai — the Taj Mahal Palace & Tower, the Taj President and Taj Lands End. Last year, they registered a turnover of Rs 30 lakh. And they have just bagged an annual contract for the current year worth Rs 1 crore.

The women had to learn the ropes of business, become entrepreneurs and compete against well-established vendors. Every morning, eight women head for Mumbai's wholesale Crawford Market to bargain over fresh pomfret, bekti and ladyfish, according to the orders given by each of the hotels. They then break up into three groups and head for the three hotels in cabs. Other women sit in a small shack close to their homes, painstakingly cracking open crab shells to prepare ready-to-eat crabmeat. This is an additional source of income for them. A year of business has transformed these women, from unassuming and unsure individuals to determined entrepreneurs, confident of tackling challenges. From deciding to wear uniform saris to approaching banks for loans and voicing their opinions, these fisherwomen are slowly but surely empowering themselves while giving their families a better quality of life. Last year they sold fish worth Rs 30 lakh and made a profit of Rs 83,000. This year they have a contract to supply 50 per cent of the hotels' seafood supply, with a projected business of Rs 1 crore. Naturally, they hope to make a much bigger profit. The plan includes investing in a delivery van, as the order size has increased. "Getting the annual contract is like a dream come true. Mr Srinivasan from the Taj group states that hopes that these unique initiatives will have a ripple effect and become a national movement that benefits many more local communities. The mutually beneficial business initiative with Shree Fish Suppliers certainly seems to have worked. Whilst giving back to the community, Mr Srinivasan and the Taj Group seem to have hauled in a prize catch. (Reproduced from http://www.tata.com/0_our_commitment/community_initiatives/articles/20060614_prize_catch.htm)

Tapuriaghata Nari Unyan Kendra, Kolkata, West Bengal

'Tapuriaghata Nari Unyan Kendra' is a registered society which has been formed under the technical guidance of CIFE, Kolkata under a two year (2001-2003) project entitled "Conceptual framework of a working model of a women fisher group at a selected village in West Bengal". Tapuriaghata is a fishing village within the city limits of Kolkata. During various focused group discussions and meetings, women of a fishing village Tapuriaghatta, were told about the benefits of working in groups. The process of sensitization to work in groups was done. Following this, a 'Fisherwomen Group' was formed. This group was further developed as a registered society 'Tapuriaghata Nari Unyan Kendra'.

This society is engaged in the socio-economic improvement activities of the fisherwomen of the fishing village Tapuriaghata in Kolkata. This society was registered on 10.01.02 by the Certificate of Registration of Societies, West Bengal (India) Act XXVI of 1961. Its registration number is S / IL / 7367. President of the society is Mrs. Bakul. Further on applying this society has also been given a registration number 210401639 as a small scale unit on 17.7.02 by Directorate of Cottage and Small Scale Industries, Government of West Bengal. This society has also audited their accounts in the last financial year.

Members of this society were provided need based training in different fishery and non fishery related activities like 'Carp breeding and nursery management', 'Preparation of value added fish products like prawn pickle, fish pickle, fish snacks, prawn papad, fish paste sandwich spread and fish papad.

Members of this society utilized the knowledge gained from these training programmes to form small scale business. The training on 'Value Added Products' have been utilized to start a small scale business. Prawn pickle, prawn papad, fish papad, fish snack prepared by them have been displayed and sold in exhibitions and profits have been earned. They have also started supplying as per the orders received. Though, lack of big orders limits the profits. With the training 'Carp breeding and nursery management' women gained information on this topic. They reported that if they are given support they have positive attitude towards participation in aquaculture as they are engaged in snail collection and duck keeping. Lack of possession of a water body was reported to be an obstacle. (Sharma *et. al,* 2003)

These activities enabled them to earn money thus empowering the women economically. This example of a working model of a 'Fisherwomen society' has trickled across to the fisher women of nearby villages.

The president along with the women of this society are also actively participating in social welfare related activities like adult education, children's education, Embroidery classes, Participation in aids awareness programmes, Anti drug campaigns. They have also attended trainings like chalk making and candle making organised by other organisations.

CIFE, acted as a catalyst in arranging for support to this society from other organisations like Technology Information Forecasting and Assessment Council, Department of Science and Technology, New Delhi. Detailed information of this society is presented in the society's website http://www.geocities.com/tnariunyankendra. This fisherwomen society is also presented as success story of Technology Information Forecast and Assessment Council, (TIFAC), DST, New Delhi fisheries projects on development of value added fish products on the website http://www.tifac.org.in/news/fish_for_all.htm.

There are strengths as well as some weaknesses of these success stories. But what is important to note is that there are a number of avenues and scope in the fisheries' sector. In most of the case studies or success stories as regards to fisherwomen it is seen that the entrepreneurial activity has been initiated by a different organization with a view of economic empowerment and community development. Though, as such this is not a critique and these efforts needs to be appreciated but what is needed is to focus on bigger challenges in the era of globalization.

The time has come to analyze the issue of entrepreneurship amongst fisherwomen with respect to confluence of factors. There are concerns as regards to the existing small. These small business development units in the era of market competition and globalization and the retail revolution taking place at a fast pace. With this respect, the conversion of fisherwomen into successful proprietors of small enterprises is one of the few politically viable tools. Fisherwomen can form their own consortiums, which would help them generate a decent regular income as well as profits.

For this, along with basic and advanced skills and training in accounting, marketing, management, and organizational development the value of high environmental and labour standards, socially useful goods and services and local ownership has to be taught to them. This has also been reported by Sharma and Das (2001) Failing to make these criteria as essential features of entrepreneurial programs, risks leaving the fishing communities behind for another generation. Small scale units require extensive management and technical consultancy. Small units have general inherent limitation in the form of scarce capital and lack of suitable equipments.

In order to facilitate the creation of entrepreneurship among fisherwomen various measures are needed. Identification and evaluation of national measures related to start-ups, information/advice, funding, training, mentoring and networks concerning the promotion of entrepreneurship amongst fisherwomen are needed. Relevant good practices adopted by other countries and successful case studies should be considered as well.

Conclusion

To conclude fisherwomen have been working since time immemorial, but they have limited themselves to the livelihood issues and small profits. There is a need to train and equip them to play a larger role as entrepreneurs for which they require capacity development and support in terms of better infrastructural support, market and financial facilities.

REFERENCES

1. Mukherjee M. (2000) In search of pasts, History, women's movements and women's studies, Published by IAWS, Calcutta.
2. Sharma A. and Radha C. Das., (2001) Functional training for women in fisheries, Aquacult, Vol. 2, No: 2, Page: 159-162
3. Sharma A. R.C. Das, S.N. Ojha, U.K. Maheshwari and P.S. Pandey (2003) 'A successful study of co-operation of women fishers', The co-operator, Vol 41, No. 2, Page: 60-63
4. Sharma A. (2004) Book Chapter: 'Fisheries sector: A Gendered Perspective' (Page: 201-205) in book 'Advances in Fish and Wild Life Ecology and Biology' by B.L. Kaul, Daya Publications, Delhi.
5. Williams. M.J., M.C. Nandeesha, V.P. Corral, E. Tech, and P.S. Choo (1998) Proceedings of the 'International Symposium on Women in Asian Fisheries', V Asian Fisheries Forum.

Chapter 27

THE ROLE OF FISHERWOMEN IN FISHING ACTIVITY : A STUDY OF THE FISHERWOMEN IN VISAKHAPATNAM, ANDHRA PRADESH

*Dr. T. Sobhasri

**Dr. G. Sanjeevayya

ABSTRACT

The socio-economic and living conditions of the fisherwomen are very low standard, because of higher degree of economic backwardness, illiteracy, abnormal family size, dependency, higher prevalence of bad habits, etc. The fisherwomen play a pivotal role in fishing activity. The time spent by fisherwomen in fishing activity being very high, which kind of activity is almost a regular feature everyday in their life. Hence, the study analyses the pattern of trade activity of the fisherwomen, fisherwomen's role in trade activity, pattern of investments by women in trade, status of the fisherwomen's trade, etc.

Introduction

Women play a pivotal role not only in the family environment, but in the working environment as well. Generally, in any kind of living kingdoms, the female species usually played a dominant role in the day-to-day activities such as the protection of the offsprings, collection and preparation of food etc. During the era of the family system in the

* Associate Professor, Dept. of Social Work, Andhra University, Visakhapatnam-530 003, A.P. email: tadisobha@yahoo.co.in.

** Teaching Associate, Dept. of Social Work, Andhra University, Visakhapatnam-530 003, A.P. email: sanjeev962001@yahoo.co.in.

primitive and folk societies, a similar trend could be noticed. In the due course of time, civilization gradually came into existence all over the world and in-turn; the working activity of women became restricted substantially and was confined mainly to the household activities. As a result, the physical, social and psychological characteristics of women have also changed and she is lagging behind when compared to men, over the period. Further, the status of the women folk is changing according to the period, civilization, religion and region. Therefore, women are forced to work only due to poverty despite the age old traditional and customary restrictions.

After the implementation of globalization and liberalization policies, the minimum expenditure of families have increased abnormally due to hike in prices of common and essential commodities. Hence, women are also rather compelled to work earning some additional income to meet the growing expenditures of their households. All these conditions are significantly responsible for increase in the share of women as a workforce, even in the traditional Northern States, which have lower participation-rates of the female workforce in the earlier periods. This sort of transformation is very high in the case of fishing communities. At present, with rapid mechanization in marine fishing adopting modern techniques in pisciculture and aquaculture, these have significantly affected the socio-economic and living conditions of the fishing communities in the coastal regions of the country. As a consequence, the fishing communities, along with their women-folk have been facing tremendous pressures both on the domestic as well as the economic fronts, as the fisherwomen play significant roles in fish-marketing aspects regularly.

Ganguli, J.M. (1967), Kalwar, A.G. (1968), Simhadri, Y.C. (1969) Moses, S.T. (1969), Plattean, J.P.H. (1974), Raghava Reddy, G. and Dasa Radha Rami Reddy, B. (1975), Hartman, W.P. (1977), Malleswara Rao, V. (1977), Suryanarayana, M., Venkateswara Rao, A. (1977), Mathur, P.R.G. (1978), Ratnam, N. V. (1979), Subba Rao, W. (1979), Panikar, K.K.P and Balaraju, K. (1981), Prasad, A.R. and Krishna, R.R. (1981), E, Nadeesha M.C. et al (1984), Ramakrishna (1984), Nalini Nayak, K.M. (1985), Pillai, N.N. (1985), Venkateswara Rao, A. (1985), etc., have assessed the socio-economic status of the fishermen communities in different regions. These studies have highlighted the household characteristics of the fishermen, fishing activity, traditional and cultural aspects, the pattern of disposal of their fish-catch, incidence of poverty, indebtedness, status and role of fisher-women in different fishing communities.

Material & Methods

The present study has made an attempt to understand the women role in fishing activity in Visakhapatnam district of Andhra Pradesh. Therefore, a random sample of 200 fisher women who actively participated in fish trade was selected from three areas i.e. Appughar, Jalaripeta and Fishing Harbour in Visakhapatnam district to collect required data during the study period of January to March 2006. The data were collected from fisherwomen through questionnaire observation, interviews and informal discussion techniques.

Results & Discussions

Table-1. It is observed that huge proportion of fisherwomen i.e., 98 per cent belong to Hindu Religion. However, it is further found that two per cent of the fisherwomen have converted into Christianity. Since fishermen belong to Hindu religion thus the data indicates that huge per cent of fisherwomen belong to Hindu religion.

The sub-caste background is one of the important social indicators, which shows great influence on the day-to-day activities of the fisherwomen. Hence, the sub-caste background of the fisherwomen is analysed and the details are as follows:

It indicates that maximum number of fisherwomen belongs to vadabalija community (57.50 per cent), followed by Jalari community (26.50 per cent) and the rest (16 per cent) are Agnikulakashtriyas. The high proportion of vadabalija is mostly due to the reason that each of sub-caste among fishermen in Andhra Pradesh is strong in one specific area. Vadabalija sub-caste is numerically strong in north-coastal districts than in other areas.

Age character is one of the important parameters to reflect the views, work culture and activities of the fisherwomen. Hence, the age composition of the respondents is assessed and the details are as follows:

It shows that the highest number i.e., 45.50 per cent of fisherwomen are found in the age-group of 31 to 50 years, followed by 36 per cent in 19 to 30 years age-group, 14 per cent are in above 50 years age-group, while the lowest (4.50 per cent) are found in the age-group of less than 18 years.

Marital status of the fisherwomen determines their day-to-day activities to a greater extent. Hence the marital status of the fisherwomen is analysed and the details are as follows:

In respect of marital status, it indicates that maximum proportion that is about 86.50 per cent of fisherwomen are married, while 8.50 per cent are widowed, 4 per cent are unmarried and 1 per cent are divorced.

The educated women play a predominant role and shows significant change in the day-to-day activities of the women. Hence, the education status of respondents is assessed.

It is found from table that 99 per cent of fisherwomen are illiterates. Whereas 0.50 per cent each (one respondent) are having primary and secondary education respectively.

Illiteracy is predominantly found in the rural women. Hence, the study analyses the levels of illiteracy of the respondents and the details are as follows:

The table shows that of the total, 78 per cent of fisherwomen neither can read nor write. However, 12 per cent can read and write and 9 per cent can only read. Though they can read and write but that doesn't mean they are educated.

The activities of fisherwomen are diverse, showing significant changes over the period. Hence, the study analyses the primary and secondary occupations of fisherwomen and the results are as follows:

The table shows that maximum proportion, that is about 96.50 per cent are with the primary occupation of only selling the fish at the local market followed by 1.50 per cent working as labour. While the rest are found in fishing-related activities such as trading, the fish at small scale 1 per cent, trading the fish at large scale 0.50 per cent and fish auctioning 0.50 per cent.

In respect of secondary occupation, about 9 fisherwomen out of 200, (4.50 per cent) have both Primary and Secondary Occupations, of which about 7 fisherwomen (3.50 per cent) in the total population have been working as coolies, with two fisherwomen (1 per cent of the total population) working as maidservants.

Family size is one of the indicators to determine the socio-economic status of the households. Hence, the study analyses the family size of the respondents. The study divided the size of the family into three types. They are small, medium and large. Small includes parents with less than two children; medium represents parents and children in between three and four. Large family includes parents with more than five children.

The table shows that 68 per cent, of the fisherwomen come from medium size. Further, it is found that 26.50 per cent of them belong to large families and very negligible per cent, that is 5.50 belong to small size family. Thus it shows that in the fishermen communities over population is a common character in their lives.

Table–2. It is observed from table that 44 per cent of the fisherwomen selling their fish in Fishing Harbour followed by 39.50 per cent in local markets. However 15 per cent of the fisherwomen sell their commodity both in the fishing harbour as well as in the local markets. Further, relatively a low proportion (1.50 per cent) of the fisherwomen sell their commodity in other areas, such as at some residential areas and colonies

In relation to the mobility of the fisherwomen to dispose their commodities, it is noted that about 72.50 per cent travel a distance between 4 to 6 Km. from their residence to the trade center, followed by 22 per cent 7 to 9 Km. and 3.50 per cent 10 to 12 Km. Only 1.50 per cent travel less than 3 Km, while 0.50 per cent travel more than 13 Km. Therefore it is found that allmost 98.50 per cent of the fisherwomen travel more than 4 Km. to trade their fish. From the data on the mode of transport used to reach the trade center, it is found that 92 per cent of the fisherwomen are using auto-rickshaws, 4.50 per cent on bus and 3 per cent on foot. In other words it is noted that utilization of public transport is highly insignificant.

As about the time-schedule of the fisherwomen, a maximum proportion i.e., about 89 per cent leave the house between 7 and 10 a.m., followed by 9 per cent before 6 a.m. further, a maximum proportion of the fisherwomen (68 per cent) return to the house between 2 and 6 p.m., followed by 7 to 10 p.m. (14.50 per cent) and 8 per cent of them return after 10.00 p.m. It can be concluded here that the fisherwomen spend more time in the trade centers.

Table-3. A huge (96 per cent) number of the fisherwomen go themselves (self) to the market to sell their fish, followed by the other family members and 1.50 per cent daughters. Moreover about 69.50 per cent of the fisherwomen go to the market once in a day whereas 30.50 per cent go twice in a day. However, 85 per cent of the fisherwomen reported that they go to the market six days in a week (except Saturday) but only 12 per cent go in all the seven days in a week.

Table-4. It is found from the table that 55 per cent of the fisherwomen invested between Rs. 2,501 to 5,000 per day. It is further noticed that 34.50 per cent invested less than Rs. 2500/-. However, 10.50 per cent invested more than Rs. 5,000/-. On the other side 84 per cent explained that the money was insufficient to run the trade where as 14 per cent felt that the money was sufficient to run the trade.

As regards the major source of finance it is observed that nearly 50.50 per cent of the fisherwomen depend on the middlemen, followed by 27 per cent moneylenders and 19 per cent on their own. Interestingly, it is found that involvement of other organizations such as Banks (1 per cent) and Governmental Institutions is negligible. With regard to the payment of interest on loans it shows that highest member (41.50 per cent) pay less than Rs. 500/- per month. However, 16 per cent pay in between Rs, 501/- and 1000/-, 12 per cent in between Rs. 1001/- and 1500/- and just 2.50 per cent more than Rs. 1500/-. It is also observed that the only 28 per cent of the fisherwomen did not pay any interest. It means they are self sufficient in their trade.

About 74 per cent of the fisherwomen felt that the fish trade brings less profit and 23.50 per cent reported that the fish trade is just profitable. Whereas only 2.50 per cent felt that it's a profitable trade. The study further probed to enquire about the reasons for continuing the fish trade even though it is not profitable. It is found that 60 per cent continuing the fish trade because of lack of alternatives. On the other side 28.38 per cent could continue because they are habituated and 12.16 per cent felt it's for their survival.

Conclusion

It is evident from the above discussion that the role of women in fishing activity is very vital, and that majority of the fisherwomen involve in almost all the activities such as acquisition of the produce, transportation of the produce to the market, selling etc., The time spent by fisherwomen in fishing activity being very high, which kind of activity is almost a regular feature every day in the fisherwomen's life. Further, the volume of trade and investment in their business is relatively on a lower scale. However, dependency on moneylenders and middlemen is very high for getting adequate finance, while the role of banking and governmental organizations in the financing of fisherwomen is negligible. Moreover, lower levels of income and a higher degree of indebtedness affect the income of the fisherwomen even though they do good business, while maximum proportion of the fisherwomen's earnings handed over to their husbands for meeting the household expenditure.

The findings of the study are showing that participation of the fisherwomen in the organizational and service sectors is relatively lower, when compared to the other working women. The main reason for this phenomenon is the heavy work of the fisherwomen. Hence, it is essential to mobilize the fisherwomen to form grous and involve them in developmental activity.

REFERENCES

1. Ganguli, J.M. (1967): *"The fishermen of Kerala",* East and West Publishers, Calcutta.
2. Kalwar, A.G. (1968): *"A Note on the Socio-Economic Survey of Fishermen Community of Thane District",* Dept. of Fisheries, Bombay (Mimeo).
3. Simhadri, Y.C. (1980): "Socio-Economic and Cultural Profiles of Coastal Fishing Village in Andhra Pradesh", *Man in India,* 60 (3-4), pp. 221-234, Ranchi.
4. Mosses, S.T. (1969): "The Valayans of Pamban", *Man in India,* 9 (8) pp. 64-76. Ranchi.
5. Plattean, J.P.H. (1974): "Impact of Mechanization of Fishermen", Voluntary Action, 16 (2-3), March-June pp. 13-19, New Delhi
6. Raghava Reddy, G. and Rami Reddy Dasa Radha (1975): "Thummala Penta Fishermen", *Kurukshetra,* 23 (11), pp. 16-18, New Delhi.
7. Hartman, W.P. (1977): "Bhandaravanipeta: A Marine Fishing Village, Andhra Pradesh", *Dept of Small Scale Fisheries in South West Asia, Colombo,* RAS/74/031-Working Paper No.16, pp. 1-35. New Delhi.
8. Malleswara Rao, V. (1977): "The Fishermen Community of Srikakulam", *Kurukshetra,* 25 (12), pp. 20-22, New Delhi.
9. Suryanarayana, M. (1977): "Marine Fisher Folk of North-Eat Coastal Andhra Pradesh", *Anthropological Survey of India,* pp. 1-14, Calcutta.
10. Venkateswara Rao, A. (1977): "Fishermen Victims of Middlemen Dragner", *The Economic Times,* 24 November, p. 4, New Delhi.
11. Mathur, P.R.G. (1978): "The Mattilla Fishermen of Kerala", A Study in Interrelationship between Habitat, Technology, Economy, Society and Culture", *Kerala Historical Society,* Trivendrum.

12. Ratnam, N.V. (1979): "Socio-Economic Organization and Problems of Technology Transfer to Small Scale Fishermen", *Workshop on Social fertility of Small Scale Fisheries Development,* September, pp. 3-8, Madras.

13. Subba Rao, W. (1979): "Economy of Marine Fishing Community: a Case Study of Jalaris in Visakhapatnam, A.P", Workshop on Social Fertility of Small Scale Fisheries Development, *Eastern Economist* 14 (10): pp. 508-11, New Delhi.

14. Panikar, K.K.P. and Balaraju, K. (1981): "Socio-Economic Status of Fishermen Community of Calicut Area", *Marine in for., Revt.,* No.33, pp. 1-12. New Delhi.

15. Prasad, A.R. and Krishna, R.R. (1981): "Helping Fishermen to a Better Life", Kurukshetra, 29 (15), pp. 25-28, New Delhi.

16. Nadeesha, M.C. *et. al.* (1984): "An Evaluation of the Socio-Economic Status of the Fishermen Community of Munfad Village of Dharwar District", *Cooperative Perspective,* 19 (3), pp. 62-68, Karnataka.

17. Ramakrishna (1984): Problems of Poor Fishermen", *Indian Express,* 10 Aug. pp. 7 & 8, Vijayawada.

18. Nalini Nayak, K.M. (1985): "Study of Fishermen in Paradeep, Orrisa", *Programme for Community Organisation,* Trivendrum.

19. Pillai, N.N. (1985): "Children of the Waters", *Kurukshetra* 3 (11), pp. 8-9. New Delhi.

20. Venkateswara Rao, A. (1985): "Victims of Middlemen and Money Lenders", *The Economic Times,* 22 September, p. 4, New Delhi.

APPENDIX

Table 1: Profile of the respondents

Characteristics	*Fisherwomen*	*Per cent*
Religion (N=200)		
Hindu	196	98.00
Converted Christians	4	2.00
Sub-Caste Category (N=200)		
Vadabalija	115	57.50
Jalari	53	26.50
Agnikulakshtriya	32	16.00
Age in Years (N=200)		
Less than 18	9	4.50
19 to 30	72	36.00
31 to 50	91	45.50
50 and above	28	14.00
Marital Status (N=200)		
Un-married	8	4.00
Married	173	86.50
Widowed	17	8.50
Divorced	2	1.00
Education (N=200)		
Illiteracy	198	99.00
Primary	1	0.50
Secondary	1	0.50
Levels of Illiteracy (N=198)		
Can only read	18	9.00
Can read and write	24	12.00
Neither can read nor write	156	78.00

Characteristics	*Fisherwomen*	*Per cent*
Particulars of Occupation (N=200)		
Primary Occupations:		
Labour	3	1.50
Fish Auctioning	1	0.50
Trade the fish at large-Scale	1	0.50
Trade the fish at small-Scale	2	1.00
Only sell the fish at local market	193	96.50
Secondary Occupation (N=200)		
Maid servant	2	1.00
Coolie	7	3.50
Nil	191	95.50
Family Size (N=200)		
Small	11	5.50
Medium	136	68.00
Large	53	26.50
Vadabalija	115	57.50
Jalari	53	26.50
Agnikulakshtriya	32	16.00
Age in Years (N=200)		
Less than 18	9	4.50
19 to 30	72	36.00
31 to 50	91	45.50
50 and above	28	14.00
Marital Status (N=200)		
Un-married	8	4.00
Married	173	86.50
Widowed	17	8.50
Divorced	2	1.00

Characteristics	*Fisherwomen*	*Per cent*
Education (N=200)		
Illiteracy	198	99.00
Primary	1	0.50
Secondary	1	0.50
Levels of Illiteracy (N=200)		
Can only read	18	9.00
Can read and write	24	12.00
Neither can read nor write	156	78.00
Particulars of Occupation (N=200)		
Primary Occupations:		
Labour	3	1.50
Fish Auctioning	1	0.50
Trade the fish at large-Scale	1	0.50
Trade the fish at small-Scale	2	1.00
Only sell the fish at local market	193	96.50
Secondary Occupation (N=200)		
Maid servant	2	1.00
Coolie	7	3.50
Nil	191	95.50
Family Size (N=200)		
Small	11	5.50
Medium	136	68.00
Large	53	26.50

Table–2. Fisherwomen and their participation in the fish trade

Characteristics	*Fisherwomen*	*Per cent*
Place of fish trade (N=200):		
Only at fishing harbour	88	44.00
At local markets	79	39.50
Both the places	30	15.00
Other places	3	1.50
Distance from residence to trade centre (N=200):		
Less than 3 km.	3	1.50
4 to 6 km.	145	72.50
7 to 9 km.	44	22.00
10 to 12 km.	7	3.50
More than 13 km.	1	0.50
Mode of transport to reach the trade center (N=200):		
On walk	6	3.00
By autorickshaw	184	92.00
By bus	9	4.50
Any other	1	0.50
Departure at the residence (N=200):		
Before 6 a.m.	18	9.00
7.00 a.m. to 10.00 a.m.	178	89.00
10.00 a.m. to 2.00 p.m.	4	2.00
Return to the house (N=200):		
Before 6.00 a.m.	1	0.50
6.00 to 10.00 a.m.	13	6.50
10.00 to 2.00 p.m.	11	5.50
2.00 p.m. to 6.00 p.m.	130	65.00
7.00 p.m. to 10.00 p.m.	45	22.50

Table-3: Fisherwomen's role in the fish trade activity

Characteristics	*Fisherwomen*	*Per cent*
Person goes to the market for selling fish (N=200):		
Self	192	96.00
Daughter	3	1.50
Other family member	5	2.50
Fisherwomen of visit go to the market to sell fish in a day (N=200):		
Once	139	69.50
Twice	61	30.50
Number of days visiting the market to sell fish in a week (N=200):		
All seven days in a week	24	12.00
Six days in a week	170	85.00
Basing on the need of income	6	3.00

Table-4. Pattern of investment by Women in Trade:

Characteristics	*Fisherwomen*	*Per cent*
Investment of amount on trade (per day) (N=200):		
Less than Rs. 2,500	69	34.50
2501 to 5,000	110	55.00
More than 5,000	21	10.50
Money to run the trade (N=200):		
Sufficient	28	14.00
Insufficient	172	86.00
Source of finance (N=200):		
Self	38	19.00
Loan from bank	2	1.00
Money-lenders	54	27.00
Middlemen	101	50.50
Government Institutions	—	—
Others	5	2.50

Amount paid towards interest (per month) (N=200):		
Nil	56	28.00
Less than Rs.500	83	41.50
501 to 1,000	32	16.00
1001 to 5,000	24	12.00
More than 5,000	5	2.50
Profitability of trade (N=200):		
Less profitable	148	74.00
Just profitable	47	23.50
More profitable	5	2.50
Reasons to continue when the trade is not profitable (N=148):		
Lack of alternative	88	59.46
For survival	18	12.16
Habituated	42	28.38

•The total is only 148 as the remarks 52 in the opinion of profitability in fish trade

Chapter 28

WOMEN IN INFORMAL SERVICE SECTOR : A CASE STUDY OF BEAUTECIANS IN VISAKHAPATNAM CITY

*Dr. (Mrs.) P. Tara Kumari

ABSTRACT

Beautician is a 100 percent women oriented and house based industry, which do not require much capital. Hence, women irre$pective of age, marital status and social status have taken up beautician as profession either to earn on their own or to increase their family income. By using simple random sampling method, 45 beauty parlours were interviewed in 2000 and discussed in this chapter. As a remarkable increase (51 percent was noticed) in the establishment of beauty parlour at Visakhapatnam city the study was carried out to find out the reason for the growth of this enterprise in the town. The study found that well educated women are engaged in this activity and they run the parlours in both residential and commercial areas of the city. Even with low investment, the women can generate significant income, which supplement family income. Again the beauty parlour enterprise is a very profit making enterprise, providing employment to a large number of women, and thereby contribute women empowerment. It is predicted hat the beautician enterprise had a wide scope for expansion and improvement in future.

* Assistant Professor, Department of Economics, Andhra University, Visakhapatnam-530 003, A.P.

Introduction

The most marked change in the economic structure of many countries in the world including India in the 20th century, particularly in its later half has become the change in emphasis from manufacture of physical goods to the production of intangible services. Many economies have transformed as service economies and USA was the first economy declared as service economy way back in 1948, followed by Canada, Australia, Japan, France, Germany, Italy, Netherlands, Sweden and United Kingdom. A popular definition describes services as any act or performance that one partly can offer to another that is essentially intangible and do not result in the ownership of any thing. Its production may or may not be tied to a physical product. There are four commonly cited characteristics of services and they are intangibility, inseparability, variability and perishability. These services can be broken down into four main components and they are physical products, service products, service environment and service delivery. The growing emphasis on services in developed and developing economies may be assigned to several reasons. Shrinkage of manufacturing sector, increase in new technologies such as information processing and telecommunications, tangible services in exports, demand for health care and such allied are seemed to be the root causes for the increasing demand for service sector.

It may be observed that, in the early stages of economic development, in India, the shift of labour force is witnessed more in favour of Industry, but as economic development gained further momentum, the service sector is likely to absorb a large share of labour force with an increasing contribution to GDP. Along with this, the percentage share of the labour force employed in the service sector is also likely to show an increase. In India the share of services have moved upwards from 43.9 per cent in 1993-94 to 47 per cent in 1999-00. This has shown a shift in GDP share in favour of services, the percentage of labour force absorbed in the service sector was also rising because of rapid industrialization and consequent growth of banking, finance, trade and commerce etc. are not only providing more employment but are generating the process of occupational shift in favour of service sector. Once the basic needs of the majority of the population are met, there is growing demand for service sector in the form of education, health, recreation and service activities.

The formal service sector considered in terms of the capital intensity, the level of technical know-how and organization they are trade, transport, communication and manufacturing. On the other hand informal service sector is extending a variety of new income generating services in an urban economy such as electrical repair, watch, clock, jewelery repair, footwear, peddlers, scavengers, motor vehicle, auto repair and transport operation etc. That is they are petty trade, transport, repair and maintenance and offering specialized services they are nothing but disguised labour. Other than these services maidservants, washerwomen, cooking, sweeping, child rearing, and mending come under personal services. Women predominantly in the specialized services as the only work that they can find are informal in nature. In recent years the trend is that more and more women are tending to personal service activities due to various advantages extended by family members and government. Encouragement by the family members to enhance their income and opportunities of loans and subsidies extended by the government agencies such as B.C, S.C corporations and national banks under various schemes like SUPUP, SUME, NRY etc. Those women who have skills and access to credit are taking up several employment activities like tailoring, petty shops, and other micro enterprises like grinding, processing and beauty parlours etc. The emerging institutions that extending vocational training short term training programes such as fashion technology and design, fabric painting, interior decoration and beautician courses etc. have attracted the women force to undergo training and establishing their own enterprise has lead to the growth of employment in this sector. Out of these, the beautician 100 percent women oriented and home based industry, which do not require much capital.

Therefore several women irrespective of age, marital status and social community have taken up beautician as profession either to earn on their own or to increase their family income. The establishment of beauty parlour as an enterprise in Visakhapatnam city has been increased two to three parlours in early 1980s to more than 700 parlours either official or non-official by 2000. About 25 beauty parlours are located exclusively in M.V.P colony, a large residential area in Visakhapatnam city. Some women run beauty parlours at their residence, with out any advertisement and provide employment opportunities to women at the rate of 2-3 persons per establishment. As this is a new line of employment by women in VSP city, it is important to know that the scope for development of this activity and its potential for generating income and employment.

Methodology

The study is based on primary data collected from a sample of beauty parlours. For selecting the beauty parlours a two stage random sampling method is used. The first stage of sampling is the region and the second stage is the beauty parlours within the selected region. The Visakhapatnam City is classified into certain regions where the beauty parlours are located. Considering the geographical extent of the city 10 per cent of the region and 5 per cent of the beauty parlours within the selected region are selected by using simple random sampling method. Thus a total of 45 beauty parlours are selected and from each of these selected parlours data are collected by canvassing pre-designed schedule during the period August-September 2000. The analysis is carried out mainly in terms of percentage and average.

Analysis

There is no systematic enumeration of beauty parlours functioning in Visakhapatnam city, the oral information sought from the beauticians and representatives who supply essential beauty care creams and oils to the parlour reveal that more 700 beauty parlours are in operation in the city. The data sought on number of beauty parlours and their establishment period indicates a humble beginning of 6.67 per cent of beauty parlours during 1970-1985 were rose to 42.22 per cent during 1985-1995 while a short duration of half a decade during 1995-2000 witnessed 51.11 per cent (Table 1). The data of the table suggests that there is a remarkable increase in the establishment of number of parlours, in fact, is the major reason for the present study to understand the socio-economic and other marketing dynamics of the beauty parlours of Visakhapatnam city.

Table 1: Establishment of beauty parlours in Visakhapatnam city.

Year	*No. of parlours*	*Percent*
1970-1985	3	6.67
1986-1995	19	42.22
1996-2000	23	51.11
Total	45	100.00

The collected data has been analyzed by classifying parameters into various clusters such as: a) social structure, b) infrastructure, c) skills and services, d) employment, e) income generation and f) customer status.

A. Social Structure

In a traditional and structural society like ours the social facts like age, education, marital status, religion, social community, languages, nativity etc. do play a role in establishing, functioning and sustaining hitherto unknown enterprises in a traditional economy. These facts have some relationship with successful functioning and development of a new enterprise. It is more in the case of beauty parlours, an enterprise of the women, for the women, by the women in service sector.

An analysis of age and education of beautician (Table 2) indicate that the graduates own 57.78 per cent parlours in the age group of 26-35 years, followed by under graduates 22.22 per cent, 4 each in the age group of 26-35, 36-45 and 2 individuals in less than 25 years of age. Post-graduate education background is noticed in 15.55 per cent and their age groups are spread over 26 to above 46 years. Professional education (MBBS) of beauticians accounts only for 4.44 per cent in the age group of 26-35 years. Graduates and post-graduates of all age groups, smaller age groups under-graduates and specific age group of professional courses indicate that the beautician profession was initially undertaken by the graduates and post-graduates but subsequently taken up by under-graduates and professional graduates in beauty care.

Table- 2 : Age and Education wise distribution of Beauticians

Education	*Age in years*					
	< 25	*26 – 35*	*36 – 45*	*> 46*	*Total*	*Percent*
Under Graduate	2	4	4	0	10	22.23
Graduate	3	13	9	1	26	57.78
Post-Graduate	0	5	1	1	7	15.55
Profession Course	0	2	0	0	2	4.44
Total	5	24	14	2	45	
Percent	11.11	53.33	31.11	4.44		100

The data on marital status and religion of the beauticians (Table-3) indicate that married women account for 68.89 per cent followed by unmarried women 24.44 per cent. The divorce and widow categories account for 4.44 per cent and 2.22 per cent respectively. The Hindu women dominate in this profession 88.89 percent followed by Christian (6.66 per cent) and Muslim (4.44 per cent). The table-3 indicates that married (29) and unmarried (8) Hindu women are more involved in the beauty care activity thus probably extending acceptance both at family and society levels, in spite of beautician profession being a new one.

Table 3: Marital status and religion wise distribution of beauticians

Marital status	*Religion*				
	Hinduism	*Christianity*	*Islamism*	*Total*	*Percent*
Un-married	8	1	2	11	24.44
Married	29	2	0	31	68.89
Divorced	2	0	0	2	4.44
Widow	1	0	0	1	2.22
Total	40 *	3	2	45	
Per cent	88.89	6.66	4.44		99.99

* Includes one each of Jain, Sikh and Sindhi.

The social community and the sociability in terms of physical touch and conversation (spoken languages) are important parameters of a beauticians work (Table 4). Women from cross section of social background are involved in beauty parlour activity as indicated by different sections of social communities. Though 28.89 per cent of beauticians come from backward communities the single largest communities are Kamma (15.55 per cent) and Kapu (13.33 per cent), followed by Brahmins (8.89 per cent), Vysyas (6.67 per cent) and Kshatriyas (4.44 per cent). The others category involves Punjabis, Rajasthanis and Sindhis and their specific social community could not be ascertained and they account for 8.89 percent. The scheduled castes account for 6.67 percent among sampled beauticians. Bilingual (66.67 per cent), trilingual (3.33 per cent) and Quadra lingual (4.44 per cent) character of the beautician is noticed in the sample and seem to have been an essential parameter to attract more customers of different lingual backgrounds in an urban setting.

Since the beauty parlour activity is gender based and is gaining momentum in its spread in recent years an analysis has been made to understand the encouraging factors at family level. Of all the parameters the education background of the beautician and their parents or husbands are more significant factor as has been presented in table 5. The data indicates that more number of beauticians have come from well-educated family background i.e. either their parents or husbands are graduates (28.89 per cent) post-graduates (20.00 per cent) or professional courses (15.55 per cent). The other category (26.66 per cent) includes mostly businessmen with only a few years of schooling. It is inferred both from the observed and analyzed data that the beautician profession is being encouraged by members of their families.

Table- 4: Social community and languages spoken by the beauticians

Social community	*Languages spoken* Single	*Two*	*Three*	*Four*	*Total*	*Per cent*
Brahmin	0	4	0	0	4	8.89
Kshatriya	0	2	0	0	2	4.44
Vysya	1	2	0	0	3	6.67
Kamma	0	5	2	0	7	15.56
Kapu	0	5	1	0	6	13.33
Reddy	1	1	0	0	2	4.44
Patnaik	0	1	0	0	1	2.22
BCs	2	8	2	1	13	28.89
SCs	2	0	0	1	3	6.67
Others*	1	2	1	0	4	8.89
Total	7	30	6	2	45	
Percent	15.56	66.67	13.33	4.44		100.00

* Include Punjabis, Rajasthanis and Sindhis.

Table-5: Education status of beauticians against their parents/husbands education status.

Education of beauticians	*Parents/Husbands education* Under	*Graduates*	*Post-*	*Professional*	*Others*	*Total*	*Per cent*
Under Graduates	3	4	0	0	3	10	22.22
Graduates	1	7	7	4	7	26	57.78
Post-Graduates	0	2	2	1	2	7	15.56
Professional Course	0	0	0	2	0	2*	4.44
Total	4	13	9	7	12	45	
Percent	8.89	28.89	20.00	15.55	26.67		100.00

* Includes B.E, B.L, C.A and M.B.B.S.

A new enterprise often believed to be initiated by new incumbents of an urban setting. In order to understand the nature of initiation and development of beauty parlour enterprise in Visakhapatnam city data are sought on the nativity and years of duration of beauticians stay in the city and the data has been presented in Table 6. Most of the beauticians are the immigrants from the other regions of Andhra Pradesh particularly Coastal Andhra (42.22 per cent), the capital city of Andhra Pradesh, Hyderabad (4.44 per cent) and the immigrants from outside Andhra Pradesh account for 11.11 per cent. It is interesting to note that though a large majority of beauticians have come from outside Visakhapatnam district a considerable percentage of (37.78 per cent) then are from the same district. The duration of stay in city indicates those who were staying for the last 6 to 25 years have taken up the beauty parlour activity. However, 26.67 per cent recent of immigrants of less than 5 years duration of stay in the city have taken up this activity suggests that the beauty parlour activity perhaps is more enterprising.

Table-6: Nativity and Years of stay in Visakhapatnam city of beauticians.

Native Place	*Years of stay in Visakhapatnam city*						*Per*
	< 5	*6 – 15*	*16 – 25*	*26 – 35*	*> 36*	*Total*	*cent*
Visakhapatnam District	5	4	3	2	3	17	37.78
Coastal Andhra Districts	6	8	5	0	0	19	42.22
Rayalaseema Districts	0	1	0	0	0	1	2.22
Telangana Districts	0	0	0	0	0	0	0
A.P. State capital, Hyderabad	0	2	0	0	0	2	4.44
Outside the A.P State	0	1	3	1	0	5	11.11
Others	1	0	0	0	0	1	2.23
Total	12	16	11	3	3	45	
Percent	26.66	35.55	24.44	6.67	6.67		100

B. Infrastructure

The success of an enterprise to some extent depends on its location, accommodation and equipment. The data collected in this direction are analyzed to understand the infrastructure of the beauty parlours in Visakhapatnam city. The beauty parlours are in operation at two levels, one is home based and the other is establishment based. These are located both in residential and commercial areas of the city. The data in this regard is presented in Table 7 and indicates that 62.22 per cent are located in commercial areas and the remaining 37.78 per cent are in residential area. The house come parlour and exclusive parlour are almost to 50 per cent each.

Table-7: Location of beauty parlours, residential vs. commercial.

Area of activity	*House cum establishment*	*Establishment*	*Total*	*Percent*
Residential area	16	1	17	37.78
Commercial area	5	23	28	62.22
Total	21	24	45	
Percent	46.67	53.33		100.00

The beauty parlour thus could be categorized into four categories such as house-cum-parlour and exclusive parlours in residential and commercial areas. Since the parlours are viable to operate in two different contexts and areas, an analysis has been attempted to derive space in use for the parlour in terms of number of rooms and the data is presented in table 8. The data indicates that parlours are in operation from a single room to as many as six rooms. However, the parlours in commercial area had more space than the house-cum-parlours, but the space and area are not showing any signification correlation.

Table 8: Location and space aspects of beauty parlours.

Type of establishment	*No. of rooms (space)*							
	Single	*Two*	*Three*	*Four*	*Five*	*Six +*	*Total*	*Percent*
House-cum-parlour in residential area	7	5	3	0	0	0	15	33.33
Parlour in a residential area	1	2	0	0	1	0	4	8.89
House-cum-parlour in commercial area	0	2	1	1	0	0	4	8.89
Parlour in commercial area	5	8	2	3	1	3	22	48.89
Total	13	17	6	4	2	3	45	100.00
Percent	28.89	37.78	13.33	8.89	4.44	6.67		

The parlours are grouped into three categories such as ordinary moderate and luxury based on their accommodation on one hand and the type of equipment including furniture on the other. The data thus arrived are presented in Table 9. It is interesting to note that two extremes ordinary versus ordinary, luxury versus luxury and in between moderate versus moderate in terms of type of establishment and type of equipment are known from the table. Among these ordinary account for 37.78 per cent, luxury account for 33.33 per cent while moderate in-between these two (28.89 per cent).

Table 9: Establishment and equipment-wise distribution of beauty parlours.

Type of establishment	*Type of equipment*				
	Ordinary	*Moderate*	*Luxury*	*Total*	*Per cent*
Ordinary	17	2	0	19	42.22
Moderate	0	10	2	12	26.67
Luxury	0	1	13	14	31.11
Total	17	13	15	45	
Per cent	37.78	28.89	33.33		100.00

C. Skills and Services

A beautician can be considered as a semi-skilled worker as she needs to undergo a formal training in beauty care practices. The training course is extended both by the government and private agencies for duration of about a year. The duration ranges between three, six and twelve months. A large majority of 86.67 per cent beauticians of the present study have undergone training in private while the remaining 13.33 per cent were trained in government sector. Out of three packages of training, a high percentage of 55.56 per cent of beauticians have undergone training for 6 months followed by 33.33 per cent for 12 months and a low of 11.11 per cent for 3 months duration. Soon after training the women need to work for some time in a parlour to enhance their skills and a few are working in big parlours as trainees by paying a nominal fee to the owners.

A wide range of services is rendered in the parlours pertaining to hair, body and skin care and make-up, the details of which are presented in (Appendix-1).

Table 10: Training component of the beauticians.

Training organization	*Duration of training* 3 months	6 months	12 months	Total	Percent
Government	1	2	3	6	13.33
Private	4	23	12	39	86.67
Total	5	25	15	45	
Percent	11.11	55.56	33.33		100.00

D. Employment characteristics

The beauty parlour activity not only provides self-employment but also generates employment to the women. The data collected for this parameter are presented in Table 11. Out of 45-sampled beauty parlours 26 have generated some employment. Of these 65.38 per cent parlours located in commercial area have generated more employment followed by 30.77 per cent by house-cum-parlours in residential area. Moreover, more number of employees is working in the parlours located in the commercial area.

Table 11: Location and No. of persons employed in beauty parlours.

Type of parlour	*No. of persons employed other than the main beautician* One	Two	Three	Four	Five	Six +	Total	Per cent
House-cum-parlour in residential area	2	6	0	0	0	0	8	30.77
Parlour in residential area	1	0	0	0	0	0	1	3.85
House-cum-parlour in commercial area	0	0	0	0	0	0	0	0
Parlour in commercial area	7	3	1	0	1	5	17	65.38
Total	10	9	1	0	1	5		26
Per cent	38.46	34.61	3.85	0	3.85	19.23		100.00

As mentioned earlier soon after the training the women work in the parlours to gain experience and to increase their skills and talents. Out of 45 sampled parlours only 8 are extending facility to the trained to have experience. Such workers are seen in both house-cum-parlours in residential area and parlours in commercial area with an exception of 1 parlour in residential area.

Table 11: Location and No. of trainees in beauty parlours.

Type of parlour	*No. of Trainees*							
	One	*Two*	*Three*	*Four*	*Five*	*Six +*	*Total*	*Per cent*
House-cum-parlour in residential area	0	0	3	0	0	0	3	37.50
Parlour in residential area	1	0	0	0	0	0	1	12.50
House-cum-parlour in commercial area	0	0	0	0	0	0	0	0
Parlour in commercial area	1	0	0	0	3	0	4	50.00
Total	2	0	3	0	3	0	8	
Per cent	25.00	0	37.50	0	37.50	0		100.00
	0				0			

E. Income Generation

The establishment of an enterprise obviously needs some input, in terms of capital and other social costs. The beauty parlours in Visakhapatnam have shown a wide range of capital investments ranging between Rs. 10,000 and more than a Lakh rupees. A uni-variate distribution of selected sample (table-13) presents about 40 percent of parlours have invested the capital between Rs. 50,000 and Rs. 1, 00,000 followed by 17.78 percent more than a lakh rupees and 15.55 per cent between Rs.40 and Rs.50 thousand rupees. The other parlours have invested the capital in the range of Rs. 10000 to Rs. 40000 thousand rupees. It is clear from the table that the pralours can comfortably be divided into two categories on the basis of capital investment into parlours of less than Rs. 40,000 and more than Rs. 40,000 capital invested. Large majority (33) parlours fall in the latter range.

The required capital is raised from both at family and institution levels. The data of the present study indicates two sources at personal level and three sources at institution level (Table-14). The self, probably from parental source (44.44 per cent) and husband (8.89 per cent) as a participant in enhancing their family income are the two sources contributing to the raise of capital at personal or family level. The banks (31.11 per cent), BC Corporation (8.89 per cent) and SC Corporation (6.67 per cent) have extended loan facility under various developmental programmes for women. Though more than 50 per cent of beauticians raised their capital at family level a considerable size (21 respondants) depended on public financing institutions.

Table 13: Size of capital

Capital	*No. of Beauty parlours*	*Per cent*
< 10, 000	3	6.67
10, 000 – 20, 000	4	8.89
20, 000 – 30, 000	3	6.67
30, 000 – 40, 000	2	4.44
40, 000 – 50, 000	7	15.55
50, 000 – 1, 00, 000	18	40.00
> 1, 00, 000	8	17.78
Total	45	100.00

Table 14: Source of capital and beauty parlours.

Sources of capital	*Beauty parlours*	*Per cent*
Self	20	44.44
Husband	4	8.89
Banks	14	31.11
BC Corporation	4	8.89
SC Corporation	3	6.67
Total	45	100.00

The data pertaining to income had some set backs in the sense that the beauticians are afraid of disclosing real income and the present study is of a preliminary survey type. However, investment costs, rent, power, services and other cosmetic items depend upon the income. The incomes of the beauticians are presented in Table-15. The data indicates that 33.33 per cent of parlours could generate only less than Rs. 5,000/- followed by 24.44 per cent less than Rs. 10.000/-, 17.78 per cent less than

Rs. 20,000/- and 11.11 per cent less than Rs. 30,000/-. 4.44 per cent and 8.89 per cent of parlours generate the income ranges of Rs. 30 to Rs. 40 thousand and Rs. 40 to Rs. 50 thousand respectively per month. It is interesting to note that there is no loss incurred even the capital investment is high, in most cases it is the self-generated for having self-employment.

Table 15: Income-wise distribution of beauty parlours.

Income groups (Rs.)	*No. of parlours*	*Per cent*
< 5, 000	15	33.33
5, 000 – 10, 000	11	24.44
10, 000 – 20, 000	8	17.78
20, 000 – 30, 000	5	11.11
30, 000 – 40, 000	2	4.44
40, 000 – 50, 000	4	8.89
Total	45	100

The positive side of income levels of beauty parlours is due to one time investment for equipment, and furniture and recurring expenditure for consumables is low. The cost of cosmetic items is always lower than the charges collected by rendering services. The expenditure details of maintaining the parlour are given in Table-16. The data shows that 36 out of 45 sampled parlours (80 percent) spend only less than Rs.5, 000/ - per month while the remaining 15.55 percent spend less than Rs.10, 000/- and 4.44 percent spend more than Rs.10, 000.

F. Customer Aspects(Demand side of beauty parlour enterprise)

The rapid growth of beauty parlours in the city indicate a higher side of demand from the customers. Several reasons are attributed to the development of beauty parlours such as health awareness, beauty consciousness, air and water pollution, chemical based cosmetics, high-density foods etc. The causes seem to have been many but the effect, for the time being is one that is mushrooming of beauty parlours in urban pockets. The inquiry into this aspect both from the demand and supply side clients indicates 'We would like to be more beautiful' and 'We are here to make you more good-looking' respectively. These twin attitudes of consumer and supplier have become inseparable and extending similar satisfaction in terms of earning money and gaining good-looking.

Table 16: Monthly expenditure for the maintenance of parlour.

Expenditure	*No. of Parlours*	*Percent*
< 1, 000	15	33.33
1, 000 – 5, 000	21	46.67
5, 000 – 10, 000	7	15.56
> 10, 000	2	4.44
Total	45	100.00

The empirical data in this regard indicates a higher percentage of middle class women (48.89 per cent) followed by higher class women (33.33 per cent) and lower class (17.78 per cent) women are utilizing the services of beauty parlours. It is further observed that 44.44 per cent of beauty parlour users are working women followed by students (31.11 per cent) and housewives (24.44 per cent). The analysis pertaining to customer visits to the parlours indicate that 44.44 per cent of customers visit ordinary parlours followed by 31.11 per cent the luxury parlours and 24.44 per cent visit the moderate parlours. The beauty consciousness has gone down below the ordinary socio-economic status as revealed by the users from a category of maidservants, fish vending women, sweepers and alike.

Conclusion

The foregone analysis on the beauty parlours of Visakhapatnam City reveals that a majority of beauticians received graduate education and they are married Hindu women. A cross section of well-educated society is represented in this activity and they can speak more than two languages. Parlours are functioning in both residential and commercial areas of the city. Even with low investment they are able to generate significant income, which is again mostly supplementary to family income. The beauty parlour enterprise is a very profit making enterprise, providing employment to large number of women, and thereby contributing for their empowerment. Since the beauty parlours require low levels of skill and capital and there is societal acceptance, any women can pursue this activity. All these servicing units are operating almost at their full capacity and there is a wide scope for their expansion.

REFERENCES

- Economic Survey-1999-2000
- Rust, R.T.Zahorik, A and T.L. Keiningham. 1999 , Service Marketing, International Student Edition, Addison-Wesley.
- Sethuraman, S.V. 1981. The Urban Informal Section in developing countries: Employment, Poverty and environment (ed) ILO, Geneva.
- Clark C. 1940: The conditions of Economic progress, London: Mac Millen.
- Madheswaran, S and D. Anita 2000; Income and Employment growth in Service Sector in India, Indian Journal of Labour Economics 43(4): 831. 839.
- Manth C. S and Ch. P.R. Reddy: 1995: Service Sector in Economic Development: An Empirical Study: Indian Journal of Labour Economics 38(4).
- Sudara Singh and Shajan Saudu 2000: Employment generation in the Service Sector: Economic and Political Weekly.
- Tara Kumari P. 1999. Women in Urben India, Allahabad, Chugh Publications.

Chapter 29

WOMEN ADMINISTRATORS IN NON-GOVERNMENTAL ORGANIZATIONS

*Mrs. Shanthi Nachiappan

**Dr. B. Dharmalingam

ABSTRACT

The chapter traces women administrators in non-governmental organizations. Although man dominate in administrative work but due to techno-social-changes the nature of work in male occupations has undergone drastic changes blurring the boundaries created by the cultural definitions. Studies have found that top women executives ere found mainly in the media, fashion and cosmetics industries. The chapter identifies sound of the successful women administrators in India, major obstacles they face and the strategies to overcome such problems.

Introduction

"The women of today are in a fair way to dethrone the myth of femininity; they are beginning to affirm their independence in concrete ways; they do not easily succeed in living completely the life of a human being. Reared by women within a feminine world, their normal destiny is marriage, which still means practically subordination to man; for masculine prestige is far from extinction, resting still upon solid economic and social foundations" – Simone de Beauvoir.

Discrimination of women from 'womb to tomb' is well known. Women throughout the world have been assigned lower positions than that of men. Similarly, the activities with prestige, power and authority

* Assistant Professor, Velammal College of Management and Computer Studies, Chennai

** Director in Charge, Centre for Rural Development, Alagappa University, Karaikudi.

have been allocated to menfolk. Social Scientists have advanced different explanations for this division of labour based on sex. A few of them basing their theories on the differences in physical strength are of the opinion that occupations which required greater physical strength came under the domain of men and activities which could be performed in or around the house were allocated to the women. (Smith-Rosenberg, 1973). Further keeping in view the biology of human body, women were given the responsibility of bearing and rearing of the children as well as the management of the household. Women are expected to give 'priority' to household work and show 'allegiance' to their family (Coser and Rokoff, 1971). It was perhaps for this reason women were not required to seek independent economic status even though they were capable of doing so. Division of labour was not on the basis of biological and physical strength of the sex but was the outcome of cultural definitions.

Psychologists feel that men and women differ in their attitudes, aptitudes and personality. In addition to their different psyche, their interests, capabilities and characteristics paved the way for creating a dividing line between 'masculine' and feminine' duties (Maccoby, 1963, Brown, 1965; Horner, 1972). The activities demanding mechanical aptitude attracted the men. Similarly, the exercise of authority came under the domain of men. Women were shy, insecure, and docile and as such could not assume the roles of leaders, because they lacked the qualities of leadership & the traditional role of child bearing rearing and managing the household also undermines the role of socialization.

When a woman attains economic independence she naturally becomes the mistress of her own body and author of her own decision. A scientific perception of women's need is essential for the process which leads to the empowering. Despite Constitutional provision of equal rights and opportunities – political, social, and educational and of employment Indian women are not allowed to enjoy the rights and opportunities bestowed upon them. Women in India are no becoming more and more conscious of their constitutional and statutory rights, even the rural and tribal women among them.

Changing Positions of women

Globally

"You can tell the condition of a nation by looking at the status of its women" said Jawaharlal Nehru

- Woman now represent forty per cent of the global labour force.
- Women hold 14 per cent of administrative and management jobs.

- ➢ The majority of women continue to earn on an average about 3/4th of the male wage.
- ➢ Women hold less than 6 per cent of senior management jobs in the world.

India

- ➢ 1/3rd of the total literate are women.
- ➢ 92 million working women, though 90 per cent of them are working in the unorganized sector.
- ➢ Work force participation rate is 37.7 per cent, where the rate for women is 22.7 per cent, which is less than half the rate of 51 per cent for men.

Women around the world have achieved higher levels of education than ever before and today represent more than 40 per cent of the global workforce. Yet their share of management positions remains unacceptably low, with just a tiny proportion succeeding in breaking through the glass ceiling.

The following strategies can be followed to empower women in a better way. They were higher literacy and education, better health care for herself and her children, higher age at marriage, greater work participation in modernized escort, necessary financial and service support, advancement into higher position of power, better consciousness of their rights, self-reliance, self respect and dignity among women.

A study conducted in UK revealing that women continue to hold only 7 per cent of all directorships and 39 per cent of UK's top companies still do not have women directors. Still women are under-represented in board rooms of many developed countries.

Women constitute nearly half of India's population but the women in management and administration position is less than 3 per cent. Out of 2709 board positions in the BSE 200 companies, only 43 are filled by women. The reasons behind it were "only women have babies and only men make rules". Women who compete like men are considered unfeminine. Women who emphasize family are considered un-committed.

In recent times, the rise of women to positions of power has become a ripe subject for scholarly analysis (Adams & Yoder, 1985). Despite enormous barriers and myths that sustain gender appropriate roles, a few women have made it to the heights in diverse fields under varying conditions. Though women administrators are still a minority, they offer a unique vantage point on the shifts in the power distribution between men and women, on the opportunities available, and deterrents that confront women in their climb to the top.

Women as Administrators

The position of the administrator/executive came under the domain of the male sex, because it was vested with prestige, power and authority. The executives were vested with prestige, power and authority. The executives were required to exhibit leadership qualities and men were considered as most suitable for such positions. It is perhaps for this reason that certain occupations are labeled as 'masculine' or 'feminine'. The 'sex typing' of certain occupations has a consequence for the persons who possess he 'wrong sex' for role assuming and role performance. It is in this context that Hughes maintained: "Society by its nature, consists in part of both allowing and expecting some people to do things which other people are not allowed or expected to do and if those who man such occupations have any sense of identity and solidarity, they will also claim a mandate to define (not merely for themselves but for others as well) proper conduct with respect to the matters concerning their work (Hughes 1968; 447).

Due to techno-social changes the nature of work in 'male occupation' has undergone drastic changes blurring the boundaries created by the cultural definitions. The separation of work from home, the introduction of push-button technology, the economic needs, the opportunity to learn formal and technical education, the change in the nature and structure of work, the changes in the orientation to work, the constitutional provisions and various other factors helped women not only to accept gainful employment in professions previously monopolized by men.

Since Management is a science, it does not recognize sex. In fact a female child is trained efficient manager. She is the builder of the family and has to be efficient in handling finance, personal management and public relations in the form of entertainment. Being a man or a woman does not really matter because one deals with situations according to one's intelligence. Women officers in administrative serves today are holding responsible positions. There is no doubt that entry to those jobs is extremely competitive. Women have entered the portals of premier institutions alongside their male colleagues to pursue a career in professional management. They are intelligent, capable and competent. They are willing to work hard, eager to work harder, eager to learn and struggle to find a meaningful role in the society. In fact, in today's society women have an added advantage. Management conscience, the need for a competent manager in a fact – moving and competitive world, and pressure from government have all provided a special edge for the women with the will and the intelligence to succeed.

In the latest survey it has been found that top women executives were found mainly in the media, fashion and cosmetics industries. It seems that the newly acquired position tallies with their femininity. Era Odehnal, manager of united women entrepreneurs, a professional association said: "If a woman does make it to the top, she is expected to look like a young woman, act like a lady, think like a man and work like a horse".

Meyer et al, studies on Europe's Women executive found that women executives in Europe have not reached the upper echelons of an entrenched business world – but they are gradually getting there. These are, however, the exceptions that prove the rule. European women are simply not on the fast track to top executives' jobs - a situation that is in sharp contrast to the United States, where women not hold more than a third of all management, professional and administrative jobs. One reason for the lag in Europe is that the feminist movement began much later than it did in America. West European countries have enacted laws protecting women from sexual discrimination, but few have enacted and sweeping affirmation – action programmes found in the United States. Since European companies are not legally obligated to promote women to managerial positions or even hire women – the dearth of women executive is in many ways self perpetuating. As a result women have been relatively invisible at the top.

"Why women still aren't getting to the top" – (Fortune July 1990 cover story): the article details evidence of glass ceiling of 4, 012 people at the highest category only 19 women. Less than one half. Women follow "Interactive Leadership" style contrasts to traditional "Command & Control" leadership style by men. One of the significant impediments to women's employment, also involving women's specific lack of access to managerial positions, has been a persistent distinction between the private world of women and the public world of men.

The longevity of sex role expectations for white upper and middle class women, which assumed that they should focus on the home while men worked in the public realm, undermined the possibility of permanent acceptance of women in the workplace, as well as in supervisory roles in that milieu.

The pervasive assessment of women as female's first rather than human beings first hindered women's progress in management throughout the years as women were viewed as wives and mothers primarily. Despite societal pressures against them, successful individual female proprietors and entrepreneurs in public sector, such as settlement houses paved the way as role models for future women's entrance into corporate world.

Women did acquire managerial positions in several ways. Managerial positions in products and services for women. Women who found employment in a new field that had no previous association with males could achieve executive status. Thus the new field of office work created the position of private secretary, which originally offered the potential of "apprentice executive". This was no longer the case after 1930, when women dominated these positions and the occupation of private secretary suffered from feminization with the result of low status and low wages. The definitions of women's work have been problematic often hiding managerial skills under gender specific categories. Each of world wars called women out of the home into workforce, including managerial positions. But this was only temporary when war ended women were encouraged to return to the home while some women entered managerial positions in the Corporate world at the beginning of 20th century. A major increase since 1970, following pressure from a women's movement and the implementation of legislatures.

Table 1: Major Obstacles to Women's Career Reported by Different Surveys in the 1980's

Factor	*% of women agreeing*
Wall Street Journal / Gallop Survey	
Family responsibilities	3%
Male Chauvinism, attitude towards a female boss, slow advancement of women, and being a woman	50%
There are disadvantages of being a woman in the business world	80%
Have been thwarted on their way up the ladder by male attitudes toward women	25%
Paid less than men of equal ability	70%
Korn / Ferry International Survey	
Being a woman	40%
Los Angeles Times Survey	
Sex discrimination	67%
Signs of racism	60%

General Problems

Structural barriers, Institutional Practices of Discrimination, Exclusionary Laws, Attitudes regarding proper sex roles (wife and mother), Negative Impact on women's advancement into managerial positions. Some other major obstacles are:

Strategies to over come the problem

1. The number of women in administration can increase only when people in authority make affirmative action, an institutional imperative. Positive recruitment strategies, change in organizational procedures to remove the hurdles and obstacles which divert or block the progress, objective appraisal, a machinery for sharing information, establishing social contact which builds on net working opportunities for developing interpersonal skills such as confidence, working with groups, net working, trust, openness and assertiveness, training in women's issues such as women's issues such as women's rights, accuracy of a stereo-types, statistics about women and their contribution to economy provision of rule models, providing a mentor, training new technology, retraining schemes, maternity leave, flexible working arrangements such as flexi time, flex place, etc.
2. Women themselves must make a commitment to their own advancement.
3. Women also need to learn to cope up with stress, combine and organize family responsibilities with office work effectively to relax as well as be efficient.
4. Women must continue to strive to reach positions of influence and power, so that their capabilities and intelligence are used to the full.

Non – Government Organisations in India

According to the Society for Participatory Research in Asia (PRIA), there are nearly 1.2 million non-profit organizations operating in India, and their total funding in 1999-00 was close to Rs. 18,000 crore - that's around one per cent of the country's GDP. Moreover, non-profits employ nearly 20 million people – some paid, others unpaid – which is comparable to the country's organized labour force. The main source of receipts for NPOs are self generated – loans, grants and donations. Foreign funds contribute only 7.4 per cent of the total receipts of NPOs. What they need is a little help in terms of professional management skills.

For many of India's NPOs, life began with one person's dream to make a difference to society. They then went out and set up non-profits that gathered steam and resources over time. But with size came the problems of age, obsolescence and irrelevance. Some of the problems faced by them today can thus be traced back to their original good intentions. "Volunteers with good intentions but poor management expertise run most NPOs. They feel that they are giving their time and, sometimes, even their money. They must, therefore, have a large say in the affairs of the organization. They do not understand that management is a science. In today's complex world, running corporations – whether for profit, or not – is not for amateurs or just the do-gooders!"

India's non-profit organizations are at the crossroads. Originally started by do-gooders and people seeking to serve community, these have now grown to a size where they need greater managerial inputs to survive and market themselves better to donors and beneficiaries. Given the competition for people, resources and mind space, they face though challenges in re-inventing themselves in order to stay relevant.

At one end, demand for their services is soaring, thanks to the slow pace of poverty reduction and a backlog of social deprivation. On the other hand, the non-profits are facing tough internal challenges – from weak leadership to organizational irrelevance, from inadequate funding to an inability to market themselves to their target audience. They also need to improve organizational motivation at a time when volunteers are being replaced by paid staff.

Being a do-gooder is not enough to run India's non-profits anymore. Admits Vyas: "NGOs have to be run like business, not mere charities". But non-profits cannot become pure businesses either, says Ramesh Srinivasan, Principa, Mckinsey & Co, who has been helping a Mumbai based NGO improve its organizational effectiveness.

What's common to non-profits organizations? To call them non-profits, or non governmental organizations is, according to Peter Drucker, only a negative definition. It tells us what these organizations are not-they are not businesses, and they are non-governmental. But then what are they? Says Drucker in his book Managing the Non-Profit Organisation: "Business supplies either goods or services. Government has discharged its functions when its policies are effective. The 'non-profit' institution neither supplies goods or services nor controls. Its 'product' is neither a pair of shoes nor an effective regulation. Its product is a changed human being. Their product is a cured patient, a child than learns, a young man or woman grown into a self-respecting adult; a changed human life altogether.

Now let us see the roles and challenges of women leaders of NGOs in India

Mother Teresa

Born August 27, 1910 in Yugoslavia, born as Agnes Gonxha Bohashiu, an Albanian nun who founded the Order of the Missionaries of Charity, Died September 5, 1997.

To get to where Mother Teresa's voyage of sacrifice began, follow Calcutta's Creek Lane through a neighborhood of humble homes and tiny businesses – a hardware store, a print shop, even a tropical fish wholesaler.

The street twists and turns like its name sake, one moment wide enough for a car, the next too narrow for a pedestrian to pass a bicycle rickshaw. At No. 14, climb two flights of stairs so old most of the paint has worn off. There waits 89-year-old Michael Gomes, his eyes clouded and hearing going, but handshake firm.

In 1949, Gomes' parish priest asked him if he would provide a home for Sister Teresa, a young woman who, the priest said, "wants to serve the poor, and wants to live with the poor."

"I did not hesitate. If you were in my place, you would not have hesitated," Gomes said.

"She was a gift from God… a very great gift".

Perhaps it's only hindsight that allows Gomes to say today that from the beginning he saw something holy in Agnes Gonxha Bojaxhir, now known to the world as Mother Teresa. The Nobel peace laureate, who founded a world wide charity, died September 5 at 87, and already the Vatican is being pressed to declare her a saint.

The Roman Catholic nun came to stay on the top floor of Gomes home-where he now lives, with his extended family sprawled throughout the two lower floors – after leaving a nearby Loreto order convent in Calcutta, where she had been a teacher since 1929.

Three years before her arrival at Gomes' home, she said, she had heard a call from God "to serve Him among the poorest of the poor."

She first moved to a home run by the Little Sisters of the Poor, but that was too far from the school she had opened in Calcutta's Motijeel slum. Gomes' home was more convenient, and likely provided the independence she needed to recruit followers. By the time she outgrew the top floor of No.14 in 1953, 28 other women had joined her work,

Gomes said. She had been granted permission to found her own order, the Missionaries of Charity in 1950.

Gomes remembers the young women were lively, once playing a game of tug-of-war on the balcony overlooking the neighborhood's muddy streets and tenement rooftops strung with laundry. "They were normal human beings, not all the time praying," he said. One room was set aside for a chapel, with an altar build by a neighborhood cabinetmaker. Today, it's a bedroom in a dark, cement-floored apartment cooled by fans and decorated with religious drawings and one pastel of Mother Teresa's familiar, smiling profile. "Mother was full of live all the time, she never looked angry-even if she was angry, she never showed to", said Polton Roy, one of her first students at the Motijeel school.

"If the school was not here, I don't know what we would have done. Because of the school, all of us have some education, we can work", said Roy, a maintenance man at lamp factory.

Mother Teresa arrived in Motijeel in 1947, asking slum dwellers whether there were children she could teach. Philomena Maiti, no in her 70s and still living in Motijeel, remembers helping to spread the word about the young nun who wanted to help, and Mother Teresa soon had scores of students learning their lessons in tin-roofed shacks.

The community later built brick-and-plaster classrooms, and, Maiti says, developed self-respect. The school has 250 pupils today, taught by five lay teachers and two members of Mother Teresa's order.

"Mother said it was her love for the poor and the needy that forced her to do her work. She put that feeling in me, too", Maiti said.

Mother Teresa attracted followers wherever she went, even when the work was hard. In 1952, she opened Nirmal Hriday, or "Pure Heart", the first of many homes for sick and dying street people. Here, Mother Teresa and her sisters cleaned maggots from the rotting faces of leprosy victims, washed the emaciated bodies of the malnourished, held the hands of the dying.

"Welcome to Mother's first love," reads a blue-on-white sign on a wall at Nirmal Hriday. Indeed, Mother Teresa seems to have found her true calling when she turned her attentions to Calcutta's most desperate.

At her death, the Missionaries of Charity had 4,000 nuns and ran 517 orphanages, soup kitchens, homeless shelters and clinics around the world.

The group is headquartered not far from where it all began, a five-minute drive from the Gomes home.

Ms. Ela Bhatt, Founder, SEWA

She founded SEWA as a trade union while working for the Textile Labour Association. She was a member of Planning Commission and a recipient of many National and International awards. She was made a member of Rajya Sabha (Upper House of Parliament). She formed SEWA Bank, run only by women, which has a turnover of more than 100 crores. She also received 'Padmasree', a prestigious National award from the President of India.

In SEWA, there is no leader. Leadership is at every level of the organization through the elected boards and committees. The members are not only the users of the programmes but also managers and owners. The main challenges of SEWA now is to change the mindsets of the middle-class who lack an understanding of the role, and hence, fail to give recognition to poor, rural women and the informal economy.

Ms. Sudha Murthy, Chairperson, Infosys Foundation

The main aim of the foundation is to help the poorest of the poor in rural areas in education and health. As a leader she said that she mostly spends her time in travelling to 8,000 villages, mostly in Karnataka in the last 6 years. She prefers travelling in second class, that's the way you get to know the people. Sometimes, she makes do with one meal a day. The meeting with villagers has become a priority with her. She loves her work and passionate about it and she felt that it was difficult to measure the impact of philanthropic work. But anyway she said that she got an idea of the work being done through her field visits and she could make it out.

The Madras Institute to Habilitate Retarded Afflicted (MITHRA)

It was inaugurated on the 19th of March 1977, by Sister Mary Theodore, an Australian Missionary. MITHRA, which also means 'friend' in Sanskrit, is an institution which serves the physically and mentally handicapped.

Sister Mary who came to Chennai 48 years ago, saw the plight of the poor in Chennai especially those families whose members were afflicted by some mental or physical disability. Their lack of financial ability, to get the right treatment was the drive to start such an institution. No one is ever turned away from Mithra, even if he or she is considered as un-helpable.

The message given to families having disabled members is, 'Accept them for what they are, and try to focus on their abilities rather than on their disabilities'.

MITHRA is a non-profit organization, its activities include:

A School housing children between the ages of 5 to 16 years.

A hospital, which provides occupational therapay

Pre-vocational section

Maintenance department.

Conclusion

"I sought my soul, but my soul I could not see,

I sought my God, but my God eluded me,

I sought my brother, and I found all three"

Are the words which are sought by the women administrators of Non Government Organisations. There are many popular women administrators in NGO sector in India who acts as a role model for the rest. On seeing them, let us hope we get many women administrators in NGO sector and in Corporate India....

REFERENCES

1. J.K Pillai, "Women Managers", in "New Frontiers in Education (1996, vol.XXVI)
2. Registrar General of India, Census Documents (71,81,91,2001)
3. UNDP, HDR 1997.
4. Frozen Thoughts - September 2004, Vol. 4 Issue 3.
5. Nandini Lakshman, Between Business and a Social Mission – Indian Management – April 2003.
6. Tarun Narayan – Good Causes – Indian Management, March 2005. (pp. 22-41)
7. Ann Stead Better, Women in Management, Prentice Hall, New Jersey, 1985
8. Chaturvedi. G., Women Administrators of India, RBSA Publications, Jaipur, 1985
9. Cooper, C. Land Davidson, Women in Management, William Heinemann Ltd., London, 1984.
10. C.P. Yadav, Empowerment of women, Anmol Publications Pvt. Ltd, 2000.
11. Louis M.J., Women Executives of Tamil Nadu, unpublished project Report, NIEPA, Delhi.
12. Mike Smith (et al) ed – A Development Programme for Women in Management, Grower, 1984.
13. Napasri Kraisonswasdi, Women Executives, Rawat Publications, 1989.
14. Vinze Medha Dubashi – Women Entrepreneurs in India, Mittal Publications, Delhi, 1987.

Chapter 30

PROBLEMS FACED BY WOMEN ENTREPRENEURS IN TIRUCHIRAPALLI

*Dr. (Mrs.) V. Gamathi

Abstract

An attempt has been made to find out the constrains faced by women entrepreneurs in Tiruchirapalli, Tamilnadu, India. Women engaged in entrepreneurial activities on their own and self-employed were selected for the study. 50 samples were selected randomly and data was collected by sing interview schedule. The women entrepreneurs are facing a number of problems, namely problems of raw material, marketing, fund shortage, competition, low mobility and high production cost. The study suggest many measures to over come the above problems.

Introduction

"TIME IS RIPE FOR WOMEN NOT ONLY TO SEEK JOBS, BUT ALSO TO ENTER INTO THE FIELD OF ENTREPRENEURSHIP".

After, Independence Government of India recognised the need for rapid industrialization of the country. It adopted several measures to develop basic infrastructure and heavy industries. Industries Development and Regulation Act 1951, Five Year planning, Industrial policy, public sector, incentives and subsidies are important measures. The Industrial Policy 1948 provided various guidelines for industrial and entrepreneurial development. It defined the responsibility of the State to promote, assist and develop industries in the national interest.

These measures led to significant change in the nature and scope of Indian entrepreneurship. A large number of established entrepreneurship diversified considerably into new industries. As a result the industrial base of the country widened considerably. The Industrial Policy Resolution

* Head, Department of Commerce, Cauvery College for women, Tiruchirapalli-620018.

1956 stressed upon the need to accelerate the development of heavy industries, machine making industries to expand public sector and to build up large and growing co-operative sector.

The period after independence has witnessed tremendous economic, social and political changes in India. These changes led to profound changes in entrepreneurship.

The independence has also brought the promise of equality of opportunity in all sphere to the Indian women and laws granting for their equal rights of participation in the political process and equal opportunities and rights in education and employment were enacted. The object of these laws was to hidden women's participation in all the areas of activity in economic, social and political life. Nehru once observed, "Freedom depends on economical conditions even more than political." If a woman, is not economically free and self earning, she will have to depend on her husband or some one else and dependants are never free."

So in order to improve the status and position of women at home and in the large society it is necessary to achieve economic independence for women. The inadequacy of entrepreneurship is an inhibiting factor to accelerate the process of industrialisation in the developing countries. The absence of an appropriate industrial and entrepreneurial climate and an industrial base coupled with lack of access of relevant technology has acted as an handicap to achieve rapid industrial development.

Entrepreneurship amongst women has been a recent concern for all of us. The hidden entrepreneurial potentials of women have gradually been changing with the growing sensitivity to the role and economic status in the society. Women are increasingly being conscious of their existence their rights and their work situation.

It cannot be claimed that women have achieved equality with men, but they are now well set on the roads towards this goal. However, the change is taking place, but the stigma still persists on the emerging entrepreneurial role with the changing time and change in the cultural norms and the increase in literacy women are gradually entering into the field of entrepreneurship the masculine job.

Women Entrepreneurs

Man power is the most important resources for any development and women constitute 50 per cent of the world population. No doubt there is growing awareness through out the world that there should be equal opportunities for women, they should be given special attention not only in granting fundamental rights but also as a necessary pre-requisite for the social economic development of the world. Women must be brought more and more into public sectors. No doubt, the role of women are in extricable, bound up with the process of modernization, but it will in turn work for the social justice, and equality and dignity of every human being.

Having realised the importance of the role to be played by women in the nation's development, the seventh Five Year plan details the plan of action for "Integration of women in Development." The role of women in productive activities in India has been increasing over the years, however the total number of enterprise run by them is insignificantly small. Women have very low participation in the work force. They are employed mostly in unorganized sector, consisting of occupation life agriculture, agro-based industries, handicrafts, handlooms, cottage based industries and construction work. Here, the employment is often seasonal.

The number of enterprises initiated being run by women in the formal sector is small. An estimate of the number of their enterprises given by National Alliance of Young Entrepreneurs is only 50,000 for the country. Women entrepreneurs in India represent a group of women who have broken away from the beaten track and are exploring new vistas of economic participation. They have long stories of trials and hardships full of challenges. They have to encounter public prejudices and criticisms. Family opposition and social constraints had to be overcome before establishing themselves as independent entrepreneurs. Appropriate education training in skills of entrepreneurship and financial support are necessary for women.

With the spread of education and new awareness, women entrepreneurs are spreading their wings to higher level of 3E's namely engineering, electronics and energy though the number of such units are not as large as it should be. But the very fact that women putting up units to manufacture solar cookers as in Gujarat, small foundries in Maharashtra and T.V. capacitors in the industrially back round area of Orissa shows that women if trained and given opportunities can venture in non-traditional industries. Even the so called socially prohibited industrial activity of wine making and selling is being done by women entrepreneurs in Bombay. So today no field is unapproachable to trained and determined modern Indian women.

But Tamil Nadu has more and more women in its nonworking population compared with the other states in India. At least six million women, capable of working are kept idle. A substantial number of them are in the rural areas with little skill and education.

Making this observation, the corporation for Development of women has called for an all out effort to bring a large number of women into the main stream of employment so as to improve the economic position.

The Tamil Nadu Government sponsored corporation in its report giving basic data and facts on their status of women in the state, has underlined the need for micro level field studies and follow up action by different agencies to improve the participation of women in each facet of development.

Significance of the Study

Tradition continues to be same kind of drag on women's activities. Even now the women the weaker sex of the society are still being dominated in the society except in few advanced countries. The argument usually advanced against employment of women is that they are too much involved in home-making, food preparation, child care and all the other domestic duties. Working women are constrained to play a dual role as a home maker and the wage earner which might affect their efficiency, concentration and devotion to the occupation chosen.

The pressing economic necessity for supplementing family income, desire for, economic freedom and the changing concept of women's role in society have led them in great numbers to employment outside the home. Even when she goes out for work due to economic and other reasons, she is never free from continuous chores of cooking, caring for home and family. Added to this is the burden of constant child bearing and nursing the sick. Thus women have got important bearing on homelife as well as the health of future generation.

So the study is undertaken in order to find out the traditional disabilities faced by them and the new opportunities available for them.

Scope of the Study

In the study an attempt has been made to find out the constraints faced by the women entrepreneurs. Places which are located within 3 kilometers in and around Tiruchirapalli such as Thillainagar, Woraiyur, Srinivasanagar, Anna Nagar and Puthur were selected for the study. The women selected are the one who are operating small scale industrial units as their own. Among the self employed, the area is limited only to those engaged in the commercial undertakings.

Objectives of the Study

1. To know the growth of women entrepreneurs and the role of women entrepreneurs associations.
2. To analyse the structure and working of small industrial units by women.
3. To find out the problems of women entrepreneurs and to give suggestions.

Methodology and Tools for the Collection of Data

In this study, survey method has been followed. Data are collected through primary and secondary sources. The main source of primary data collection was an interview schedule. The secondary sources include the reports, and magazines of District Industries Centre, Tamil Nadu Industrial Investment Corporation and Small Industries Development Corporation.

Sampling Design

For this study information was collected from the women entrepreneurs. Places which are located within 3 kilometers in and around Tiruchirapalli Town such as Thillainagar, Woraiyur, Srinivasanagar, Puthur and Anna Nagar have been selected for this study. In each area, 10 respondents have been selected at random. The following table clearly shows the sample selected for the study.

Table - 1 : Sample selected for the study

S.No	*Location*	*No. of Respondents*	*Percentage*
1.	Thillainagar	10	20
2.	Woraiyur	10	20
3.	Srinivasanagar	10	20
4.	Anna Nagar	10	20
5.	Puthur	10	20
	Total	50	100

Geographical Coverage

This study covers the area of 3 kilometers in and around Tiruchirapalli Town.

Women Entrepreneurs in India

Due to the growth of industrialization, urbanization, education and democratic system in the country, the tradition bound Indian society is now undergoing a change and women are now seeking gainful employment in several fields. It is only during the last 5-10 years women have started becoming entrepreneurs and started industries and business and they are yet to go a long way to be equal with men

Having realised the importance of the role to be played by women in the nation's development, the seventh Five year plan details the plan of action for "Integration of women in Development." The new Industrial policy of Government of India has highlighted the need for conducting special entrepreneurship programers for women to enable them to start small scale industries to uplift their status in the economic and social fields

It is believed that entrepreneurs are born and not made. However, some recent researches showed that this view is not really correct. Entrepreneurship can be planned and developed and the need for providing appropriate environment to promote entrepreneurship is of vital importance in the case of prospective women entrepreneurs. The spirit of entrepreneurship can be nurtured to some extent by an appropriate pattern of education and training programme. Such education should impart knowledge of facts on the one hand and motivation on the other.

The argument usually advanced against employment of women is that they are too much involved in home-making, food preparation, child care and all the other domestic duties. Working women are constrained to play a dual role as a home maker and the wage earner which might affect their efficiency, concentration and devotion to the occupation chosen.

The pressing economic necessity for supplementing family income, desire for economic freedom and the changing concept of women's role in society have led them in great numbers to employment outside the home. Even when she goes out for work due to economic and other reasons, she is never free from continuous chores for cooking, caring for home and family. Added to this is the burden of constant child bearing and nursing the sick. Thus women have got important bearing on home life as well as the health of future generation. Hence, society is primarily concerned with the conditions of their employment. Prevention of exploitation of working women is the aim of all the legislations regarding women.

Historically, women had never been exclusively domestic workers. Before Industrial Revolution women had been participating in productive work of all kinds in agriculture, fishery, handicrafts and cottage industries. After the Industrial Revolution began in Uk and spread over to western Europe and USA, women were recruited for employment in the organized sector. Now women workers are found in administrative, managerial, technical, research, engineering and other departments. Women working is not a new phenomenon. The only difference is that women in earlier days worked along with their men in the fields, while now they work in the factory or as domestic servants. Actually the new phenomenon is the advent of high and middle class women taking part in the sphere of man's activities.

Selection of Industry / Business

It depends upon the following factors

1. Family background
2. Education
3. Attitude and
4. Special training if any she had received.

Industries/Business that could be established by women entrepreneurs.

1. Agarbathi making
2. Papad making
3. Pickle making
4. Bedspread making
5. Embroidery making
6. Running Restaurants, soft drink stalls.
7. Running working women's hostel
8. Running crèches
9. Service centre like Radio/ T.V. repairing
10. Xeroxing Firms
11. Photographic studios

Broadly speaking, there are two ways by which the training could be obtained.

1. On the job training and
2. Undergoing EDP, conducted by banks and other organizations.

If a women entrepreneur decides about a particular line of business, it is desirable that the undergoes training in a similar industry already functioning and learns all aspects of that particular business. This could be arranged by institutions like Federation of chamber of commerce and Industry through their members. Now a days, the banks are conducting special programmes for development of entrepreneurial skills and persuade participants to set up independent business ventures.

Role of Women Entrepreneur's Associations

With the growth of women entrepreneurs, a few associations of women entrepreneurs have been set up both at international and national levels. The main purpose of these associations is to create a congenial environment for developing women entrepreneurship in rural and urban areas. These associations seek to achieve the following objectives,

(1) to provide a meeting ground for women entrepreneurs;

(2) to promote and develop feelings of unity and brotherhood among the entrepreneurs;

(3) to develop self-confidence and hope among female entrepreneurs;

(4) to prevent the problems of women entrepreneurs before the concerned authorities for consideration and redressal;

(5) to secure various concessions, subsides and assistance for women entrepreneurs;

(6) to conduct EDP for women;

(7) to organize seminars and conference on entrepreneurship with the help of other national and international bodies;

(8) to secure wider dispersal of entrepreneurship among women:

(9) to establish useful contacts for promoting women entrepreneurs;

(10) to perform other activities to improve the operational efficiency of women entrepreneurs.

Analysis

The following aspects are covered in the analysis.

1. Reasons for starting the business
2. Sources of ideas
3. Training Programme

4. Sources of financial assistance.

Reasons for Starting the Business

The pressing economic necessity for supplementing family income, desire for economic freedom and the changing concept of women's role in society have led them in great numbers of employment outside the home. This is clearly shown in the following table.

Table–2 : Reasons for Starting the Business

S.No	*Reasons*	*No. of Entrepreneurs*	*Percentage*
1.	Challenge and Adventure	5	10
2.	Liking for independent occupation	25	50
3.	Financial Difficulties	14	28
4.	Family circumstances	6	12
	Total	50	100

From the above table it is clear that 5 entrepreneurs have started the business for challenge and adventure, 25 entrepreneurs for self-employment, 14 entrepreneurs due to financial difficulties and 6 entrepreneurs due to family circumstances.

Sources of Ideas

Since the entrepreneurs will be with a number of problems, it is suggested that the entrepreneur should take utmost care in selecting a project. In simple words, the success of the entrepreneur depends on the careful selection of the project.

Table-3 : Sources of Ideas

S.No	*Sources*	*No. of Entrepreneurs*	*Percentage*
1.	Trade Fairs	5	10
2.	Government Agencies	15	30
3.	Competitors	20	40
4.	Friends & Relatives	10	20
	Total	50	100

Source: Primary data

From the above table it is clear that 5 entrepreneurs got the idea from the trade fairs, 15 entrepreneurs got from Government agencies, 20 entrepreneurs from the competitors and 10 from their friends and relatives.

Training Programme

If a woman entrepreneur decides about a particular line of business, it is desirable that she undergoes training in a similar industry already functioning and learns all aspects of that particular business. This could be arranged by Institutions like Federation of chamber of commerce and Industry through their members.

Table 4 explains the training undergone by the women entrepreneurs.

Table-4 : Training Programme

S.No	*Category*	*No. of women Entrepreneurs*	*Percentage*
1.	Trained	30	60
2.	Untrained	20	40
	Total	50	100

Source: Primary data

Of the 50 women entrepreneurs 30 (60%) entrepreneurs have undergone training and 20 (40%) entrepreneurs have not undergone training.

Sources of Financial Assistance

Finance is the life blood of business, without finance nothing can be done. This assistance is given by various financial institutions which is explained below

Table-5 : Sources of Financial Assistance

S.No	*Sources*	*No. of Entrepreneurs*	*Percentage*
1.	Banks	25	50
2.	Other Institutions	16	32
3.	Parents	5	10
4.	Friends and Relatives	4	8
	Total	50	100

Source: Primary data

It is obvious from the above table that 25 (50%) entrepreneurs got their financial assistance from Banks, 16 (32%) entrepreneurs from other institutions, 5 (10%) entrepreneurs from their parents and 4 (8%) entrepreneurs from their friends and relatives.

PROBLEMS

She is a Woman

The biggest problems or difficulty of a woman entrepreneur is that she is a woman.

Inspite of the constitutional equality and legal equality, in practice the attitude of men, not only of tradition bound village men but even those who are responsible for decision making, planning and research is not of equality. They still suffer from male reservations about a women's role and capacity. This attitude or reservation creates difficulties and problems at all levels, that is family support, training, banking, licensing and marketing.

Women in non-urban areas have to suffer still further. They have to face not only resistance or reservation of men but also of elderly women who are ingrained with this attitude of inequality.

It is not that women do not have skills or capacity but they are not properly trained or inculcated in craftsmanship because it is felt that if a skill is imparted to girl, it is wasted because when she gets married, she takes away the skill with her. Therefore, a woman can only act as helper, she cannot function independently.

Training is basic for any entrepreneurship facilities are available many institutions are imparting training under various scheme but again social attitude keeps women away from them, both in urban and rural areas. Secondly, part time training facilities especially during afternoon will attract more women to acquire skills. To enable women to acquire skill, certain facilities like stipend, crèches for their children, transport facilities need to be given and mobile training centre will attract more women as sending women away from family for training is not liked by family members.

Though women are equally qualified as men to succeed as entrepreneurs they suffer from initial lack of confidence in their own abilities. The tradition of acceptance of a sub-ordinate status and the strict role segregation have stopped women to venture boldly into new initiative.

Procurement of Raw Materials

One of the difficulties faced by the small scale units is in the procurement of raw materials in time and at reasonable prices. Large scale units obtain their supplies of stock directly from the manufacturers, but small units have to share the small quantities available at the stock yard of the state Industrial corporation. Thus, the distribution of materials in proportion to stocks, cuts in to the actual availability of materials to small units, and major purchases have to be from the open market at high prices.

Marketing of the Product

The problem of marketing the products is a big hurdle for women. Competition, inability to honour contracts on time, depending on one buyer alone and slumps in the market have all led to piling up of stock and loss. If it is possible for large industries to identify items required by them and if it is possible that these items be contracted out or given to women entrepreneurs for manufacture, some of these marketing problems could be solved.

Shortage of Funds

Another major difficulty of women entrepreneurs is finance or capital. Money or finance is the blood stream of any enterprise. It has to be made available at the right time in right amount. It is true that, one can borrow finance from banks and other financial institutions. But the biggest catch is that of collateral security which is required to get bank credit. And women generally do not have any property in their names. They may have some jewellery but they cannot give them as security without the consent of the husbands or male members of family. In addition, procedures of bank loans and delay prevent many women from venturing.

Collection of Money

Another difficulty faced by women is in collecting payments against sales. Again and again, we have to approach customers for payment. They have received the goods, yet ask us to come tomorrow and yet another tomorrow.

Stiff Competition

Many of the women enterprises have imperfect organizational set up. They have to face severe competition from organized industries and male entrepreneurs.

Family Responsibilities

In India it is mainly women's duty to look after the children and other members of the family. Her involvement in family leaves little energy and time for business. Married women entrepreneurs have to make a fine balance between business and home. Their success in this regard also depends upon supporting husband and family. Without the support and approval of husband, the female entrepreneurs cannot succeed. There arises a role conflict in many women entrepreneurs. Such conflict prevents them from taking prompt decisions in business. Despite modernization, tradition and family responsibilities slow down the movement of women. Occupational background of families and educational level of husbands have a direct impact on the development of women entrepreneurship. The development of kinder gardens, day nurseries and creches and family planning have to some extent helped women entrepreneurs to carry on business without affecting the social prestige of their husbands.

High Cost of Production

Another problem which undermines the efficiency and restricts the development of women enterprises is the high cost of production. Government assistance in the form of grants and subsidies, to some extent enables them to tide over this difficulty. However to ensure their ultimate survival it is necessary to increase efficiency, expand productive capacity and thereby reduce the cost.

Low Mobility

One of the biggest handicaps for women enterprises is mobility or traveling from place to place. Women on their own find it difficult to get accommodation in smaller town. A single woman asking for a room is still looked upon with suspicion. Some of the women entrepreneurs complain them as women are believed to be less able to go through complicated court proceedings.

Lack of Education

In India literacy among women is very low. Due to lack of education, majority of women are unaware of technological developments, marketing knowledge and the like. Lack of information and experience creates further problems in the setting up and running of business enterprises.

Low Need for Achievement

Need for achievement, independence and autonomy are the pre-requisites for success in entrepreneurship. But women are proved to back in the glory of their parents, husbands and sons. Their pre-conceived notions about their role in life inhibit achievement and independence. In the absence of the required urge to achieve few women succeed as entrepreneurs.

Suggestions

1. Emergence of entrepreneurship in a society depends to a great extent on the economic, social, religious, cultural and psychological factors prevailing in the society. Development of women entrepreneurship needs proper environment, so healthy and sound entrepreneurial climate is a must.
2. Lack of information and skills for choosing an activity is another major hurdle for development of women entrepreneurship. So training programmes should provide special assistance for selection of produce/service so that women entrepreneurs can be in a position to perceive and respond to various profitable opportunities.
3. There is an urgent need to educate women for taking up entrepreneurship and for stressing benefits of entrepreneurship. This awareness can be achieved through conferences, seminars, training programmes, refresher courses, awareness camps and other related activities.
4. Success stories of women entrepreneurs from varied backgrounds should be popularized through text books of schools and colleges. All possible media should be used to project these role models.
5. When women work outside their home they face problems of childcare, Governmental and other non-Governmental organizations should make efforts to provide facilities in the form of childcare institutions like crèches, nurseries and child-care facilities. These facilities should adjust timings, location as per the convenience of women entrepreneurs.
6. The procedures should be simplified. Procedural delays, tedious formalities should be avoided. Moreover, the required documents should be minimized. All the documents should be in local languages.
7. It is observed that women deal with traditional activities, which are more or less feminine in nature. They generally choose

activities like food preservation, beauty services, tailoring, embroidery etc. that fit with their stereotyped role. In addition to these activities, there are some unexplored areas which provide flexible working hours and convenience of working at home. Such avenues should be explored. There is tremendous scope for agro based industries like animal husbandry, poultry, dairy, bakery, food processing, sericulture, agriculture, horticulture etc.

8. Outlets should be provided for marketing of products of women entrepreneurs since in open competition they cannot compete with big manufacturers. Similarly protection should also be provided for acquiring raw material at concessional rates from Governmental agencies.

Conclusion

In rural areas, where agriculture is prominent activity, agro-based industry like food preservation, bakery, dairy, poultry could be taken up by women.

In areas, where forest predominates forest preservation, planting and looking after the trees can be entrusted to them. Weaving or power loom can also be given to them.

In districts where industries are located spare parts and ancillar industry can be managed by women. They should also be encouraged in mechanical and electrical activities. ITI (Industrial Training Institute) can train girls and encourage them to start on their own.

In urban parts, electronics, computer services and needed informative and consultative services, advertising agencies and the like are the areas which women entrepreneurs can explore. What they need is little training, finance and large quantity of co-operation and encouragement from all men at home, in society and in governmental organizations. That will enable women entrepreneurs to enter the main stream of country's economy, which in turn will speed up the economic development of our country.

Chapter 31

MARKETING PRACTICES AND CONSTRAINTS IN WOMEN ENTERPRISES

*Dr. K. Selvarani

ABSTRACT

The major objectives of the study is to identify some of the constraints faced by women entrepreneurs in marketing their products. Primary data was collected from 150 women entrepreneurs at Virudhunagar District. The sample comprises of women entrepreneurs engaged in manufacturing, namely wax carving, match boxes, five works, rice mills, trading such as groceries, stationary, cosmetic; and servicing like beauty parlour, tailoring, Xeroxing and repairing shop. Statistical tools such as chi-square techniques and spearmans rank correlation co-efficient technique was used for analyzing the data collected. The major problems are competition from large scale units, high marketing cost, low sales promotion techniques. The study suggests proper entrepreneurial skill and marketing training to the women entrepreneurs.

Introduction

Marketing is the key co-ordinating role as it plays between the linked process of production, selling and distribution. Marketing is nothing more or less than the total business function of producing a salable product. In spite of an extensive potential market, the woman entrepreneurs were most reluctant towards efficient marketing technique and consequently have met with utter failure on the front of marketing their products.

* Reader in Commerce, V.V. Vanniaperumal College for Women, Virudhunagar.

Women entrepreneurs find it difficult to capture the market and make their products popular. In order to make a success of a venture, women entrepreneurs need to have good marketing plan. In the marketing plan, the important factors to be considered are building up on image for venture, location, policy, planning the stores and channels of distribution of goods/services, advertising, promotion strategies and the selling skills.

Modern marketing whether it is urban areas or rural areas it values movement of the entrepreneurs. In certain economic activities the movement for marketing their products on services is easy. For example, women engaged in enterprises like, vegetables, fruit vendors, papad, garment, handicraft items etc., But if they are in non-traditional enterprise like washing powder, matchbox, stappler pins, wax curving, fire works etc, then movement for business is necessary and often difficult.

Hence, an attempt has been made to analysis the marketing strategies adapted by the women entrepreneurs to market their products and the problems faced by them in the managerial functions of marketing.

Methodology

The present study is mainly based on primary data and secondary data. The primary data has been collected from the women entrepreneurs in Virudhunagar District with the help of pre-tested interview schedule. The primary data collected are analyzed by using appropriate statistical tools such percentage analysis, mean, chi-square techniques and spearman's rank correlation co-efficient technique. The data has been collected from 150 women entrepreneurs derived from DIC, Virudhunagar, spread over all the areas of Virudhunagar District. The sample comprises the women entrepreneur who engage themselves in manufacturing [86 (57.3%)], like wax carving, match boxes, fire works rice mill etc., trading [33 (22%)] like, groceries, stationery, cosmetics etc. and servicing [31 (20.7%] like beauty parlor, tailoring, Xeroxing, repairing shop etc.

MARKETING PRACTICES

Identification of Scope for the Market

The survey throws light on whether women entrepreneurs identified the scope for the marketing for their products before starting the units. If the scope of marketing is not identified it may lead to problems in the introduction of the product.

The investigation reveals that 48 per cent of the women entrepreneur units identified the scope of marketing and the rest of 52 per cent had established the units without identifying the scope of marketing. The following table exhibits the respondent's identification of market scope.

Table 1 : Identification of Market Scope

Particulars	*No. of respondents*	*%*
Yes	72	48
No	78	52
Total	150	100

Further investigation reveals that a great majority of women entrepreneurs manufacture only a traditional products. So it is not necessary to identify the scope of market. Very few entrepreneurs state the reason for not identifying the marketing scope is the lack of business experience.

Problems in Product Introduction

The introduction stage is the first stage in the life of a product. The initial stage needs large amount of investment. All the business units especially, the small entrepreneurs units are exposed to many problems at this stage of survival. During the study an attempt was made to magnitude the nature of problems faced in the introduction of the product in the market by women entrepreneurs units.

Table 2 : Problems in Product Introduction

Particulars	*No. of respondents*	*%*
Yes	109	73
No	41	27
Total	150	100

This study reveal that a majority (73%) of women entrepreneurs faced problem of product introduction.

Reasons for Problems in Product Introduction

The survey explores the factors responsible for the problems in the product introduction. The study has brought to sharp focus that the 'Heavy competition' is the foremost constraints which caused problem to 62 units (42.47%) in the product introduction. Among the reason 'availability of labour' and maintenance of quality were the problem to 53 (36.30%) units and 31(21.23%) units respectively. The following table exhibits the reasons for problems in product introduction.

Table 3 : Reasons for Problem in Product Introduction

S.No.	*Problems*	*No. of respondents*	*%*
1.	Heavy competition	62	41
2.	Availability of labour	53	35
3.	Maintenance of quality	31	21
4.	No answer	4	3
	Total	146	100.00

The study identified that women entrepreneurs have to face a stiff competition for marketing their products with both organized sector and their male counterparts.

Area of Market

In order to ascertain whether the women entrepreneurs sell their product in wide area or limited area. The market is divided into different location – Local, Taluk, District, State and Country.

Table 4 : Area of Market

S.No.	*Area*	*No. of responses*	*%*
1.	Local	83	30.29
2.	Taluk	45	16.42
3.	District	64	12.36
4.	State	68	24.82
5.	Country	14	5.10
	Total	274*	100.00

* Note : Since each respondents answered more than one area, the number of respondents has outnumbered the number of respondents.

From the above it is clear that women entrepreneurs in Virudhunagar District serve the customer in wide area including other States and Country.

Branding

A brand is word, letter, group of words or letters or combination of any or all of these used to identify the goods or services of a seller or group of sellers. Branding is the practice of establishing brand names, marks or trade name for a product and it is the process of finding and fixing the means of identification. Branding strategy involves around ensuring that the brand name will stick in the consumer's minds. If it does, the chance and fairly good that, other things being equal, the product will do well; According to one study made by Willard H. Doyle, if it does not and chances are about 200 to 1 that it will not the product will probably fail. Considering the entrenched position of the established brands and consumer's preference for the known and popular brands, small entrepreneurs has to make concerted efforts to get better sales.

The study sheds light that, the study participants, namely 65 (43%) units branded their product. The products of remaining 85 (57%) were not branded.

Basis for Selecting Brand Name

Each respondent has different opinion in connection with selecting brand name. But normally the brand name should be simple and easily recorded in the minds of consumers.

Table 5 : Basis for Selecting Brand Name

S.No.	*Basis*	*No. of responses*	*%*
1.	Related with other units name in your area	10	15.4
2.	Very lucky name	26	40.0
3.	God name	13	20.0
4.	Easy to tell & remember	16	24.6
	Total	65	100.00

It is clear that a majority of women entrepreneurs selected brand name as 'Very lucky name".

Registered and Unregistered Brads

Many brand users seek to register their brands in order to prevent other sellers for using those brands. When a brand name or brand mark is registered and legalised it becomes a trademark. A trademark is occasionally used to indicate a registered brand, but this use is not to be preferred. Better usage is to equate brand, trademark and distinguish between whether they are registered or not by calling them 'registered or unregistered'. An effort was made to study whether brands used by the sample women entrepreneur units are registered or unregistered.

Table 6 : Registration of Brand

Particulars	*No. of respondents*	*%*
Yes	7	10.8
No	58	89.2
Total	65	100.00

Labelling

Label is a part of a product, which carries verbal information about the product or the seller. It may be a part of a package, or it may be a tag attached directly to the product. Label identifies the quality of a product by a letter, number or word. Label give written or illustrative objective information about the characteristics, use, construction, care performance or other features of a product. If a substance is poisonous, the label must tell the user what steps to take if any is ingested and must list the antidotes. Label is also a indicator of brand name of the product.

The investigation discloses the number of respondents fixing label on the products. Out of 150 women respondent, a majority of 118 (79%) respondents gave special attention to fix label on the product and the remaining 32 (21%) respondents expressed that 'no need' to fix label on the product.

Nature of Information Provided in the Label

The information such as contents of product, quantum of contents, brand name, price, method of storing, method of using etc., should be clearly provided in the label.

The study also sheds light on the information provided by the respondents on the label used by them.

Table 7 : Nature of Information Provided in the Label

S.No.	*Nature of information*	*No. of respondents*	*%*
1.	Product contents	40	17.24
2.	Quantum of contents	50	21.55
3.	Brand name	48	20.69
4.	Price	44	18.97
5.	Method of storing	14	6.03
6.	Method of using	36	15.52
	Total	232*	100.00

*The number of responses exceeded more than one from each respondent.

Cost of Labelling

The cost of labelling differs from one unit to another unit. The entrepreneurs spend a smaller portion of amount against label out of the selling price.

The survey sheds light on how much amount being spent for labelling by the study participants.

Table 8 : Cost of Labelling

S.No.	*Cost in %*	*No. of respondents*	*%*
1.	Upto 0.5%	40	33.8
2.	UPto 0.75%	36	30.5
3.	Uptot 1%	25	21.2
4.	More than 1%	17	14.5
	Total	118	100.00

Pricing Objectives

Price fixation is of great importance to marketing planner for several reasons. Price plays a pivotal role in the regulation of the entire spectrums of economic activities to an enterprises. A pricing policy must act as a motivating force for the accelerated growth of industries. Proper and careful pricing and the adoption of a proper price policy are some of the important steps towards the success of small scale industries.

The process of establishing objectives is structured by the firm's internal environment. A very large number of price objectives are available, the objectives must be consistent with the organization's internal thrust and compatible with the external environment.

Table 9 : Pricing Goals of Sample Women Enterpreneurs

S.No.	*Pricing objective*	*No. of Units*	*%*
1.	Maximisation of current profit	32	21
2.	Minimum return on investment on Sales	30	20
3.	Target sales volume	20	14
4.	Deeper penetration of market and find new market	32	21
5.	Keeping competition week	36	24
	Total	150	100

The pricing objective is always to make profit, but often building a high sales volume has priority. The pricing can yield the maximum contribution towards overheads and profits. The study brings to limelight the pricing goals of sample women entrepreneurs.

Pricing Policies and Pricing Method

The pricing policies and pricing methods followed by a firm emanate from the pricing objective of the firm. The various methods of pricing known to most of the sample women entrepreneurs can be grouped under the following three categories.

1. Cost based pricing – cost plus pricing
2. Demand based pricing – fixing at the highest level what the traffic can bear.
3. Competition based pricing – pricing below or above competitive level.

The study brings to lime light the pricing goals of sample units.

Table 10 : Method of Price Fixation

S.No.	*Pricing method*	*No. of respondents*	*%*
1.	Based on cost plus margin	84	56
2.	Based on competitors price	40	27
3.	At the highest level that market can bear	26	17
	Total	150	100.00

Discount

Discounting policy is often a collateral policy to help to achieve a price objective like target, return on investment. Discount is often an important part of the price policy. Difference in size of purchases, type of customer, geographical area and transport, consideration may result in legitimate discounts to reflect economies of scales, competitive situations on the cost of serving different segments.

The small women entrepreneurs units though do not apparently establish any price discrimination, but make differentials in price by allowing the buyers certain discounts on reduction from the selling price. The enquiry unearths that among 150 sample units, only 69 (46%) units offered discount to their buyer. The remaining 54 per cent of respondents did not provide any discounts.

Kinds of Discount Offered

In the light of the previous finding, an attempt has been made to ascertain the nature of discount offered to the buyers. The most common are the quantity discount, based on quantity purchased; the trade discount based on trade status of the buyer; and the cash discount, allowed for prompt payment.

Table 11 : Kind of Discount Offered

S.No.	*Kind of Discount*	*No. of respondents*	*%*
1.	Trade Discount	15	21.8
2.	Cash Discount	37	53.6
3.	Quantity Discount	17	24.6
	Total	69	100.00

It is lucid that cash discount is offered by maximum number of units than any other type of discount.

Distribution Channel System

One of the key decisions for an entrepreneur concerns what distribution channel to use. A channel of distribution, some times called a trade channel is the route taken by the goods as they move from producer to consumer. According to Jakate, marketing problem of small scale industries vary not only by the size of these units but also by the nature of demand and the pattern of distribution channels necessary to reach the customer.

The link between the producer and consumer are varied; therefore a small scale entrepreneur has to select the best channel which will allow a small manufacturer to reach the market most profitably is often narrowed down to three choice.

Table 12 : Type of Distribution Channel of Sample Units

S.No.	*Type of Channel*	*No. of respondents*	*%*
1.	Direct Selling	47	31.3
2.	Through intermediaries	70	46.7
3.	Combination of both	33	22.0
	Total	150	100.00

The study reveals that the use of different type of distribution channel depends upon the type of goods manufactured. The survey indicates that only 31.3 per cent of sample respondents select the channel direct selling.

Direct selling has not become a powerful channel. According to an estimate, even less than 3 per cent of total consumer sales are made in their channel due to spending handsome amount in training, maintaining and supervising a large number of staff.

Advertising

Marketing has changed substantially from the time when producers and intermediaries could talk directly with their customers, who were virtually within a shouting distance. Small entrepreneurs, actually amount for advertisement. The smaller the adverting budget the lesser is the problem in utilizing the limited fund effectively. Becoming competent in advertising is, therefore, for more important for the small businessmen than the person planning to climb the corporate ladder in large enterprise.

Advertising consists of all the activities involved in presenting to a group of non personal, oral or visual, openly sponsored message regarding a product, service or ideas, this message, called on advertisement disseminated through one or more media and is paid for by the identified sponsor.

The study throws light on the women entrepreneurs unit's practice of advertising. It is disclosure that out of 150 sample units, an appreciable number standing for 56 (37%) units used advertising as a tool for marketing their product 94 (63%) units were not using any advertising technique.

Media of Advertisement

Several media of advertising are available for a woman entrepreneur and she has to select one or more of these media for her product to be advertised. Media choice are mainly influenced by the purpose of advertising, nature of the product, the types of consumers to be approached and the cost of the media.

An analysis of the survey data unfolds that among 94 responses obtained from 56 units which used advertisement.

Table 13 : Media of advertisement

S.No.	*Media*	*No. of units*	*%*
1.	Newspaper	14	14.9
2.	Wall poster	14	14.9
3.	Banner advertisement	20	21.3
4.	Cinema and theaters	14	14.9
5.	Bit notice	32	34.0
	Total	94	100.00

Sales Promotion

Sales promotion has been the fastest segment of the promotion mix and a major factor in the success of marketers during the turbulent economic times of the past decade rather than competing with either advertising or personal selling. Sales promotion activities are complementary to them. Their purpose is as their name suggests to 'promote sales'. Sales promotion should not be dismissed as a miscellaneous part of promotion. To some sellers, it may be the single most important type of promotion. The decision of a small industrial unit makes to emphasize on dealer promotion or consumer promotion will be crucial to the success of the entire marketing programmes.

The investigation unveils the sample unit's adoption of sales promotion programmes. An analysis of the survey data brings to limelight that out of 150 study units, only 72 (48%) used sales promotion programmes.

Methods of Sales Promotion

The various sales promotion methods that markets have at their disposal include providing samples, price reductions, free gifts, prize coupons, contacts, shows and exhibits and so forth.

Table 14 : Sales promotion methods adopted by sample units

S.No.	*Methods*	*No. of respondents*	*%*
1.	Price deduction	34	47.2
2.	Free gift	13	18.0
3.	Samples	25	34.8
	Total	72	100.00

From the above analysis it is lucid that the offer of 'Price deduction' is the usual sales promotional device adopted by the women entrepreneurs units in Virudhunagar district.

The statement placed herewith point out the association and significant level of marketing practices adopted among the units of different industry group with the help of chi-square value.

Table 15 : Chi-Square Analysis of Marketing Practice on Nature of Business Wise

S. No.	*Marketing Practices*	*df*	*Calculated X^2 value*	*Table X^2 value*	*Significant or not significant*
1.	Identification of market scope	2	15.047	5.991	Significant
2.	Problems in product Introduction	2	1.810	5.991	Not Significant
3.	Area of market	8	107.755	15.5	Very significant
4.	Branding strategy	2	48.378	5.991	Significant
5.	Labelling strategy	2	74.823	5.991	Significant
6.	Method of price fixation	4	55.259	9.49	Significant
7.	Sales promotion programme	2	1.279	5.991	Not significant
8.	Advertisement	2	18.852	5.991	Significant

It is a significant revelation that is most of the marketing practices, the variances among the women entrepreneur's units on nature of business basis are significant. So women entrepreneur's units have exerted its influence over the employment of business tools and technique.

Constraints in Marketing

During the survey, it is observed that the sample women enterprises were exposed to a host of drawbacks in the field of marketing. In the light of the previous findings, an attempt was made to analyse the problems faced in the spectrum of marketing.

The investigation unveils that in order of importance, the problems 'Heavy competition among the small scale units', 'Competition from the large scale units', 'High credit sales', 'High distributors margin', 'High marketing cost', 'Low sales promoting knowledge', 'Cheaper competitive substitutes', 'Cost plus pricing not feasible', 'Low brand preference', prevailed in the midst of women enterprises and ranked 1,2,3,4,5,6,7,8 and 9 respectively.

Respondent's Ranking of Marketing Problem – Nature of Business Wise Analysis

An attempt was made to find out whether any correlation exists in ranking the problems in the sphere of marketing by the sample women entrepreneur units. For this spearman's rank correlation co-efficient (r_s) was used. The following table exhibits whether the manufacturing, trading and service organization have a close approach in ranking the common problems in marketing.

Since the co-efficient of rank correlation is negative (-0.37) in the judgment of first and second judges namely manufacturing and trading group units. So they have a negative approach to the common problems in the area of marketing. It is also noted that rank correlation co-efficient between first and third judgment i.e., manufacturing and service group units and the judgment of trading and service group units are positive. So they have a nearest approach to the common problem in marketing. A discussion of various kinds of problem encountered by the study participants in the realm of marketing is made in the following passages.

1. Heavey Competition among the Small Scale Units

Excessive competition among the Small-Scale Units is the first and fore must marketing problems to the sample women entrepreneurs. The marketing team should be dynamic, aggressive, in tune with contemporary needs, one better than that of the competitors. Competition, it is remarked improves efficiency but due to under development economy and imperfect market condition, this effect of competition is negligible. Women enterprises have imperfect organizational setup. Due to this, they have to face server competition from organised sector and entrepreneurs.

During the survey, it is observed that the problem in the area of marketing as faced by the women entrepreneurs is the existence of unhealthy competition among small entrepreneurs themselves and specifically among manufacturing and servicing unit.

Women entrepreneurs in the areas reported that, in these days face stiff competition, a lot of money is required for adverting and fail to adopt innovative sales promotion scheme, which entail heavy expenditure. There are no proper organized associations among the small units to avoid cut throat competition.

2. Competition from Large Scale Units

Small enterprises are poor in all the competitive marketing attributes like packaging, branding, standardization, distribution and after sales service. When competing with large-scale enterprises, problems may also is developed from inadequate resources, at the disposal of small industries for identifying market outlets and marketable characteristic of the product. Because of their small size and lack of resources, small units are unable to adopt modern marketing methods.

Many good products do not automatically lead to marketing success. Small units face more difficulties for proper positioning and promotion of products than larger ones. Women entrepreneurs in Virudhunagar District said that, it is difficult to produce, market and render services to their customer at cheapest cost. The main causes and lacking and compete with the large sector was diseconomy in scale of production, unable to follow moderisation in production technology, exploitation of middleman, undue credit sales etc. Further the small industries are faced with problem of costly transport.

3. High Credit Sales

It was found that most of the women enterprises are making sales on credit basis. They sell the goods on credit in order to maintain sales and compete with male entrepreneurs. Owing to non-availability of adequate and timely credit facilities from commercial bank to match the working capital requirements arising out of unavoidable credit sales, the small units find it difficult to continue production without interruption. Women entrepreneurs reported that it is difficult to collect debt from the customer. Loss on bad debts is increasing every year.

4. High Distributors Margin

Here, it is impossible to avoid sharing profit with the middleman because nearly 66 per cent of the products are disposed through middleman. It is also found that, the margin of profit retained by the intermediaries or distributors may be higher than the women entrepreneurs. Women entrepreneurs reported that, without middleman, it is difficult to search customer and market the product, particularly in case of food production ventures.

5. High Marketing Cost

Advertisement of the products, through the elaborate sales promotion methods such as cadres of trained salesmen, advertisement in cinema slides, posters, papers, magazines and so on has become increasingly fashionable to entrepreneurs. But, small industries lack the required resources as well as knowledge. Further, volume of production and selling is very much limited which lead to heavy marketing cost.

Small entrepreneurs are unable to cope with the unequal contest in the faces to powerful rivalry of large-scale units. In Virudhunagar district most of the women enterprises are generally owned and controlled by individuals. So they unable to meet heavy marketing of cost due to lack of financial support and moral support.

6. Low Sales Promotion Knowledge

Majority of women entrepreneurs do not adopt any promotional strategy. Due to lack of qualitative education, women are not aware of

Table –16 : Respondent's Ranking of Marketing Problem – Nature of Business Wise

S. No.	Problems	Mean Score of the rank Sfx/eF			Rank awarded			R1 & R2	R2 & R3	R1 & R3
		Manufac-turing	Trading	Service	M R1	T R2	S R3	D2 $(R1-R2)^2$	D2 $(R2-R3)^2$	D2 $(R1-R3)^2$
1.	Cheaper competitive substitutes	4.51	3.91	3.77	6	8	6	4	4	0
2.	Low Brand preference	3.88	3.98	2.95	8	7	9	1	4	1
3.	Cost plus pricing not feasible	3.65	5.27	3.52	9	1	7	64	36	4
4.	Heavy competition among the small sale units	5.67	3.90	4.38	2	9	4	49	25	4
5.	Competition from the large scale units	4.82	5.23	6.00	4	2	1	4	1	9
6.	High credit sales	5.72	4.00	3.48	1	6	8	25	4	49
7.	High distributors margin	5.05	4.72	4.10	3	4	5	1	1	4
8.	Low sales promotion knowledge	4.40	4.91	5.05	7	3	3	16	0	16
9.	High marketing cost	4.53	4.68	5.24	5	5	2	0	9	9
							ΣD^2	164	84	96

market knowledge. It is observed that only 37% women respondents adopt advertising technique and 48% respondents follow sales promotion method.

Women entrepreneurs reported that, it is unnecessary to adopt any promotional strategy because they sell the goods only in limited area of marketing.

7. Cheaper Competitive Substitute

During the survey, it has observed that women enterprise face a number of difficulties because of cheaper and superior competitive substitute. Consumers usually go for low priced products. The entrepreneur of such units informed that the customers normally prefer the products manufactured in the large-scale units having reported brand names.

8. Cost plus Pricing Not Feasible

It is noteworthy here that all the women entrepreneurs know the cost of production of their units through one way or another; of course, in general the costs records are not maintained accurately and systematically.

It is reported by the women entrepreneurs that the products are kept lower than the market prices of other similar brand named products in the market in order to entice the customers having an inclination for products with the brand name. New entrants are particularly keen to fix the prices of their products on a somewhat lower level than the prevailing market prices for the said reason.

9. Low Brand Preference

It is reported that by the entrepreneurs that 'brand consciousness' of the customers is a big hurdle in marketing the goods produced in the small sector. Absence of brand name is a problem faced by the small women entrepreneurs. Many of the entrepreneurs do not have any knowledge on the branding strategy. Besides, most of the brands used by the sample women entrepreneurs units are not registered, thus paving the way for the competitors to copy the brand.

Conclusion

Women entrepreneurs do face many challenges in today's business world. The process of developing marketing skill is rather not so slow as compared to early eighties. The present study clearly indicates that marketing practices by the women entrepreneurs and their outlook on business must still go a long way to catch up with the rapid technical and industrial advancement that is taking place in India. Proper entrepreneurial skill and marketing talent are to be given to the women entrepreneurs through proper training programmes for carrying entrepreneurial activities successfully. If they are given proper education and awareness about entrepreneurial activities they will become an important source for the economic development of our nation.

Chapter 32
WOMEN ENTREPRENEURSHIP PROBLEMS—CASUAL TRENDS

*Dr. G. Varadharajan

ABSTRACT

Problems faced by women as an individual or as a group member or as in institution is discussed in this chapter. The problems faced by women entrepreneurs in the initial stages include poor credit availability, weak collateral position, lack of business training, lack of respect for women in business and problems on the legal and personal fronts. The paper suggest active institutional involvement of both government and non-governmental organization for their supportive involvement for the growth of women entrepreneurs.

Introduction

The social condition of women in our society had been an acute problem since several centuries. They were not accorded equal with men, rather their status was quite low in our society. One can think of several approaches to remedy the gender inequality and imbalances in development, but one substantive approach could be promoting entrepreneurship among women. The usefulness of this approach depends on how seriously and faithfully it is translated into action. Unless there is something exclusive answering the cause and improving the economic conditions of women, any grand designs, formulation of polices and diluted approaches in the name of women development will hardly bear fruits.

The biggest problem of a woman entrepreneur is that she is a woman. Women entrepreneur have to face difficulties at all levels i.e. family

* Director G.V. Siddha & Herbal Research Foundation, Kainangarai, Mathur(po), Kulathur, Pudukkottai (Dt)-622515.

support, training, banking, licensing and marketing. Women in non-urban areas have to suffer still further. It is not that women do not have skills or capacity but they are not properly trained or inculcated in craftsmanship. It is well known fact that the women, entrepreneurs' development is necessary for economic development. The relation between women entrepreneurs' development and National development is a two-way process.

Women in Society

In the historical evolution of mankind, woman has been an economic partner to man, besides her biological and social roles. It is said that it was the woman who discovered the possibility of domesticating plants for food and beginning the rudiments of home-culture. It was so when man was in the hunting and gathering stage. Since then, through agricultural and industrial revolutions, she has been an economic partner in the family of man. She started the enterprise of food cultivation and later adopted bartering the food articles for other necessities of life.

In the recent past, as a result of increase in women's education, industrialization, urbanization, social and occupational mobility, the emergence of nuclear families, westernization, politico-social movements and changes in the value system, some educated women have taken to certain careers. Some, compelled by economic necessity, have taken to small business and trade.

Women clientele could be categorized into several groups, based on residence; education, family occupation or profession, socio-economic level and employment. Based on the above criteria, we can think of the women in terms of: (*a*) rural, (*b*) urban, (*c*) educated employed, (*d*) educated unemployed, (*e*) land owning, (*f*) landless, (*g*) tenant farmer, (*h*) artisan groups, (*i*) supporting the family economically, (*j*) just keeping the house, (*k*) enjoying considerable leisure; and (*l*) just thinking of doing some small business or activity to supplement the family's income.

Women as Human Resources

The effective utilization of human resource is a necessary condition for the development of any economy. Women occupy about 50 per cent of the total Indian population and they constitute an important segment of human resources. Through women have undergone many kinds of exploitation and oppressions, after independence there is some notable change in their status, specially in terms of breaking the age old customs and traditional bondages.

Women have been identified as potential contributions for fostering the pace of economic development. But the opportunities that exist are in occupations that are insecure and low paid. Agriculture is the major sector in which 70 per cent of the female working population is engaged. It is also a low wage occupation and income potential from agriculture depends on favourable climatic conditions. Alternative employment opportunities are inaccessible to women due to their poverty and unskilled nature.

Role of Women in Economic Development

It has resulted in a pervasive sexual division of labour, which reinforces the notion of the male having more power and relegates low status occupations to women. This leads to waste of female potentiality.

A women who earns as much as 50 per cent or sometimes 100 per cent of the household income is still regarded as a supplementary earner, And almost in all cases and in all levels (except to a large extent in the organized sector which accounts for a very small percentage of women) they do not get equal wages for equal work, nor do the conditions of work offered to them take into account their dual roles.

Amongst the poorer sections of the rural community, women are frequently expected to shoulder the burden of the survival of their families.

Women are principally engaged in agriculture or in the unorganized informal sector as construction workers, petty hawkers and vendors and in traditional home based occupations such as basket and mat weaving, beedi making, lace making, agarbathis etc. Women are also involved in marketing in certain traditional areas.

Marketing of agricultural products, however, is traditionally undertaken by men. Women are involved in fish trading, vegetable and flower vending and other areas of petty market trading. Similarly, women involved in handicraft occupations such as basket making, etc., will frequently market their products in the local shandies (bazaars).

Women carry out the bulk of the work in agricultural production. Around 70 per cent to 80 per cent of all fieldwork is done by women whilst most post harvest and processing tasks are solely their responsibility. There, however, strict sexual/ division of labour in agricultural work. All operations involving machinery and draught animals are performed by men. All activities involving direct manual labour are assigned to women.

In addition, the women are exposed to financial exploitation by traders and middlemen who provide credit or raw materials and take back the finished product, cheating the women through providing insufficient or sub-standard raw materials and then making unreasonable deductions for poor quality.

Concept of Women Entrepreneurs

The Government of India has defined women entrepreneurs based on women participation in equity and employment of a business enterprise. Accordingly, a women entrepreneur is defined as "an enterprise owned and controlled by a woman having a minimum financial investment of 51 per cent of the capital and giving at least 51 per cent of the employment generated in the enterprise to women"

In nutshell, women entrepreneurs are those women who think of a business enterprise, initiate it, organize and combine the factors of production, operate the enterprise and undertake risks and handle economic uncertainty involved in running a business enterprise.

According to Schumpeter an entrepreneur is one who introduces something new into the economy. In Indian context, entrepreneur is more an adapter or 'initiator' than a true innovator. Therefore any woman who initiates, innovates or adapts an economic activity may be called woman entrepreneur".

Importance of Women Entrepreneurs

Women entrepreneurs are the dynamic element and an important component in the process of economic development. Though India is primarily an agrarian society, she is one of the ten largest industrial powers of the world. Women's share in self-employment is not only very low but predominates, overwhelmingly, in the unorganized sector. Presently, a trend is visible in India where more and more women are venturing as entrepreneurs in all kinds of activities. This is due to pull and push factors.

The developing countries like India, the presence of entrepreneurs, that too women entrepreneurs are of vital necessity, to achieve a rapid, all round and regionally and socially balanced economic growth through industrialization. It also helps in tapping the inherent talent prevailing among them and act as a panacea for many problems faced by them, such as dowry death, low recognition in society, poverty, unemployment and excessive dependence on male members.

Factors Influencing the Women Entrepreneurship

The general observation and several studies reveal that two factors influence the women entrepreneurs in India:

Pull Factors

Pull factors imply the factors, which encourage women to become entrepreneurs. They include desire to do something new in life, need for independence, availability of finance, concessions and subsidies.

Push Factors

Push factors are those, which compel women to become entrepreneurs. They include financial difficulties, responsibility in the family, unfortunate family circumstances like death of the husband or father, divorce etc. However, the influence of this factor on women in becoming entrepreneurs is low than the former factor

Types of Women Entrepreneurs

Women entrepreneurs can be classified into four groups depending on the driving motivational factors.

Natural Entrepreneurs

Those who take business as a profession on their own either by self preplanning or motivated through profit/money factor and also for keeping themselves busy.

Created Entrepreneurs

Those who have been encouraged and trained through specialized training programmes such as entrepreneurship development programmes to set up independent business.

Forced Entrepreneurs

Those who are compelled by circumstances such as the death of father or husband with responsibilities falling on them-to take over the existing business.

The Benami Entrepreneurs

Those who are acting as a facade for business of their husband or brother.

(*i*) Problems Faced by Women Entrepreneur

The problems of entrepreneurial development are of individual, group and of institutional nature. Ultimately, it is the individual who has to take the initiative to decide on, start and manage his enterprise. He also needs the approval and support of his kin-group or community. The individual and the group constitute the client system. The institutions are to stimulate the client system towards entrepreneurial activity. The institutions are the various governmental and autonomous agencies that are concerned with entrepreneurial development. They are the source of several commissions and omissions that impede and slow down the process of entrepreneurial development. We may briefly look into some of the problems that centre around the individual, group and the institutions.

Individual

1. Lack of motivation.
2. Shyness and inhibition.
3. Ignorant of opportunities that he can avail himself of.
4. Lack of requisite managerial skills to start and manage his enterprise.
5. Lack of finance for initial investment.
6. Lack of familial and community support for his enterprise.
7. Scared of the cumbersome and time-consuming process in establishing the enterprise.
8. Even if she starts the enterprise, she is not sure of sustained support from the promotional agencies in terms of timely and adequate credit and marketing of his products.

Group

- Lack of awareness.
- Preference for traditional occupations and professions.
- Don't think of alternative avocations.
- Apathy, sense of fear and insecurity towards government initiated and sponsored programmes.
- Ignorant of their own potential: material and human.
- Economically and politically weak.
- Lack the freedom to choose and pursue their choices as a consequence to the power- sway of the local elite or the dominant caste.
- They are more tradition-bound, and their values are, to continue *with* their institutionalized familial occupations.
- They prefer to be what they want to be.

Institutional

1. Vague and unrealistic policies, and policies not supported by action.
2. Lack of teamwork and internal coordination in the agencies.
3. Lack of inter-agency coordination.
4. Bureaucratic style of working.
5. The functions of the personnel are not vested with the requisite power and authority.
6. Overlapping and duplication of functions both at the apex and operational levels.
7. A multiplicity of agencies performing a more or less similar task.
8. The field-level personnel are not supported in their, promises and performance by the higher-ups in the organizations.
9. Lack of work motivation and commitment to their task.
10. Lack of relevant training on the part of the EDP personnel.
11. Lack of appreciation of the importance of human factors in development.
12. Lack of knowledge of technical know-how on the part of the personnel.

Other problems of entrepreneurial development are in respect of provision of infrastructural facilities, including finance and marketing.

The problems mentioned above though are stupendous and complex, are not insurmountable, an inter-disciplinary and multi-pronged approach is required to find

Solutions to these Problems

The problems listed above are not inherent or unchangeable. Through gradual entrepreneurial education, organizational and institutional support provided to the people in terms of motivation, incentives, infrastructural facilities, supply of certain inputs, credit and market support, the neo-entrepreneurs will gain confidence through their experience and success and they would be the factors creating congenial entrepreneurial climate. These problems are interrelated and they are to be looked at by the industrial development agencies and the community leaders. As mentioned above, entrepreneurial education through entrepreneurial activity and training provided to the development personnel and potential entrepreneurs would gradually create conditions favouring a positive change in the problems listed above.

(*ii*) Problems of Women Entrepreneurs

Women entrepreneurs encounter two sets of problems, viz. general problems of entrepreneurs and problems specific to women entrepreneurs. These are discussed as follows:

Problem of Finance

Women entrepreneurs suffer from shortage of finance on who counts. Firstly, women do not generally have properly on their names to use them as collateral for obtaining funds from external sources. Secondly, the banks also consider women less credit- worthy and discourage women borrowers on the belief that they can at any time leave their business.

Scarcity of Raw Material

Most of the women enterprises are plagued by the scarcity of raw material, and necessary inputs. Added to this is the high price of raw material, on the one hand, and getting raw material at the minimum of discount, on the other.

Stiff Competition

Women entrepreneurs do not have organisational set-up to pump in a lot of money for canvassing and advertisement. Thus, they have to face stiff competition for marketing their products with both organised sector and their male counterparts.

Limited Mobility

Unlike men, women mobility in India is highly limited due to various reasons. A single woman asking for room is still looked upon suspicion. Cumbersome exercise involved in starting an enterprise coupled with the official's humiliating attitude towards women compels them to give up idea of starting an enterprise.

Family Ties

In India, it is mainly a woman's duty to look after the children and other members of the family. Man plays a secondary role only. Her total involvement in family leaves little or no energy and time to devote for business. Accordingly, the educational level and family background of husbands positively influence women's entry into business activities.

Lack of Education

In India, around three-fifths (60%) of women are still illiterate. Due to lack of education and that too qualitative education, women are not aware of business, technology and market knowledge. Also lack of education causes low achievement motivation among women.

Male Dominated Society

In the Male-dominated Indian society, women are not treated equal to men. This in turn serves as a barrier to women entry into business.

Low Risk Bearing Ability

Women in India lead a protected life. They are less educated and economically not self-dependent. All these reduce their ability to bear risk involved in running an enterprise. Risk -bearing is an essential requisite of a successful entrepreneur.

In addition to above problems, (*a*) inadequate infrastructural facilities, (*b*) shortage of power, (*c*) high cost of production, (*d*) social attitude, (*e*) socio-economic constraints, (*f*) late commencement of women entrepreneurs in India, (*g*) producers of bank loan and delays, (*h*) discrimination in selection for entrepreneurs development training and inferiority complex among lower and middle class women also hold the women back from entering in to business.

Trends for Future

Entrepreneurs are well-known to live in the future and the future is uncertain and predictable to some extent. Circumstances always forces the entrepreneurs to play the safe game and to stay at the top always and to be the agents of change. The emergence and popularity of electronic commerce as a medium of exchange signifies the importance of this information age. Traditional activities and jobs are being revolutionized as the ever changing economy demands all these changes periodically. The fast changes of the technology forces all the economies to have thorough changes and reshaping their society, economically, commercially and socially for the days to come

Conclusion

The foregoing discussion provides a brief a glimpse of how 'entrepreneur' and 'Entrepreneurship' have been theoretically examined and analyzed in economic thought. Reviewing the major theories and expositions from cantillon to krizner, spanning space, time and problems orientation, the entrepreneurs is seen as performing various functional roles as risk- taker, decision maker, organiser or coordinator, innovator, employer of factors of production, arbitrageur and allocator of resource to alternative uses. Women entrepreneurs expressed their deficiency in some management skills. The problems in the initial stages included credit availability, weak collateral position, lack of business training, lack of respect for women in business, and problems on the legal and personal fronts. Where as both female and male entrepreneurs are equally affected by the non-availability of finance, the rural and semi-urban areas suffered more than the reliability better-off towns. The higher the level of education, better was the difficulty in securing finance. The suggest active institutional involvement of both Government and Non- Government Organisation should be encouraged and support of women Entrepreneurship.

REFERENCES

- **Balu.V (2001),** Entrepreneurship and Management of Small Business, Sri Venkateswara Publications, Chennai.
- **Gupta.C.B, Srinivassn. N. P., (2001),** Entrepreneurial Development, Sultan Chand & Sons, New Delhi.
- **Hisrich peters, (2001),** Entrepreneurship, Tata Mcgraw Hill Publishing Company Ltd, New Delhi.
- **Khanka.S.S, (2001)** Entrepreneurial Development Sultan Chand & Company Ltd, New Delhi.
- **Saravanavel.P,** Entrepreneurial Development, ESS pee Kay Publishing House, Madras.
- **Dahiya. L.N August (2000)**, Emerging Profile of Women Entrepreneurs and Workers in India, Southern Economist, Bangalore.
- **Rathakrishnan.L, Sellammalle.B August (2001)**, Women Entrepreneurs in India, Southern Economist, Bangalore.
- **Setty.E.D. (2004)**, Clinical Approach to Promotion of Entrepreneurship Women, Anmol Publication PVT. Ltd, New Delhi
- **Santha Rani. G, (May, 2006)** Promotion of Entrepreneurship for Women's Development, Southern Economics, Vol.45, No.1 Bangalore.

Chapter 33

WOMEN ENTREPRENEURSHIP IN INDIA—PROBLEMS AND PROSPECTS

*Dr. D. Pulla Rao

ABSTRACT

The chapter traces the significant contribution made by the women entrepreneurs in the economy and global scenario. However, they encounter many problems the problem may be related to shortage of finance, supply of raw materials, training facilities, market the finished products and so on.

Introduction

Entrepreneur's fast reinforce the capitalist tendencies in the context of globalization. The economic history reveals that it is the entrepreneurs who holds key of economic development. But unfortunately innovative entrepreneurs as conceptualized by Schumpeter are a rare tribe to be found equally in all parts of the globe. The large the number of entrepreneurs the greater the economic growth rate is the experience of the advanced countries like U.K., U.S.A., Germany, France and Japan.

The supply of insufficient number of entrepreneurs is holding back economic development in developing countries like India. For entrepreneurial activity is an adventure backed by resource endowment to fully exploit the markets at local, National and Global levels. Entrepreneurial traits are rather not widely visible in the Indian context and not to speak of women entrepreneurs in particular.

Although women's population is almost equal to that of men, their active participation in economic development seems to be insignificant till 1990. The women in India did not enjoy social freedom so as to freely

* Reader, Dept. of Cooperation & Applied Economics, Andhra University, Visakhapatnam.

mingle with the mainstream of life sharing the nation building activity through realizing their full potentials.

Keeping the above background, it is very clear that the entrepreneurship for women group is essential and it is to be developed. Indeed, there have been several women in the history of our country who have successfully ruled their kingdoms. Even in the modern times also there have been several women leaders such as Mrs. Sorojini Naidu, Mrs. Durgabai Deshmukh, Miss. Padmaja Naidu, Mrs. Sucheta Kriplani and Madam Indira Gandhi who could equal their men counterparts in intellectual capabilities and statesmanship. Now-a-days there are several women political leaders in our country who could show their talents and abilities in the administration on par with men. All these would only prove that women are in no way inferior to men in any walk of life and they can be as good entrepreneurs as men.

Having realized the importance of the role of women in the Nations development, in the Sixth Five year plan, a special chapter on women's development has been included and the chapter explains the plan of action for "Integration of women in development". Further, the New Industrial Policy of Government of India has especially highlighted the need for conducting special entrepreneurship programmes exclusively for women group. These programmes would be in the nature of product/process oriented courses meant for women entrepreneurs to enable them to start small-scale industries. It shows that the objective of this course is to give representation to women group in the field of small industry development with view to uplift the economic and social status of women.

Indian society, though tradition bound in the past, now it is undergoing through a change and women are seeking gainful employment in all fields in increasing numbers. Even then it cannot be said that women entrepreneurship movement has taken off the ground and it is felt that the movement is still in a transition period. It is during the last 10 -15 years women have started becoming entrepreneurs and started industries and business and they are yet to go a long way to be on par with men. The situation is quite understandable, as women have to play a dual role as a housewife and also as an income earner. Despite the modernization and other factors mentioned above, the weight of tradition and the responsibilities of the women have to discharge to their children as mother slow down this movement. Further, occupational backgrounds of the families and the educational attainment of the husbands have a direct bearing in the development of women entrepreneurship. Limiting the size of the family help the women entrepreneurs to some extent to enable them to enter business in such a manner that husband's prestige is not affected in any manner.

It is believed that entrepreneurs are born not made. However, some recent researches on promoting entrepreneurs seem to show that this view is not really correct. Entrepreneurship can be planned and developed and the need for providing appropriate importance in the case of prospective women entrepreneurs. The spirit of entrepreneurship can be nurtured to some extent by an appropriate pattern of education and training programme. The curriculum design for women's education needs re-orientation and the philosophy of "Good enough for women" should be given a go-by.

For instance, the present emphasis in any women's polytechnic is on stitching, embroidery, house decoration, etc., which are the women's traditional role rather than aiming at imparting new skills which would help them to become entrepreneurs by starting small-scale industries or setting up business. Some recent researches conducted indicate that several women are now willing to become entrepreneurs due to various factors. These factors can be broadly classified under heads, namely, "pull factors" and "push factors". Under the first category, the women entrepreneurs choose a profession as challenge and adventure with an urge to do something new and to have an independent occupation. The other category of women take-up business enterprises to get over financial difficulties and responsibility is thrust on them due to family circumstances.

However, in sum, the problem of entrepreneurship among women is a question of the family outlook on the role to be played by the women, and the estimation of capabilities by women themselves. Much depends upon the courage and determination of women to become entrepreneurs and with the facilities offered by Government, Banks and Financial Institutions to women, they should now start setting up business ventures in large number in many parts of the country.

Definition of Women Entrepreneurship

The term women entrepreneurship refers to socio-economic and political upliftment of women-folk making them equal to their men counterparts in all respects. These include social status, self-sustenance and participation in decision-making mechanism starting from gross-root level to the national level. In this context International Labour Organization

(ILO) describes that "entrepreneurs are people who have the ability to see and evaluate business opportunities, to gather the necessary resources to take advantage of them and to initiate appropriate action to ensure success".

World Bank defines empowerment as "the process of increasing the capacity of individuals or groups to make choices and to transform those choices into desired actions and outcomes. Central to this process or set of actions which both build individual and collective assets and improve the efficiency and fairness of the organizational and institutional context which govern the use of those assets".

This definition explains freedom of choice and action in all spheres to shape one's life and the life of fellow citizens. Women must have to secure control over resources and decisions. Due to gender inequality, such control is often severely curtailed. Hence, at the individual level, women empowerment require a set of assets and capabilities like health, education and employment and at the collective level they secure the ability to organize and mobilize to take action to solve their problems.

A women entrepreneur is one who owns and controls an enterprise having a share capital of not less than 51 per cent as partial / shareholder / directors of private limited company / members of co-operative society. The functions performed by a woman entrepreneur are categorized as risk-bearing organization and innovation. In India, where its population maintains almost equal ratio of male and female, the emergence of women entrepreneurs have great relevance and importance. Otherwise it will be amounting to neglecting 50 per cent of the entrepreneurial talent of the country.

Confidently speaking the creative entrepreneur is the back-bone of a nation's industrialization and economic development. There is no gender for the entrepreneur. Women entrepreneurs are managing the fast developing USA's 40 per cent business and it is likely to be further more in the Third Millennium.

Need For Women Entrepreneurship

Primarily, the Indian women are generally under valued and considered inferior to males. Creating and developing more women entrepreneurs in India is nothing but giving them their due share of recognition and social respect. Under the suppressed socio-economic conditions women entrepreneurs did not prosper in the 50 years of independence. There has been a little movement in the growth of women entrepreneurship. With the advent of liberalization policy, there is lot of scope for the growth of entrepreneurship under the private sector and at the same time the circumstances to develop women entrepreneurship have become congenial.

With growing awareness and spread of education over the years, women have started engrossing to modern activities like engineering, electronics and energy. In certain business, women entrepreneurs are doing exceedingly well.

Most of the women entrepreneurs carry on small or medium sized business and many of them operate in the informal sector. The management styles adopted by women differ from men due to difference in skills and experience. The prosperity of women entrepreneurs largely depends on association, networking and mutual support.

Functions of Women Entrepreneurs

The women entrepreneur is a key to economic development.

Frederick Harbison has enumerated the following five functions of a women entrepreneur:

(*i*) Exploration of the prospects of starting a new business enterprise.

(*ii*) Undertaking of risks and the handling of economic uncertainties involved in business.

(*iii*) Introduction of innovations or imitation of innovations.

(*iv*) Coordination, administration and control.

(*v*) Supervision and leadership.

The emergence of women entrepreneurs in a society, depends to a great extent on the economic, religious, cultural, psychological and other factors. For developing countries like India, the presence of entrepreneurs, that too women entrepreneurs are of vital necessity, to achieve a rapid, all round and regionally and socially balanced economic growth through industrialization. It also helps in tapping the inherent talents prevailing among them and act as a panacea for many problems faced by them, such as dowry death, low recognition in society, poverty, unemployment and excessive dependence on male members.

Characteristics of Entrepreneur

To be a successful entrepreneur, a person has to acquire and develop certain qualities, which can be included by training and motivation. The essential entrepreneurial traits/qualities are:

1. High achievement motivation
2. Insatiable drive and persistent enthusiasm
3. Readiness to face challenge
4. Persistent problem solving
5. Goal setting
6. Dealing with failure
7. Technical background
8. Experience in the line
9. Willingness to introduce something new (Sprit of innovation)
10. Taking initiative and seeking personal responsibility
11. Competing against self imposed standards
12. Tolerance to ambiguity and uncertainty
13. Hard working
14. Regularity and dedication to work
15. Self control
16. Self confidence
17. Confidence in self capability
18. Use of feed back
19. Willingness to take advice
20. Time management
21. Money as a measure
22. Drive and energy
23. Long term involvement
24. Total commitment and immersion

Entrepreneurship development among women can be considered a possible approach to economic empowerment of women. A woman as entrepreneur is economically more powerful than as a mere worker because ownership not only confers control over assets (and liabilities) but also gives her the freedom to take decisions. This will also uplift her social status significantly.

Status of Women Entrepreneurs In India

It is evident that women constitutes around 50 per cent of the world's population, do the two-third of world's work hours, receive 10 per cent of world's income and own less than one per cent of world's property (ILO Report 1980). Women owned business are becoming increasingly important in the economies of almost all countries. To the U.S. economy, they contribute more than $250 billion annually and create new business opportunities at two to three times the rate of their male counterparts.

Similarly, in India, women constitute nearly 50 per cent of national population and a very important human resource for the nation's development. According to Survey Report on Indian women, women entrepreneurs constitute 47 per cent of the total urban population. The participation of women in the economy's GDP is as low as 8 per cent, though their work participation was 19.7 per cent in 1981. In India, according to the census 2001, the female labour force participation, rated in their total population, is 25.7 per cent but it is 31 per cent in rural and 11.6 per cent in urban areas. They are engaging in different sectors.

It is estimated that the invisible work of housewives contributes nearly one-third of Indian's GNP. Over the last few decades, women have come forward to establish their own enterprises. Earlier studies revealed that economic role played by women couldn't be isolated from the framework of development. The contribution of women in the socio-economic development particularly in the rural areas has been vital. Around 77 per cent of the total female population of the country lives in rural areas. Out of the main workers as many as 80 per cent are live in rural areas and the percentage of women engaged in cultivation was 33.2 per cent. As major part of the agricultural operations like breaking clods of earth, manage weeding, transplanting, harvesting, threshing and winnowing women do most of the work. In household industries, it is 46 per cent against the male percentage of 43.7 per cent working in the same sector. They also extend their helping hand in other small industries like rope and basket making. Pottery, handloom, weaving and food processing indicating that women playing multi-dimensional role in the society. However except some cases, it is an indisputable fact that out of more than 370 million women in the country almost 150 million are below the poverty line.

The national policy for empowerment of women was adopted in 2001 with the objective of ensuring women their rightful place in society by empowering them as agents of socio-economic change and development. Empowerment of women is therefore, an important approach adopted in the Tenth Five-year plan for development of women. The new industrial policy has stressed the need for conducting a special Entrepreneurship Development Programme (EDP) and some other programme supporting and promoting entrepreneurial skill. Government financial institutions and national banks also have special cells to assist women entrepreneurs.

Problems of Women Entrepreneurs

Apart from the facit assumption that women are frail and indecisive, women entrepreneurs encounter many problems in their efforts to develop the enterprises they have established. The main problems faced by the women entrepreneurs may be analysed as follows:

Shortage of Finance

Women and small entrepreneurs always suffer from inadequate financial resources and working capital. They are lacking access to external funds due to absence of tangible security and credit in the market. Women do not generally have property to their names.

Inefficient Arrangements for Marketing and Sale

For marketing their products, women entrepreneurs are often at the mercy of the middlemen. Although the middlemen exploit the women entrepreneurs, the elimination of middlemen is difficult.

Shortage of Raw Materials

Women entrepreneurs find it difficult to procure raw materials and other necessary inputs.

Stiff Competition

Many of the women enterprises have imperfect organizational setup. They have to face stiff competition from organized industries and male entrepreneurs.

High Cost of Production

Another problem, which undermines the efficiency and restrict the development of women enterprises, is the high cost of production. Government assistance in the form of grants and subsidies to some extent enables them to tide over this difficulty.

Low Mobility

One of the biggest handicaps for women entrepreneurs is mobility or traveling from place to place. Women on their own find it difficult to get accommodation in smaller towns. A single woman asking for a room is still looked upon with suspicion.

Family Responsibilities

In India it is mainly a women's duty to look after the children and older members of the family. Her involvement in family leaves little energy and time for business. Married women entrepreneurs have to make a fine balance between business and home. Their success in this regard also depends upon supporting husband and family.

Social Attitudes

The biggest problem of a women entrepreneur is the social attitude and the constraints in which she has to live and work. Despite constitutional equality, there is discrimination against women in a tradition-bound society, women suffer from male reservations about a woman's role and capacity.

Low Ability to Bear Risk

Women have comparatively a low ability to bear economic and other risks because they have led a protected life. Sometimes they face discrimination in the selection for entrepreneurial development training. Some of them lack entrepreneurial initiative or specialized training.

Lack of Education

In India literacy among women is very low. Due to lack of education, majority of women are unaware of technological developments, marketing knowledge etc. lack of information and experience creates further problems in the setting up and running of business enterprises.

In addition to the above problems inadequate infrastructure, shortage of power and technical know-how and other economic and social constraints have retarded the growth of women entrepreneurship in India.

Suggestions for Improving the Status of Women Entrepreneurs

The problems of women workers in India are multifarious and multidimensional. These problems can be solved through changes in the attitude of family, society and nation towards the women. Some suggestions are given below.

Financial Cells

Special cells may be opened for providing easy finance to women entrepreneurs in various public financial institutions and banks. These cells should be manned by women officers and clerks. Efforts should be made to provide finance at the local level.

Marketing Cooperatives

Encouragement and assistance should be provided to women entrepreneurs for setting up cooperatives. These cooperatives will pool the inputs of women enterprises and sell them on remunerative prices. Such cooperatives will help to eliminate the middlemen.

Supply of Raw Materials

Scarce and imported raw materials may be made available to women entrepreneurs on priority basis. A subsidy may also be given to make the products manufactured by women entrepreneurs as cost effective measure.

Training Facilities

Training and skills are essential for the development of entrepreneurship. Training schemes should be so designed that women can take full advantage. Family members do not like women to go away to far off places for training. Women have the potential and the will to establish and manage enterprises of their own. What they need is encouragement and support.

Education and Awareness

Many efforts were taken to improve the position of women by increasing the literacy rates. Now, both government and non-government organizations are taking steps to promote entrepreneurship among women. But the results are not in commensurate with the efforts. A recent study of the Town and country planning reveals that self-employment is a powerful motivating factor. It should motivate her to set up an enterprise.

It is necessary to change negative social attitudes towards women. Elders particularly, mothers and mother-in-law need to be made aware of the potential of girls and their dual role in society. There shall be compulsory education for women. When she is educated, she can manage her dual responsibility at home and work.

Seminars

More seminars, conferences and workshops on women should be organized. They should be encouraged to participate and express their views.

Part Time Jobs

Another suggestion is to increase part time jobs for women in various organizations, which will give a sense of dignity and identity to the women.

Wage Gap and Medical Facilities

Wage gapes between men and women should be reduced. Better medical facilities and congenial atmosphere should be provided to them. Maternity benefit schemes should be enhanced in private sectors also.

Change of Attitude

The attitude of the husband and family members should be changed towards working women. Husband should come forward to share her burden. Women should change their attitude about themselves. They should be self confident in their approach.

Baby Care Centres

Baby care centres should be opened at the work place where she can leave her child.

Constitutional and Legal Rights

Women should be made aware of their constitutional and legal rights both in their work and in the social sphere.

Conclusions

Now working women have become a major part of labour market of India and hence their problem cannot be ignored. When they are engaged in gainful employment and contributing to the household and national economy, they should be given the due respect and status they deserve in the family and the society. In the changing socio-cultural environment of India, women are entering in a new era. But they are still over-burdened with the household cores. So some measures should be introduced to reduce their household burden. This requires a drastical change in the mind set of the men folk towards women in general and working women in particular.

Hence, it becomes necessary for the society and Government to find remedies for the problems of women entrepreneurship. Already the Central and State Governments and non-governmental organizations have taken so many steps to solve the problems of women entrepreneurs, yet they have to provide special incentives and subsidy. As entrepreneurship opportunities will be more in small and medium scale industries, the sector should be given prominence and proper marketing strategy of such products should be planned and implemented, which will give scope for women entrepreneurs. If Indian women's talent will be utilized properly, one day India will become an ideal country to others.

REFERENCES

- Bhatia, B.S. and Batra, G.S. (2003): Entrepreneurship and small Business Management, Deep and Deep Publications Pvt. Ltd., New Delhi.
- Birley, S. (1989): "Female Entrepreneurs: Are they really any different", Journal of small business management, 27 (1), pp32-37.
- Dhameja, S.K. (2004): Women Entrepreneurs, Deep and Deep Publications Pvt. Ltd., New Delhi.
- Garg, R.B.L. (2004): "Women Entrepreneurs: Problems and Prospects", Social Welfare, 50 (12), March, pp16-18.
- Khurana, I.R. (1988): "Strategy for Rural Development", Khadi Gram Udyog, 34 (8), pp335-344.
- Mohiuddin, A. (1987): "Entrepreneurship in Rural Women", Kurukshetra, 35 (12), pp22-25.
- Nelson, R.E.(1985): Entrepreneurship and Self Employment Training, Asian Development Bank, Manila.
- Rao, S.K. (1976): Entrepreneur Development in India - Is achievement training the answer, Laghu Udyog, 4. pp 9-12.
- Sinha, Poonam. (2003): "Women Entrepreneurship in the North East India: Motivation, Social Support and Constraints", Indian Journal of Industrial Relations, 28 (4), April, pp 425-41.
- Sundaram, I. Satya. (2004): "Encouraging Women's Entrepreneurship", Social Welfare, 50 (12), March, pp15-19.
- Vidyu Lata. (1990): Developing Rural Women, Discovery Publishing House, New Delhi.
- Vitz, M.D. (1987): Women Entrepreneurs in India, Mittal Publications, New Delhi.